P9-DWD-176

MAY 27 2003

THE HERO
and
THE OUTLAW

THE HERO
and
THE OUTLAW

Building Extraordinary Brands
Through the Power of Archetypes

MARGARET MARK
and
CAROL S. PEARSON

McGraw-Hill

New York   Chicago   San Francisco   Lisbon   London
Madrid   Mexico City   Milan   New Delhi   San Juan   Seoul
Singapore   Sidney   Toronto

McGraw-Hill

A Division of The **McGraw·Hill** Companies

1 2 3 4 5 6 7 8 9 0   DOC/DOC   0 9 8 7 6 5 4 3 2 1

ISBN 0-07-136415-3

It was set in Janson by Binghamton Valley Composition.

Printed and bound by R. R. Donnelley & Sons Company.

McGraw-Hill books are available at special quantity discounts to use as premiums and sales promotions, or for use in corporate training programs. For more information, please write to the Director of Special Sales, Professional Publishing, McGraw-Hill, 2 Penn Plaza, New York, NY 10011-2298. Or contact your local bookstore.

 This book is printed on recycled, acid-free paper containing a minimum of 50% recycled, de-inked fiber.

Contents

Foreword

In October of 1987, I had to make a rush business trip to Toronto. After I landed at Pearson Airport, I ran for the first taxi in line. From the rear seat, I could see that the driver wore a tattered mackinaw and a wool cap with earflaps pulled down over wisps of straggly hair. In the mirror, I could see a crusty, days-old beard.

As he pulled away from the curb, he suddenly braked, turned to me, and spoke with urgency: "Did you hear the news?"

I sucked in some cold air. "No, what?"

"Awful. The Hang Seng stock index went down nine percent this morning."

In that instant, I knew the long-awaited era of global communications had actually been born.

All the world, rich and poor, was fixated on the collapse of the financial markets in real time. And there was *real* worry in the cabby's eyes, which reflected fears around the world.

What was the story? No one seemed to understand why the markets were in free fall. What did it mean, this October collapse? Neither President Reagan, nor Margaret Thatcher, nor the secretaries of the treasury or exchequer, nor any other leader of reputation had stood up to tell us what the story was. So, in the absence of a new story, millions of people fell back on the last usable story: the stock market collapse of October 1929. And the quotes chased each other down and down.

Eventually, after scooping the cream out of millions of portfolios, the markets bottomed out, well above depression levels, because it wasn't actually 1929 all over again.

Today, as I write in another October, markets are roiling as never before. Brands are being born faster than ever before. The media are glutted with much more data, news, entertainment, and advertising than they were 13 years ago.

Without a good "story" for us to latch onto, to give meaning to the message, most of it slides by, vaguely seen or heard, but surely not absorbed.

We all love stories, and we need them. From fables to novels, from musicals to advertising, we instinctively crave stories which can provide the human context for forces that are often vast, ancient, and abstract. Stories are the best teachers.

This is a book about finding the right story. It provides a fresh framework for understanding how brands and companies gain and lose meaning, attention, value, and share of market in these hectic times.

In 30-odd years in the business of advertising and marketing, I have met no more original thinker or articulate researcher than Margaret Mark. I have had the good fortune to work with her for nearly two decades, during which I have watched her constantly tear up the hard sod of accepted wisdom and break new ground for the great benefit of her clients. Now, she has joined forces with Dr. Carol Pearson, a uniquely gifted scholar who has not only been delving deeply into archetypal studies for years, but has been applying her insights in a practical fashion as a consultant to major organizations. Together, they have fused a remarkable thesis that, in the end, is all about strengthening the value—even the market value—of brands and companies.

I could not help but think of Margaret and Carol on the last Super Bowl Sunday, as a fresh phalanx of dot-coms paraded their million-dollar-per-half-minute commercials in front of the nation's richest TV audience. Most of the commercials were witty, novel, and spectacular in effect. And most lacked anything close to "meaning." Their millions were wasted.

This book illuminates the most ancient grooves in our mental architecture, which Carl Jung described as "archetypes," and shows how they can be employed to bring meaning and profit to a brand. There is a nascent power here that, if understood correctly, can bring a rare vitality to a brand or a corporation.

But let me post the "warning label" up front. In my opinion, meaning is not something that can be grafted onto a product, particularly an inferior one. To attract and keep customers, meaning must be true to the intrinsic value of a brand—that is, what the product really is and does. Thus, the management of archetypes must begin long before an ad is begun. It starts with the development of a product or service that provides a real benefit.

This idea is not new. For centuries, creative individuals have discovered the right archetypes for a brand by hunch and by genius. From the raw beginnings of advertising, they have told stories in their ads. But never before has the search for the right archetype and the right story been made systematic or scientific. With this book, it becomes both.

In fact, the book itself is a new story that makes sense out of marketing brands in a confusing new world.

Alex Kroll
former Creative Director,
CEO, and chairman of
Young & Rubicam

Acknowledgments

Very special thanks go to Peter Georgescu, much-admired friend and colleague, whose early support for the premise underlying this book helped bring it to life. Thanks also for the invaluable encouragement of Jane Brite, Jayne Evans, Dick Upson, Dirk Metzler, Susan Royer, Linda Srere, and Ed LeBar, as well as students and faculty at the C. G. Jung Institute in Switzerland and at the Saybrook Graduate Institute. Also, we offer our gratitude to Rosemarie Murray, for initially seeing the connection between Margaret's ideas and Carol's work.

The authors would like to thank as well Mary Glenn, our editor at McGraw-Hill, and our agent, Stephanie Tade, for championing our book; Michael Brennecke, for his time, professionalism, and elegant illustrations; Letty Phillips and Carol Spranger, for tirelessly helping us pull the manuscript together; Dawn Barhyte, for her resourceful research into companies' histories; Maura Gallagher, for her late-night rescues when the computer system crashed; David Merkowitz, for his kind willingness to help with editing, Part 1, McGraw-Hill's Paul Sobel, editing supervisor, for overseeing the editing of the manuscript, and Brian and Abigail Baker of Write With, Inc., for copyediting; Paul Fox and Ed LeBar, from Young & Rubicam's Brand Asset Valuator Group, for releasing to us their innovative analyses supporting the power of archetypal brands; Peter Murray, for his invaluable help with conceptualizing the artwork; Gail David, Susan Royer, and Rosemarie Truglio from Sesame Workshop, for their timely assistance in guiding us to the creative origins of "Sesame Street"; Joe Plummer, brilliant strategist and researcher at McCann Erickson, for his input on viewer reward theory; Carla Gambescia, president of Artful Enterprises, for generously sharing her insights regarding category gender; Mary Giammarino, Doug Staples, and Dr. Virginia Howse, from the March of Dimes, for their thoughts regarding the evolution of their organization; Grant McCracken, visiting scholar at McGill University, for his eloquently expressed insights and for his comments on segments of the book; Stewart Owen and Young & Rubicam, for allowing us to use

McCracken's inimitable "Riggens" piece; Denise Larson, from The Lord Group, for taking the time to review the Entenmann's case; Paul Wolansky, professor of film at the University of Southern California, for reviewing material and sharing his wonderful perspective on story patterns; and Ami Ronnberg, at the C. G. Jung Center in New York, and Professor Josephine Withers, of the University of Maryland Art History Department, for their help in researching illustrations.

We extend our appreciation to the busy and enormously talented folk who found the time to read and comment on the book: Bob Wehling, Proctor & Gamble's global marketing officer; Peter Georgescu, chairman emeritus, Young & Rubicam; Ruth Wooden, president of the National Parenting Association; Linda Kaplan-Thaler, president and CEO of The Kaplan-Thaler Group; Murray Stein, Jungian analyst and pioneer in applications of Jungian thought to the business world; Margaret Wheatley, consultant and author of *Leadership and the New Sciences*; Arlene Brickner, vice president of Creative Services for Coach; and Anna Maria Cugliari, senior vice president of Strategic Marketing and Brand Management, Sesame Workshop.

Finally, we are deeply indebted to Alex Kroll, for having taken the time to read and critique the manuscript and to lend his incomparable brainpower to this endeavor.

"*All that happens is symbol, and as it represents itself perfectly, it points to all the rest.*"

Goethe, 1818

Primal Assets

A System for the
Management of Meaning

Brands are as much a part of our daily lives as our workplaces and neighborhood landmarks.

Big, enduring brands become icons—not just of corporations, but of whole cultures. Coca-Cola not only has the most recognized logo in the world, but the logo also has become a symbol of the Western way of life.

Today the brand is a repository, not merely of functional characteristics, but of meaning and value. But if we are to identify and effectively leverage the essential elements, or "immutables," of our brands, we must become fluent in the visual and verbal language of archetypes.

The creators of great brands have intuited this simple truth. For example, superstars in the film and entertainment industry, and the agents who manage them, understand that their continued popularity does not hinge simply on the quality or success of the films they make or the visibility they attain. Rather, it depends on creating, nourishing, and continuously reinterpreting a unique and compelling identity or "meaning." Madonna changes her lifestyles and hairstyles, but she is always the outrageous Rebel. Offscreen and on, Jack Nicholson is the bad-boy Outlaw. Meg Ryan and Tom Hanks imbue every role they play with the spirit of the wide-eyed Innocent.

These identities are not only consistent—they are compelling. Love 'em or hate 'em, you can't help but notice 'em. In fact, we can't help but be mesmerized by who they are and what they implicitly stand for. In an era of declining network viewership and 300 cable channels, the trial of O. J. Simpson commanded record viewership on a continuous basis. Was it the sensationalism of the crime? The glamour of Beverly Hills? The racial subtext?

Although each of these played a part in getting people's attention, it was the deeper archetypal meaning that kept them tuning back in, day after day. Regardless of the reality of his personality or his life, Simpson, as a brand, was seen as the fierce warrior, able to defeat any competitor. The revelations of abuse and violence that emerged during his trial led many to conclude, despite his formal acquittal, that he had murdered his wife. Instead of a popular figure, he became an object of scorn and contempt. Thus, O. J.'s story fits the classic mold of Shakespeare's Othello—the warrior undone by the destructive power of his own jealous rage.

In her life and in her death, Diana Spencer held sway over the world. The power of her tale may remind you of the magnetic appeal of the Cinderella story—the beautiful, but vulnerable, girl who gets the prince, but must live under the ever-watchful eye of the withholding stepmother. Even in the aftermath of her divorce, Diana's story evolves in Romeo-and-Juliet style: She breaks social convention to find love and meets with an untimely death.

The case of Princess Di also shows how compelling people find the evolution of an archetypal story. What happens if the girl marries Prince Charming, but does not live happily ever after? She divorces, adjusts, and becomes a great lover of humanity, motivating humankind to show its love for her.

Even though Diana's life story has many chapters, styles, and reifications, it always dances around the archetypal theme of the princess lover. Absent this essential archetypal unity, she would not have captured our attention so profoundly.

The story of Elián González, the young Cuban boy who became the object of an international tug of war, made headlines for weeks.

In a world filled with orphans, why did this little boy's plight so grab us? Was it the sheer drama of his having been left alone at sea after his mother and his other boat mates drowned? Did the controversy inspired by the decision to return him to his father's care, and thus to Castro's Cuba, reflect a basic conflict between the values we attach to freedom of opportunity, on the one hand, and family and relationship, on the other? Did this controversy highlight the need to let go of Cold War thinking and enter a new time? Undoubtedly, it was all of these—and each has its archetypal theme.

Commenting on the symbolic nature of the news, *Washington Post* reporter Paul Richard links Elián's story to the mythic pattern of the archetypal Hero: "Young Moses in the bulrushes and the young Elián on his inner tube are to some degree related. We expect them to drown. Such sea births seem a blessing; such deliverances miraculous. The child will become a man."[1] Thus, Elián holds the promise of cultural redemption. Richard notes that "Moses . . . spent prosperous years in Egypt before heading to the Promised Land," implicitly raising the question of whether Elián was here to rescue Americans from materialism or Cubans from Castro and poverty.

News stories that really grip public attention always have an archetypal quality, Richard observes. "When the next big story breaks, we'll all be caught again," he says, because each story that so mysteriously grabs us is some version of "Once upon a time . . ."—a mythic tale acted out in real life.

Richard's point is illustrated by how the news media covered the tragic death of John F. Kennedy, Jr. By placing this event in the context of the deaths of other beautiful and charismatic Kennedy males (Joseph, John Sr., Robert), the stories called up deeply held archaic human beliefs: in the family curse and in the redemptive power of the sacrifice of the most perfect man of his time. It matters little that in ancient times, the beautiful youth was sacrificed in a religious ritual, not by tragic accident or assassination; some chord in the human psyche still is moved by this story of martyrdom.

Similarly, films that are box office hits almost always have archetypal structures. The six most recent Academy Award winners for

1. Paul Richard, "Big News: The Sagas with Staying Power," (*The Washington Post*, April 26, 2000), p. C1

> ### What is an archetype?
>
> Forms or images of a collective nature which occur practically all over the earth as constituents of myths and at the same time as individual products of unconscious origin.
>
> —C. G. Jung, *Psychology and Religion*
>
> The concept of archetypes was borrowed by Jung from classic sources, including Cicero, Pliny, and Augustine. Adolf Bastian called them "Elementary Ideas." In Sanskrit, they were called "subjectively known forms"; and in Australia, they were known as the "Eternal Ones of the Dream."
>
> —Joseph Campbell, *The Hero with a Thousand Faces*
>
> Jung to some extent took the opposite approach to that of the behaviorists, that is, he did not observe people from the outside, did not ask how we behave, how we greet one another, how we mate, how we take care of our young. Instead, he studied what we feel and what we fantasize while we are doing those things. For Jung, archetypes are not only elementary ideas, but just as much elementary feelings, elementary fantasies, elementary visions.
>
> —Marie-Louise Von Franz, *Psyche and Matter*

"Best Motion Picture" all exemplify classic archetypal stories: *Forrest Gump* (1994), the power of the Wise Fool; *Braveheart* (1995), the triumphant Hero; *The English Patient* (1996) and *Titanic* (1997), the transformative Lover; *Shakespeare in Love* (1998), the Creator (writer) transmuting the suffering of lost love into ennobling art; and, finally, *American Beauty* (1999), the Regular Guy as mystic (a midlife crisis in which the dark night of the soul leads to the experience of mystic enlightenment—and, sadly, in this case, death).

Sometimes the writer, director, and producer simply intuit the archetype. Sometimes they are guided by a conscious system. The *Star Wars* series—as well as spin-off action figures and other products—holds endless appeal. In making these films, George Lucas has been guided by Joseph Campbell's *The Hero with a Thousand Faces*, which outlines all the rich and evocative stages of the Hero's journey.

Nike, the winged goddess, was associated with victory, as is the brand that bears her name.

The popularity of each episode is derived in large part from the way Lucas consciously crafts the entire series to convey archetypal characters and mythic plots.

Products grab—and keep—our attention for the same reason: They embody an archetype. For example, throughout the ages, cleansing rituals have signified more than physical cleanliness: They also symbolize the removal of sin or shame, bestowing rectification and worthiness upon the person who has performed the ritual. Ivory soap has drawn from this well. Ivory is not just about getting clean; it is about renewal, purity, and innocence. Over the years, Ivory has changed the details of its ad campaigns, updated the cultural references they employ, and diversified the ages and cultures of the bathers they depict. Nevertheless, the central message of the ads—their meaning—has remained deeply symbolic and constant. Ivory succeeds because its brand meaning is consistent with the deep essence of cleansing.

Brands that capture the essential meaning of their category—and communicate that message in subtle and refined ways—dominate the market, just as Princess Di, O. J., Clinton/Lewinsky, and Elián dominated the airwaves.

The First System—Ever— for the Management of Meaning

ADVERTISING ALWAYS HAS USED archetypal imagery to market products. The Jolly Green Giant is, after all, the archetype of the Green Man, a figure associated with fertility and abundance. The judicious use of such symbolism can fuel a leading brand. Brand icons go further. It is not just that archetypal symbols and images are used to position the brand, but that, over time, the brand itself takes on symbolic significance. Ivory is not merely associated with innocence; it embodies it. Mothers wash their children with Ivory not only to keep them safe from germs and irritating chemicals, but also because Ivory just "seems right" for precious infants and toddlers. To comprehend the power of this phenomenon, we must understand the nature of symbols. Some symbols have the deepest religious or spiritual meaning. For example, within Christianity, Baptism is the ritual of purification, while Communion provides a ritual for the acceptance of divine grace. It would, of course, be sacrilegious to exploit any faith's particular symbolism in order to sell products. Yet both sacred and secular symbols of renewal exist on a continuum unified by an archetype. While the conscious power of a religious symbol is inordinately greater, the unconscious power of an archetype, even in an entirely secular context, is immense.

Meaning as a Brand Asset

Understanding and leveraging archetypal meaning, once an interesting "bonus" to effective marketing, is now a prerequisite. Why?

There was a time when successfully creating, building, and marketing brands required neither endless inspiration nor endless capital. Demand exceeded supply, and markets were uncluttered. In the main, products were physically different from each other, and brands were built on those differences.

Such was the case, for ages and ages, in the marketing, or selling, world. But once competition reached a certain threshold, every business—whether a multinational cola company or a neighborhood dry cleaner—encountered a new challenge. No matter how effective the company's manufacturing and distribution systems, or how state of the art its dry-cleaning processes, its competitors could imitate or duplicate them. In this circumstance, businesses found that they had only two broad strategic routes to go: reduce their prices or imbue their products with meaning.

Clearly, the creation and management of meaning was the more desirable option.

Ironically, though, as critical as meaning has become, no system has been developed until now for understanding or managing the meaning of brands—be they products, services, companies, or causes. We have had manufacturing systems for producing products, message development systems for creating candidates' platforms, and business systems for marketing goods, but no system for managing what had become a brand's most leverageable asset.

Why not? Partly because the need to manage meaning was a relatively new phenomenon. If you were the only soft drink in town (as you might be in, say, Hangzhou, China), you could market your product on the basis of its features and benefits. And if you were the only dry cleaner in the neighborhood, you could market your store on the merits of its convenience, environmentally sound packaging, and effective cleaning.

However, in increasingly crowded and highly competitive categories, the cases in which brand differentiation could be based on discernible product differences became rare or nonexistent. And even if a corporation was successful in creating a legitimate product-based point of difference, it was quickly imitated and duplicated by competitors.

As early as 1983, Paul Hawken identified a profound change in the relative importance of product "mass" versus product "meaning" that required a corresponding shift in our business model. Soon after, Wall Street made a comparable discovery, whereupon whole corporations were acquired simply to obtain their powerhouse brands— even though other brands offered virtually identical products. Something new was happening. Hundreds of millions of dollars were being spent to purchase certain brands because they possessed a trait or property that was not fully understood and that caught the purchasers totally off guard.

The truth was that these brands had become phenomenally valuable not only because of their innovative features or benefits, but also because these properties had been translated into powerful meanings. They were worth millions of dollars because they had gained a kind of meaning that was universal, larger than life, iconic.

Whether the new managers understood it consciously or not, they had become the stewards of archetypal brands. The meanings these brands hold are like primal assets that must be managed as carefully as financial investments. And most companies have not been prepared to do so, because, quite simply, no system was available to guide them.

Levi's, once a strong and clear Explorer brand, drifted from Outlaw to Hero, back to Explorer, then to Regular Guy or Gal, then to

Jester—and sometimes presented a patchwork quilt of archetypal identities all at once, reflective of the confused management of both the parent and the subbrands (501, Five Pocket, Wide Leg). The company's market share declined accordingly.

Nike, one of the great Hero brands of all times, became clichéd and self-conscious in that role and publicly demonstrated a loss of confidence, changing advertising agencies and brand managers— when the real solution was to tap more deeply and surely into the Hero's Journey, a never-ending source of inspiration for the Hero archetype.

These companies had some of the most sophisticated and talented marketing professionals at their helms; nevertheless, they lost their way. The result was chaos, similar to what would happen if CFOs tried to manage money by making everything up as they went along, without any system of financial management or accounting,

Meaning management is relevant not only to the for-profit world: In a somewhat more subtle way, nonprofit organizations and political candidates face the same dilemma as the one we have just described. While a particular cause may seem unique to its advocates, potential contributors are besieged with requests for money. Their decision on which good cause to support is based largely on some sense that the meaning of a particular organization is the best fit with their values. Similarly, most candidates from the same party have at least similar stands on the issues. To get nominated, they must connect with voters in a way that offers the meaning promise appropriate to the particular time. John F. Kennedy did this effectively by invoking Camelot.

The meaning of a brand is its most precious and irreplaceable asset. Whether you're selling a soft drink or a presidential candidate, what your brand means to people will be every bit as important as its function—if not more so—because it is meaning that tells us "this one feels right" or "this one's for me." Meaning speaks to the feeling or intuitive side of the public; it creates an emotional affinity, allowing the more rational arguments to be heard.

North Star Marketing

Marketing without a system for managing meaning is analogous to ancient navigators trying to find port in treacherous seas on a starless night. What they need is an enduring and reliable compass—a fixed place that illuminates both where they are and where they must go. For marketers, the theory of archetypes can act as this compass.

We have written *The Hero and the Outlaw* to communicate the first system—ever—for the management of meaning. And like many sound ideas, it borrows from very ancient and eternal ones.

Imprints, hardwired into our psyches, influence the characters we love in art, literature, the great religions of the world, and contemporary films. Plato called these imprints "elemental forms" and saw them as the idea structures that formed a template for material reality. Psychiatrist C. G. Jung called them "archetypes."

In the marketing world, we have had no comparable concept or vocabulary. Yet brands are, in truth, among the most vibrant contemporary expressions of these deep and abiding patterns. Whether through conscious intent or fortunate accident, brands—be they candidates, superstars, products, or companies—achieve deep and enduring differentiation and relevance by embodying timeless archetypal meaning. In fact, the most successful brands always have done so.

This phenomenon is not about "borrowing" meaning in an ephemeral advertising campaign, but rather *becoming* a consistent and enduring expression of meaning—essentially becoming a brand icon. Powerhouse products have done so: Nike, Coke, Ralph Lauren, Marlboro, Disney, and Ivory, to name a few. So have films—*Star Wars, E.T. The Extra-Terrestrial*, and *Gone with the Wind*—and personalities—Lady Di, Jackie O, Joe DiMaggio, and John Wayne. Brands that have achieved this status, accidentally or as a result of fabulously gifted instinct, have captured and held the imagination of the public. And, if they are wise, their marketers have stayed the course simply because what their brands have come to represent resonates with the public so well and so consistently.

But reliance on genius goes only so far and lasts only so long. Sooner or later, brands suffer from the fact that there has been no science related to the development and management of meaning. When business as usual takes over, there is no compass to guide the inevitable choices or decision points that determine a brand's fate: How to keep pace with the times without losing the brand's essence? How to survive fierce competitive assaults? How to appeal to multiple segments—perhaps numerous cultures—without violating the brand's "core" meaning? How to market responsibly and in a way that does not exert a negative influence on the customer or the times?

In the absence of such a science or compass, irreplaceable and invaluable repositories of goodwill—brand meanings—are squandered.

This book addresses the critical need, and the tremendous opportunity, to create, preserve, protect, and nurture brand meaning by leveraging its deep archetypal roots.

We do this first by dignifying the process of managing meaning. Today, even in the most sophisticated companies, this most critical of processes is left to chance, to the whim of an art director and copywriter, or to the serendipity of casual brainstorming: "Should we be friendly and accessible, or aloof and alluring?"

Developing the most critical element of what our brand represents too often is a careless or frivolous process. Thus, it is no wonder that marketing teams keep reinventing the brand and, in doing so, dilute or destroy its meaning.

We have written this book to share our experience developing and utilizing the first systematic approach to meaning management. Our collaboration began with the awareness that archetypal psychology could provide a more substantive source for the science of creating effective advertising. What we found was a far deeper truth: Archetypal psychology helps us understand the intrinsic meaning of product categories and consequently helps marketers create enduring brand identities that establish market dominance, evoke and deliver meaning to customers, and inspire customer loyalty—all, potentially, in socially responsible ways.

These are not simply pie-in-the-sky ideas. Carol Pearson has spent 30 years developing a sound, reliable psychological framework that integrates concepts from Jungian and other psychological systems and applying them to leadership and organizational development as well as marketing. Margaret Mark has equivalent experience applying deep human insights and constructs to marketing with clients, first at Young & Rubicam and now at her own company. As a result, we are confident that the approaches described for you in these pages consistently have produced results without negative side effects. Our system already has affected the marketing approaches of leading brands in the financial services business, the soft-drink, apparel, and snack categories, tele-

Archetypes and Their Primary Functions in People's Lives		
Archetype	**Helps people**	**Brand example**
Creator	Craft something new	Williams-Sonoma
Caregiver	Care for others	AT&T (Ma Bell)
Ruler	Exert control	American Express
Jester	Have a good time	Miller Lite
Regular Guy/Gal	Be OK just as they are	Wendy's
Lover	Find and give love	Hallmark
Hero	Act courageously	Nike
Outlaw	Break the rules	Harley-Davidson
Magician	Affect transformation	Calgon
Innocent	Retain or renew faith	Ivory
Explorer	Maintain independence	Levi's
Sage	Understand their world	Oprah's Book Club

Figure 1.1

vision programming, cause marketing, and many other industries and has defined or redefined organizations' brand identities in both the for-profit and not-for-profit sectors.

The system we have developed, and that we share with you in this book, offers a structure for describing the archetypes that already have provided powerful identities for numerous winning brands. By using this system, you do not have to step out on a limb to implement archetypal branding strategies in your company. Rather, you can follow a theoretically sound, proven method for establishing a brand identity for your product, your service, your company—or even yourself. As we explored the archetypal basis of successful brands, we discovered the 12 major archetypes expressed most often in commercial activity today.

Figure 1.1 names each of the archetypes, describes its primary function in people's lives, and gives one example of a leading brand or brand icon with that identity.

The Missing Link: Archetypes and Customer Motivation

Archetypes provide the missing link between customer motivation and product sales. Virtually all marketers know that they need to understand human motivations. Until now, however, no scientific method has been available that would allow them to link the deepest motivations of consumers with product meaning. The missing link is an understanding of archetypes. An archetypal product identity speaks directly to the deep psychic imprint within the consumer, sparking a sense of recognition and of meaning.

Archetypal images signal the fulfillment of basic human desires and motivations and release deep emotions and yearnings. Why do you suppose our hearts leap up, our throats choke, or we begin to cry at certain moments? An Olympic athlete winning a gold medal (Hero); an elderly African-American man in the audience instinctively rising when his grandson's name is called to receive his college diploma (commercial for the United Negro College Fund—triumph of the Regular Guy); a mother being handed her newborn for the first time (Johnson & Johnson spot): Each of these ads draws from the same well.

One psychological explanation for such responses is that either we are unconsciously reliving critical moments in our own lives (for example, the separation scene at the end of *E.T.* calls up our own experiences of loss) or we are anticipating them. These archetypal images and scenes call people to fulfill their basic human needs and motivations (in the previous examples, freedom and identity, achievement, and intimacy, respectively). In an ideal world, the product serves a mediating function between a need and its fulfillment.

A System That Integrates Motivational and Archetypal Theory

In brief, motivational theory can be condensed into a focus on four major human drives positioned along two axes: Belonging/People versus Independence/Self-Actualization, and Stability/Control versus Risk/Mastery. (See Figures 1.2 and 1.3.)

In everyday human terms, this means that most of us want very much to be liked and to belong to a group. At the same time, we also want to be individuals and go our own way. Both of these desires are deep and profound human urges, yet they pull us in opposite directions. The desire to belong makes us want to please others and

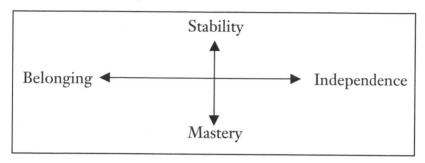

Figure 1.2

conform, at least to some degree. The desire to individuate causes us to spend time alone and make decisions or act in ways that those close to us may not understand.

Similarly, most people have a deep need for security and stability. Such desires are fulfilled by routine, comfort, and staying with the tried and true. We are responding to them when we buy insurance, stay in a job for the pension plan, or religiously take our vitamins. Yet, however much people want safety, most also are energized by their ambition and the desire to exert mastery. If we want the exhilaration of accomplishment, we must take risks. So, motivated by the wish to leave a thumbprint on the world, we take a controversial stand, start a business, or try other new and risky ventures.

Life requires constant negotiation along these poles. When we sacrifice one end of one of these continua to the other end, there is a tendency in the psyche to seek balance. That's one of the reasons some people experience midlife crises; they have gotten out of balance, and some part of them that has been suppressed for too long seeks expression.

Both of us have used a grid like the one in Figure 1.2, with two axes and four primary desires emerging independently in a person's thinking, in our prior work. We both found that our clients instinctively understood the grid's meaning and importance, because they have experienced those tensions in their own lives. The grid also has provided a quick diagnostic test for recognizing the underlying motivation to our clients' organizational mission and their brand identity. When the two of us began to collaborate, we altered the terms

Human Development Stage Theories and Motivational Categories

Theorist	Stability/Control	Belonging/Enjoyment	Mastery/Risk	Independence/Fulfillment
Kegan's subject/object structure	Imperial (2)	Interpersonal (3)	Institutional (4)	Interindividual (5)
Maslow's hierarchy of needs orientation	Safety (2)	Belonging (3)	Esteem/Self-Esteem (4)	Self-Actualization (5)
Wilbur's correlation	Material Exchange (1)	Emotional Exchange (2)	Mental Exchange (3)	Soul/Spiritual Exchange (4, 5)
Erickson's developmental challenges/ virtues	Trust vs. Mistrust = Hope (infancy) Generativity vs. Stagnation = Care (age 35–65)	Autonomy vs. Shame = Will (age 2–3) Intimacy vs. Isolation = Love (age 19–35)	Initiative vs. Guilt = Purpose (age 3–5) Industry vs. Inferiority = Competence (age 6–12)	Identity vs. Confusion = Fidelity (age 12–18) Integrity vs. Despair = Wisdom (age 65 and above)

Figure 1.3

a bit, so that we were using the same language, but the fundamental categories we were using were, and remain, the same.[1]

Although both of us view each of the previously described desires as a strong motivational factor for most people today, a number of theorists associate several of the desires with different stages of development. By their way of thinking, some motivations are more fundamental than others.

Our categories of motivation link most closely with the stages defined by Abraham Maslow (*Motivation and Personality*, 1954), who has influenced both of us profoundly. Maslow is best known for defining the "hierarchy of needs," which describes how human desires evolve as more primary needs are met. The chart in Figure 1.3 summarizes Maslow's findings, as well as those of the three other major motivational psychologists of the twentieth century. Eric Erickson, who also has influenced our thinking about human desire, identified developmental issues in the life cycle, the resolution of which helps people form major character virtues.[2] Robert Kegan, a leading educational psychologist and Harvard professor, developed a theory of personality development that balances meaning-making and social development. (See *The Evolving Self*, 1982.) Ken Wilbur, the leading theorist in the field of transpersonal psychology, identified stages in the development of consciousness as people evolve from an ego orientation to more spiritual (transpersonal) approaches to the world. Figure 1.3 outlines these theories for those readers interested in connecting our motivational categories with developmental models. (When Stage 1 is missing from the chart for a particular model, it is because the stage is too focused on fundamental issues of survival to be relevant to contemporary consumer behaviors.)

Archetypes mediate between products and customer motivation by providing an intangible experience of meaning. Figure 1.4 iden-

---

1. Carol Pearson also has been working with John Corlett on a short publication on archetypes in organizations. Here she had the same experience. Dr. Corlett had been mapping the basic motivations within organizational cultures. He, too, had independently identified these four quadrants as most fundamental, although again, his language was somewhat different.

2. Eric Erickson, *Childhood and Society* (New York: Oxford University Press, 1963) and *Identity: Youth and Crisis* (New York: Norton, 1968).

Archetypes and Motivation			
Motivation: **Stability & control**	**Belonging & enjoyment**	**Risk & mastery**	**Independence & fulfillment**
Creator	Jester	Hero	Innocent
Caregiver	Regular Guy/ Gal	Outlaw	Explorer
Ruler	Lover	Magician	Sage
Customer Fear Financial ruin, ill heath, uncontrolled chaos	Exile, orphaning, abandonment, engulfment	Ineffectuality, impotence, powerlessness	Entrapment, selling out, emptiness
Helps People Feel safe	Have love/ community	Achieve	Find happiness

Figure 1.4

tifies the archetypes most important to the fulfillment of the four basic human needs.

Heroes and Outlaws shows how archetypal theory provides a sound, proven methodology for establishing a memorable and compelling brand identity, one that can withstand the test of time, cross lifestyle and cultural boundaries, and translate into success that endures.

Archetypes

The Heartbeat of
Enduring Brands

I N ANCIENT GREECE AND ROME, archetypes formed
the basis of myths, in which they were depicted as gods and goddesses. These deities, together with those of other ancient cultures,
provide some of the specific images associated with the 12 archetypes
described in this book. Even though the actors in today's mythic
stories are mere mortals, not gods, the same plots fascinate us. Why
was President Clinton able to withstand the Lewinsky scandal?
Think of the ancient Greeks' fascination with stories of Zeus's (the
Ruler's) sexual exploits and the suffering and faithfulness of his wife,
Hera. Just so, Clinton's Zeus-like exploits captivated the country
without causing his downfall. Since he was widely perceived as an
effective president, faithfulness to his constituents was regarded as
more important than marital fidelity. More surprisingly, Hillary
Clinton's popularity soared, at least for a time, as she came to per-
sonify the Hera-like wronged, but faithful, wife.

Whatever their party, presidents succeed when their brand identity is clear and consistent. Grandfatherly Ronald Reagan was known as the "Teflon President" for his capacity to remain popular in the face of scandal and controversy. As an actor, Reagan knew the importance of branding. Most likely, he maintained his paternal Caregiver archetypal identity quite consciously, providing constant reassurance to the country that all would be well.

Conversely, many politicians who fail to get either elected or reelected never establish a consistent archetypal identity. For example, President George Bush, a man of vast government experience, initially positioned himself as the Wise Ruler. When running for reelection, however, he vacillated between Warrior and Orphan and lost his bid for a second term.

Similar patterns hold with corporations. Apple has made many serious business mistakes, but repeatedly has been saved by the great loyalty of its customers, who tend to love the company anyway. The firm's motto, "Think different," its logo of an apple with a bite out of it (suggesting Adam and Eve's disobedience in eating from the Tree of Knowledge), its reputation for innovation—each calls up the archetype of the constructive, independent Outlaw. In contrast, Microsoft's identity became synonymous with Bill Gates's Ruler-gone-amuck persona, wandering into the dark side of the bully and jeopardizing public support.

The Product as Prop in an Archetypal Drama

When archetypes are active, they evoke deep feelings. Sometimes those feelings have a spiritual resonance. In our religious traditions, foods frequently take on numinous significance—e.g., the "bread" and "wine" in Christian Communion or the Paschal Lamb in the Jewish Seder. In a more everyday, secular way, foods accrue symbolic cultural meaning. For example, in the United States it is traditional to serve turkey on the Thanksgiving holiday. This practice is so prevalent that the presence or absence of turkey can determine whether it feels like Thanksgiving. On a deeper level, turkey as a cultural symbol is one of the many expressions of the archetype of cornucopia, or the horn of plenty, that appears in harvest celebrations throughout the world.

Similarly, entire product lines can take on a meaning that gives them symbolic power in all of our lives. A tuxedo (black tie) signifies that an occasion is important. Champagne says that we are celebrating. It used to be that a golden ring signified marriage, but a successful advertising campaign has helped to confirm social convention, so that now, "A diamond is forever."

Some product lines also feel right as gifts in certain circumstances, because they serve as props in the story someone is just entering: a pen for the bar mitzvah boy, an attaché case for the MBA, a car for the young man or woman coming of age, a household item for the newlyweds. Buying a taco kit for a child signals that she or he is competent to make something to eat, even if mommy and daddy are busy.

The Pinocchio Effect

When you understand the potential archetypal power of your product, marketing becomes much simpler, more rewarding, and worthier of respect. The management of meaning is about selling products, but it also is about selling meaning with integrity. If companies fulfill their meaning promise to the same degree that they deliver quality products, they help customers in two ways: (1) by providing a functional product or service and (2) by helping people to experience meaning in ordinary life. If they do not, they are unlikely to compel brand loyalty.

Archetypes ennoble life by highlighting its meaning. For example, someone might feel attracted to another person without experiencing meaning, but the moment they connect with the love story, the archetype of the Lover is evoked and the world comes alive. Similarly, you might have a good time on a cross-country trip, but if you undertake the journey to find your long-lost father (or to discover the soul of America, get in touch with yourself, or seek your fortune), the archetype of the Pilgrim or Explorer is activated, and the experience becomes filled with meaning.

In a way, archetypal meaning is what makes brands come alive for people. Think of stories like *Pinocchio* or *The Velveteen Rabbit*, wherein an inanimate object comes alive. Archetypes are the heartbeat of a brand because they convey a meaning that makes customers

Nicknames Express the Ownership the Public Feels for Archetypal Brands	
Budweiser	Bud
McDonald's	Mickey D's
Coca-Cola	Coke
Federal Express	FedEx
AT&T	Ma Bell
Volkswagen Beetle	The Bug; and, more recently, the Buggie
Kentucky Fried Chicken	KFC*

*(The brand name was eventually changed to KFC, in part to acknowledge the consumers' nickname in the "official" name of the brand.)

relate to a product as if it actually were alive in some way. They have a relationship with it. They care about it.

One expression of the intimacy that develops between customers and archetypal brands is how users tend to give these brands nicknames, signaling, as they would with friends or relatives, a special, closer relationship. Coca-Cola has long been called "Coke"; Budweiser, "Bud"; McDonald's, "Mickey D's"; the Volkswagen Beetle, "the Bug"; and so on. True emotional "ownership" of the brand becomes ambiguous. Customers assert their "rights" to the meaning of their brands with the fury they expressed at New Coke, or their insistence that new stage interpretations of beloved classics such as *The Wizard of Oz* or *A Christmas Carol* remain absolutely true to the story lines of the originals. Don't mess with this, they say in so many words. It is part of my life, of my memories, of my history—and you have no right to change it.

Some products have succeeded easily at this because a clear, verifiable, and deliverable meaning is intrinsic to their function. Harvard, Yale, MIT, and other elite colleges generally market a Sage meaning, implicitly promising that if you go to such a school, you will know more, think more clearly, and be smarter than you were before entering. To use archetypal language, you will awaken the Sage within you by the time you graduate from one of these colleges, they claim. Intangible "meaning" and tangible results are so interconnected that to fail, you would have to undermine the institution's ability to deliver—by refusing to study, cheating, etc.

It may be less obvious that more everyday products (like dishwashing soap or cheese) can deliver on the archetypal promise of their message. But in every category, brands that come alive for consumers *can* do things you would not expect any inanimate, "heartless" object to accomplish.

Why do medical researchers always set up control groups to guard against the "placebo effect"? Because a condition can improve simply because the patient believes in the pill or the doctor. The researchers need to ensure that it is the drug they are testing that actually causes the cure. Similarly, we all need to develop products that actually do what they promise. However, in the meaning arena, the placebo effect is important because the meaning *itself* can have a positive effect on a consumer. For example, a woman buys a new dress and feels beautiful, like a goddess. A man (or woman) wanting to impress others pulls out an American Express card, pays the bill, and feels like a king (or queen).

After a psychologically contaminating or emotionally violating experience, many people will take a shower—as if the water could literally wash away feelings as well as dirt. Or, some people might shower just to wash away the cares of the day. Although rationally they may know that the water cleanses only their skin, in truth, the emotional meaning they attach to this practice transforms ordinary experience into a ritual that cleanses the soul as well as the body. If they have incorporated into their souls the brand meaning of renewal and purity in a bar of Ivory soap, it will take on a mediating function in the process, helping them to feel spiritually and emotionally (as well as physically) clean.

This is the placebo effect in its positive guise. Instead of filtering out the placebo effect, marketers would be advised to understand it so that they can use the power of belief not only to sell products, but also to help people and thus command brand loyalty. The important point here is that archetypal meaning, whether experienced consciously or unconsciously, triggers this placebo effect.

Often, the best corporate logos echo ancient symbols. Apple's logo, for instance, evokes the first act of rebellion in the Garden of Eden, a powerful distillation of the brand's iconoclastic identity.

Archetypal Meaning as the Driver of Product Development

Leveraging archetypal meaning is not simply about indiscriminately "attaching" meaning to a product. While it is true that archetypal meaning can play a role in differentiating commodity brands, this role is not its best or highest use. Brands that become truly iconic are archetypal through and through.

Perhaps one of the best contemporary illustrations of this principle is the Volkswagen Beetle, both in its early life and in its recent reincarnation. Sixties counterculture brought an interesting dilemma upon itself. Cars, especially the big living-room-on-wheels variety of their mothers' and fathers' generation, represented all that the children of the sixties rejected: excessive comfort, overt appeals to status, and unnecessary fuel consumption. Yet, they valued mobility, and hitchhiking could get them only so far.

The answer came in the form of a little car called the Volkswagen Beetle, or "Bug," which delivered on the Innocent principle in every way. The car was tiny beyond belief by then-Detroit standards, and its lines were so round, it was almost cuddly. It had no bells and whistles or excessive frills of any kind. It was wonderfully fuel efficient. It was cheap to buy, easy to fix, and seemed to run forever. And its style never changed. Bill Bernbach's brilliant advertising positioned this new "anticar" in ways that captured its unique spirit. His clever, humorous, award-winning commercials showed the Innocent "Bug" outwitting big gas-guzzlers: Little David getting the better of big Goliath.

Today, we look at the highly successful reincarnated version of the Beetle and want to smile. We may not know exactly why, but we feel that it would be really great to own and drive one. For some inexplicable reason, we are attracted to the bright, bold colors in which it is painted, like those on the color chart we first saw in kindergarten. As consumers, what we intuit, but cannot express, is our delight that the Innocent has been resurrected in such a clever new way.

How can this wholehearted expression of a relevant and, in its time, highly differentiating archetype be compared with that of an inadequate product upon which an archetypal identity has simply been "grafted"? The answers lie in the annals of marketing history. The best archetypal brands are—first and foremost—archetypal *products*, created to fulfill and embody fundamental human needs.

Quantitative Analysis Supports the Archetypal Basis of Winning Brands

Our early examinations of the world's most successful brands convinced us that their meaning was qualitatively different from that of ordinary brands; the meaning was expressive of timeless and universal archetypes. But even though our observations seemed incontrovertible, we also knew how much was at stake for our clients. We wanted an objective, quantitative test of our theory, grounded in real data. Fortunately, Young & Rubicam shared the same interest and had a powerful database that could be used to explore the theory.

First as an executive vice president and then as a consultant to Young & Rubicam, Margaret Mark had access to the company's BrandAsset Valuator (BAV), the most in-depth, extensive study of brands in the world. Comprising 75 investigations conducted in 33 countries, BAV enables Young & Rubicam continually to explore consumer attitudes toward more than 13,000 brands. To fully assess each brand's position, the BrandAsset model evaluates it in the context of an extensive cultural "brandscape" covering at least 100 categories of products and employing more than 55 measures per brand. Over 120,000 consumers have been interviewed for this study to date.

Working with Ed LeBar and Paul Fox at Young & Rubicam's BrandAsset Group, Margaret developed an algorithmic system for determining the extent to which consumers' perceptions of brands are aligned with archetypal identity. Weights are assigned to some 48 descriptive attributes included in BAV: obliging, rugged, carefree, authentic, daring, etc. Consumers' ratings are normalized within and across brands, and each brand is given a cumulative distribution score on each archetype. In this way, it can be determined whether a brand is strongly associated with any archetype and, if so, its primary archetypal identity, secondary identity, and so on.

Scoring of Archetypes

On the chart on the next page, archetypes are scored as follows:
- Scores are normalized within and across brands.
- Each brand receives a cumulative distribution score for each archetype (the percentile linking it to the archetype in the context of the full "brandscape").
- In an actual analysis, scores would be filled in on the following sample chart (shown for the rental-car category):

Sample Brands:	Hero	Joker/Jester	Innocent	Explorer	Outlaw	Caregiver	Regular Guy/Gal
Hertz							
Avis							
Budget							
Alamo							
National							
Dollar							
Enterprise							

Once brands are classified by archetype, the breadth and scope of BAV allows for explorations across a far-reaching consumer base and "brandscape," enabling examination of multiple industries, consumer segments, and types of brands.

Margaret, LeBar, and Fox began to generate hypotheses about the archetypal identity of brands and then tested the hypotheses against the database. The results were always illuminating, and the algorithm seemed to classify brands appropriately, suggesting that the hypotheses have a good deal of face validity. For example, the data showed that consumers saw Coke as an Innocent brand, which helped to explain many things, such as how much the sweet, playful "Polar Bears" commercial had caught on when so many others had not, during an explosive exploration of creative alternatives. It also helped to illuminate why earlier successes had included optimistic expressions of solidarity and love, such as "Mean Joe Green" and "I'd Like to Teach the World to Sing." Each commercial, in its own way and for its own time, had expressed the wish of the Innocent—to make the world a better, happier place. The data helped explain why the original bottle is so important to the brand's identity, as is the original Coke! As was demonstrated by Coca-Cola's abortive "New Coke" campaign, replacing the Innocent is much more a violation or betrayal of trust than are other kinds of substitutions. By way of contrast, the data showed that consumers viewed Pepsi as a Jester— an identity that shed light on why that brand, over time, was allowed to be changeable, and why it always is at its best when it good-naturedly pokes fun at sanctimonious Coke.

Because BAV is a longitudinal study conducted over an extended period, we also were able to explore how brands' archetypal identities have evolved, for good or for ill. For example, we conducted a BAV archetype analysis to try to diagnose why a leading brand of apparel was losing both sales and cultural prominence. The data revealed that, as recently as 1997, the brand was viewed strongly and consistently as a "Hero" across all age groups from 15 to 50+, as shown in the following table:

Apparel Brand's 1997 Index on the Hero Archetype	
Age:	
15–17	100.12
18–29	101.12
30–49	102.55
50+	95.41

Just two years later, the brand's Hero identity plummeted within only one group—unfortunately, the most important one, in terms of both its current "cultural cachet" and its future vitality: teenagers. The 1999 figures are shown in the following table:

Apparel Brand's 1999 Index on the Hero Archetype	
Age:	
15–17	33.62
18–29	104.00
30–49	101.06
50+	104.72

The Y&R Team concluded that the brand needed to reclaim its tough, competent, Heroic image and interpret it for a new generation.

While the case studies always were dramatic and insightful, the most powerful test of the archetypal theory would need to go far beyond the simple "classification" of any individual brand and instead explore broad patterns of how archetypal brands work and how they affect multiple criteria for success. It was with that intent that Young & Rubicam's analysts discovered that the strength of a brand's association with an archetype makes a significant difference in at least one fundamental indicator of true economic worth: asset valuation.

The BAV researchers were working with some pioneering concepts of economic performance developed by Stern Stewart, a highly respected financial consulting firm. Their analysis showed that brands associated with archetypal identities positively and profoundly influence the real asset valuation of their companies.

The measures involved are Market Value Added (MVA) and Economic Value Added (EVA). MVA is a measure of how much value a company has added to, or subtracted from, its shareholder investment. In other words, MVA measures whether investors expect that future profits of the corporation will be greater or less than the cost of capital. An increasing MVA indicates that the company is producing (or is likely to produce) higher rates of return than the cost of capital. A decreasing MVA shows that a firm has fallen short of expectations or has committed capital to new investments that the market does not expect to be justified.

EVA is the financial performance measure that comes closer than any other measure to capturing the true economic profit of an enterprise and is the measure most directly linked to the creation of shareholder wealth over time. EVA is an estimate of net operating profit minus an appropriate charge for the opportunity costs of all capital invested in the enterprise. As such, EVA is reflective of true economic profit, or the amount by which earnings exceed or fall short of the required minimum rate of return that shareholders and lenders could get by investing in other securities of comparable risk. A positive change in EVA reflects a company's internal progress in creating real value.

These measures are critically important because while most companies appear profitable under conventional accounting, many, in fact, are not. As Peter Drucker put it in a *Harvard Business Review* article, "Until a business returns a profit that is greater than its cost of capital, it operates at a loss. Never mind that it pays taxes as if it had a genuine profit. The enterprise still returns less to the economy than it devours in resources. Until then, it does not create wealth, it destroys it."

The Young & Rubicam analysis explored changes in EVA and MVA from 1993 to 1999 for a set of 50 well-known and highly regarded brands, such as American Express, American Greetings, Fruit of the Loom, Disney, Kodak, Sears, Heinz, Harley-Davidson, and The Gap. The relationship of changes in these fundamental financial indicators was profiled among two sets of brands: those with "tightly defined" archetypal identities, whose closest secondary relationship was 10% or more below the first, and a "confused" set of brands, whose secondary archetype was within this 10% boundary. Each set consisted of an equal number of brands.

The analysis showed that the MVA of those brands strongly aligned with a single archetype rose by 97% more than the MVA of confused brands. Also, over the six-year period under study, the EVA of strongly aligned brands grew at a rate 66% greater than that of the EVA of weakly aligned brands.

Of course, being believers, the researchers were enormously gratified (though not surprised) by the results. But the implication of these findings was quite impressive: Identities that succeed at striking an essential human chord affect the most fundamental economic measures of success. And what may be even more startling is what the data reveal about the importance of a single coherent archetype in successfully determining identity and influencing performance. Archetypes defy the "pick some characteristics from column A and some from column B" practice of creating brand identity; rather, these ancient psychic imprints are whole and complete concepts, demanding to be fully realized and deployed.

We now know that brands that consistently express an appropriate archetype drive profitability and success in real and sustainable ways. And in a very positive chain of causality, they can do this at no cost to the consumer or the culture. Indeed, such brands address deep and abiding human needs. The Young & Rubicam study demonstrates, without a doubt, the importance to marketing of understanding and maintaining an archetypal identity as a primary business asset.

How Archetypes Affect Consciousness

Not only conventional products and services, but also superstars, films, and public figures have achieved exceptional success by stumbling into archetypal territory. In fact, anyone associating meaning with a product already has moved onto archetypal terrain. The problem is that most marketing professionals have not been trained to understand the archetypal dimension. Consequently, they are dabbling in powerful material without fully comprehending it. But creating an archetypal identity, nourishing it, and managing it can and *must* become a deliberate, insight-based process. To use this theory, it is essential to understand what an archetype is and what it does.

One way to begin is by examining the great story patterns we see repeated throughout literature and film. One such scenario might involve a sexual encounter. Another might be about rising on the corporate ladder. Still another might begin with a character skipping work and going to the beach. While these stories and the fantasies upon which they are based may or may not have literary merit, you can easily recognize the plot structure as variants of the romantic love story, the rags-to-riches tale, or the take-me-away-from-it-all escape narrative, respectively. Although Freud assumed that our fantasies resulted from our experiences and conditioning only, Jung noted that fantasies are quite predictable, following well-known narrative patterns. Jung's perception was that all human beings share a common psychic heritage that undermines apparent differences of time, space, and culture.

One measure of how deeply these myths express elemental human concerns is the extent to which they are both timeless and universal. Mythologists and anthropologists see the same themes, situations, and stories played out again and again, across the ages and around the globe.

Perhaps the underlying reason that archetypes are so enduring is that, in essence, they reflect our inner realities and struggles. The external particulars may vary, but the essential journey is always the same.

Joseph Campbell and other students of mythology maintain that the various myths and archetypes found all around the world are basically expressions of the inner human drama: We can understand them as different expressions of an eternal impulse to find a human meaning in the mystery of creation. We "recognize" them because we have been programmed to do so. If you have only a few seconds to get your message across—as in a television commercial, print ad, or Web page—you can do so more effectively if your message taps into the stories we all know already. In the view of Jung, Campbell, and others, we come into life instinctually resonating to these archetypal stories because of the very ways in which our minds are configured. Therefore, the meaning of a product can be communicated very quickly simply by evoking a story or a concept that calls forth the viewer's instinctual recognition of some fundamental, recognizable truth.

Archetypes are the "software" of the psyche. One archetypal program or another is active and engaged at all times. For example, some people live constantly from the perspective of the "don't fence me in" Explorer, or the "my way or the highway" Ruler. These archetypes can be seen as the "default mode" for such individuals, just as an e-mail or word-processing program might be the default mode on our computers. Brands that are associated with each of these archetypes will feel right and comfortable to the people who express them and lend meaning to their lives in some interesting way.

Imagine a computer preloaded with a package of software programs. You cannot open and learn them all at once. Like software, archetypes lie dormant in the unconscious until they are opened or awakened. Just as software helps us do things such as write a book, create a spreadsheet, or produce transparencies, archetypes help us to fulfill ourselves and develop our potential. For example, if the Hero in us is awakened, we can learn to call up our courage to fight for others and ourselves.

Sometimes archetypes emerge because we are in a certain phase of life that evokes them: The child becomes a teenager and suddenly experiences the Explorer's need to be different—to separate from parents and learn about the greater world. However, dormant potentials may not be experienced until an outer event or image awakens them. For example, the grip of the me-first, narcissistic Explorer consciousness of the 1980s and much of the 1990s was relaxed when people responded with such strong feeling to the examples of altruism set by Princess Di and Mother Teresa—both of whom died just as the archetype of the Caregiver was attaining new life in the more general culture.

A young man may be ready for adventure, but that desire may remain latent until triggered by an ad for a car, an airline, or a motorbike. Soon he purchases a vehicle that will serve as the trusty steed on his adventure. The encounter with archetypal images in the external environment—in literature, art, movies, TV, or advertising—tends, over time, to move an archetype from dormancy to action. Archetypal images in advertising awaken archetypal stories—similar to the way clicking an icon on a computer screen opens a program.

Of course, the social implications of commercial communication awakening dormant archetypes are enormous and terrifying. However, we have no responsible way to avoid the potential pitfalls of this process but to learn what we are doing and why. Anyone engaged in the management of meaning already is operating at the archetypal level and affecting the consciousness of individuals and of our time. It is best to do so with caution, integrity, and—most of all—*knowledge* of the archetypal terrain. We predict that in a few years, it will seem as irresponsible to practice meaning management without archetypal knowledge as it now seems to practice medicine without understanding anatomy. While certainly it is less heinous to kill a brand than a person, it is not desirable to do so—and incompetence can still the heartbeat of even the best brand. Moreover, the meaning of a product cannot be sold without our actions affecting the collective consciousness of the age. If we are going to reinforce certain meaning patterns in a mass audience, we at least should know what impact we are having.

The Warning Label

Before continuing, it is important to caution the reader. Archetypes are powerful forces in the collective and individual psyche. As illustrated by O. J. and President Clinton, when they are active in a person, they can pull him or her into an unpleasant or even tragic story just as easily as a happy one. When you tap into the archetypal dimension—deliberately or by accident—these energies become activated in and around you. Whether or not they are expressed in a moral and healthy way depends on the consciousness of the person (or the company) evoking them. The more knowledgeable you are about archetypes, however, the more they can serve, metaphorically speaking, as your allies. Once you can name an archetype, you can choose whether and how to express it in your life, your work, and your marketing strategies. It is less likely to sweep you up and take you over.

Many marketers have stumbled—unawares and ill-equipped— onto archetypal territory. Because advertising is such an important and pervasive medium in our culture, it is only to be expected that it will be loaded with archetypal freight. That is a primary reason we have written this book—so that meaning management will not have negative side effects. We recognize that some people might use this information in manipulative ways. We have been concerned about this possibility, not only because we do not want the system to be misused, but also because we believe that doing so is dangerous to both the consumer and the perpetrator. Remember the great scene in the Disney movie *Fantasia* where Mickey, as the Sorcerer's Apprentice, creates mayhem? That is the most likely outcome of both naïve and unprincipled use of archetypal meaning.

3

Postmodern Marketing

VIRTUALLY EVERYONE writing about consumers today acknowledges that something radically new is going on. The modern age is over, and we are in a postmodern time, where the old rules do not necessarily hold. The new breed of consumer is not as trusting, as loyal, or as malleable as those of the past. Buyers today are savvy, deeply skeptical of advertising hype, and more concerned with finding and expressing their individuality than conforming to societal norms. They seek meaning, but they do not expect to find it in any kind of cultural consensus. Although they are pressed for time, they take time to be informed about their purchases and, when possible, like to call the shots. Also, they value independence and authenticity highly and are hard to fool. Access to the Internet gives them information about brands and companies, so what you say had better be the truth. If not, they surely will find out.

While this new breed throws many marketing professionals off stride, it does not have to throw you. Think about it. We are living in a time of great affluence, wherein many people have access not only to virtually any product they want, but also to education, travel, and information. Yet, to a great degree, cultural consensus about values has broken down. We have few if any shared sacred stories to give our lives meaning. Joseph Campbell put it this way: "The problem of mankind today, therefore, is precisely the opposite to that of men in the comparatively stable periods of those great coordinating mythologies, which now are known as lies. Then all meaning was in the group, in the great anonymous forms, none in the self-expressive individual; today no meaning is in the group—none in the world; all is in the individual."[1] As a result, people are thrown back on their own devices. They have to find themselves and know what they think, feel, want, and stand for. For brands, this means that the archetypes of the Explorer (for finding identity) and the Sage (for exploring one's inner world) likely are salient motivators. In addition, when people aspire to be unique individuals, capable of independent choice, they are attracted to higher levels of other archetypes than they might have been before.

For instance, the Cinderella story is one archetypal narrative pattern associated with the Lover archetype. That the narrative still packs an archetypal punch is apparent from the fact that many movies employing variants on this theme enjoy box office success—*Pretty Woman* being just one example. The level of sophistication of the culture, however, affects the interpretation of the story. At the lower level of this archetype, people can read the story rather shallowly and think that Cinderella needs only to get a great dress and a sporty car (i.e., carriage) to attract the modern-day prince—who himself does not have to have much besides good looks and great wealth. Indeed, the ratings attained by a television show like "Who Wants to Marry a Multimillionaire?" demonstrate that this level of the archetype still works—at least among the contestants. Yet, even here, some of the fascination for viewers undoubtedly was seeing women who actually would marry a man they did not know just for the money, and a seemingly successful man who would marry a woman primarily on the basis of looks. This behavior, in the contemporary context, is odd enough to entice interest.

It is important to recognize that a critical mass of people no longer are so shallow as to believe that love results just from using

---

1. Joseph Campbell, *The Hero with a Thousand Faces* (New York: The World Publishing Company, 1949), p. 388.

the right products. They do not think that the combination of a beautiful dress, face, and body on her part and a large bank account on his is a formula for true love. Rather, they expect both Cinderella and the Prince to be self-actualized individuals with personalities, values, strengths, and weaknesses—if only because they have watched Oprah.

Perhaps, having absorbed the lesson taught by our society's high divorce rate, most thinking people know that if the Prince marries the dress and Cinderella marries the castle, soon they will wake up disillusioned to the reality of a flesh-and-blood human being.

This does not mean that good ads cannot employ the Cinderella narrative. Such archetypal stories bear repeating. You can tell them over and over, and people will not be bored. That's what it means to tap into an archetypal story pattern. However, as human consciousness evolves, people interpret the stories differently. Embedded in the fairy tale is an emphasis on character that is recognized easily by a complex person, even though someone who is more shallow and undeveloped may miss it. Along with a loving nature, Cinderella has the capacity for virtue and hard work. The prince is not only "charming"; he also has enough soul and perseverance to search throughout the kingdom for a woman he met only once. If your customer base is even relatively sophisticated psychologically, your ads will be more compelling if they tap into the deeper aspects of archetypes, not just their superficial trappings.

As illustrated in the Cinderella example, were you to choose a brand meaning of Lover, but emphasize a kind of belonging that compromised your identity, modern consumers would be put off in a way that their mothers and fathers might not have been. So, too, if you choose the brand identity of the Ruler, you have to realize that modern consumers are willing to be constituents, but not subjects. The progression from monarchies to democracy (like the progression from arranged marriages to romantic love) is connected to the evolving capacity of ordinary people to individuate themselves and therefore to expect rights of self-definition.

Within each archetype is a wide range of behaviors, some very simple and others more evolved. For example, within the Lover archetype, you will find (1) simple awakening of lust; (2) the desperate desire to attract a lover; (3) the attainment of deep and abiding romantic love; (4) the capacity for intimacy with family, friends, and colleagues; and (5) spiritual love for all of humankind or even all sentient beings.

As we researched archetypes in ads and brands today, we discovered that the largest percentage of ads is designed as if this change had not taken place. In fact, they communicate with the reader at the lower stages of each archetype—the forms in which the archetype is expressed when a person is *not* self-actualized. For example, everywhere we looked, we found Explorer ads. Marketers clearly understand that this archetype speaks to people today. Yet, we were disappointed that so few of them tapped into the deeper and more interesting level of the archetype. The overwhelming majority of the Explorer ads we surveyed focused simply on either being out in nature or feelings of alienation. Few were designed to help people with the deeper learning task of the archetype—that of truly finding oneself.

Ironically, when people do not develop the capacity to make meaningful choices in a society that offers practically an infinite number of options, they tend to blame society for their own defects. Consequently, they rail against the materialism of society and the corporations that produce consumer goods, instead of taking responsibility for their own purchasing decisions. Paradoxically, corporations that do not help consumers gain a capacity for self-definition and responsible choice will be prey to consumer backlash.

Beyond Market Segmentation, Beyond Stereotyping

Even more importantly, because most people in the field of marketing do not understand archetypes, and because they think in terms of market segmentation, they have an unfortunate tendency to reduce archetypes to stereotypes. For instance, imagine a high-achieving executive. She ordinarily might be attracted by ads for Ruler products, which reinforce her sense of status or power and help her make her mark on the world. Reading an airline magazine, she might perk up at an ad that offers her a more effective planning calendar, an innovative computer program, or a power suit. While a variety of products might help her achieve and maintain power (or just feel powerful), what will signal their appeal to her is the underlying symbolism of regal power, status, and control. If marketers think in terms of market segments, it may be tempting to stereotype such a person, mentally confining her to a very narrow motivational category.

However, if we realize that she is a full human being, then it isn't difficult to recognize that from time to time, she might feel trapped by her high-powered life. Like many of us, she may be working so hard that she has begun to feel too driven. Every human being has a basic desire to achieve, and this desire may have taken over her life. In addition, we all have a need for pleasure and adventure. Our executive might not even be conscious of this sense of yearning or the need for balance. Yet, despite this lack of awareness, she is suddenly attracted by advertising images that connote freedom.

The Jester could appear to her through an ad in which people are having a wonderful time drinking a particular beer, an airline is taking a couple to exotic places, or happy people are riding in a convertible by the beach. Whether or not she analyzes her responses and concludes that she needs more balance in her life, she might well respond to the archetypal pull by buying the beer and throwing a party, booking her next trip on the airline, or purchasing the convertible (even if she never actually takes it to the beach).

The woman who is juggling multiple roles may be empowered by the ability of the archetypal Hero to overcome great challenges or the Ruler to maintain order when chaos threatens. But she also may be attracted to archetypes that give her what she is craving, rather than those that simply reflect what she is experiencing. Thus, she may respond to the peace and simplicity of the Innocent or the erotic intensity of the Lover.

Instead of connecting with empowering images, the representation of the modern "superwoman" in advertising today has become clichéd and stereotyped. Most women are simply annoyed when they encounter yet another portrayal of the overworked, frantic wife–mother–career woman. They do not feel known. Rather, they feel trivialized, just as they once felt demeaned by stereotypical images of the housewife.

People's eyes glaze over when confronted by messages that do not meet them where their compelling issues are. This may be *the* primary reason marketers have trouble getting the attention of consumers who are facing challenges that require them to be complex and real, and who are not living out the boring stereotypes that often are implicit in market segmentation categories and simpleminded assumptions about human motivation. To do archetypal branding well, it is advisable to tap into the deeper, more humanly compelling quality of archetypes, rather than treating them in an incidental manner as lifeless stereotypes.

Crossing Boundaries

While the archetypes are universal, the "valance" surrounding them changes on a cultural basis. In the United States, for instance, a shared value of individualism reinforces the Explorer archetype with an emphasis on discovering and expressing one's own uniqueness. Other cultures are more relational. In Latin America, children live with their parents until they marry. The culture reinforces fidelity to family and community over individualism. This predilection also is strong in the former Soviet republics, as well as in China and Japan. Relational cultures are living out a different story than individualist cultures.

Even within the United States, different workplaces reflect different mores and archetypal plots. For example, many for-profit firms (Microsoft, for one) are living out the value of becoming the premier company in the entire industry (the Ruler). By contrast, most nonprofit organizations are more likely to stress making a difference to the world (the Caregiver). Colleges and universities emphasize learning and the discovery of truth (the Sage), while many companies in the fields of entertainment, dessert (Ben and Jerry's), and recreation (Patagonia) accentuate pleasure and fun (the Jester). Values are different. These differences become clear when companies articulate their vision, values, and mission statements. At least in the best companies, the bottom line is never just profits and revenue.

In the past, the image a company conjured up might result in part from conscious marketing decisions, but even more so from the unconscious assumptions of people in the field. You know people who go into nursing because they are caring. So, too, corporations whose products support health and healing (think Johnson & Johnson) may have Caregiver values. A young, ingenious hacker may enjoy a line of work that involves continuous learning and endless innovation. A technologically innovative computer firm may be energized by the same Sage archetype motivations.

Quite unconsciously, the management of these companies tends to be attracted to brand identities consistent with the archetypes that simultaneously are shaping their own behavior and the corporate culture. This is how some leading companies happen onto archetypal identities and manage to retain them over time—especially if they have leadership that trusts their own insides and their intuitive hunches. They like brand identities that are like them. However, if they don't—and if marketing firms convince them to follow every fad or public whim—they inevitably will drift from one identity to another, creating no clear lasting impression.

Marketing and advertising firms also have their unconscious biases. Within the field, individuals and firms have quite different reasons for getting out of bed in the morning. We all know people in advertising who have a novel in the drawer or ideas for making videos or films. They are in advertising because the field offers a well-paid way to express their creativity and artistry. We also may know people who love the competitive aspects of marketing—and are propelled onward by their enjoyment of the contest. Still others like the mental stimulation of marketing strategy. In archetypal terms, these examples reflect the archetypes of the Creator, the Hero (as competitor), and the Sage. If people in the field are uneducated about archetypes, the approaches they try to sell may simply reflect their own unconscious predilections and not be optimal for the client.

To determine the brand identity a company will like, it is best to find out who the firm thinks it is—in terms of the archetypes it is living out. The biographies of successful business leaders demonstrate that, generally, they are drawn to a field or a product for some reason. Even in a societal context, where money and success are primary, individuals' deeper values are reflected in the details of their ambitions—the dreams that propel them forward. These values and dreams create an identifiable organizational culture, which is then reflected in its brand identity (e.g., IBM vs. Apple). We can trace the values to the underlying archetypes (in this case, Ruler and Outlaw/ Rebel, respectively), making it possible to factor the archetype of the organization into discussions of brand identity.

Individuals, societies, and organizations frequently have different archetypes that are dominant, but each has at least some access to all archetypes. While a CEO might have a dominant Ruler archetype, he may buy a toy for his son that appeals to his own fun-loving Jester or his desire to nurture a child (Caregiver). He may be motivated to buy a necklace for his wife to express his Lover, or to spend more time developing the technological side of his industry in service of his Sage. Similarly, successful companies are so generally because all the archetypes are expressed somewhere within them. Organizations that thrive have at least one active archetype in each quadrant helping them to find their unique mission (individuality), create the feeling of community (belonging), get the work done (mastery), and create stabilizing structures (stability).

Yet, for a brand identity to be compelling, it needs to be simple and easy to recognize. This means that brand identities are forged best by identifying solidly with one—and only one—archetype. The archetype within the brand serves as a beacon for the corresponding motivation in all of us. In practice, with the high rate of product innovation, it generally is prudent to brand the company, not just the product or services. Companies do best when they are explicit about the archetype that is truest to their values, mission, and vision—and allow that archetype to shine, like a beacon in a lighthouse, drawing others to their shores.

Until now, in most companies the link between organizational culture, corporate values, and brand identity has been informal and largely unconscious. The system we describe here can provide a means to discover, articulate, and strengthen that connection. Brand identity for an organization is like the persona for an individual. It is the image we present in the world. When an individual's persona is too different from the reality of the self, he or she becomes neurotic. So, too, with organizations: If their brand identity and their actual corporate culture, policies, and procedures are discordant, they become unhealthy. As a consequence, both employee morale and credibility with customers begin to plummet.

As with the individual, an organization does not have to show the world everything and certainly does not have to display its dirty linen. Nevertheless, in a world where people from all over are chatting on-line with your employees, the more congruent you are, the better off you will be. Understanding and aligning the archetypal core of your values, your organizational culture, and your brand identity—and having a logic and a language to help you do so—allows you to manage meaning in a way that can prevent scandal and embarrassment, while also inspiring employee and customer loyalty.

Customer Loyalty and the Experience of Meaning

The most profound change affecting marketing for the new millennium is the quasi-priestly role it plays in a society without sacred stories to provide our whole culture with shared meaning. In part, the lack of such stories offers us a kind of personal freedom never before experienced. Anthropologists tell us that in the developed world, for the first time in the history of the human race, the story of our lives cannot be predicted by our gender and our social station at birth. We are free to define ourselves for ourselves and to choose our own life path.

Of course, this freedom brings tremendous power and exhilaration. But it also creates an unprecedented degree of stress. We have to figure everything out on our own. If we are working mothers, many of us have no role models to guide us. If we are men who want to play an active role in parenting, we may not be able to draw on much from our own experiences growing up with our fathers. For one thing, they worked away from home, where we could not see them. For another, they lived by a male ethic that, like the traditional female ethic, has become anachronistic.

Life really did shift radically in the 1960s. Baby boomers and every other cohort since that decade now are living lives much different from those of their parents. Many whose parents were doctors or lawyers have chosen to become social workers and shopkeepers, and many whose parents were laborers have gone on to become doctors and lawyers. It is wonderful to have such opportunity for self-definition and self-determination, but it also is burdensome, because we have to be pioneers in the journey of life. The personal icons and heroes who once provided models for how to live one's life have largely been replaced by friends and relatives who, however valued or beloved, may not set a relevant or useful example.

Adding to our predicament, we are engaged in this quest at a time when civilization provides us with almost no cultural guideposts. The village elders, the Bible, the great oral tradition, the classic stories—all have fallen by the wayside, just at the time we need them most.

But the human need for archetypes to guide us does not evaporate; rather, it grows. And as with all human needs, when the original source of satisfaction is absent, something fills the void. For our young people, it's peer groups and gangs. And for all of us, it's Hollywood and Madison Avenue, the great Myth Machines of our times, spewing forth a steady stream of "meaning" into the culture, without a clue or a thought as to what they are doing. We are creating meaning without managing meaning.

It's no wonder, then, that the public appetite for meaning, particularly archetypal meaning, is so strong that archetypal brands, in the form of personalities, public figures, and corporate offerings, are fervently embraced and fiercely defended.

All products have the potential to be mediators of meaning, somewhat like ritual objects. A child hugs a teddy bear and feels loved. Actually, the bear is just an inanimate object. It does not love the child. But it does represent the mother's love of the child, and the child releases his or her own love in the hugging. Similarly, a young, somewhat stressed career woman steps into her convertible and experiences a sense of freedom. The truth may be that she is just driving home. But the sensation of her hands on the wheel and the wind in her hair is liberating.

The freedom this woman feels is not a surrogate for some other experience or the result of some false-advertising promise; it's the real thing—at least for that moment. The meaning carried by the brand addresses a deep psychological need or yearning.

How does this differ from addiction, which keeps people coming back for more in a destructive way? We become addicted to substances that promise what they cannot deliver and thus manipulate the psyche. Archetypal marketing, on the other hand, is rooted in product truth and actually fulfills people's deeper yearnings.

People need authentic meaning. Deepak Chopra cites research suggesting that a lack of meaning is correlated strongly with heart attacks. Victor Frankel credits a sense of meaning with enabling people to survive in concentration camps.

Of course, people derive meaning in their lives primarily from their faith, their families, or their sense of purpose. If they do not do so, their lives will have a void that commerce can never fill. However, with commercial messages, products, and services infiltrating every single aspect of our lives, it is important that they carry significance and values as well—especially if marketers understand that the meaning most products deliver to people is of a much lower order than the experiences people have in their lives.

Consciously utilizing brands and the products that bear their names to provide meaning not only creates customer loyalty, but also helps people experience greater fulfillment in their lives and their work, at least in small ways that incrementally improve the quality of everyday life. That's how to build strong and resilient customer loyalty.

Imagine—just imagine—that we could do so consciously, responsibly, and well. We could be the first generation of marketers to address timeless and universal human needs in a way that builds timeless, universal, commercially effective—and *psychologically constructive*—brands.

The Telescope and the Artichoke

The ancients employed their native human abilities in pattern recognition to group stars into constellations that they then used to navigate difficult waters. Similarly, this first system for the management of meaning provides a kind of telescope to help you see the patterns that unify the "stars" in the branding world. Without a system, you may not see these patterns—or you may connect the dots in ways that are unique to you, but that do not resonate with others.

Parts 2 through 5 will help you recognize the underlying patterns that explain why archetypal brands and archetypal communication have such power. These chapters focus on the 12 archetypes within the four motivational categories, exploring how each archetype is expressed in typical advertisements (many of which do not reflect a coherent brand concept), brand identities, customer motivation, organizational cultures, and marketing strategies. (For more information on these archetypes as they play out in the psyches of individuals, see Carol Pearson's *Awakening the Heroes Within*. For more information on their roles in forming organizational cultures, see her book *Invisible Forces*.)[2]

Most of the examples we use represent ephemeral brand communication, not a fully sustained identity. In addition, these chapters are written in a value-neutral way and in no sense should be taken as an endorsement of any of the brands, advertisements, or organizations we mention.

Parts 6 and 7 are more like an artichoke. When eating an artichoke, you strip away extraneous leaves until you get to the core. Similarly, to determine which archetypal meaning is best for your brand, you will need to strip away surface information to discover the deeper core meaning that can make your product, service, or organization a winning brand, as described in Chapter 16 in Part 6. Chapter 17 shows you how to tell your brand story in a compelling way—not just in advertising, but in everything you do. Chapter 18 puts all of the information described up to that point together in a case-study format, highlighting how archetypes helped provide a renewed sense of mission for the March of Dimes.

Part 7 shows you how to recognize the archetype most essential to your brand's product category (Chapter 19), how to align your brand identity with your corporate culture (Chapter 20), and how to consider the deep ethical issues relevant to the marketing of meaning (Chapter 21).

Overall, *The Heroes and the Outlaws* provides an in-depth understanding of the impact of brand meaning on consumer psychology and on the collective consciousness of our time. It is written primarily for professionals in the field of marketing and executives who

---

2. See Carol S. Pearson, *The Hero Within: Six Archetypes We Live By* (San Francisco: HarperSanFrancisco, revised edition, 1998); *Awakening the Heroes Within: 12 Archetypes That Help Us Find Ourselves and Transform Our Worlds* (San Francisco: HarperSanFrancisco, 1991); and *Invisible Forces: Harnessing the Power of Archetypes to Improve Your Career and Your Organization* (Gladwyne, PA: Type and Archetype Press, 1997).

make marketing decisions. It also is useful for people in the organizational development field, as well as others in management, who can help to align an organization's policies, procedures, and culture with its brand identity. In addition, *The Hero and the Outlaw* can be helpful in developing consumer literacy.

II

The Yearning for Paradise

Innocent, Explorer, Sage

R EMEMBER BRIGADOON? Just a glimpse of paradise, and then people are doomed to endure ordinary life. Today's consumers all have some recollection, some experience of a wondrous moment when the perfect, good life seemed possible. For much of the rest of their lives, they seek to fulfill a longing for some ideal place where they can feel fully themselves and at home.

Some psychologists explain this yearning as a desire to reexperience the safety and oneness of the womb. In a more spiritual context, it can be seen as a result of the nostalgia we feel because we left a spiritual place for a material world. In "Intimations of Immortality from Recollections of Early Childhood," the English Romantic poet William Wordsworth suggests that, as young children, we remember a glory that we have known, but gradually we forget it and settle for ordinary life: "Heaven lies about us in our infancy! Shades of

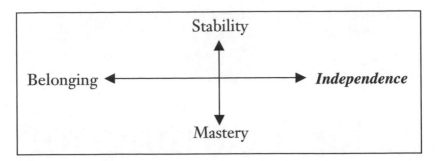

Figure 2.1

the prison-house begin to close/Upon the growing boy . . . At length the man perceives it die away,/And fade into the light of common day." By the end of the poem, however, Wordsworth recaptures spiritual rapture on the mountaintop and feels as if he has reentered paradise.

In fact, many consumers today do live in a kind of paradise. In material terms, we currently enjoy greater affluence than humankind has ever known. Yet happiness evades many of us because consciousness has not kept up with our material advantages. We have so many choices, in terms of how to pursue our individual destinies, but so few guideposts to help us find the way. That is why archetypes and archetypal stories that provide a road map for self-actualization are more relevant than ever before.

The three archetypes that are central to this chapter provide different strategies for the pursuit of fulfillment. The Innocent is a bit like the lovely little child or the wise mystic, filled with wonder at the beauty of it all, still believing it is possible to live in paradise right now. At the lower levels of the archetype, people feel that this is their birthright and therefore become angry when life seems to let them down. At a higher level, the Innocent makes choices for a simpler, more values-driven life and moves into paradise by acting on this decision.

We see the Innocent's consciousness in society today in the strong desire parents have to make their children's lives perfect—to deny them nothing, to require little of them, and to allow them to express themselves as free spirits. We also see it in the revival in the 1990s and beyond of a concern for spirit or values as the basis for a sane and happy life.

The Explorer is driven by a sense of not quite belonging, like the Ugly Duckling seeking its own kind. Explorers suffer from an underlying dissatisfaction and restlessness, as if they are constantly seeking something better, but again and again saying "not this" and hitting the road. Like the Hebrews leaving Egypt, the Explorer may wander in the wilderness for 40 years (a metaphor for "as long as it takes") before reaching the Promised Land.

Developmentally, this archetype helps with the task of finding oneself. All that outer seeking really is a strategy for exploring experiences, settings, relationships, and products that resonate with the Explorer's inner truth. Along the way, Explorers have wonderful adventures.

While the Innocent seeks fulfillment in the here and now, and the Explorer hits the road in search of it, the Sage tells us that happiness is the result of education. Living with the level of freedom and abundance we now have requires a high level of consciousness and the attendant ability to make choices. The Sage archetype helps us gain the consciousness to use our freedom and prosperity to enhance our lives.

At the more everyday level, the Explorer looks for products and services that advance the journey of self-discovery, the Innocent looks for those that provide the experience of peace and goodness right now, and the Sage seeks those that are adjuncts to learning or wisdom.

As consumers, Explorers are independent minded and curious. They like to try new things, so to gain their loyalty, it is important to provide continual novelty and improvements in products. (Software companies have this one down.) Innocents, by contrast, like to find a brand they can trust and stick to it, believing that "If it ain't broke, don't fix it." They also like brands that make life simple (user-friendly computers, for example). Sages like to have all the relevant information they need to make informed decisions about brands. They also enjoy learning, so products that require a learning curve (like computers) appeal to them.

All three archetypes emphasize self over others and autonomy

The Jolly Green Giant echoes the natural purity of the Green Man, a mythic image of the abundance of nature, transferring the Innocent ideal to Green Giant's frozen, "farm fresh" vegetables.

over belonging. (See the motivational grid in Figure 2.1.) They often play out in opposition to the archetypes in Part 4, which place a higher value on belonging than on authenticity. Of course, to enter the Promised Land, it is necessary to find ways to balance the desire for individuation with the desire to connect.

CHAPTER 4

The Innocent

Motto: "Free to be you and me."

Every culture has myths of a golden age when life was perfect and utopian visions of how it might become that wonderful again. Symbols like the Star over Bethlehem announcing the birth of the Christ child, the Holy Grail appearing to the knights of the Round Table, or a vine-covered house with a white picket fence suggest that it is possible to find happiness through the triumph of a kind of simple purity or goodness. The Innocent in each of us wants to live in that perfect land where we are "free to be you and me."

The promise of the Innocent is that life does not need to be hard. You are free to be yourself and to live out your best values right now, right here, just by following simple guidelines. Best-sellers such as *Chicken Soup for the Soul* (in all its variations) and *All I Really Need to Know I Learned in Kindergarten* speak to the part of us that trusts in an ultimate kind of simplicity. The Innocent is extraordinarily attractive in this hectic, stressful age because it promises that you can get out of the fast lane, relax, and truly enjoy your life.

Innocent brands include movie stars Doris Day, Meg Ryan, and Tom Hanks, the movies *Baby Boom* and *Local Hero*, the PBS network, Keds, Disney, Breyers, Ronald McDonald, Baskin-Robbins, the Pillsbury Doughboy, Ivory, cotton ("the fabric of our lives"), and most

> **The Innocent**
>
> **Core desire:** to experience paradise
> **Goal:** to be happy
> **Fear:** doing something wrong or bad that will provoke punishment
> **Strategy:** do things right
> **Gift:** faith and optimism

whole or organic foods. Such brands promise the experience of returning to innocence—that life can be simple, uncomplicated, and good.

The movie *The Accidental Tourist* plays on this Innocent hope that it is possible even to travel without experiencing the slightest inconvenience, while implicit in *Forrest Gump* is the faith that it is possible to experience all the challenges of the sixties, seventies, and eighties and remain unscathed if we keep the simple sweetness and love of a true Innocent. While none of us wants Forrest's limited IQ, the incredible success of the movie tells us that we do appreciate his purity of spirit and his simple power to endure.

Historically, many brands appeal implicitly to the Innocent by promising a predictable rescue from an imperfect world. Ads that show a man with dandruff, a shirt with ring around the collar, or a proposal that may not arrive by mail by the deadline appeal to people's desire for rescue. "This is an unfair, unsafe world. You can get rejected, abandoned, fired, or exiled if you do not do it right. But Eden can be restored if you buy our product—your scalp becomes healthy and attractive, your clothes look immaculate, the proposal gets accepted, and life is secure once more." However, contemporary consumers respond less well to such blatant promises of simple answers. Nevertheless, in its more subtle forms, the Innocent archetype still has strong appeal. In fact, as life becomes more complex, that appeal is growing.

Innocent films include many Disney movies (as well as Disneyland and Disney World) and most Warner Brothers children's movies. Classic songs that reveal the yearning for Innocence include "Someone to Watch Over Me," "Summertime," "The Age of Aquarius" ("We've got to get ourselves back to the garden"), and "Don't Worry, Be Happy."

People who resonate to the Innocent archetype long to have the perfect work, the perfect mate, the perfect home, perfect kids, and the ideal life. The primary promise of the Innocent is that life can be Eden. Think of Christmas and most Christmas specials and the attendant sense of wonder and hope that life can be beautiful, especially if we simply believe in its possibilities and choose to do right ourselves. The secondary promise is that if any fall from Eden occurs, redemption is possible: Unpleasant or challenging events can lead eventually to a happy ending, and stagnation can lead to renewal.

> The Innocent also may be known as Pollyanna, *puer or puella*, utopian, traditionalist, naive, mystic, saint, romantic, traditionalist, dreamer.

Of all the archetypes, the Innocent has the most levels, because people experience it at both the beginning and the end of the journey. (See box, "Levels of the Innocent," below.) Initially the Innocent has a childlike quality of naivete and a simple, even unconscious, dependence. Children should be able to take it for granted that their parents and other relatives will care for them. However, many people carry that outlook over into adult situations where such trust is not necessarily warranted. For example, today, more workers than one might have an anachronistic expectation that their employers will take care of them—regardless of whether they are effective in their jobs. Such assumptions can lead to an extreme sense of disillusionment when management does not do so.

At the highest level, the Innocent is the mystic. A famous example is Thomas Merton, the modern Trappist monk who lived most of his life in a monastery, retired from the world; yet his books profoundly affected his time. In a more ordinary sense, people who

---

Levels of the Innocent

The Call: a desire for purity, goodness, and simplicity
Level One: childlike simplicity, naive, dependent, obedient, trusting, idyllic
Level Two: renewal, positive, reinventing, reframing, cleansing, reentering the Promised Land
Level Three: an almost mystical sense of oneness, whereby Innocence comes from values and integrity, not outer experience; being, not doing
Shadow: denial, repression

choose to follow a mystic path in retirement are responding to the truth that innocence beckons the very young and the very old. In either case, the gift is trust in life and faith in a spiritual power greater than ourselves that holds us and keeps us safe, even beyond death.

The Promise of Paradise

The idea of an earthly paradise retains a tremendous hold on the imagination of the modern world, so much so that Ernest Hemingway once said that all American literature was a search for paradise— "the great good place." In many myths, the ideal place is symbolized by a domesticated landscape: a garden, a sacred grove, a pasture. Life is always easier in these places: Death, pain, and suffering do not exist there, and you do not have to work hard to survive.

In paradise you do not want for anything. The Balinese, for example, tend to think of Bali itself as an earthly paradise. Because they are certain that they will have everything they need, they live happily and simply, requiring very few possessions. At the same time, they are not competitive, cooperating with one another even in the production of art. Spirituality infuses everyday life, so that a very simple life is full of meaning. Of course, the natural environment, too, is idyllic in its beauty. Yet it also is true that the Balinese belief that they live in paradise is a self-fulfilling prophecy.

Even in a more materialistic and competitive society, the Innocent archetype is associated with simple pleasures, basic values, and a wholesomeness that make it the meaning of choice for natural products (think cotton, for example), soap, breakfast foods (especially oatmeal and whole-grain cereals), and other domestic products. Folgers coffee, for example, has come to embody the domesticated Eden the Innocent yearns for—a cheerful, comfy house, the smell of coffee brewing, the promise of a new day.

Possibilities for ads invoking the perfect experience are endless. Doubletree Hotels appeals to this desire explicitly, running idyllic pictures and the words "the perfect getaway." Nortel Networks runs an ad quoting Carlos Santana saying "A road to a world with no borders, no boundaries, no flags, no countries—where the heart is the only passport you carry." The promise is that the Internet provides the metaphoric path to the perfect world.

Some brands acknowledge the limits of their ability to create Eden, appealing to consumers who recognize the reality that it is quite an accomplishment to make *any* part of life wonderful. Rockport Shoes pictures a comfortable pair of shoes with the tag line "Life is perfect, at least from the ankle down." The investment brokerage Morgan Stanley Dean Witter ran an ad with a lovely, natural-looking, mature woman—cotton shirt, flowing hair—invoking an Innocent yearning, but with a surprising twist: "How do you measure success? I have someone to watch over me. Me." The ad recognizes the Innocent's desire to be cared for and implies that the company does some of the watching, but it also appeals to women's desire for independence: This woman is not waiting for the white knight to rescue her; she helps to create the perfect life by taking responsibility for her own.

In today's complex world, even the most sophisticated and jaded parents feel a strong pull to keep their children as innocent as they can, as long as they can. For many, this takes the form of trying to give them everything they could ever want, so that they never have the experience of lacking anything. Babystyle lightheartedly jokes about the appeal of such innocence to parents. Under a picture of a totally captivating baby is the caption "He'll make you laugh. He'll make you cry. He'll make you buy him lots of stuff."

There is often something unabashedly childlike even about ads appealing to adults when the Innocent archetype is being evoked. Before its bankruptcy, e-retailer Value America had ads showing a picture not just of comfy slippers, but of pink, bunny-eared ones. The company's explicit promise was hassle-free shopping. ("Forget where you parked your car. Ignore pushy sales clerks. Lose your tolerance for limited selection. But wear your shopping shoes"—the slippers.) The implicit promise of pink bunny slippers is way beyond easy shopping; it is an escape from power suits and soccer-mom car pools to being a kid again. J. C. Penney's ads and catalogues similarly highlight women and children in soft, pastel, frilly clothing. Land's End runs an ad of a white room with French doors leading to a natural backyard, with a woman dressed all in white dancing unself-consciously. The caption says, "You don't just want clothes. You want clothes that make you feel completely at ease with yourself. Like when you were six."

The Innocent often wants to go back to nature and natural living. Clairol Herbal Essence pictures spring leaves and flowers, promising "a totally organic experience with style." You can think of Thoreau in America advocating the simple, natural life, or Gandhi, in India, who advocated a return to simplicity in ways that would free that country from British rule. Similarly, you can remember the back-to-nature hippie impulse in the 1960s. In today's affluent, but rather driven and fast-paced society, the urge to go back to a simpler life takes on a rather different emphasis. A magazine like the upscale *Real Simple* promises "low-stress living, one-dish dinners, simpler skin care, clothes that work, nurturing friendships, [and] serene spaces," yet delivers on this promise by advertisements for extremely expensive, but nostalgic, clothing.

Real Simple (motto: "do less, have more") has been created with the Innocent visual effect. Colors are soft pastel. Images are simple, uncluttered, and classic. The page layout provides a refreshing amount of white space that keeps the text and the message from being overwhelming.

Sometimes, new technologies wisely capitalize on the promise of the Innocent to help translate what can be off-putting features of a product into something that feels natural and wholesome. For years, the Jolly Green Giant, created by Leo Burnett, epitomized the fresh, wholesome qualities of the frozen vegetables bearing that name. Never mind that frozen felt less than perfect; the evocation of the Green Man and his lush, abundant valley helped to convey the idea that flash-frozen vegetables could bring even more of the farm to your table. Likewise, the Pillsbury Doughboy, also a Leo Burnett creation, embodies all of the natural wholesomeness of "baking," even as the word was being redefined to mean removing a product from a tube and putting it into the oven. Even in a hurried, technology-driven time, the act of taking something warm out of the oven (however it got there!) conveys a feeling of "life as it should be," as it was before we were all so busy and distracted.

Even in the so-called "vice" categories, the Innocent archetype has been used effectively. For example, in the early days of its national rollout, Coors beer's reliance on the pristine imagery of the Rocky Mountains set it apart from a meat-and-potatoes category and led drinkers to imagine John Denver and rushing streams of pure water. More recently, regional beers have succeeded in conveying this spirit. Instead of imagining a huge factory when thinking of the production of these brews, consumers picture a small brewery, full of local color, and they believe that the characteristics of the locale are somehow delivered in the experience of drinking the beer.

The marketing of environmentalism is a natural for emphasizing the Innocent archetype. America's electric utility companies have run an ad with a picture of a lovely little girl in a sunlit, idyllic forest and the following words superimposed on the image: "We're doing our part to make sure our children inherit a world where the wood thrush still has a reason to sing."

Back to Basics

The poet W.H. Auden wrote that people come in two varieties: Utopians, who imagine the perfect world in the future, and Edenists, who, if life is not perfect now, believe it once was in the past. Innocent ads, then, often appeal to nostalgia. An ad for Belvedere Vodka runs a picture of a wonderfully alive old man with the words "The same way my father made it. The same way his father made it. The same way his father made it. . . ." The ad explains further that the vodka is "drafted using traditions over 500 years old." The revival of Rheingold beer, which traced its roots to Brooklyn in 1835, was fueled with the energy of nostalgia, as was the reintroduction of the Volkswagen Beetle. Early Rheingold ads also played on the Innocent's optimism, saying "Suddenly the world's glass is half full again."

Like a good child, the Innocent is always trying to get life right. An ad for Maxwell House—with the requisite Innocent pastel colors and a sweet-looking young woman with a white blouse and soft blue coffee cup—resolves, "I will forgive my husband for snoring. I will stop finishing other people's sentences. I will buy myself sunflowers and anemones. I will send my parents on an Alaskan cruise. I will read everything ever written." At the bottom is the promise of paradise: "Make every day good to the last drop."

The Innocent is not only allied with the past; it is also associated with getting back to fundamental values and simple pleasures. An ad for Crystal Light (low-calorie) lemonade pictures a woman dressed in white, with a soft yellow shawl, standing on a beach, looking ecstatic. The caption, which is written in script to look like a note that might be from a friend, reads, "because a single-digit dress size does not guarantee happiness, an afternoon of piggyback rides beats a day on the treadmill, a moment of laughter is the best therapy, do what works for you. That's the beauty of Crystal Light." Papyrus stores pictures a woman—again all dressed in white, on a soft yellow rug, reading a card illustrated with delicate lavender flowers. The card says, again in handwriting, "an oasis in the information age." Continuing in print, it remarks, "The simple pleasure of the act of writing remains. That is because the most memorable messages are those written by hand."

As the pace of life picks up and technology defines more and more of our lives, the Innocent wants peace, ease, naturalness, and, most of all, to have some things endure. The Innocent explains the appeal of tours to Amish country, of Shaker furniture, and of Ikea, which, the ad tells us, means "common sense."

Coke: An Innocent Masterpiece

Coca-Cola has generally been brilliant in its consistent understanding that it is an Innocent brand, although the framing of that brand identity happened primarily as a side effect of a decision to connect the brand with America.

A character in a Nancy Mitford novel called *The Blessing* sums up the meaning of Coke this way: "When I say a bottle of Coca-Cola, I mean it metaphorically speaking. I mean it as an outward and visible sign of something inward and spiritual, I mean it as if each Coca-Cola bottle contained a djinn [spirit], and as if that djinn was our great American civilization ready to spring out of each bottle and cover the whole global universe with its great wide wings."

During the Second World War, Coke made a compelling case for the importance of a cool, refreshing, nonalcoholic drink for soldiers. Dwight D. Eisenhower was a strong believer in the motiva-

tional power of Coke. In fact, after a key invasion, Ike asked the
company to set up sufficient production facilities to provide 3 million
bottles for the troops.

Postwar Coke became associated with a particularly global kind
of Americanism, distinguishable from the Harley-Davidson kind by
its idealism. In the early 1970s, Coke hit a home run with the following words from its theme song: "I'd like to build the world a
home and furnish it with love/Grow apple trees and honeybees and
snow white turtle doves." The song was so popular, it ran for six
years.[1]

Even the slogan "Coke, it's the real thing" suggests the emphasis
within the archetype on honesty and authenticity. The firm's one real
mistake—the introduction of New Coke—ended up rebounding to
its benefit, as customers demanded Classic Coke, demonstrating an
enviable amount of customer loyalty.

The Promise of Renewal

The United States is not only associated with enduring, wholesome
values; it is also integrally associated with new beginnings. From the
immigrants coming to the New World to wagon trains going west,
America has promised that people could start over and, when necessary, reinvent themselves. "Go west, young man," urged journalist
Horace Greeley during the latter part of the 19th century. Horatio
Alger stories written in the early 20th century invested that onward
and upward energy into entering an economic system that rewarded
merit.

Walt Disney's Mickey Mouse cartoons typically illustrated how
persistence transmutes defeat into success. Disney himself had en-
dured many failures before ultimately gaining enormous success, as
had his family before him. In inventing the famous mouse, his intention was to reinforce the best of the American rags-to-riches tradition and to teach values of optimism and persistence. Before he
died, Disney summed up the impulse behind his films this way: "I

---

1. Bernice Kanner, *The 100 Best TV Commercials . . . and Why They Worked* (New York:
Times Business, 1999), pp. 18–19.

hate to see downbeat pictures. . . . I know life isn't that way, and I don't want anyone telling me it is."[2]

Our research among older Americans has shown that even more than the population at large, they love seeing babies and children in advertising. For them, the innocence of children has a special poignancy; it is the best of new beginnings, validating one's own existence and the continuity of life.

A Procter & Gamble report entitled "Celebrating 100 years of Ivory soap as America's Favorite" begins by recognizing that Ivory continues a "tradition that six generations of Americans have enjoyed. That tradition is reborn each time a new generation reaches for a bar of Ivory; it is reborn each time Ivory keeps its promise of quality, first made a century ago." Ivory, however, does not just embody renewal within continuity; it also promises something like redemption.

We know the way that religions offer spiritual renewal. Scholar Mircea Eliade explains that one of the central rituals in primitive cultures is an annual rite in which the world is symbolically re-created. Christianity speaks of the renewal of Easter and of grace washing away sin. In the Catholic practice, confession and penance allow for the forgiveness of sins. The period between the Jewish New Year and the Day of Atonement calls for Jews not only to reflect on the ways they have broken the laws but also to make amends as best they can so that they can go into the New Year with a clean slate.

It is not at all surprising that religions teach us how rituals of forgiveness can restore our simple faith, optimism, and goodness. It is more surprising that a product like Ivory soap has managed to establish a secular meaning not unlike the religious one. Company legend has it that Harley Procter, one of the founders of Procter & Gamble, was sitting in church thinking about how to market a new soap that accidentally floated. When the minister began reading the 45th Psalm, Procter felt that the Edenic words were just for him and his quandary: "All thy garments smell of myrrh and aloes and cassia out of ivory palaces whereby they have made thee glad." Hence came the name "Ivory" and the idea that this soap could be associated with

---

2. Thaddeus Wawro, *Radicals & Visionaries: Entrepreneurs Who Revolutionized the 20th Century* (Irvine, CA: Entrepreneur Press, 2000), pp. 109–114.

purity, goodness, and renewal "so pure, [that] it floats." The first wrappers were white with black writing, updated to white and blue later to convey an image of crisp cleanliness. The slogan, of course, was "99 and 44/100 percent pure."

Procter & Gamble had the wisdom to align this brand meaning with the company's early business practice. A 19th-century Ivory plant was named Ivorydale and was dedicated to the ideal that a plant should be a pleasant place to work. It had massive windows to let in light and air and also featured well-kept lawns, flower beds, and recreational areas. For 100 years, ads consistently showed lovely babies, as well as wholesome images of children and mothers with beautiful, fresh complexions that the firm promoted as the "Ivory look." The consistency of this approach, over time, allowed Ivory to take on a meaning that translated its physical purity (as having relatively few defects) into a kind of metaphorical spiritual purity. And in some special way, that purity was associated with America, with family values, and with all that is right with the world.

The Innocent Organization: The Case of McDonald's

Innocent organizations include mom-and-pop shops, small neighborhood businesses, and any organization that is unself-consciously dedicated to practicing simple values. Short on innovation and long on loyalty, they emphasize predictability more than change.

The Innocent archetype is also connected to the concern people feel about large, anonymous conglomerates buying or closing out small, community-based, values-based businesses, as is dramatized in movies like *You've Got Mail*. The shift to global businesses is often seen by the Innocent as the end of a way of life. Ironically, the Innocent consumer rarely sees the connection between this trend and his or her own desire for inexpensive products. It is that very desire that forces businesses to get big in order to attain the critical mass necessary to compete. One way they resolve this dilemma is the franchise.

One Innocent marketing masterpiece can be seen in the growth of McDonald's as not only a widely successful business but also a prototype for a whole type of business. Designed for children and families, McDonald's promises a fun place—a variant on the "great, good place." Arches are wonderfully consistent symbols for the entrance into a Promised Land, and McDonald's golden arches announce the availability of "food, folks, and fun." To some people, McDonald's golden arches are reminiscent of a well-known Sunday school illustration of the tablets containing the Ten Commandments. Although it is unlikely that the McDonald's Corporation had that intention, the fact that people make this association links the arches with the Innocent archetype's faith that if we would all just follow the rules, Eden could be restored.

The Ronald McDonald character, Happy Meals, and primary colors all appeal to children, as does the play equipment. McDonald's philanthropic efforts also are consistent with the desire to make the world a bit better for children: Ronald McDonald Houses help children and their families cope with critical illnesses.

Ernest Hemingway's classic short story "A Clean, Well-Lighted Place" illustrates the desire many people feel to escape, temporarily at least, the ambiguity and uncertainty of modern life. McDonald's has that same appeal. McDonald's restaurants not only are consistently clean and well lighted; they also serve exactly the same food— at least in the continental United States. Nor do they confuse the customer with many choices. And their core dish is the most identifiable American food (other than fried chicken): the hamburger.

The Innocent likes predictability and certainty. Anywhere you travel in the United States, you know exactly what you will find at McDonald's: the same menu, the same décor, and even the same specials. In the late 1940s, two brothers, Dick and Maurice (Mac) McDonald, recognized the speedup in American life that made fast food and drive-through windows important. They also understood that customers may want their meals fast, but also predictable. Ray Kroc helped the McDonald brothers franchise their fantastically successful restaurant.

Kroc realized that the franchise had to be a version of the mom-and-pop store. The best owners were not rich people, but people willing to bet their lives and life savings on one break, often a husband-and-wife team. Quality control became an internal company religion. Franchise owners were trained to do things exactly the same way. The result was a seemingly paradoxical situation, but one intrinsic to the Innocent archetype. McDonald's sought out people who were entrepreneurial enough to want to try running their own small business, but who were not especially innovative. They had to be willing to do things the same way, the right way. In short, these were people captivated by the ambitious American dream, but who also did not want to change anything. They had to believe that the perfect world of McDonald's had already been invented and did not need to be improved—at least not by them.[3]

Although McDonald's does not pay its employees especially well, it does provide opportunities for teenagers and immigrants to find jobs and begin to learn good work habits—including punctuality, good customer service, and, most of all, predictable delivery. Innocent employees like to know exactly what is expected of them and, to some degree at least, like to be taken care of by management. Often they behave like good children, and are willing to be obedient and follow the rules in exchange for some reasonable certainty of having a job.

The Innocent organization exists not just in franchises, but also in multilevel marketing structures such as Amway and Mary Kay, which encourage ambitious salespeople to make their fortunes by enlisting their friends and relatives in not only buying the product, but also selling it. Often the company is selling not just a product, but explicit values. As Mary Kay expresses it, "God, then family, then Mary Kay." In such cases, employees are willing to take enormous risks because they believe in the values of the company and the promise of success through persistence and hard work.

The Innocent as Mystic

Advertising for products is taking on a more spiritual tone, sometimes in a tongue-in-cheek manner. Most people today are aware of spiritual practices that people follow for their whole lives before achieving the desired enlightenment. The lower level Innocent wants the outcome without the discipline and hard work. An ad for Taster's Choice, sporting a cup of coffee sitting on the sand, reads, "Some meditate for hours searching for inner peace. Others find it instantly. Serenity. Tranquility. Balance. It's all right here—made fresh in your

3. Wawro, pp. 250–253.

cup. Rich, smooth Taster's Choice." Taster's Choice, of course, does not expect customers actually to believe that a cup of coffee is equivalent to years of meditation, but it does offer the moment of peace available to them now. Reading the ad can provide a chuckle of recognition: "Maybe someday I'll do what it takes to be enlightened. Right now I can stop to smell, and taste, the coffee."

People today are tired. The driven pace of modern life, the striving of the Hero, and the restlessness of the Explorer leave people little peace. This means that just slowing down itself can feel spiritual. Buddhist monk Thich Nhat Hanh, for example, teaches exhausted Americans to slow down and be in the moment. Commercials appealing to the Innocent need to be slower than those aimed at the Explorer and less crisp. You can think Impressionist paintings, natural sounds, and gentleness in approach and imagery.

The Innocent Customer

When the Innocent archetype is active in an individual, a person is attracted to certainty, to positive and hopeful ideas, to simple, nostalgic images, and to the promise of rescue and redemption. The Innocent also strives for goodness, which can mean finding the "right" product, but it also means choosing moral over immoral behaviors and kindness over greed. People who are high in Innocence often are very trusting and, in some cases, unconsciously dependent and childlike. They place faith in authorities and institutions and expect them to deliver on their promises.

At the same time, people with a high degree of Innocence have a capacity for great independence from the dominant society. If customers believe that a product or an organization can deliver on promises of paradise or that it is based on eternal values, they are willing to step out of the dominant society and its values in order to experience something they conceive to be of greater worth. The paradox is that Innocent consumers are both traditional—in wanting to connect with the values of the past—and also willing to sacrifice belonging to the larger society to connect with more enduring values than those they see as informing that society. Examples of Innocents are, in most extreme form, the Amish in the United States, fundamentalists in any religion and in any society, and people who "drop out" of a high-pressure, achievement-driven culture to experience the joy of the simple life.

On the other hand, all this rushing about and resultant depletion of their energy can make Innocents regress, so some of them may evidence the lower levels of the archetype. In a large number of consumers, innocence is associated with a certain narcissism and childishness. Many customers today are impatient and do not like to wait. They want things when they want them and the way they want them. Speed is therefore of the essence, as is superb customer service.

Immature Innocents tend to dislike people who complain about or dwell on their problems. In fact, they dislike anyone who makes them see the negative potential in life (without providing a solution), which includes corporations that make excuses for their lack of responsiveness. The majority of Innocent consumers today expect to be the center of value for the corporation: Their wishes are the corporation's command.

There also may be the shadow of rage in the Innocent against whatever forces in the world they identify as being responsible for the breakdown of values and civility in modern life. Conservatives blame liberals. Liberals blame conservatives. Majority Innocents may blame minorities, while minorities blame racism.

Innocents also have a tendency to go into denial about problems and not face them until they escalate, simply because they want life to be perfect—now. The most extreme example of this is Nazi Germany, where most good people were in denial about the Holocaust. In the United States, analogous situations would be the annihilation of the buffalo and the systematic destruction of American Indian civilization. How does this attitude influence commerce? What it means is that the Innocent is self-involved and may not empathize with your dilemma. For example, many consumers today expect perfection in their dealings with corporate America. If you do not fulfill this fantasy, they happily go elsewhere. But at the same time, customers who respond to the appeal of the Innocent archetype are likely to be loyal to your brand if their experience is positive, simply because, unlike Explorers, Innocents like predictability more than novelty. Innocents may, for example, remain loyal customers of L. L.

Bean, because of the company's almost flawless customer service and the image it purveys of a pure store somewhere in Maine that has not been "corrupted" by corporate greed.

If you compare the new Innocents with those in the 1940s and 1950s, you can see a major change. In the forties and fifties, Innocents really were innocent—trusting, loyal, even willing to have expert voice-overs talking down to them. In the sixties, innocence got more complicated. The back-to-nature hippie movement was fueled in part by the Explorer's belief that the dominant society was shallow and materialistic. Innocents within this context emphasize the importance of quality goods—they want fewer—and handcrafted, not mass produced, things. By the 1980s, Innocent energy was channeled into the New Age—which was a utopian spiritual movement. Some New Age thinking has reflected the immature Innocent's desire for deliverance—like the belief that aliens are going to rescue us or that forces are operating on the planet that are automatically creating a more spiritual time, without human effort. According to more grounded New Age thinking, however, the perfect world is created by a change of consciousness. In this context, the Innocent just becomes more sophisticated, through the utilization of skills and abilities available from a variety of spiritual traditions—from yoga to meditation to native rituals.

In the 1990s, the Innocent's hopes and dreams were focused on two possibilities: first, the Y2K computer "bug," widely predicted to cause the breakdown of a technological and materialist society, followed by a more cooperative, community-based, caring society; and second, a cultural transformation resting on technological advancements, especially the Internet.

We can hear the voices of many archetypes in different people's reflections on the World Wide Web and its impact on our lives. However, those with an Innocent cast typically take on religious imagery and a utopian tone. Margaret Wertheim, in *The Pearly Gates of Cyberspace*, quotes Mark Pesce:

> Let us begin with the object of desire. It exists, it has existed for all of time, and will continue eternally. It has held the attention of all mystics and witches and hackers for all time. It is the Graal. The mythology of the sangraall—the Holy Grail—like the archetype of the

revealed illumination withdrawn. The revelation of the graal is always a personal and unique experience. . . . I know—because I have heard it countless times from many people across the world—that this moment of revelation is the common element in our experience as a community. The graal is our firm foundation.[4]

Pesce describes his first experience of learning about cyberspace as a "moment of revelation," like a religious epiphany. While this characterization is extreme, many people write about the Web as offering the potential to create a harmonious and egalitarian world. It is seen as making oneness tangible, so that all people can get to know one another across distances and national boundaries.

To our knowledge, no one overtly developed a scheme to provide a spiritually utopian brand identity for the Web. It happened because many have seen it as a tool for the realization of their most noble dreams of human potential. However, Internet-related businesses can capitalize on the halo effect gained by association. The Web gives us infinite capability to connect with one another, making the dream of oneness realizable. As Wertheim points out, for centuries humankind has believed that life in the body drags us down. Interaction on the Web is purely a communication among minds. The body is completely irrelevant to it. It can be experienced as the place where minds or spirits touch, unhindered by physical reality. This vision, too, inherently requires greater sophistication, because even Innocents need to learn to use such technologies and actually connect with others different from themselves before any of their utopian fantasies can be realized, even in part.

Our point here is *not* that we are about to enter paradise. Rather, it is that those in marketing need to understand that people still have the yearning for paradise characteristic of the Innocent, even though they are no longer simple or naïve. You can actually observe the history of Innocent consciousness in the 1990s simply by tracking the Academy Award for best picture during that decade. We went from *Forrest Gump* early in the nineties to *Titanic* (a metaphor for the threatened end of civilization as the millennium approached) and,

4. Margaret Wertheim, *The Pearly Gates of Cyberspace* (New York: W.W. Norton & Co., 1999), p. 254.

The Innocent archetype provides a good identity for brands that

- provide a relatively simple answer to an identifiable problem.
- are associated with goodness, morality, simplicity, nostalgia, or childhood.
- have functions associated with cleanliness, health, or virtue—and that are infinitely replicable.
- are priced moderate to low.
- are produced by a company with straight-arrow core values.
- desire to differentiate from a product with a tarnished image.

finally, *American Beauty*. The new Innocent is savvy and skeptical, as well as weary. Yet, the more jaded people get, the bigger is the pull of the great dream. Innocence is not really about reality; it is about keeping hope alive.

In *American Beauty*, the hero leaves the emptiness of his career (in marketing, ironically), recognizes the pathology of his dysfunctional family, and escapes into regressive patterns of slinging hamburgers in a fast-food restaurant and lusting after a teenager. By the end, he has the quintessential Innocent mystic vision, recognizing that the simple pleasure of living his life is, in fact, enough. His expression of profound gratitude for the gift of being alive—as well as audiences' unexpected appreciation of the film—suggests a new level of the Innocent in the world today, one that is able to see the beauty in life even while recognizing its limitations.

CHAPTER

5

The Explorer

Motto: "Don't Fence Me In."

W HILE THE INNOCENT EXPECTS to be able to live in paradise, as a right or by virtue of a shift in consciousness, the Explorer goes out seeking a better world. The journey Explorers are experiencing is simultaneously inner and outer, because they are motivated by a deep desire to find what, in the outer world, fits with their inner needs, preferences, and hopes.

The Explorer's story is at the root of the success of the whole genre of travelogues (including immigrant narratives); fairy tales (such as *Hansel and Gretel*) in which the protagonist goes on a journey, gets entrapped in some way, and finally escapes; science fiction (about exploring the universe); coming-of-age stories; narratives about leaving marriages, jobs, or town; expatriate literature; literature about seeking the promised land; and all absurdist literature demonstrating human alienation.

Great Explorer-brand literature includes Mark Twain's *The Adventures of Huckleberry Finn*, F. Scott Fitzgerald's *The Great Gatsby*, Jack Kerouac's *On the Road*, Ralph Ellison's *The Invisible Man*, T. S. Eliot's "The Waste Land," and, of course, Homer's *The Odyssey*. Famous Explorer-brand television series are "The Lone Ranger" and "Star Trek" ("To Boldly Go Where No Man Has Gone Before").

The old cowboy classic may be the Explorer anthem: "Give me

> ## The Explorer
>
> **Core desire:** the freedom to find out who you are through exploring the world
> **Goal:** to experience a better, more authentic, more fulfilling life
> **Greatest fear:** getting trapped, conforming, inner emptiness, nonbeing
> **Strategy:** journey, seek out and experience new things, escape from entrapment and boredom
> **Trap:** aimless wandering, becoming a misfit
> **Gift:** autonomy, ambition, ability to be true to one's own soul

> The Explorer also may be known as the seeker, adventurer, iconoclast, wanderer, individualist, pilgrim, quester, antihero, rebel.

land, lots of land, 'neath the starry skies above. Don't fence me in," although the country classic "Take this job and shove it" vies for second place. Folk music is an Explorer genre.

Products and services that successfully embody the Explorer archetype must serve in some way as useful props on Explorer journeys in order to compel any kind of brand loyalty. This starts at the level of literal journeying and moves into its more figurative versions.

Props for the Journey

One expression of the Explorer is the simple desire to hit the open road and to be in the wild, wide-open spaces of nature—to experience the joy of discovery. Products, then, that serve naturally as props on the Explorer's journey are often automobiles (Ford Explorer, "No Boundaries"); any kind of off-road vehicle (Jeep Wrangler, "Take your body where your mind has already wandered"); and boats of various kinds.

If you think of the typical ad for such a product, you know the Explorer's most natural setting: big open skies; the appeal of the open road; nature in all its variations, but especially mountains, asking to be climbed; the compelling quality of the receding horizon, always removed, no matter how far you travel; the night sky, speaking volumes about the infinite possibilities of outer space.

Of course, Explorers often like sports, but not necessarily for competitive reasons. Instead, they tend to favor individualistic or even solitary pursuits, such as kayaking, skiing, biking, or long-dis-

> ## Levels of the Explorer
>
> **The Call:** Alienation, dissatisfaction, restlessness, yearning, boredom
> **Level One:** hitting the open road, going out into nature, exploring the world
> **Level Two:** seeking your own individuality, to individuate, to become fulfilled
> **Level Three:** expressing individuality and uniqueness
> **Shadow:** being so alienated, you cannot find any way to fit in

tance running—activities that get them out in nature and give them time to clear their heads. Backroads is a travel agency that books weeklong and longer trips, featuring these experiences throughout the world, clearly attracting the Explorer in each of us.

To create great Explorer brands, of course, you have to get into the Explorer story—not just the setting, but also the costumes. What kind of clothes would an Explorer want to wear? Sturdy ones, of course, that give you room to move. (Think, for example, of brands like Levi's REI, Patagonia, and Land's End.)

Explorers' desire for freedom makes them wary of being tied down by anything—including big mortgages or time payments. Currently, Yamaha motorcycle ads use the lead "Declare your independence. Not Chapter 11."

Music is great solace on the road. Sony has made hay with this urge, first with the Walkman—the Explorer's own music, in his or her own space—and now with the Memory Stick ("Your digital images. Your music. Your work. Your ideas." Programmed into the stick). You get hungry, you stop at Burger King, which, catering to Explorer types, lets you "have it your way."

What might you want to drink when you're on the road? A great cup of coffee! Traditionally, coffee has been a Caregiver product category (Think of Folgers' Mrs. Olsen, in her own homey kitchen, dishing out motherly advice as she pours another coffee.) Starbucks, however, saw an opportunity for creating a compelling Explorer coffee brand, in part by emphasizing the exotic quality of coffee as an import from foreign lands.

Starbucks, an Explorer-Brand Masterpiece

Starbucks, listed by Interbrand as "one of 25 great global brands of the 21st century" and by *Fortune* as one of the "100 Best Companies to work for," is a contemporary success story and an Explorer archetype masterpiece, not only because the brand expresses the archetype consistently—in its name, logo, packaging, retail shops, product, service, and mythology. The Explorer theme starts with the Starbucks name, which is a classic literary reference to the American novel *Moby Dick*, by Herman Melville. Starbuck was the first mate on a whaling ship, the *Pequod*. Despite the commercial nature of the voyage, the captain, Ahab, became so obsessed with killing Moby Dick (in revenge for the whale having bitten off his leg), that he forgot his responsibilities to his stockholders. At the end, the *Pequod* is lost, and almost all its crew are dead.

Starbuck is the solid, stable foil for Ahab's obsessive craziness. In the modern world, Ahab's frenzied attack on the whale can be likened to the devastation of the environment, while Starbucks' (the company's) evenhanded appreciation of nature and responsibility to the consumer could provide a modern ecological ideal. Starbucks reinforces its association with proenvironment values and with exotic places by donating a percentage of the company's profits to environmental causes in coffee-growing countries. Starbucks also stresses environmentally friendly construction and design materials for its stores and always includes a cart for recyclables.

The masculine name—Starbucks—is complemented by the logo of a sea goddess with long spiraling locks (anthropologist Angeles Arrien links spirals with a subconscious desire for becoming), with the result that Starbucks has a particularly androgynous feel (like adolescents today). The color green reinforces the ecological, natural imagery, while the Starbucks décor, combining metal piping and wood, is reminiscent of a sailing ship.

Starbucks, of course, imports fine coffees and makes them available for all the restless folks who need either a quick, comfortable place (patterned on the coffeehouses of Milan) to rest (and perhaps chat) for a bit or a quick cup to take on the road.

The number of available choices of coffee, milk, and syrup makes the ordering of coffee a statement of personal identity (one ad cam-

Starbucks' logo supports the sea theme of this Explorer brand. The logo is reminiscent of this sea goddess depicted in a 1659 French woodcut.

paign explicitly presented ordering coffee as a statement of the customer's uniqueness), and the upscale quality of the place implies a sense of personal taste. You never stand in too long a line—because, after all, Explorers get restless. And Starbucks is everywhere—at least in the mainland United States. Almost anywhere you are, you can stop for a *latte* to go.

Starbucks has gone international and, in the United States, has teamed with airlines and ferries (emphasizing the on-the-road Explorer theme), with Barnes & Noble bookstores (where people come looking for ways of self-improvement and to explore new ideas), and with colleges (as the Explorer is often active in young adults). The

Explorer in all of us is youthful. By touting a *latte* that is three-quarters milk, Starbucks even manages to promote a product that exemplifies how children traditionally first drink coffee—and to make ordering it cool!

Starbucks is now such an important part of American culture that Magic Johnson is investing his money to open stores in such places as Harlem and South L.A., secure in the belief that just having one in a depressed area will bring a greater sense of hope and upward mobility.

How did Starbucks convince people to pay over two dollars for coffee? Simple: the Explorer archetype, artfully expressed in every detail—the product, the packaging, the shops, the logo, the name, and the very experience of placing an order. Such is the power of that archetype.

The Feel of the Journey—at Home

Even if you are not literally taking a trip, Explorer products can provide the feel of wide-open spaces. For example, Trex Decks has a wonderful Explorer ad showing a series of round overlapping decks spiraling from the home to overlook a huge canyon. You can see for miles and miles, and the caption says "How Far Would You Go if Nothing Was Holding You Back?" Timberpeg, promoting those wonderful Western glass, wood, and stone homes (generally sporting a view to die for) uses the slogan "You don't always have to go outside to enjoy the wide-open spaces."

Today the Explorer can sit at home alone and surf the net, exploring not so much physically, but through a whole world of information. Amazon.com's name calls up the image of sailing the Amazon River as you actually sit comfortably in your home. Catering to the individualism of the Explorer, it promises 24-hour access to books and music from an astounding array of sources, keeps track of individual customer purchases, and recommends what else they might enjoy. In short order, the company is likely to begin publishing the books their customers most want to read. While Amazon.com may or may not find a way to be profitable, its product launch indisputably provided an example of almost instant brand identity.

The archetypal Amazon name also conjures up images of the legendary warrior women of ancient Greece, providing an association with great feminine power. A majority of readers are female, and many (though, of course, not all women) channel their desire to seek out new experiences and find their identities less into hitting the road than into hitting the books. The name, then, also has a particular appeal for women.

By this time, it may go without saying that the image of the Amazon is deeply archetypal. So it is not surprising that one of the first companies to establish a true brand identity on the Web did so, in part, by adopting an archetypal name that evoked an appropriate meaning.

What country makes the most supportive home for the Explorer? One could make a case for Australia, but all in all, the United States is the quintessential Explorer-brand country, with its immigrant heritage and emphasis on political rights. The country was founded on the Declaration of Independence, asserting each person's right to "life, liberty, and the pursuit of happiness." Even the Constitution was carefully drafted to provide checks and balances to be certain that no part of the government would gain enough power to curtail freedom. U.S. history begins with the Pilgrims, and its dominant mythology is captured in the settling of the West. The slogan "Go west, young man" that sent young men (and women) out to settle the West gave a literalness and direction to the restless ambition of the American character.

Part of the attraction of American exports, then, is the spirit of the Explorer archetype. Whether it is a teenager in China buying a can of Pepsi or someone in Romania finding a pair of black-market Nikes, part of what they are buying is a small and fleeting sense of freedom and possibility.

The Explorer Goes Global

In an increasingly global marketplace, it is important to remember that not every country shares the Explorer's values, either because of political limitations or because of the pure force of culture. Asian and Latin American cultures, for example, tend to be far more relational and affiliating, placing greater value on the group than on the individual. This does not mean, however, that people within these cultures do not have access to the Explorer archetype. Indeed, part of the appeal of American Explorer products may, in fact, be that they reinforce the validity of finding yourself, even if your primary culture undervalues this important developmental task. The simple assumption that the rights of the individual should be protected is one of America's most compelling exports, a value that is often sold unconsciously along with U.S. products. (Of course, Americans also benefit from the value exports of other countries. For example, Asian cultures have exported meditation techniques to the United States and, in doing so, have encouraged the expression of a particularly peaceful aspect of the Sage archetype underdeveloped here.)

Because the Explorer so loves to travel, virtually any imported products can have a bit of an Explorer brand's allure, especially products from more primitive or exotic countries. Even domestic products with a global meaning have appeal. For example, long before Starbucks emerged on the scene, General Foods (now Kraft Foods) launched a line of flavored instant coffees called General Foods International Coffees.

In the seventies and eighties, while most coffee brands were perceptually grounded in the kitchen of the homey housewife, these "international" coffees offered flavors such as "Orange Cappuccino" and "Swiss Mocha." Their early spokesperson, a celebrity named Carol Lawrence, was featured in the ads breezing back from Europe with her latest "discovery." The line used in the campaign was "General Foods International Coffees—as much a feeling as a flavor."

Not only was the brand successful, but it was able to sustain profit margins much higher than the norm for the category. Why? Partly because the Explorer archetype was able to powerfully differentiate the brand from those in the rest of the category. Also, because the brand tapped into—and perhaps even gently nurtured—the emerging Explorer archetype in its female customers.

The Youthful Explorer

Any archetype can be expressed in a person of any age. However, adolescents and twenty-somethings in virtually any culture are likely to have an Explorer side to them because it is their developmental task to figure out who they are and what they want to do. Whatever fashions they adopt (long hair and tight jeans in the sixties; body piercing and loose jeans in the nineties) are chosen because they confront the older generation's sense of propriety and establish the younger generation's personal style. All products, of course, that help them do so will prosper. Folk and rock music did this in the 1960s; rap music and MTV do today.

The Explorer identifies with the Outsider. This explains why adolescent styles of the 1960s were influenced by American Indians—headbands, for instance—and why teenagers in affluent suburban neighborhoods were quick to jump on the bandwagon in the 1990s when inner-city kids started wearing baggy pants.

Brands that are attentive to the Outsider influence on the fashion of the young also subtly—and largely unconsciously—help to integrate outsider values and manners into mainstream culture, and vice versa. While Anglo kids in affluent suburbs were beginning to wear high tops and low-slung baggy pants, preppy Tommy Hilfiger clothes were catching on like wildfire in the inner cities, as each group of teens integrated the sensibility of the "outside" culture into their own lives. Although most of us share a concern about the number of young people who are taking up smoking, it is still a sign of the power of the Explorer archetype that Virginia Slims has been so successful with the slogan "Find Your Own Voice." Unfortunately, it is the very need to identify with the countercultural message that makes it difficult for young people to sort out the difference between harmful products and benign outsider brands.

For many young people, the Explorer archetype is associated with the experience of leaving home and going off to college. However, some students are more influenced by the individualistic Explorer than others. Certain colleges vigorously promote themselves as Explorer brands—most notably Goddard, Hampshire, and Antioch, all of which allow students to structure their own majors. The catalogues of these schools emphasize the enormous freedom available to students to forge their own paths.

The other stage in life during which the Explorer becomes powerfully reactivated is middle age. In story or fact, the Explorer may literally take off. (See, for example, Ann Tyler's *Ladder of Years*, in which a restless middle-aged wife and mother goes for a walk on the beach and, without ever formally deciding to do so, just keeps going and doesn't come back.)

The Explorer as Individualist

The Explorer may be expressed in the desire for self-sufficiency. FreeAgent.com personnel services makes explicit the desire to flee from the corporate expectation of company spirit, advertising that the firm is "Saving the world from the indignities of the company picnic. One person at a time."

Libertarian politics are prevalent in Silicon Valley, where Explorer values emphasize laissez-faire attitudes and products that give enormous power to the individual. Computers and the World Wide Web not only have given the individual enormous power to access information; they also have equalized the playing field—at least among those affluent enough to own a computer and educated enough to know how to use it.

Although not all Explorers are libertarians, they tend to be critical of the establishment. However, whereas the Hero may fight to change the world, the Explorer more typically simply lives by his or her own lights. This may mean setting up—or shopping at—a different kind of business. You might expect cosmetic companies to sell Lover brands, but not The Body Shop. Anita Roddick founded a cosmetic shop with no hype and no promises to transform her customers. Rather, she counted on finding customers who would share her global awareness, environmental consciousness, and concern with animal, as well as human, rights.

Explorers tend to see themselves as—and often are—ahead of their time and definitely willing to take tough stands for something they believe in. The Body Shop combines this cutting-edge image with the Explorer's fascination with all that is exotic and foreign. Organic products are made with ingredients from the Amazon rain forest. Roddick's philosophy is "Trade, not aid," so she helps create incomes for economically stressed communities while also working to stop the burning of the rain forest. The Body Shop reminds employees that "goals and values are as important as our products and profits" and that "the Body Shop has soul—don't lose it."

The Explorer archetype has a spiritual side. Think about the Knights of the Round Table, each entering the wilderness, where there was no path, in search of the Grail. In the 1990s, such seeking has grown to epidemic porportions, giving rise to a plethora of spiritual books, workshops, and products. (Think of the Mystic Trader and other New Age catalogues, for example, or the New Spirit Book Club.)

Walking in the Moccasins of the Explorer Customer

When the Explorer archetype is active in customers, their call is to explore the world and, in the process, to find themselves, so that they know who they are. Some Explorers demonstrate great exuberance and a sense of adventure. Others, like Dorothy in *The Wizard of Oz*, seem reluctant about all this journeying, wishing all the while to find a place to call home. Plainly, the Explorer's inner self is sometimes not as confident as the face he or she presents to the world.

To market an Explorer brand effectively, it is best to empathize with the Explorer story from the inside, imagining, for example, what it's like to feel trapped by your life, to yearn for more excitement and adventure, to feel "bigger" than your life, as though it is constraining you. (Teenagers in Beijing in the 1980s often sported T-shirts that read "New York, Paris, Rome," literally "advertising" their desire to break free of their sometimes suffocating circumstances.)

You might also consider the part of you that wants to belong as dangerous, sacrificing your integrity to your desire to fit in. If this feeling is strong, you may consciously do things to set yourself apart—as adolescents do with pink hair, tattoos, or pierced body parts. It is as if your appearance is yelling "I'm different" so that you will resist the impulse to conform. However, the more you do this, the more lonely you feel, so the more intense will be your desire to belong. The stronger it gets, the scarier it feels, so you back off more and more . . . and so on. Even if you have experienced this only a little, you can extrapolate from it enough to know how someone locked in such a dilemma might feel.

Most people have had some moment when they were afraid that if they were true to themselves, they would lose the support of someone they cared about. Often, as we are growing up, we discover our individuality only when our true proclivities brush up against those of parents, teachers, and peers. To empathize with what this feels like, you might remember a time when you stood up to a parent, teacher, or boss and how essential it seemed to do so, even if the person saw you as an opponent. You also might recall a time you had to walk away from something to save your own soul, and what courage it took to do so.

You might even tap into the memory of standing on the top of a mountain or skyscraper, looking at the expanse of the view or the night sky and feeling a complicated mixture of awe, joy, and loneliness—a quintessential Explorer feeling.

It is important to remember that the underlying desire of Explorers is to finally find the Promised Land, the place where they can be completely true to who they are—and belong. Children's stories like "The Ugly Duckling" and adult religious texts like the Bible's relation of the Exodus from Egypt into the Promised Land embody the power of this longing.

Undoubtedly, you also have experienced the more optimistic and enthusiastic Explorer, who is not necessarily alienated at all. Perhaps you are simply eager to experience as much life as possible, seeking opportunities to travel and spend time in nature doing what you love, even though doing so will not get you anything other than the sheer joy of the journey itself.

In developing advertising for Explorer brands, you may want to subtly deal with the loneliness of the Explorer by placing him or her in the company of other people. The Explorer, of course, often has one or more sidekicks, like the Lone Ranger's Tonto, or Dorothy's Toto (as well as the Cowardly Lion, the Tin Man, and the Scarecrow).

You may also be able to imagine, by extrapolating from your own experience and from Explorer narratives, how the Explorer relates to other archetypes. For example, the congenial Jester, Regular Guy/Gal, or Lover may invite the Explorer to become part of a group or a couple and end up dismayed or hurt when the Explorer runs for his or her life. To the Explorer, becoming close can feel like a threat to the self. On the other hand, Rulers who lay down the law see themselves as doing so because they know what is good for people.

They are therefore put off when the Explorer gets angry and takes off. A Caregiver who creates a guilt trip for the Explorer for being self-involved can be experienced as the enemy, while one who packs a care package for the journey is welcomed as a friend.

The Explorer may seek out the Hero, Outlaw, or Magician as a potential supporter, but is almost always disappointed in that role model, eventually leaving to find his or her own truth. In fact, the Explorer will learn for a time from almost anyone who has a new insight or experience to offer, but soon sees the person's Achilles' heel and hits the road.

The Explorer Organization

Explorer organizations value individuality, de-emphasize rules and hierarchical decision making, and tend to equalize opportunity as much as is workable. We can see the influence of the Explorer archetype in newer, flatter, and more democratic organizations; in individualistic policies like flex-time; and in empowered workers making as many decisions as possible at the most local and involved level. In such organizations, workers are typically hired for their expertise and, once on board, expect to be allowed to go their own way for the most part. Even if outcomes are set by management, workers are permitted to use their own judgment about how to reach them.

When the Explorer awakens in individuals, they often start their own small business, become consultants, or seek out a pioneering or scouting role in their company. The companies or units they run are often more freewheeling and decentralized than the traditional hierarchical organization. Typically small, Explorer organizations have as few rules as possible and hire competent professionals who control their own hours and their own time. Of course, the "virtual office" is making this work style more possible than ever before.

Even if the company is large, dress may be outdoorsy and rugged or suitable for travel, but certainly workplace casual. Organizational values stress independence and the ability to respond quickly to new opportunities, tailoring products or services to fulfill unique needs. Independence and self-direction are generally shared corporate values. In many cases, the work that is done is pioneering and groundbreaking.

Healthy Explorer organizations provide enough structure to hold the enterprise together. In unhealthy Explorer organizations, when things go wrong, the enterprise tips into the dangerous area of anarchy. But the best Explorer organizations can tolerate a great deal of fluidity.

Rockport Shoes, which might have "Comfortable shoes for the journey" as its motto, is famous for being one of the first organizations to reorganize in two days, using the structure of Harrison Owen's innovative Open Space Technology. Following this approach, all employees gather together in a large room for a couple of days and organize themselves into groups that discuss any idea an employee has any passion about. Whatever a person's role, he or she has the same power as anyone else, and everyone is allowed to vote with their feet where they want to be and where they don't want to be.

During the Rockport Open Space experience, a custodian allegedly convened a group, attended by the president of the company, that came up with the idea for an innovative, and ultimately highly successful, product line that made a big difference to the company's future.

In the new economy, many people affiliate with virtual organizations. This means they no longer even *go* to work in the conventional sense. They work from home offices using fax, e-mail, phones, etc., to connect with coworkers they may rarely see. They may create a formal organization, or simply partner with one another as needed on particular projects or to achieve particular aims. These decentralized, nonhierarchical, and temporary allegiances maximize personal freedom, flexibility, and effectiveness, while minimizing structure and schmoozing.

Explorer Marketing and the New Customer

In *The Soul of the New Consumer*, David Lewis and Darren Bridger describe this person in ways that suggest that he or she is invoking the Explorer archetype in purchasing decisions. While the old consumer, Lewis and Bridger argue, makes purchasing decisions based on convenience and conformity, the new consumer seeks authenticity in the product as a way of expressing individuality. At the same time, the new consumer is better informed, intimately involved in purchasing decisions, skeptical of any kind of advertising hype, highly restless, easily distracted, and chronically short of time.

People's orientation toward identity and freedom today lead them to want to be as free as the wind—to try everything and be limited by nothing. The result is a collective speedup. Lewis and Bridger cite NASA Administrator Daniel Goldin's motto for the space program: "faster, smaller, cheaper, better." People today not only move quickly; they also can process information rapidly (especially those under 30). Most are comfortable with hyperkinetic pacing in film and television, "cutting between scenes so rapidly that many images remain in view for less than two seconds." If the pace isn't quick, they get bored.

The media most facilitative of this restless desire to experience and know everything and to do so instantly are, of course, e-mail, the Web, chat rooms, and all the other instantaneous and interactive modes made possible by modern communications. The vision is expansive: People who have reached this level of development typically take a global view.

Moreover, these same consumers habitually critique what they see and hear, viewing all tried and true ideas, institutions, and products, including advertising, with suspicion. For this reason, "buzz" can be more effective in marketing than hype. Even so, these new consumers value change more than consistency, so brand loyalty is not a natural value for them. This does not, however, mean that they cannot become loyal when the right archetypes are evoked, as we can see from the avid fans of "Star Trek" ("trekkies") or people who use only cosmetics from The Body Shop or who drink only Starbucks coffee.

People who are living in Explorer stories are most likely to be loyal to products that carry the archetypal meaning of authenticity and freedom—if they are to be loyal at all. Such products reinforce the deeper longings of customers with a strong freedom orientation (as most of us have in adolescence and midlife, if at no other time).

These archetypes also connect with the "dormant" freedom-loving part of customers who more habitually express their desires for stability, belonging, and mastery. A relatively traditional and conformist individual might, for example, express that freer potential by buying a motorcycle or a mountain bike.

In the 2000 Academy Awards, it was clear that the Explorer archetype was active in the country and the Academy. Some of the big winners were from smaller independent production companies (albeit some of those companies are owned by larger parent brands).

Remember also that younger Explorers like to search out the Internet and prefer to find you rather than have you find them. Make it easy for them to do so. And realize that they will be influenced by counterculture icons more than by mainstream celebrities. Best of all, create a buzz. Explorers are deeply skeptical of advertising hype. They like products that seem as authentic as they are, and they are influenced by people who seem real. In the early 1990s, Hush Puppies' classic suede casual shoes were about to be dropped from the Wolverine World Wide product line until word spread that youths in New York's Greenwich Village were buying up Hush Puppies from resale shops. Company executive Owen Baxter examined the fad and discovered that kids were seeking the authenticity of being able to say "I am wearing an original pair." Suddenly, Hush Puppies were hot everywhere because the cool, individualistic Village young people liked them. Pretty soon, fashion designers were wearing them and, of course, they remained a valued part of the line.[1]

In one of the hippest of Ralph Lauren's new flagship stores, located in Soho in New York City, vintage pieces of apparel are mixed in with the new items. Next to brand-new cargo pants may be a well-worn old flannel work shirt, or a 50-year-old faded classic Levi's denim jacket. The vintage pieces lend an unmistakable air of authenticity to the shop and to everything in it—Ralph Lauren is not just selling his own designs; he is "honoring" best-of-class designs from other classic companies such as Levi-Strauss. The "mix" in the store is made even more unusual by the designer's featuring surprising combinations on the models and on the racks—for example, a taffeta ball skirt and buffalo plaid halter top, with a bomber jacket casually tossed over the shoulders.

As a result of both the vintage items and the unusual mix, the experience of shopping in the store is one of searching, exploring,

---

1. David Lewis and Darren Bridger, *The Soul of the New Consumer: Authenticity—What We Buy and Why in the New Economy* (London: Nicholas Brealey Publishing, 2000), p. 93.

The Explorer archetype might provide a brand identity for your brand if

- your product helps people feel free, is nonconformist, or is pioneering in some way.
- your product is rugged and sturdy or is appropriate for use in nature, on the road, or in dangerous settings or occupations.
- your product can be purchased from a catalogue, the Internet, or another alternative source.
- your product helps people express their individuality (e.g., fashion, furnishings).
- your product can be purchased and consumed "on the go."
- you seek to differentiate your brand from a successful Regular Guy/ Gal or other more conformist brand.
- your organization has an Explorer culture.

and discovering. And tying this well-integrated retail concept together are the following words imprinted on the window next to the entrance to the store: "Polo Sport: Explorers, Travelers and Adventurers, Since 1970."

If Lewis and Bridger's analysis in the *Soul of the New Consumer* is accurate, the Explorer archetype is strongly influencing consumer decisions at the beginning of the 21st century. Perhaps this is because we are all living in a new millennium. Suffice it to say that this seems to be a particularly propitious time for Explorer brands.

The Sage

Motto: "The truth will set you free."

SAGES HAVE THEIR OWN WAY of finding paradise. Their faith is in the capacity of humankind to learn and grow in ways that allow us to create a better world. In the process, they want to be free to think for themselves and to hold their own opinions. The most obvious example is the scholar, researcher, or teacher. However, it can also be the detective, nightly news anchorperson, or any expert sharing knowledge, including the classic disembodied male voice telling homemakers about the science behind a successful laundry detergent. Famous Sages include Socrates, Confucius, the Buddha, Galileo, and Albert Einstein . . . but also George Carlin, Phyllis Diller, and Oprah Winfrey. We see the Sage in all mystery stories—Sherlock Holmes figuring out the case; in science fiction, such as any of Asimov's thrillers; and in informative books, magazines, and ads.

The popularity of "The X-Files" (which almost begins with the statement "The truth is out there") illustrates the perseverance of the Sage in trying to sort out truth from illusion and the paranoia that can result when the answer is not clear or easy to find. In politics, the Sage is associated with clear thinking, but may lack charisma and social graces. Al Gore, teased unmercifully for his stiffness, is one example. Einstein is another. (He was known for tuning out a whole party in his honor because he got interested in the pattern of the tea leaves floating in his cup.)

Sage brands include Harvard University, MIT, high-end consulting firms such as McKinsey and Arthur Andersen, and the Mayo Clinic (known for its diagnostic prowess), as well as the Educational Testing Service, and innumerable companies, research laboratories, and journals dedicated to discovering and disseminating truth.

Stanford University, at one point in its history, decided to become "the Harvard of the West" and consciously developed a public relations campaign, supported by investment in the research aspect of the university, to establish a prestigious intellectual image. And it worked.

Popular Sages include Oprah Winfrey and Walter Cronkite, who educate and guide their respective audiences, and Erma Bombeck, who provided wisdom through humor. In decades past, many brands embodied Sage identities and provided a strong educational role—for example, Betty Crocker on homemaking or Oil of Olay on skin care—but many have since gone the way of the 15-second sound bite. In fact, print campaigns of the 1950s often included some piece of information or advice. Advertising, in general, attempted to be

---

The Sage

Core desire: the discovery of truth
Goal: to use intelligence and analysis to understand the world
Greatest fear: being duped, misled; ignorance
Strategy: seek out information and knowledge; become self-reflective and understand thinking processes
Trap: can study issues forever and never act
Gift: wisdom, intelligence

Levels of the Sage

Call: confusion, doubt, deep desire to find the truth
Level One: search for absolute truth, desire for objectivity, looking to experts
Level Two: skepticism, critical and innovative thinking, becoming an expert
Level Three: wisdom, confidence, mastery
Shadow: dogmatism, ivory tower, disconnection from reality

helpful—to provide some piece of knowledge or wisdom as a kind of "quid pro quo" for the attention of the reader.

Currently, there is an opportunity to renew the Sage role in marketing, especially since the Internet offers such an effective vehicle for contemporary Sage brands.

The Sage as Expert

Sage brands may provide information, as do *The New York Times*, *Consumer Reports*, National Public Radio, and CNN. Typically, they help the customer make smarter decisions. One ad by Charles Schwab's investment firm (motto: "creating a world of smarter investors") shows two worried-looking women reading books entitled *Keep Ahead of the Sharks* and *How to Get Rich*, while a self-satisfied-looking man reads *Boy, Am I Happy*. The caption explains: "You can always tell the investor who's had a Schwab Portfolio consultation. They feel smarter, more informed, more in control."

> **Also Known As**
>
> Expert, scholar, detective, oracle, evaluator, advisor, philosopher, researcher, thinker, planner, professional, mentor, teacher, contemplative

The picture of the Sage as interpreter of the news has changed in significant ways in recent times. Once, oral communication, and later, the written word, was the conveyor of news beyond the confines of one's village or town. Visual information, describing what it "looked like" outside of our own normal routines, was scarce. Much later, in America, people waited on street corners for the arrival of *Life* magazine, then the primary vehicle for "seeing" what things were like on the outside.

With the advent of TV news reporting, and especially TV's intensive, day-to-day reporting of the Vietnam War, everything began to change. For the first time ever, television was the most trusted source of news reporting. Americans began to believe that "seeing was believing," and the role of the anchorperson, journalist, or commentator was transformed.

The basic source of the information that described our lives switched, in a very short time, from being orally and then verbally based to visually based. Yet the question remained, were we "visually literate"? Did we, as a nation, naively believe that "seeing was believing," or did we understand that the business of visual literacy was as important as, if not more important than, verbal literacy? For example, even beyond the interpretive biases of the photographer, every day the capabilities of digital photography were making it possible to superimpose images and to change them. Who would be our Sages or guides in this new, visually based world? Sage brands promise that they can help you discriminate better and think more effectively. A press release from Arthur Andersen quotes former managing partner Jim Wadia as saying "traditional models of wealth creation and management are not enough in a world that values speed, networking and information. With our global reach and seamless delivery of services, Arthur Andersen helps clients realize value from both tangible and intangible assets."

Such companies typically emphasize their own research and development. Procter & Gamble stresses innovative breakthroughs resulting from ongoing research, promoting the fact that the firm holds over 25,000 patents worldwide. A typical ad (in this case for Swiffer mop sponges) shows "one concerned P&G scientist," "one innocent [a baby] in a dirty world," a mop referred to as "one dirt magnet," and a package of Swiffer with the caption "A mop with a mission." The descriptive material names the P&G scientist and describes the breakthrough that created "a unique fabric of hydro-entangled fibers that generates an electrostatic charge that works like a magnet to attract dust, hair and common allergens." Such ads appeal to the desire of moms and dads to be informed about the latest ways to keep their homes state-of-the-art clean.

Sage brands may even congratulate customers for being informed and intelligent. Oldsmobile ran an ad saying, "Wanted: drivers with a firm grasp of torque, traction, and verb tense," implying that people in the know will choose their brand. Similarly, Infinity asserts, "It's not just a new car. It's all the best thinking." Toyota tells us that the Prius is "a car that sometimes runs on gas power and sometimes runs on electric power from a company that always runs on brainpower."

In a print campaign for Sesame Street, little anecdotes from the show that seem entirely playful at first glance are highlighted in terms of the learning opportunity they provide regarding problem solving, pattern recognition, and so on. As a result, the "invisible" research-based curriculum that drives the development of each show becomes apparent to the adult. It is assumed that if the parent or caregiver understands the Sage quality that drives the delightful escapades of each episode, she will better appreciate what makes this show truly unique in the world of "quality" children's programming.

The Sage is an excellent brand identity for computer hardware and software. Adobe Systems Incorporated, for example, positions itself as a tool for Sages, helping "to bring ideas to life on the Web, the printed page, and video." Any brand that helps people be or act smarter is also a legitimate tool in the Sage's story. Examples include Lean Cuisine ("Eat smart. Cook simple.") and CNN ("You are what you know.").

Where Can We Turn for Advice?

How did Oprah Winfrey become the most influential woman in America? Knowing what it means both to be poor and to be rich, she can empathize with anyone. Born on a farm in Mississippi, she learned to read when she was just two from a grandmother who also encouraged her speaking abilities. When she was six, she moved to Milwaukee, where her mother worked as a domestic. After being sexually abused by several different men, she began to act out. Her father, who had thus far not been much of a factor in her life, stepped in and changed things. In her words, he "turned my life around by insisting that I be more than I was and believing I could be more." His "love of learning showed me the way."[1]

After college, she became a news coanchor at CBS's Nashville affiliate, but she was so empathic, she often had to fight back tears when reporting touching stories. A new manager saw the gift in her seeming shortcoming and gave her a chance to try a talk show. The rest is history. Oprah visited with the usual array of interesting, troubled, and way-out people who were the rage on all talk shows. What she did with them, however, was different. She would empathize with them, analyze their situation, and work through their problems, as though she were a trusted friend or family member.

1. Wawro, p. 437.

Since 1986, her show has been the number-one talk show in America—and the source of guidance to people of all races and economic groups. In recent years, she has begun to shape culture. Books she features instantly become best-sellers. Musicians who appear on her show sell records. People who hear her emphasize health, spirituality, and personal responsibility practice what she preaches.

Oprah became the mother, the aunt, the big sister for a nation. At the same time, she carried the archetype of the Black Madonna, who scholar Robert Graves tells us is black because the color black is archetypally associated with great wisdom. All these figures carry the same energy as the biblical figure of Sophia (whose name means "wisdom") and the Greek goddess Persephone, who understood the secrets of the underworld (death) as well as of ordinary reality.

Jungian analysts Marion Woodman and Elinor Dickson, in *Dancing in the Flames*, quote the call of this goddess (from the Bible's "Proverbs") in words as relevant to today's man and woman as they were to the ancient Hebrews:

> O people; I am calling you. . . .
> Listen, I have serious things to tell you,
> And from my lips come honest words.
> My mouth proclaims the truth . . .
> All the words I say are right,
> Nothing twisted in them, nothing false,
> All straight forward to the one who understands,
> Honest to those who know what knowledge means.
> Accept my discipline rather than silver,
> Knowledge in preference to gold.
> For wisdom is more precious than pearls,
> And nothing else is so worthy of desire.[2]

How typical of 20th-century America that the Dark Goddess/Sophia Wisdom speaks to us through a wonderfully savvy talk show hostess and Sage-brand icon.

Is Oprah aware of her Sage brand identity? Of course she is. It

2. Marion Woodman and Elinor Dickson, *Dancing in the Flames: The Dark Goddess in the Transformation of Consciousness* (Boston: Shambhala, 1997), p. 11, quoted from Proverbs 8:4–11.

clearly governs her decisions regarding how to leverage her success. Rather than develop a line of cosmetics or fashion, Oprah continues to guide the American public through her book club and now a magazine. The archetypal congruence of her new enterprises with her talk show role makes her brand identity all the more clear and convincing. Even though she is the wealthiest woman in the media, she is never seen as self-serving. Rather, she is seen as a woman with a mission.

It is not surprising that spirituality has become an important priority for Oprah. Spiritual Sages have entered a market economy in the 21st century. While churches still pass the collection basket, people now pay gurus from a variety of religions to speak and give workshops. People are hungry for spiritual wisdom and willing to pay to learn yoga, meditation, and spiritual perspectives from different traditions. The goal here is not only wisdom, but also peace. Deepak Chopra, for example, is as much a Sage brand as MIT is. Speaking with an Indian accent, Chopra can easily embody the image of the wise Indian guru in the public mind, which gives everything he says additional credibility.

Advertising for products is taking on a more spiritual tone, sometimes in a way that seems gratuitous, as the religious imagery has nothing to do with the product. Some products, however, without the cover of humor, risk offending readers by associating religious symbols with their brands. For example, Antron carpets, by Du Pont, ran an ad with a picture of the Buddha, with text that said, "a daringly different backdrop of geometry and patterns that subtly frames, defines, and provides a new metaphor of harmony and strength. It's Zensual. It's zenduring." As customers click on the company's Web site, they are advised to "Pick a mantra. And don't forget to breathe."

Barnes & Noble: Marketing Savvy for Booksellers

Leonard Riggio purchased Barnes & Noble when it was struggling and he was a nobody. However, he understood that the action in bookstores was expanding the market. His initial strategy was shocking to other bookstores, because he used tactics similar to those of Wal-Mart, cutting prices every way he could. He made enough from doing so to keep purchasing his competition. At the same time, he kept the Barnes & Noble name, a name that conjures up the old monkish image of the small, dedicated bookshop, run by and for people who just love books.

The temple of the Sage archetype has to be either the library or the bookstore. Even when Barnes & Noble was conducting slash-and-burn price reduction as a strategy to defeat the competition, the firm's image still conjured up the archetypal bookstore ideal.

Over time, the introduction of the superstore updated this image to provide a book-buying experience, speaking to the full needs of the book lover in each of us. Understanding the absence of the village green, Riggio recognized that bookstores were a natural place for people to gather, particularly people who like to talk about ideas. He therefore began to offer Starbucks coffee, provide comfortable chairs, expanded store hours, book discussion groups, and readings by authors. Eventually, he learned to deliver an experience that Sages would enjoy. Barnes & Noble even became a place for young people who loved ideas to meet each other—a veritable dating service!

Getting into e-commerce just shortly after Amazon.com, Riggio also was quick to see the possibilities of the Internet. He predicts that, in time, on-line services "will allow shoppers to download and print all or part of a book," making changes that will revolutionize the industry.[3] His ability to hold firm to a Sage identity while updating the business of book marketing has made Barnes & Noble the biggest and most successful book chain in the world.

Marketing That Makes People Think

Marketing expert Bernd H. Schmitt, in *Experiential Marketing*, identifies "think campaigns" as a major way to market a brand, and we would add that think campaigns are ideal ways to market Sage brands. Genesis ElderCare, for example, differentiates from others offering care for the elderly by stressing the company's capacity to analyze what each individual needs and tailor a program just for them. At the same time, to strengthen the firm's image of intelligence, it also portrays the elderly in unusual ways. Undermining stereotypes about older people as dependent or victims makes people stop and think and also leads them to associate independent thinking with ElderCare. The Discovery Channel store displays a model of a

3. Wawro, p. 355.

Tyrannosaurus rex and many other interactive educational displays. Tourneau in New York teaches customers about the history of watches. Eddie Bauer simply posts words like "inspire," "imagine," and "insight" in retail stores to position its clothing so that it is more likely to be associated with imaginative and intellectual people.[4]

Ads where something is missing make you think to fill in the gap. For example, both Target and Nike have run ads that include their logos, but not their names, causing the consumer to stop, think, and realize that they know the names. This, of course, captures the customer's attention, but, more importantly, also makes the customer feel smart for knowing. Ads for Kenneth Cole shoes inevitably make reference to current events, associating the brand with being "in the know." Brands as different as *The Wall Street Journal*, Hewlett-Packard, and Dewar's Scotch sell the image of the customer as refined, intelligent, and knowledgeable. Perhaps in an even more topical way, tapping into our newfound need for visual, as opposed to verbal, literacy, Absolut vodka has created a magnificent campaign that relies on the reader's interest in, and ability to recognize, visual patterns and interpret them appropriately.

Intel established its brand identity through association with already respected brands. Intel offered computer companies a discount for its chips if they would write "Intel inside" on their product. Consumers, seeing so many brands labeled "Intel inside," assumed that the computer companies were bragging. Intel must be really great, they inferred, if big-name brands added its name to their labeling. Intel does not tell the customer that it has the best product on the market. Rather, the company creates a situation which encourages customers to assume that it has.[5]

The Sage customer enjoys the process of research, finding out about brands. Sages will go onto the Web and see what is available, and they trade information about the tools of the technological trade. Netscape and Yahoo! established their brand identities without spending money on advertising. Rather, they linked to appropriate sites on the Web and paid for banners. Then they let customers find them.

4. Bernd H. Schmitt, *Experimental Marketing* (New York: The Free Press, 1999), pp. 142.

5. Agnieszka M. Winkler, *Warp Speed Branding* (New York: John Wiley & Sons, Inc., 1999), p. 67.

More typically, Sage marketing is dignified and subdued, with an elite air to it. Think, for example, of the way Ivy League colleges are promoted. Public relations efforts focus on getting out the word about important research projects conducted at the college, the accomplishments of faculty and graduates, and the difficulty of getting hired for a job there or being admitted as a student. The message is "Not very many people are smart enough to be here." Furthermore, although scholarships are designed to make certain that meritorious students from moderate circumstances can attend, the high cost of tuition gives out the message: The education provided here is expensive because it is the best available. Similarly tasteful and elite marketing approaches are characteristic of museums, like the Corcoran or the Smithsonian in Washington, DC, and of symphonies, ballet companies, and other places offering cultural opportunities.

Even in the world of conventional brands, an air of mystery or mystique can contribute to the aura of the Sage brand. For example, for many years, Bell Labs carried an aura of "communication genius," even though most people didn't have any idea what was done there. But its very existence "lifted" parent AT&T, as a result of the assumption that it was somehow "ahead of the curve" in terms of scientific understanding.

Of course, the most convincing way to appeal to Sages is to have your brand recommended by an expert. The Palm Pilot (which, in other ways, is a Creator brand) was launched by demonstrating the product at industry conferences and offering it at half price to opinion leaders. Predictably, experts in the field spread the word, with the result that it took just a little more than a year to sell a million Palm Pilots.

The Sage Organization

Sage organizations are often found in universities, research labs, think tanks, and companies that see themselves as learning systems (as described by Peter Senge in *The Fifth Discipline*)[6]—that is, organizations whose structure and values promote continuous learning.

---

6. Peter Senge, *The Fifth Discipline: The Art and Practice of the Learning Organization* (New York: Doubleday/Currency, 1990).

Emphasis is placed on analysis, learning, research, and planning. Quality is seen as resulting from the expertise of employees, whose freedom of opinion must be protected. The pace is measured, because thorough study is considered essential before change takes place—except in the case of newspapers and newsletters, where information must be gathered and published quickly. Dress styles and the environment tend to be understated. The dominant colors are generally gray, beige, white, and light blue. Emphasis is on the collection and analysis of data, and the chief item of value is expertise.

As employees, Sages have a high need for autonomy. If you think of universities and research labs as the quintessential Sage environments, you can see that Sages want to come and go as they please (no time clocks, thank you), they like to do the work in their own manner, and they prefer peer to administrative evaluation. They are often skeptical of the ability of any mere manager to know enough to make educated decisions about their work.

The Sage organization typically has a very decentralized structure, emphasizing the development of expertise rather than control. Employees are expected to know what they are doing and therefore are free to make autonomous decisions. Usually, a small administration handles the business and marketing side of things, but most of the major decisions—about the curriculum, teaching strategies, and even promotion and tenure decisions—are made primarily by the faculty, generally through a cumbersome set of committees. Faculty are completely free to come and go as they please, as long as they teach their classes and hold office hours. They conduct whatever research interests them, under the protection of academic freedom.

Even in corporate America, research and development teams often have greater freedom than is allowed other corporate entities, because they simply cannot keep researchers if they are overly hemmed in. Most doctors today see themselves primarily as scientists, and they are used to managing themselves and making independent decisions. This is, of course, why managed care has so demoralized them, working as it does with a Ruler archetype bias—limiting reimbursable time and requiring approval of treatment modalities.

For-profit Sage organizations also typically have decentralized and rather democratic governance. VISA was founded by Dee Hock as the first "chaordic" (his coined word, combining "chaos" with "order") banking organization. VISA is a loose confederation of banks that agree to certain basic principles and systems. Any bank can pull out at any time, so no one can tell it what to do. Representatives meet annually to make decisions almost as citizens make decisions in political caucuses or community forums. According to Hock, the glue that holds chaordic organizations together is a common philosophy. That is why he advocates taking time to create a constitution that describes the ideas members hold in common. The organization is held together not by hierarchy or security, but by fidelity to common ideas. Other organizations based on chaordic principles include the Society for Organizational Learning and United Religions.[7]

Ray Anderson, the CEO of Interface, turned his company into a learning organization when he became committed to redesigning the company so that it was 100 percent sustainable. To do this, he turned Interface into a closed loop of resources, so that the company not only turned raw materials into products but also turned products back into raw materials with no negative impact on the environment. This meant that the firm could no longer engage in business as usual. Rather, everyone had to rethink absolutely everything in light of the new consensus that every decision would be sustainable for the natural world, the company, and its customers.

To do this, Anderson trimmed the company's hierarchy and created "permeable boundaries"—see-through walls connecting administrators, lab technicians, and the design studio. Now, customers can see employees working, and workers can see customers buying. Also, the back wall of the plant is made of glass, allowing workers and customers alike to remain aware of the beauty of the landscape around them. At the same time, information was made to flow freely. The result was not only the establishment of the first ecologically sustainable carpetmaker but also savings of millions of dollars through greater efficiency.

The Sage Customer

When the Sage is active in the lives of customers, they are keenly interested in learning for its own sake. Freedom and independence

---

7. Michael Toms, interview with Dee Hock, *The Inner Edge: A Resource for Enlightened Business Practice* (Feb./Mar. 2000), pp. 5–7.

The Sage archetype might provide a suitable identity for your brand if

- it provides expertise or information to your customers.
- it encourages customers or clients to think.
- the brand is based on a new scientific breakthrough or esoteric knowledge.
- the quality of the brand is supported by hard data.
- you are differentiating the product from others whose quality or performance is questionable.

are valued as a means of keeping one's objectivity (as in the case of universities, whose faculties support academic freedom). One individual might be more interested in inner knowing and another in knowledge of the external world, but in any event, both feel that it is essential to think for oneself and have one's own opinions. The Sage part of a person agrees with the statement "I think, therefore I am." When the Sage is dominant in someone's character, learning is a compelling motivator. The accompanying fear is of being duped by misinformation and therefore misinterpreting data or a situation. At worst, the Sage is dogmatic, arrogant, and opinionated. At best, he or she becomes a genuinely original thinker and achieves real wisdom.

In appealing to a Sage, it is important to establish your credibility. Otherwise, why would they listen to you? Moreover, never talk down to the Sage, and never use a hard sell: They want to feel competent, smart, and in charge of the transaction. If they feel that you are pushing them, they are likely to distrust you and walk away. To Sages, a purchase is a rational transaction. They want you to provide information about the quality of the good or service being sold and its cost. Then they simply want to make a logical decision based on the information. However, if, in the process, you help them feel like an expert, they are more likely to buy than if they feel confused, incompetent, or pressed. Reinforce their wisdom, and if you have a product that is demonstrably of high quality, they will reward you with their loyalty.

Leaving a Thumbprint on the World

Hero, Outlaw, Magician

W E SELDOM SPEAK of the Hero, the Outlaw, and the Magician in the same breath, but they are, in fact, powerful archetypes cut from the same cloth. In classic film and literature, they are often fearless protagonists who realize their own special power and go on to take great personal risks in order to change their reality. In day-to-day life, these powerful archetypes provide a structure that can release the ability of ordinary people to rise to challenges, take risks, break rules, and transform their lives. They help them develop the quality of mastery, requiring them to embrace risk and change, which can trigger an inner conflict with the need for safety, structure, and security. They are each, in their own way, magnetic, because they are about *change*—with all of its accompanying anxiety and exhilaration. The outcome can be socially positive (consider Churchill

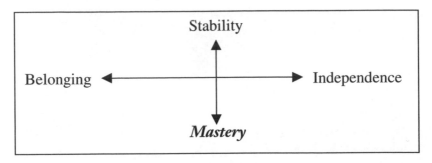

Figure 3.1

and FDR as Heroes), disruptive (Outlaws Annie Oakley and John Dillinger), or purely magical (Houdini, Jackie O, and Harry Potter); the effect is similar. Such figures seem beyond the powers of the normal person, but they raise the motivating question, *Could I do that as well?*

Children's stories abound with these figures, but in more subtle form, adults are mesmerized by them as well. Box office hits could include any Indiana Jones film, *Goodfellas*, and *Heaven Can Wait*. These archetypes are magnetic, and more: In today's cultural climate, they are useful as well.

Changing times require people who are energized by risk and who want to prove their own capacities through rising to challenge after challenge. The ability to take risks and to persevere to the point that we really accomplish something of consequence results in high self-esteem and social validation. When these archetypes are active in people, they want to take action to have an impact on the world. Emotions related to such aspirations tend to be fiery and energetic, ranging from anger, to ambition, to fierce determination. The Hero, the Outlaw, and the Magician use this energy to leave a thumbprint on the world or to mobilize in order to destroy or transform rigid, enervating structures. If these figures are missing in our personal lives—as they often are—we crave their presence in the marketplace and in the media.

In some ways, the distinction between the Hero and the Outlaw rests with history. Benjamin Franklin reminded the U.S. founding fathers, "We must all hang together, or assuredly we shall all hang separately." Had the United States lost the war, the revolutionaries would likely be remembered in British history books as Outlaws, not Heroes. In marketing, it is useful to realize that the negative pole of the Hero bleeds into the Outlaw, as the most primitive Hero is really about winning at all costs—a goal that is, often, hardly noble or pretty.

It is also important to remember that in American culture, perhaps because this country began with a revolution, Heroes often have a slightly rebellious quality to them, and Outlaws—at least the ones people like—carry on the wilder, more rambunctious qualities of American life without actually undermining the society.

The Hero, the Outlaw, and the Magician all take a stand against some limiting, restrictive, or harmful reality. The Hero (who is often seen as a Warrior) takes a great personal risk in order to defeat evil forces to protect society or sacred values. The Outlaw acts as a disruptive force, violating cultural norms and rules for the good of others (like Robin Hood), for adventure and personal gain (like Bonnie and Clyde), or out of desperate alienation (like Thelma and Louise). The Magician acts as a catalyst for social or institutional transformation or healing. In all three cases, the underlying desire is to take action and exert power. The underlying fear is of allowing life to just happen to you—of being a victim or a wimp.

We live in an achievement-oriented society in which people are expected to take great risks and develop competence in order to contribute to the society (Hero), while technological advancements such as computers, the Internet, and genetic engineering bring magic into everyday life (Magician).

At the same time, large numbers of people seem increasingly alienated to the point that they identify with outsiders if not actual Outlaws. So many people use or have used illegal drugs that it is now routine to ask presidential candidates about their drug use. In fact, it is enough for a candidate to affirm that he didn't inhale or did not use drugs in recent years to confer a reasonable amount of respectability. Just listening to rap or hip-hop lyrics is enough to show that there is a strong strain of the Outlaw in African-American youth culture, which is now being adopted by white youth as well. Tattoos and body piercing are prevalent with young people of all ethnic groups. Both liberals and conservatives (especially those opposing abortion) practice civil disobedience—which is an Outlaw strategy for change. You might think of militia groups in Montana,

Pegasus is a mythic winged horse, ridden by conquering heroes, but also throwing off those who are unprepared to ride across the sky. Mobil's logo evokes the mastery and power of the Hero, but also warns of the cost of the Hero's possible arrogance and desire to conquer, rather than work with natural forces.

the Klan in the South, and skinheads throughout the world to understand the importance of the Outlaw archetype to the identity of far-right groups.

The Hero, Outlaw, and Magician, as power archetypes, focus consumer attitudes and actions relevant not only to achieving one's aims, but also to changing the world. They therefore provide natural brand identities for products and services that have a marked impact on their time and place.

7

The Hero

Motto: "Where there's a will, there's a way."

Everything seems lost, but then the Hero rides over the hill and saves the day. There are infinite variations on this story, but in every one the Hero triumphs over evil, adversity, or a major challenge, and in so doing, inspires us all.

To get a sense of the Hero, think John Wayne, John Glenn, or Susan B. Anthony, and at a lower level, James Bond and the Mission Impossible team. Virtually all superheroes—Superman, Wonder Woman, Batman, etc.—fit this just as their adversaries are classic Outlaws.

John F. Kennedy was a Hero president, running on his bravery in the military and challenging us to send an expedition to the moon "because it is there." So were Teddy Roosevelt and Dwight Eisenhower. Famous generals from MacArthur to Colin Powell qualify as Heroes also, as do culturally transformative figures like Martin Luther King, Jr., and Nelson Mandela. Movies like *Star Wars* and *Saving Private Ryan* provide us with the basic archetypal structure of the hero's story, as do classic television shows like "The Lone Ranger," "Star Trek," "Superman," and, more recently, "Xena" and "Homi-

The Hero

Desire: prove one's worth through courageous and difficult action
Goal: exert mastery in a way that improves the world
Fear: weakness, vulnerability, "wimping out"
Strategy: become as strong, competent, and powerful as you are capable of being
Trap: arrogance, developing a need for there always to be an enemy
Gifts: competence and courage

The Hero also may be known as the warrior, the crusader, the rescuer, the superhero, the soldier, the winning athlete, the dragon slayer, the competitor, and the team player.

cide." We see the Hero in any crusader for a cause or in efforts to rescue the victim or defend the underdog.[1]

The natural environment for the Hero is the battlefield, the athletic contest, the streets, the workplace, the political jungle, or anyplace where difficulty or challenges await courageous and energetic action.

The Hero wants to make the world a better place. His or her underlying fear is failing to have what it takes to persevere and prevail. This archetype helps us develop energy, discipline, focus, and determination.

Distinctive Hero brands include the Marines, the Olympics, the space program, the National Organization of Women, Nike, Federal Express, the Red Cross, and most video games. (The chief notable exceptions are Outlaw video games.) Because the Warrior aspect of the Hero archetype is so strong in the culture, many health and social initiatives are framed as wars, like the War on Poverty or the War on Drugs.

Imagery associated with the Hero includes natural terrain requiring skill and agility; machines and offices where things are getting done; horses, cars, planes, people, or anything moving fast; and anything powerful, hence strong colors and defin-

---

1. In *The Hero Within* and *Awakening the Heroes Within*, Carol Pearson made the case for the Hero's journey encompassing all 12 archetypes, decrying the popular confusion of the Hero with the Warrior only. Here, however, we are acknowledging that, in our society today, the Hero and the Warrior are synonymous, and the term "Hero" helps people identify with the more positive aspects of this archetype. Warriors may simply be combative, but the Hero fights for a principle, a cause, a way of life, or a future vision.

> ### Levels of the Hero
>
> **The Call:** the bully kicks sand in your face or someone tries to intimidate or abuse you; a challenge beckons; someone needs you to help defend him or her
> **Level One:** the development of boundaries, competence, mastery, expressed through achievement, motivated or tested through competition
> **Level Two:** as with a soldier, doing your duty for your country, organization, community, or family
> **Level Three:** using your strength, competence, and courage for something that makes a difference to you and to the world
> **Shadow:** ruthlessness and obsessive need to win

itive lines and shapes. Hero attires and environments are functional, not lavish. In fact, too much comfort is perceived as dangerous because it can make you soft. The Israeli kibbutz and Army boot camp are each a prime example of an environment that prepares the potential Hero through austerity and hard work.

When the Hero archetype is active in individuals, they may be ambitious and seek out challenges—think astronauts, Marines, or athletes—or they may be more reluctant Heroes who recognize an injustice or problem and simply rise to the occasion to do what needs to be done to remedy it. Either way, the Hero is invigorated by challenge, feels outraged by injustice, and responds quickly and decisively to difficulty or opportunity.

Heroes pride themselves on discipline, focus, and an ability to make tough choices. They are the instinctive protectors of those they see as innocent, fragile, or legitimately unable to help themselves. (Think of the Hero who rescues the damsel in distress.) All others, they prefer to shape up.

In politics, think of Martin Luther King (especially in the "I Have a Dream" speech) inspiring Americans of all races to live up to the cultural ideal of equality of opportunity. Heroes often evince qualities that heighten consciousness in everyone around them. In fact, their secret is who they are, not just what they do. In a recent tribute to Nelson Mandela, he was celebrated for forgiving his jailers after having been incarcerated for 27 years, and in doing so, helping free people not only from apartheid, but also from hatred. Now that's heroism!

At their worst, Heroes become arrogant or bullying, or they drive themselves into an early grave. At their best, they accomplish great things. Paradoxically, Heroes do not think of themselves as Heroes, because to do so seems presumptuous. More typically, they see themselves as just doing their jobs. If there is anyone they really dislike, it is not so much the villain as it is the wimp. Therefore, they are vulnerable to taking a dare or a challenge even if it may be foolish.

There is, of course, a negative potential within the archetype, just as there is within all archetypes. The conquering Hero can be a horrible bully. Attila the Hun may be celebrated as a Hero because he conquered many peoples, but the experience of the conquered is of being victimized—slaughtered, raped, pillaged. At the lowest level, the Hero archetype simply wants to prevail. The opponent is devalued as the enemy or as someone deserving to be victimized. The Nazis, for example, had a heroic image of themselves, but it resulted in heinous consequences for people in concentration camps. Within the more normal range of behaviors, you can see this negative tendency in hostile corporate takeovers. The acquiring companies may feel like winners, but others' lives may be devastated in the extreme. The trap within the Hero can be that you see yourself as heroic, but others see you as a villain. When this occurs, it behooves you not to dig in your heels, but to stop, see what they see, and correct your course.

Nike: The Creation and Testing of a Hero Brand

Nike began with a partnership between a University of Oregon graduate student and his track coach. Their goal was to design shoes that improved one's running performance while being affordable. Nike's brand identification with the Hero has been long standing, consistent, and well executed. The company's central mission is to understand and inspire the soul of the athlete, and its current slogan, "Just do it," promotes the heroic virtue of the courage to act.

As with many brands that have forged a strong identity in relatively recent times, the name of the product is itself archetypal. Nike is the winged Greek goddess of victory. The Nike company was built by athletes who loved the contest and believed in running. Its initial success coincided with the jogging craze, which promoted an ideal not only of health, but also of the runner as a heroic individual.

In the 1990s, the company's campaign relied strongly, but not exclusively, on the well-loved sports hero Michael Jordan, as well as on donating Nike shoes to top professional and college teams and convincing coaches to give them to the players. The message, of course, is that the best athletes wear Nikes.

However, the focus on Jordan has been carefully balanced with ads with real people (and researching the tastes and preferences of "cool" kids). Nike also championed the importance of female participation in sports and invited women to identify with the heroic ideal. Some ads also featured Little League football and high school soccer teams. By connecting the swoosh with women, everyday cool kids, and Michael Jordan, Nike uses celebrity in a healthy way. Ordinary people are encouraged to "feel like Mike." To help promote this image, Nike also featured Jordan in an ad in which he was rather unsuccessfully trying to play minor league baseball, thus making him seem more human and accessible than when he is showing such exceptional ability at basketball. Wearing Nikes, then, is aspirational: Consumers wear them not necessarily because they have the qualities of heroism, but because they *want* to have those qualities.

Jonathan Bond and Richard Kirshenbaum, in *Under the Radar*, posit a similar connection when "Nike sponsors an urban playground competition and the black-and-white swoosh logo is affixed to the chain-link fence. The playground is automatically turned into a professional sports arena—with only two nylon-fabric signs. That's the power of branding!"[2] Bond and Kirshenbaum go on to state that "People spend years working out ways to get a job at Nike," and their employees are so loyal that many "tattoo the famous Nike swoosh on their inner thighs." They do not just work at Nike; it's a driving force in their lives.[3]

2. Jonathan Bond and Richard Kirshenbaum, *Under the Radar: Talking to Today's Cynical Consumer* (New York: Adweek Books, 1998), p. 82.

3. Bond and Kirshenbaum, p. 189.

Nike's strategy has relied heavily on what David A. Aaker, in *Building Strong Brands*, calls "strategic opportunism," introducing hundreds of shoes each year for some 30 sports.[4] Cemented by a strong heroic identity, the firm can target specific shoes not only to different sports, but to different market segments, without defusing its identity.

On the other hand, over time, Nike became so well recognized that it began to run ads with only the swoosh (and Jordan or a shoe)—no Nike, no message. Was this a sign of confidence or of arrogance? The classic Hero of ancient tragedies had larger-than-life qualities, but also had a tragic flaw—often, but not always, hubris, or pride—that caused his or her downfall. Oedipus and Antigone are examples from Greek drama; King Lear, Othello, and Hamlet from Shakespeare's plays; and Nixon and O. J. Simpson in our own times. At the turn of the new century, Nike's ultimate fate was still uncertain, but the company has definitely been living through both the triumphs and the liabilities of the Hero archetype. The public scandal over Nike's use of child labor in China has escalated as Nike has reneged on gifts promised to universities that are supporting the student-led group working to impose standards for the protection of the international labor force. Nike's lack of political finesse in dealing with this scandal might have been predicted from the company's mission: "to experience the emotion of competition, winning, and crushing competitors." However much or little the resulting backlash hurts Nike's sales, the firm's reputation has been tarnished.

Traditionally, Nike has run wonderfully idealistic and noble ads encouraging athletes to protect the environment, boosting character in athletes, and recognizing the ways that athletics prepares women to control their own lives and participate more fully in a highly competitive economy. During the scandal, however, Nike ran an unusual ad. It showed a man running through a world that seemed to be coming to pieces. Cities were burning, missiles were falling, and he just kept running. He stoically ignored everything with the single exception of one other runner. This ad reveals an ambiguous strength of the archetype. On the one hand, the Hero's ability to persevere in dangerous circumstances is a wonderful thing. On the other hand,

4. David A. Aaker, *Building Strong Brands* (New York: The Free Press, 1996), p. 256.

the tendency to just keep going, filtering out useful criticism or defending against criticism (no matter how relevant or useful) is a serious danger within the archetype. One cannot help but wonder whether the ad expressed the company's feeling of being under siege.

What is sad about all this is that, had Nike understood archetypes, it might have recognized the negative potential within the Hero and protected against its own insistent aggression and arrogance. Every archetype has such a trap. To the degree that you fully understand the archetype that fuels your own organization's efforts, you can guard against its negative potential and save yourself from such embarrassing and brand-damaging publicity.

Hero-Brand Organizations: The U.S. Army and FedEx

Hero organizations often are either committed to a worthwhile cause or devoted to helping their customers and employees to "Be all that you can be," as the U.S. Army ad states. This "all," of course, means tough, resilient, ambitious, effective, competitive, and, ideally, principled. Such organizations push people hard in order to develop their full capacities. In the private sector, they are typically very competitive places with sales figures as a running scorecard of achievement. Entrepreneurial in the extreme, they not only expect, but in fact demand, continuous growth. In the public and nonprofit sectors, dedication and commitment to the cause are required. In either case, people who cannot take the heat are expected to get out of the kitchen.

The best-known prototype of such an organization is the U.S. Army. The military has perfected hierarchy as a mechanism to develop strong fighters, highly coordinated teams, and the capacity to act quickly and flexibly, as circumstances require. Ironically, although the military is not at all democratic, it has become a place where men (and, increasingly, women) from diverse races and often deprived circumstances can participate fully in the society at large— partly through GI education benefits, but also through the training and development offered by the Army itself.

Whether in the Army or in Hero companies, standards are high and employees are expected to be tough and do whatever it takes to succeed. In the for-profit world, companies in highly competitive fields often have Hero organizational cultures in which all are valued as long as they produce, but the moment they fail, they are out. Consequently, these firms often burn people out through unflagging demands that they perform at a high (and perhaps unreasonable) level and the expectation that good employees remain stoic performance machines. It may make sense to do whatever it takes, as long as it takes, if you are on the battlefield, but such expectations can be harmful in the corporate world. Soldiers always get R & R, but lawyers in high-pressure firms often do not. Crusaders in mission-driven nonprofits, moreover, may drive themselves equally hard. Over time, the results of unremitting demands can breed heart attacks, cause depression, and undermine families (and, if children are neglected, eventually, also whole communities).

Well-developed, healthy Hero organizations, however, develop winning employees and teams, much as a good coach manages and directs the efforts of a sports team. It is expected that goals and standards will be met, but good employees are well compensated, well trained, and highly valued. Consequently, they take care of themselves and one another. People share a sense of pride in being part of a winning operation, and a commitment to quality guides their actions. The highest-level Hero organizations are also principled and have clearly articulated convictions that inform practice and are not just rhetoric.

Virtually all Hero organizations are good at motivating people (like coaches firing up the team for victory) and releasing energy by convincing people of the importance of winning in the economic contest. Employees who sign onto the organizational mission generally have a strong sense that their efforts matter and that, whatever happens, they should not let their team down.

Originally, the U.S. Postal service was a heroic brand par excellence—"Neither snow, nor rain, nor heat, nor gloom of night" could keep the mail from being delivered. Unfortunately, this heroic identity was not adequately maintained. Fred Smith, the founder of Federal Express, got the idea in the mid-1960s for an overnight delivery service when he was a student at Yale. When he wrote a paper about it, his professor gave him a C on the basis that the idea was not feasible.

Smith knew about the Hero's perseverance. Born with a congenital birth defect, he walked with braces and crutches as a youth, until finally he gained the ability not only to walk on his own, but to play basketball and football. Eventually, he was healthy enough be a marine platoon leader in Vietnam. Federal Express was not an instant success, but Smith believed in the idea and stayed with it, investing in an ad campaign emphasizing the famous line "FedEx—when it absolutely, positively has to be there overnight."

Marketing campaigns first were directed at middle and senior management and later were expanded to appeal to secretaries and mailroom personnel. Initial ads highlighted actual experiments sending packages of sand by FedEx and its primary competitor—in which, of course, FedEx won. Later ads emphasized the fast-paced, competitive quality of modern business and featured Spleen—a fast-talking, intense manager who strung together hundreds of words per minute to illustrate the urgency of on-time package delivery. The message was that, in order to keep up with competitors today, you need FedEx. The organizational culture of FedEx reinforces its heroic identity. Although Smith was from an affluent background, he was impressed with the heroism of blue-collar folk in the Marines. In his business, he wanted to be fair to them. FedEx employees are expected to have a heroic commitment to quality results, so that those packages really are delivered intact and on time. In return, they are treated with respect and fairness—and they have a voice: Managers are evaluated by their employees as well as by their bosses.

FedEx has been cementing its success and its iconic status with appearances in big box office movies. In Steve Martin's *Bullfinger*, a filmmaker knows he is a success when the FedEx truck pulls up. Receiving the overnight package is portrayed as if he had been visited by the Grail. In *Runaway Bride*, Julia Roberts takes off from one of her weddings by hopping onto a FedEx truck. A character then quips words to this effect: "I don't know where she's going, but she'll definitely be there by 10:30 tomorrow."

"Be a Hero"—Brands

Unlike the pure archetypal Hero brands cited here, many brands today "dabble" in explicit or implicit calls to heroism. For example, ITRadar.com ("The eMarket for IT Services") runs a picture of

World War I soldiers relaxing near a plane with these words: "Who will be tomorrow's business heroes? Maybe you." The ad urges consumers to "move fast" to "apply information technology." For the Hero, the sky is the limit. Fujitsu appeals to such ambition by saying "Be limitless" (and buy one of the firm's notebooks). FTD.COM florists say "Be a hero," or at least be seen as one by someone—perhaps your mother—who receives flowers from you.

Marlboro clothes the call to heroism in nostalgia, inviting readers to "Marlboro Country" and the mythic land and life of the cowboy. One of the most successful Marlboro ads of all time showed the Marlboro man carrying a calf across a creek, illustrating the Hero's willingness to help anyone in need. Consumers who know the old "Mission Impossible" television show or have seen the movie cannot miss the call to heroism in the Kodak ad that reads "Your mission, should you choose to accept it, begins at www.kodak.com/M12/Digital."

Often, though, the incentive is fear—of falling behind or of not being up to the task. PricewaterhouseCoopers ("Join us. Together we can change the world.") ran one of many such ads, saying "The biggest risk is being left behind." An Army ROTC ad pictured a shark saying, "Only the strong survive. So, take the smartest college course you can. Then go out into the world and tear it up." Outdoor Research camping gear promotes its bivy sacks with a picture of a lightning storm over a lake surrounded by forest: "Five went in, None survived." The ad gets your attention with the thought that people died, but as you read, you find out:

> It was a long, wet night after we got rained off of the East Face of Mt. Whitney a few years back. Our five different brands of bivy sacks all leaked. There had to be a better design, so in the morning I began scratching one out in the sand. I knew that creating a truly advanced bivy sack would be difficult, and it turned out to be way worse than I feared! The designing was tough, the engineering was tougher, and it took three years to get the patent.

This urgency of the call to act also fuels a Planned Parenthood ad: "Accidents happen . . . if you have unprotected sex. You have 72 hours to reduce your risk of getting pregnant. It's called emergency contraception. Got questions? Call Planned Parenthood."

Brands as Heroic Guides and Props on the Journey

In some cases, the company is pictured as providing the heroism you may lack. Upside, a Web site for dealmakers, runs advertising that asserts, "Ambition and will to succeed aren't part of everyone's DNA." Dealmakers who read this publication can learn what they might lack. It is not uncommon for services to be cast as guides that can teach you to be a Hero. J. P. Morgan Securities promotes hostile takeover insurance with this language: "In today's hostile business environment, ignoring the possibility of a takeover bid means your company may be less prepared to challenge one successfully. There are steps you can take now—before a hostile bid is made—which can improve your chances of surviving one." Many such ads picture the economy today as essentially a battlefield or an athletic contest. Deutsche Bank markets itself as "winning the game" of achieving positive returns on investment and then sharing with consumers how to do it.

An ad for Calico ("eBusiness for Leaders") shows a man in a three-piece suit with a Viking hat on his head with these classic words: "Don't just compete. Conquer." Such an ad is an example of how a number of companies are using archetypes in obvious, but not very effective, ways. Just wearing the hat makes the man look a bit silly. To invoke the archetype, it should better call up the power of the Hero—the inner drama of feeling and being heroic. An ad for the Marines, for example, that ran repeatedly on national television evoked the hero powerfully. It begins with the image of a great hero fighting a monster. The image could have been from *Star Wars* or many other truly heroic tales. Then, suddenly, the warrior morphs into a U.S. Marine, standing at attention. The message is clear: You can be a real hero if you sign up.

Market research by the U.S. Army revealed the fact that young people did not join the Army just for scholarships. They joined out of a heroic desire to develop their discipline and character. The "Be all that you can be in the Army" slogan has strong drawing power. There is a yearning within people—especially the young—to meet real challenges and prove their mettle. The Army provides an arena for realizing that desire.

Similarly, the Women's National Basketball Association targets young girls and the mothers and fathers who support the organization's desire to have their daughters be in the company of strong, confident, winning athletes. And Teach for America challenges potential participants to be tough enough to do some real good: "Before you go to Harvard Business, Yale Law or Stanford Med, consider applying to a really tough school." The ad concludes, "Take two years of your life to change a few kids' lives forever. Not to mention your own."

Other ads identify the consumer as a Hero and offer props for the journey. An ad for beef, clearly aimed at the working mother, shows toy soldiers—every one of them female—in various contemporary female activities: running, doing laundry, going to work, shopping, and holding a baby. The copy reads, "Your kids need you. Your office needs you. Call in the reinforcements"—the reinforcements being the nutrients in beef. America's pharmaceutical companies see themselves as conducting wars on disease. One ad reads, "Cancer. It's a war. That's why we're developing 316 new weapons" (i.e., medicines, gene therapies, and "magic bullet" antibodies).

Anything associated with liberation for women can be marketed as a heroic product, even tampons. An ad for Tampax ("The revolution continues") reads, "It is a symbol of strength. Beauty. Resilience. Spirit. It is a representation of body. It is a frame of mind. It is progress. Advancement. Innovation. It is your sister, your mother, your daughter. It is woman. It is you."

Nike ads aimed at women often counter the cultural stereotype that heroism is for men only. The company's famous campaign—"If you let me play"—attempted to influence not only women, but society at large, by pointing out that girls who are involved in athletic pursuits are much less likely to get pregnant, use drugs, etc. Another ad says, "Why are too many muscles manly? We were all born with muscles. They don't belong exclusively on men, any more than skin belongs exclusively on women. Isn't it possible for femininity and physical power to coexist? Isn't it possible that the more we embrace our bodies, the more womanly we become? Embrace your body. And find out." Of course, Nike apparel helps you do so.

Whether for men or for women, the Hero archetype is associated with exacting standards, perseverance, and the ability to set boundaries. Similarly, a Lady Foot Locker ad with women working out says, "When training, I demand one thing from myself. MORE." Avia shoes shows a lovely muscled woman and advises, "With her routine, she gained definition in her arms. And her life."

Gazelle.com sells pantyhose with a picture of a woman astronaut on the moon saying, "one small step for women, one giant leap for womankind." Certainly, for women in corporate America, pantyhose are tools of the trade. Beauty products are also sometimes marketed as weapons in the battle between the sexes and the war on aging. For example, L'Oreal face cream is called "Wrinkle Defense Cream."

One major prop is the heroic steed, second only to the Explorer as the brand of choice for automobiles. An ad for Cadillac Seville brags that the car is "more than a pretty face;" it is "a force to be reckoned with." To rub it in, the ad, which appears near the front of a magazine, continues, "Just how powerful is the 300-hp Northstar V8? This ad started out in the back of the magazine." Ford Trucks ("We Race. You Win.") enjoins the reader, "In the last few miles, it doesn't matter how talented or smart or rich you are. What matters most is how determined you are," reassuring the customer that as grueling as off-road racing is, "Ford trucks not only survive, they thrive." Nissan Xterra is promoted as "Jack of all trades. Master of every single solitary one." Chevy S-10 shows Carlos Sandoval, veteran navy officer, crawling through a dark swamp. The ad assures us that he thinks this hardship is "cool," but if you deprived him of his rugged Chevy, he would get "cranky."

Both the Explorer and the Hero archetypes require a considerable amount of journeying, but for the Hero, the emphasis is on proving rather than finding yourself. Thus, its products are marketed for their toughness and resilience. Nissan goes on, "If you can think of it, it can do it. Up for some mountain biking in Moab? Done. How about skiing in Jackson Hole? No problemo. Surfing at Mavericks? Your wish is its command." Pontiac puts it this way: "The problem: suddenly the going gets tough. The solution: Rock on in the 2000 GrandAm SE with Solidform Design. It's built with enough solid steel reinforcements to make Pittsburgh jealous. Because the road of life can be a pretty rough place, and out here you need the right armor." The ad shows drivers playing car hockey near the edge of a cliff with the words "Not that you would, but you could." In fact, the tough prop for the Hero's journey is so prevalent in the automotive industry that it likely no longer differentiates among cars.

Sifting through ad after ad hyping car toughness, we found it a relief to come upon a Yakima Loadwarrior system ad with a more lighthearted approach, spoofing the Hero's classic stoicism. The ad reads, "The key to happiness is to stop carrying everything inside." The picture shows a top rack with a bike and other heroic paraphernalia.

Competition and Challenge

A lighthearted ad for Intel recognizes the often knee-jerk competitiveness of the lower levels of the Hero archetype. It shows a young man by his computer expressing the sentiment "How much speed does my PC need? More than my friend Bob's." Aethersystems ("Wireless Solutions for a Portable Planet") says, "PCs and laptops talk real big about business. Until we ask them to step outside."

Homestead, a Web-site developer ("It's a new world. Make your place.") recognizes the Hero's desire to brag about his exploits. In the epic poem *Beowulf*, for instance, heroes wile away their evenings swapping stories about the monsters they have slain and the countries they have conquered. Homestead gives you a way to join them, picturing the rough-and-tumble of team sports: "Winning hurts. Making the website to brag about it doesn't."

In more earnest guise, the Hero archetype is also at the root of all horror flicks and video games. Sega Dreamcast, promoting Resident Evil, dares the viewer to be up to the challenge of facing its horror:

> *You may laugh in the face of fear. But it'll be a nervous, unconvincing little laugh . . . If you enjoy Resident Evil (you sick pup), then kill the lights and immerse yourself in two disks—over 40 hours of the most vile, mutated, flesh-eating terror yet. New weapons, 3D graphics, and P.O.V. battles bring the horror to life like never before. Which means you'll get to see how brave you really are.*

In the same vein, Half.com shows a bruised and battered young boy and suggests he buy *Bruce Lee's Fighting Method* to be prepared for the next battle.

There is also real aggression in people that can be channeled in a positive or a negative direction. An ad for Lugz shoes leaves it ambivalent, showing a young man kicking a metal door. The only explanation is the single word "Conquer." The Hero archetype helps channel that aggression and will into positive expression. At the mid-range levels, this can mean athletic or economic competition rather than physical aggression. Thus, Equitable Life ASA financial services associates its expertise with developing "strong will, stronger leadership."

The higher level Hero, of course, uses strength to be a peacemaker. In a lighthearted ad, Symphony, an Internet connection firm, pictures a family engaging in a tug-of-war over Internet access. The company offers a cordless home network that "allows everyone to surf the Web wirelessly," thus stopping "the war over Internet access." Volvo runs an ad differentiating its "my car is safe and rugged" campaign from others' by associating with peace, not war: "The first missile that truly makes the world a safer place." In fact, the Hero is the archetype for almost all actual peacemaking efforts throughout the world.

At the High End

In increasingly spiritual times, the courage and perseverance of the Hero can be promoted as necessary to spiritual attainment. An ad for Danner boots reads, "The road to Nirvana is not paved." The scene of snowcapped peaks conjures up the hardships of trekking in order to attain spiritual enlightenment (perhaps in Nepal). The copy continues, "No one said Nirvana would be easy to reach . . . so strap on a pair and get there before somebody tries to turn paradise into a parking lot."

Similarly, the American Cancer Society is countering the image of the cancer patient as victim with a marketing campaign designed to promote an alternative image of the Hero. One great ad pictures a nice-looking middle-aged woman and says, "She is a mother who finally found a way to help her daughter stop smoking. [She] is a patient who calms her own fears by talking with others who care. [She] is a wife whose newfound strength has given her husband hope."

Finally, green innovation is perfect for a Hero-brand identification, because the higher levels of the archetype are focused primarily on making a positive difference in one's time and for the planet. Green Mountain Energy ("Choose wisely. It's a small planet.") runs an ad saying, "Some people dream of making a difference. Others actually do." Rather than focus on the heroism of the company, the firm wisely portrays its customers as Heroes, making "renewable facilities" possible "as a direct result of customer choice."

One of the most successful ads of the Partnership For a Drug Free America was "The Long Way Home," in which a young boy, going home from school in a truly tough neighborhood, climbs over high fences and cuts through alleys and backyards to avoid the drug dealers. This ad—which shows wonderful empathy with the plight of the inner-city kid—says that "just say no" is not so simple. The boy says " . . . and maybe the dealers are scared of the police, but they're not scared of me. And they sure don't take no for an answer." Rather than promoting simple-minded solutions, this ad is empathic with the plight real kids face, while still portraying them as Heroes with options. Subsequent research by the Partnership indicated that the ad increased children's confidence in their ability to resist drugs and drug dealers.[5]

Marketing to the Hero

When asked about Western civilization, Gandhi responded that he thought it was a good idea. People widely experience our time as one adrift and lacking in values and convictions. Consumers—especially those who express the higher levels of the Hero archetype—are hungry for convictions and attracted to people, companies, and brands that have them. In *The Dream Society*, Rolf Jensen predicts that before long, brands will be seen as the owners of meaningful stories, not products. The most compelling stories are those which

---

5. See also the discussion of the March of Dimes as a Hero brand, examined in detail in Chapter 6.

> The Hero identity may be right for your brand if
>
> - you have an invention or innovation that will have a major impact on the world
> - your product helps people perform at their upper limit
> - you are addressing a major social problem and asking people to step up to the plate to help address it
> - you have a clear opponent or competitor you want to beat
> - you are the underdog and want to rival the competition
> - the strength of your product or service is its ability to do a tough job efficiently and well
> - you need to differentiate your product from one that has problems with follow-through
> - your customer base identifies itself as good, moral citizens

communicate some value that ennobles life. "The battle of the twenty-first century," he writes, "will be fought on a microfront where the bone of contention is the individual's attention." "Companies," he continues, "will gradually enter the market for convictions" primarily because the "customer wants it. When you are no longer that preoccupied with politicians' vast smorgasbord of ideological systems and more or less vapid visions, then you no longer just vote in the polling booth on election day; you vote every day, with your shopping cart."[6]

Customers, he notes, are already taking companies to task, "asking questions like, 'Does your company have no heart, no feelings? Are you nothing but a rationalistic, profiteering machine?'" Ironically, companies that value nothing but competition and the bottom line are also evincing the Hero archetype in its more primitive warriorlike stages. What we can see from this is that when the archetype is expressed in the public at a higher level, people reward brands with their business.

We see the triumph of the higher level of the Hero archetype in the emergence of cause-related marketing and the increasing con-

---

6. Rolf Jensen, *The Dream Society: How the Coming Shift from Information to Imagination Will Transform Your Business* (New York: McGraw-Hill, 1999), pp. 111–113.

sumer expectation that companies will engage in philanthropic activities. The backlash against Bill Gates started long before the antitrust suit against Microsoft scandal revealed his bully tactics. The initial criticism resulted from his failure to engage in philanthropic activities, given his massive wealth, until challenged by public opinion to do so. Although he then did so, many thought it was too little, too late.

Most companies today articulate their values, mission, and vision in a clear way. Increasingly, the public and the consumer expect those corporate visions to reflect some sense of social responsibility. To deal with this expectation, Jensen recommends that a company "have a political platform roughly equivalent to that of a presidential candidate. The only difference will be that companies face election daily and not just every four years."[7] When marketing to the Hero, know that you are being evaluated not only by the quality of your product or services, but also by the strength and ethics of your convictions.

7. *Ibid.*

8

The Outlaw

Motto: "Rules are meant to be broken."

T HE VILLAIN IN THE MELODRAMA curls his mustache and smiles, and young girls are caught between dread and attraction. The siren sings and the sailor is lured to his death.

The Outlaw has the enticement of forbidden fruit. Recently, at a conference, Carol Pearson attended a workshop on "Being the Outlaw or Dating One." There was standing room only! It seems that the more well-behaved and responsible we are, the more we yearn to be an Outlaw, at least a little bit, some of the time.

Certainly, we see the Outlaw in its most positive form in figures like Robin Hood or Zorro. Finding their identity outside the current social structure, such Outlaws are faithful to deeper, truer values than the prevailing ones. Such Outlaws are romantic figures, ready to disrupt a society that has succumbed to tyranny, repression, conformity, or cynicism. In modern history, we can think of the demonstrators at Tiananmen Square in China and the participants in the civil rights and antiwar movements in the United States—they are some of the revolutionaries who changed the world to the one we know today.

Of course, we also see the Outlaws who lack such principles— who are just alienated, angry, and willing to victimize others to get what they want. People who give up on getting what they want in a healthy and socially acceptable way may turn to illegal or unethical

> **The Outlaw**
>
> **Core desire:** revenge or revolution
> **Goal:** to destroy what is not working (for the Outlaw or the society)
> **Fear:** being powerless, trivialized, inconsequential
> **Strategy:** disrupt, destroy, or shock
> **Trap:** to go over to the dark side, criminality
> **Gift:** outrageousness, radical freedom

strategies in order to prevail. They may not feel moral, but they at least feel powerful. While the Hero wants to be admired, the Outlaw is satisfied to be feared. At least, fear implies power of some sort. The styles differ. Each in his or her own way, a mobster, a revolutionary, a skinhead, and an adolescent with numerous tattoos or body piercing may feel powerful making others scared or uncomfortable.

Any kind of effective action against them dispels the fear of victimization, so the cowboys with the black hats ride in and shoot up the town with no more of a goal than simply to disrupt things and feel powerful. Both the Hero and the Outlaw feel anger. The Hero takes action when he or she is outraged by injustice. The Outlaw's anger tends to be provoked by being slighted as a person. Whereas Heroes identify with their community, Outlaws feel deeply estranged from it. You might imagine the typical villain in *Superman* or *Batman* comics—Lex Luthor or the Joker—who often has become evil as a result of being humiliated or exiled (for being different, maimed, or defective in some way).

The natural habitat for the Outlaw is places that are hidden and shadowy—out of the way. Psychologist C. G. Jung described the way in which individuals and cultures have Shadows—qualities that are judged unacceptable and hence are hidden and denied. People do not want to acknowledge their own Shadows, even to themselves, so they often project them onto others, seeing those others as the problem.

> The Outlaw may be known as the rebel, the revolutionary, the villain, the wild man or woman, the misfit, the enemy, or the iconoclast.

The Outlaw holds the shadowy qualities of the culture—that is, the qualities the society disdains and disregards. In this way, the Outlaw can release society's pent-up passions—as, in more ancient times, festivals allowed great license (for example, in England, on Beltane, all sexual restrictions were off for just that one night) and operated as a release valve that, in fact, helped stabilize the culture. In modern times, Woodstock held the positive image of the Outlaw culture, prefiguring the potential for a more utopian time, while Altamont illustrated the more dystopian potential for an Outlaw society to crumble into violence.

One need only think of the success of Outlaw novels and films to know how powerful a force this archetype is in society today: Some, such as *Rebel Without a Cause* or Jack Kerouac's *On the Road*, chronicle alienation from the culture that leads to breaking cultural norms and taboos. The resonance of such movies and books tells us that some part of every one of us feels some degree of alienation from the dominant culture, particularly when we are young. Other films, such as *Bonnie and Clyde* or *Butch Cassidy and the Sundance Kid*, show the Outlaw as a somewhat glamorous figure and the breaking of rules as liberating. Still others, like *The Godfather*, *Goodfellas*, or *Eyes Wide Shut*, trade on the simple allure of criminal or forbidden behaviors. The hippies of the 1960s introduced countercultural, Outlaw values into the culture, and as baby boomers have come of age, such values have become mainstream, and with them magazines such as *Rolling Stone*. Rock music, which was once a countercultural statement, is now the music of choice of an aging middle class.

In every generation, adolescents flock to Outlaw products. Just a few years ago, purple hair dye would fall into that category. Today, tattoos and body piercing fill this need, as do mosh pits, many forms of hip-hop and rap, and (attractive to Outlaws of any age) Harley-Davidsons. Outlaw brands include MTV, which is why kids tend to love it and parents worry about it. It is also there in a more subtle way on Fox, which, of the major commercial networks, leans more to shocking and edgy content than do ABC, NBC, or CBS. Although one could see Calvin Klein as a Lover brand, since its imagery is so sexual, the company also has Outlaw qualities because of the way it pushes the edge of what social propriety will allow.

Hoards of people listen to Howard Stern or watch "Politically Incorrect"; drink Tequila, Jack Daniels, or Southern Comfort; or smoke Winstons. The pirate-like eye patch on the man in the Hathaway shirt adds just enough sense of the Outlaw to spice up what is, after all, quite a proper shirt. In the women's movement, educated professional women—motivated by books like Clarissa Pinkola Estes's *Women Who Run With the Wolves*—try to recapture the lost instinctual wild woman within, while Robert Bly and others take men to the woods seeking their wild man.

When Outlaw consciousness is present, people are more acutely aware of the ways civilization limits human expression. Nathaniel Hawthorne's classic American novel, *The Scarlet Letter*, contrasts Puritan society with the freer life of the forest, which is linked with sexuality, vitality, sin, and, paradoxically, also transformational virtue. American novels and movies that offer critiques of the society often show how good people are forced to break the law in order to do the right thing. A well-known example of a classic novel that exemplifies just such a theme is Mark Twain's *Huckleberry Finn*, and the theme appears as well in modern movies like *Thelma and Louise*, *Fried Green Tomatoes*, and *The Cider House Rules*, in which groups feel so unprotected by society that they are forced to break the law to survive. Historical figures like Lenin or Malcolm X illustrate what happens in a society in which leaders of disempowered groups become alienated enough to be willing to espouse or practice violence.

In an everyday way, celebrities like Brad Pitt, Jack Nicholson, and Madonna succeed because they break outdated rules in a manner that feels liberating to people. By acting in a sexually liberated, even promiscuous way while wearing a cross and the name of the Virgin, Madonna's brand identity blatantly challenges the historical distinction between the virgin and the whore. Such a brand identity requires a capacity for risk. It can be wildly successful if the society is ready for its values to be challenged. It can also generate serious backlash, criticism, and shaming if society is not ready.

In the Soviet Union, capitalist behavior was outlawed, yet circumstances necessitated participation in the black market (which was, of course, capitalist in the extreme). Over time, a nation of Outlaws was created, and it was only a matter of time until communism, at least in that form, collapsed.

The threat of the Outlaw, however, is that an individual, quiet rebellion will break out in ways that begin to destroy the society, either eroding it from within or demolishing it in a violent eruption. The negative pole of the archetype is evidenced in characters like

Darth Vader and other villains who have gone over to the dark side. The negative Outlaw, then, thrives in organizations that allow profit and competition to outweigh any kind of moral value or sense of social responsibility and in the ever-present danger that hostile takeovers will destroy the identity (and hence the soul) of healthy companies.

Carriers of Outmoded and Revolutionary Behaviors

Outlaw brands have a complicated role. They can reinforce soulless, cynical behaviors when values are absent. But they can also assist in bringing down an oppressive establishment, help to open and ease social restrictions, or serve as a safety valve that allows people to let off steam, thus protecting the status quo. In addition, they can reinforce real revolution, breaking through staid and repressive thinking to champion a whole new way.

The 1960s can be seen as an Outlaw era, with both countercultural heroes and the cowboys and cowgirls they offended ultimately holding values of freedom for the whole culture—even though their respective definitions of freedom differed. As baby boomers have come into power, they have brought many of these alternative values with them.

Ads for NetZero feature mock McCarthy hearings, in which a congressional committee is investigating the Internet, which its members see as un-American because it is free. The brave witnesses, however, speak for the American tradition of free speech and advocate the people's right to free access. Indeed, overall, the new world of e-commerce has a wonderfully liberated, rule-breaking Outlaw quality to it. Yet brands like Compuserve and AOL lost customers because they blithely signed up more subscribers than they could serve. This new world simply does not operate by the established rules. Indeed, it is a bit like the Wild West, with the rule of law and order not yet firmly established. At this point, only the strongest and the cleverest survive.

Many cultures have sacred trickster figures, which act almost completely on the basis of primitive instinct—what Freud would call the id. The coyote figure in American Indian lore, for example, cons people in order to get food, dislodges his penis and sends it ahead

to rape women, and generally acts in ways that are entirely determined by greed, gluttony, and lust. Such figures have a wonderfully
cathartic role in culture. They hold behaviors that are still current
in people's inner lives, but are neither socially nor morally acceptable.
When we see these behaviors and laugh at them, they are acknowledged, their energy is released, and hence their hold on people is
lessened.

Some Outlaw images are darker and may either release or reinforce potentially dangerous energy. It is hard to know for sure how
they function. The Internet and media today have a trickster quality
to them, with an almost-anything-goes attitude. The most basic and
primitive emotions are allowed full play. We do not yet know
whether the upshot of such license will be a release of more primitive
emotions so that people can live in a more civilized way with one
another or whether we are witnessing the decline of a civilization.
Do pornographic Web sites siphon off oppressive behaviors, or do
they abet rape and incest? Do violent and misogynous lyrics in rap
and other music act as a catharsis to vent frustration, or do they aid
and abet violence, sexism, and antisocial behavior? We do not yet
know for sure.

When the Outlaw is active in individuals, they may feel estranged
from the dominant culture and contemptuous of its rules. They may
engage in self-destructive behavior (drug use, body piercing, attire
that sets them outside the bounds of normal society) or actions that
flagrantly disregard general standards of ethics, health, or propriety.
While the Explorer also stands at the edges of society, Explorers just
want to be free. By contrast, the Outlaw actually wants to disrupt
things, shock people, ferment a revolution, get away with something,
or just feel the excitement of being a little bit "bad." Both may feel
somewhat alienated, but the Explorer experiences this disconnection
with sadness and loneliness, while the Outlaw does so with anger,
outrage, or the exhilaration of breaking out of or through society.

Most young people feel a bit alienated from the culture simply
because their developmental task is to find themselves. If this alienation is relatively minor, they will identify with the Explorer. If it is
not so minor, they will identify as Outlaws or at least rebels. The
word "rebel" in our society is used in an ambiguous way that can
carry either archetype. If the rebel is merely operating in an individ-

ualistic way, we are seeing the Explorer at work. But if the rebel is ready to break convention or the law, then it is carrying the archetype of the Outlaw.

In a more everyday way, responsible, hardworking people may also be attracted to Outlaw archetype brands—not because they will ever disrupt anything or shock anyone, but as a way of letting off steam. A generally virtuous mother may get a thrill from wearing Opium perfume, but never actually break the law. The successful lawyer or doctor may ride a Harley-Davidson or be attracted to ads for SUVs in which a frustrated driver stuck in traffic suddenly swerves off the road and drives through the countryside, thus breaking the rule that you have to stay on the highway.

I'm Mad as Hell and Won't Take It Anymore

The Explorer is lonely and seeks his or her identity. The Outlaw feels helpless and seeks the experience of power, even if only in the ability to shock or defy others. Nintendo ran an ad invoking barbarians wearing purple loincloths, painted faces, and fierce expressions, clearly about to ravage a village. The ad says, "In the dark ages, one's choice of colors reflected his personal style of madness, mayhem, and mass destruction. It still does." What follows are pictures of Nintendos in six new colors. One might infer that children and adolescents must be feeling particularly powerless and angry if they are attracted to such violent imagery. Diamond video games provides a message that is even more graphic: Accompanying a picture of a man aiming a pistol in front of a world in flames, the copy reads, "Speeds up

---

Levels of the Outlaw

Call: feeling powerless, angry, mistreated, under siege
Level One: identifying as outsider, dissociating from the values of the group or society in a way that flies in the face of conventional behaviors and morality
Level Two: behaving in shocking or disruptive ways
Level Three: becoming a rebel or a revolutionary
Shadow: criminal or evil behavior

your assault. Speeds up your annihilation. And if you suck, it also speeds up your retreat."

The Outlaw archetype stands out of time. It can hold future values that promise (or threaten) revolution, as well as offering a form to continue archaic qualities in the culture. Teenage gangs and the Mafia are organized in the same ways as feudal societies were. Once, it was an acceptable form of social organization, but now it is not. We can see the Outlaw in a mild way in the popularity of someone like Howard Stern, whose politically incorrect remarks seem to let off steam for some people. Such remarks would not have seemed so outrageous just a few decades ago, but because they are now generally unacceptable, many people find their free expression exhilarating. (Others, of course, find that they reinforce views they still secretly, or not so secretly, hold.)

We also see the continuing appeal of anachronistic practice in much more extreme behaviors. For example, Attila the Hun was once a Hero figure, but his ruthlessness could now only be seen as criminal. Certainly, any modern war tribunal would find him guilty of crimes against humanity. Nevertheless, such behaviors are alive and well in modern video games (as well as in certain parts of the world, like Rwanda and Kosovo).

Sega Dreamcast advertises a soundtrack by Rob Zombie as "A gory revenge. An extremely gory revenge." Infogames promotes "Hogs of War," saying, "This little piggy joined the army. This little piggy stayed home. This little piggy had grenades. This little piggy had none. This little piggy went BAM, BAM, BAM and blasted all the other pigs into bacon!" We could go on and on. This is just the tip of the iceberg.

Although many ads by reputable companies portray African Americans as responsible and middle class, numerous ads also aimed at blacks are violent in the extreme, perhaps reflecting a corporate belief that they "are mad as hell and won't take it anymore." A record label called "Murder Inc." advertises an album called *The Murderers* with pictures of angry and sullen black faces. Historically, the Outlaw archetype in its more primitive forms was projected onto both blacks and Indians (who also carried the romantic image of the Noble Savage for the culture). Whether such ads are developed by whites or blacks, they certainly reinforce anachronistic and racist images.

Camelot music company similarly promotes a CD called *Cypress Hill Skull and Bones*, with the reassurance that the firm is "still F**kin' up the program." Of course, since the 1980s, it has been fashionable for rock bands—white and black—to destroy their instruments and the set before leaving the stage. Rage is in today—on the stage and on the highways. Commander Salamander, a shop in Washington, DC's fashionable Georgetown neighborhood, sells products to adolescents that include jewelry with satanic imagery mixed in with trendy clothes. Similar shops are found all over the world and are enormously popular with teenagers, many of them from upper middle class neighborhoods and affluent, professional families.

Even with children, action figures are getting more and more grotesque. Today, monsters are as attractive as Heroes, especially to boys. Codemasters promotes Micro Maniacs, "Reckless, destructive, wicked, aggressive, manic fun! Micro Maniacs punch, kick, and fight dirty as they run wild through the house. No principles, no prisoners, just 12 mutant characters devastating anyone and anything that comes between them and winning. It's multiplayer mayhem at its maniacal best."

Destruction, Metamorphosis, and the Shadow

Outlaw brands love to be identified with things that are bad for you. Hard Candy Lipstick ads, picturing a very young girl with vampish makeup, include a prominent warning label, much like that on cigarettes, to caution consumers that, because "caffeine lipstick may be addictive, apply and re-apply as needed." Warning labels on cigarettes may, in fact, add to their appeal with youth.

Captain Morgan Rum is marketed in a more lighthearted way, with an image of a pirate. Most brands of Tequila have an Outlaw imprint. Patron Tequila pictures a gorgeous but scantily clad woman with the caption, "Ladies love outlaws." Yet, the classic dead worm in the bottom of some brands not only attests to the strength of the alcohol content, but also subliminally hints at courting death through drinking the product.

It almost goes without saying that all restricted substances—like cigarettes and alcohol—have an Outlaw attraction for the young. And, of course, actual illegal substances have even more such appeal, which may be why so many young people experiment with illegal drugs, learning only later that their impact is hardly glamorous.

To understand the appeal of the Outlaw archetype, it is important to recognize, as Freud did, that Thanatos (the death wish) is about as strong as Eros (the life force). Particularly during major life transitions—like adolescence and midlife—the psyche is calling upon people to "die" with respect to what they have been and be "reborn" into another identity. At such times, images of death can be very appealing.

The danger here is that symbols of death and destruction reinforce the concrete, literal desire to die. David Oldfield, director of the Midway Center for the Creative Imagination, found that adolescents who were suicidal or at high risk for suicide often drew images of death. His theory is that in a society that does not teach people to think metaphorically, the inner yearning for death is channeled not into metamorphosis, but into annihilation. Thus, at critical points in the life span, people drink too much, drive fast, take drugs, attempt suicide, or engage in other life-threatening behaviors when what is needed is real transformation. There is, of course, a real need for products and services that aid in such transitions rather than fostering dangerous behaviors.

Of course, even healthy activities can have an Outlaw imprint. Take running, for example. Tattoo running shoes have evil-looking flames and dragons on the soles and are advertised with images of tattoo-sporting guys running through desolate terrain. Such images meet alienated young people where they are and invite them into a healthy activity. A few ads, of course, blatantly take on the appeal of death by confronting it directly. One, geared toward motorcycle safety, warns men that women love scars, but not holes where your eyes used to be. If that doesn't scare a motorcyclist into safe driving, we don't know what would.

The Lighthearted Outlaw

The Outlaw can be associated with the persistent cultural interest in extraterrestrials—which are likely the ultimate Outlaws. Like Outlaws generally, aliens are often pictured as dark, dangerous figures that may well destroy the planet. On the other hand, they can be pictured as technologically and spiritually ahead of us and therefore here to provide rescue from our own self-destructive impulses.

Products, of course, generally associate with the latter. IPIX Internet Pictures Corporation sports a picture that calls up alien monster images—a head with eyes all over it—on a man with a fiercely determined expression, saying, "See everything!" Similarly, Sony promotes the new Walkman's advanced technology with an ad showing an FBI report deeming it a sign of alien invasion—the product is so advanced, it must come from another planet.

Sometimes the Outlaw image is used in a lighthearted way, as with the Frito Bandito. Milky Way Midnight, for example, is advertised as "dangerously bold chocolate" that is "finally out on parole." The association of the Outlaw with secret, shameful behavior serves as a great leverage point for lighthearted ads, spoofing this whole tradition. Microsoft ran an ad in which a blurred image of a person, clearly wanting to be disguised, confesses, "I own a PowerMac G4 with all the trimmings. And yes, I use Microsoft Office. Sometimes I say that just for the shock value."

One of the most successful New York Lotto ads of all times begins with a typical boardroom meeting, interrupted by the news that the company has been acquired by Chuck from the mail room. Having won the lottery, he buys the company and lets the former CEO know how he likes his coffee. This ad, fueled by research that said most lotto players were motivated by job dissatisfaction, plays on the desire to break the rules of the work ethic—and turn the tables on the boss.

Harley-Davidson: An Outlaw Masterpiece

Harley-Davidson is an American icon—but, paradoxically, one that captures the Outlaw rather than the heroic character of American life. The idea today of a motorcycle company sponsoring a racing team is obvious enough, but it was a radical notion in 1915, when Harley-Davidson sponsored The Wrecking Crew, whose daredevil antics were so dangerous, they led to frequent accidents and some fatalities. Harleys were also used in the military and by the post office to deliver mail.

The Harley-Davidson motorcycle was in serious trouble some

years ago because the Japanese were selling a better product at a cheaper price. The company regained its market share by marketing meaning. By promoting the personality of the brand, moreover, the firm was able to expand from building motorcycles to selling a line of clothing and accessories linked not by function, but by archetype.

Harley-Davidson cycles are not inexpensive, so their owners are often professional people who want to express their wild side. Harleys also are associated with the Hell's Angels and other Outlaw groups. The personality is complicated. For example, it is associated with patriotism, but not as a Hero would see it. One study found that riders thought that riding a Harley-Davidson was "a stronger expression of patriotism than is obeying the law." This form of patriotism is the old nationalistic kind for Harley-Davidson riders, sometimes associated with Japan bashing.

The macho image was aided by the bikers in Marlon Brando's *The Wild Ones* in the 1950s and has grown since, although the "ladies of Harley" make up 10 percent of riders. As one might expect, not only do many customers sport tattoos, but "the most popular tattoo in the United States is the Harley-Davidson symbol." Riders see Harleys as more than a motorcycle—more like a whole set of attitudes, a lifestyle that is not just about freedom (as the Explorer might be), but freedom from mainstream values and conventions. A typical ad shows a remote cabin with the tag line, "If you didn't have to answer to anyone, what would you do?"

Harley riders often sport black leather, heavy boots, chrome, conspicuous weaponry, long hair, boots, and body piercing—as well as tattoos. Harley gatherings have the character of Outlaw bands coming together, in contrast to the wholesomeness of RegularGuy/Gal Saturn reunions.[1]

The Harley Web page challenges riders to answer one question:

> *Suppose time takes a picture—one picture that represents your entire life here on earth. You have to ask yourself how you'd rather be remembered. As a pasty, web-wired computer wiz, strapped to an office chair? Or, as a leather-clad adventurer who lived life to the fullest*

---

1. David A. Aaker, *Building Strong Brands* (New York: The Free Press, 1996), pp. 138–141.

astride a Harley-Davidson? You can decide which it is, but think quickly.
Time is framing up that picture, and it's got a pretty itchy shutter finger.

Power to the People: Apple and the Revolutionary Organization

The story of Adam and Eve in the Garden of Eden tells us that humankind fell from grace because the pair ate an apple from the tree of the knowledge of good and evil. Leaving the garden meant that people would no longer live in paradise (which we might think of as "blissful ignorance"), but it also meant that they would have free will. That is one reason theologians refer to this episode as the "fortunate fall."

The Apple logo—an apple with a bite out of it—calls forth these associations. Its motto, then, admonishes customers to "Think different," and ads run pictures of iconoclastic creative geniuses in a variety of fields, including Albert Einstein, Martha Graham, Maria Callas, Amelia Earhart, Rosa Parks, Buzz Aldrin, Muhammad Ali, Richard Branson, and John Lennon and Yoko Ono. Apple is also known for technological innovation and the revolutionary step of making such user-friendly software that virtually anyone could become expert enough to use the company's computers almost immediately.

Founder Steve Jobs puts it this way: " 'Think Different' celebrates the soul of the Apple brand—that creative people with passion can change the world for the better. Apple is dedicated to making the best tools in the world for creative individuals everywhere." The Super Bowl ad that put Apple on the map opened with the famed 1984 dystopian society, clearly linked with Ruler archetype IBM, portrayed as Big Brother. Zombielike, gray-uniformed people shuffle into a huge assembly hall, dominated by a huge screen. Big Brother delivers the party line from the screen, "We are one people. With one will. One resolve. One cause. Our enemies shall talk themselves to death. And we will bury them with their own confusion. We shall prevail!" Suddenly, a young, athletic woman appears, wielding a sledgehammer, and shatters the screen. The announcer then says "On January 24, Apple Computer will introduce Macintosh. And you'll see why 1984 won't be like '1984.' "

Apple is associated in the public mind with computer hackers and, generally, business-as-unusual innovators, giving power to the people by making computers more user friendly. The company is more closely connected with computers and a love of innovation than with pure profit mongering. It is also associated with the radical potential of computer technology to return power to the people. Apple's early company decision to focus on educational and home uses more than business ones also established a progressive, populist image. Customers purchasing an Apple are identifying themselves with an image of independent thinking, and with intellectual, trend-setting pioneers. Apple customers are loyal almost to the point of fanaticism, and the image of the "noncorporate corporation" needed to be backed by reality. When the board of directors decided to replace founder Steve Jobs with a more traditional manager, employee morale sank and sales plummeted. Only bringing back the freewheeling founder saved the day. And when he returned, he also rehired Chiat/Day, the advertising company that developed the blockbuster 1984 Outlaw ad.[2]

Apple catalogues are rather cramped, utilizing bright colors and almost cartoon shapes, and look like they might be from some kind of discount house, in contrast to the more dignified IBM look with more white space and genteel print. The latest Apple coup is the success of the iMac—once again breaking the unwritten rule that computers have to be gray. This time they come not only in colors, but in a see-through case.

Living in Revolutionary Times

In times of rapid transition, the status quo stops being privileged. The future is always lurking on the edges, and it is not clear which social experiments will become the new establishment. In the 1990s, as the last millennium was winding to a close, Outlaw organizational development strategies privileged nothing. Everything was up for grabs. Zero-based budgeting, reengineering, and all other strategies weeded out everything that was not working, appealing to the Outlaw revolutionary spirit while striking terror into the hearts of those

2. Tom Cannon, *The Ultimate Book of Business Breakthroughs* (Oxford, UK: Capstone, 2000), pp. 123–126.

who prefer stable, secure times. Some believed that the predicted Y2K computer bug would wipe out civilization as we know it. Although that did not happen, the business sphere did change radically as a result of all the weeding of the economic garden. Businesses that were not viable tended to fold. Yet, as the death of winter is necessary for spring, the result has been a flowering of prosperity.

At the same time, the curricula of major universities have emphasized a deconstructionist critique of society that has encouraged a whole generation to see the establishment as an enemy and to identify with Outsiders. In a scathing article in the *Atlantic Monthly*, Alston Chase posits that a Harvard education may have created the Unabomber. He argues that

> It was at Harvard that [Ted] Kaczynski first encountered the ideas about the evils of society that would provide a justification for and a focus to an anger he had felt since junior high school. It was at Harvard that he began to develop these ideas into his anti-technology ideology of revolution. It was at Harvard that Kaczynski began to have fantasies of revenge, began to dream of escaping into wilderness. And it was at Harvard, as far as can be determined, that he fixed on dualistic ideas of good and evil, and on a mathematical cognitive style that led him to think he could find absolute truth through the application of his own reason.[3]

His point is, of course, that the curriculum which created a killer also fueled a time in which the elite are alienated from their own culture and are both inclined to deconstruct it and intellectually skilled at tearing it down. Will this dismantling of the traditional culture result in a Renaissance? It may be too soon to tell.

Marketing to the Outlaw

An extreme example of Outlaw marketing is the promotion of raves—one night countercultural dances. Perhaps because of the drug use associated with them, they often are publicized by flyers

---

3. Alston Chase, "Harvard and the Making of the Unabomber," *Atlantic Monthly* (June 2000), p. 43.

and distributed only in music stories featuring ambient, trance, and heavy-metal music. If you do not frequent such places, you do not even know a rave is occurring.

Outlaw products are best marketed in special-interest magazines or through flyers, personal ads, and other formats designed to find Outlaws. This does not mean that you cannot reach a large audience; MTV, for instance, reaches adolescents everywhere, but still is experienced as a countercultural and alternative medium.

Images used can have a dark, shadowy quality to them and often also feature quite intense colors. Moreover, this archetype likes things that shock, on a continuum from the mildly surprising joke to the truly disturbing. The Outlaw is the archetype most suited to sustaining an edgy identity and to the creation of edgy ads that really work.

The Outlaw in each of us also wants to get away with things. Therefore, slash-and-burn sales are great marketing strategies, as are various kinds of cash kickbacks for buying a certain product. Events held to launch or promote Outlaw products need to allow people to kick back and feel free; they may even seem a bit racy or on the edge of violating propriety. A fund-raiser for the Democratic National Committee, broadcast live on CNN, probably was designed to counter likely presidential nominee Al Gore's image as overly stiff and proper. Gore and President Clinton dressed in blue jeans, and comedian Robin Williams not only roasted Gore, Clinton, and the donors in the "posh pit," but also used the "F word." While this is a debatable tactic for a presidential candidate, it would be a great strategy for any genuine Outlaw brand.

David Brooks's comic look at American culture, *Bobos in Paradise: The New Upper Class and How They Got There*, makes a compelling case that the attitudes and behavior of educated, affluent citizens now completely integrate sturdy bourgeois standards with nonjudgmental bohemian ease. In this new world, a person's status comes from his or her net worth, combined with antimaterialistic values, and countercultural references drive the ads of capitalist companies, so that William S. Burroughs may appear in a Nike ad and Jack Kerouac in one for The Gap.[4] Mass marketing to the Outlaw, then, requires the

---

4. David Brooks, *Bobos in Paradise: The New Upper Class and How They Got There* (New York: Simon & Schuster, 2000), passim.

The Outlaw may be a good identity for your brand if

- customers and employees are feeling very disaffiliated from society or identify with values at odds with those of society at large
- the function of your product is to destroy something (actually, like a bulldozer, or virtually, like many video games) or is genuinely revolutionary
- your product is not very good for people, so that using it is akin to thumbing your nose at society's ideas of what constitutes health
- your product helps retain values that are threatened by prevailing ones or pioneers new and revolutionary attitudes
- your product's price is low to moderate

understanding that most people identifying with this archetype are, in fact, actually responsible, good citizens. And the truth is that Harley-Davidsons are so expensive that they are often owned by doctors, lawyers, and high-level managers. This means that mass marketing to the Outlaw works—if you remember not to go too far. As Calvin Klein and others have learned, it is easy to go too far and harm or offend someone. As Bob Dylan put it, "To live outside the law, you must be honest."

9

The Magician

Motto: "It can happen!"

THE EARLIEST IMAGES of the Magician were the shaman, the medicine man or woman, and the village witch or wizard. Later we had the alchemist, seeking to turn lead into gold. Still later, we had scientists probing the fundamental secrets of the universe, psychologists studying the workings of human consciousness, and gurus offering to share spiritual success secrets. Most basic to the Magician is the desire to search out the fundamental laws of how things work and to apply these principles to getting things done. The most typical applications of magical lore are to heal the mind, heart, and body; to find the fountain of youth and the secret of longevity; to discover ways to create and maintain prosperity; and to invent products that make things happen.

Perhaps the most famous Magician in Western culture is Merlin, who looks in his crystal ball and predicts the potential for Camelot. Aware, however, of the counterpotential for doom, he extends his energy to ensure the most ideal outcome. He does this, in part, by talking about his vision for a peaceful and just society, developing his talents (as legend has it that he did with King Arthur), and crafting or finding magical objects (the Round Table, Excalibur, the Grail) that support desired values of community, valor, and enlightenment. In the process, he also studies astronomy, natural science, and engineering.

Merlin, the great Magician of King Arthur's court, retreated to his cave when he needed to reflect or do magic. The cool, dark interiors of today's Tudor and adobe-style homes provide Magicians with the cave's modern equivalent.

The wildly successful Harry Potter series demonstrates children's and adolescents' fascination with the Magician. In fact, this series has actually motivated kids to read!

In contemporary film, we see Yoda of *Star Wars* teaching Luke Skywalker to "trust the force"; the witches in *Practical Magic* invoking true love; the antics of Mary Poppins; any number of angel shows or movies, such as *City of Angels* or "Touched by an Angel," in which the spirit world intervenes in this one; or movies like *Field of Dreams*, which help us believe that miracles do occur. In Mexico, a genre of film and fiction called magical realism has resulted in such movies as *Like Water for Chocolate*. In the United States, we have the growing genre of metaphysical films, including big box office hits like *The Sixth Sense*.

The Magician
Core desire: knowledge of the fundamental laws of how the world or universe works
Goal: make dreams come true
Fear: unanticipated negative consequences
Strategy: develop vision and live it
Trap: becoming manipulative
Gift: finding win-win outcomes

Magician brands include all those that foster "magical moments": sparkling water, champagne, Sony, General Foods International Coffees, Calgon ("Take me away"), many cruise lines, Jackie O, spas, and many chic hotels. They also include many cosmetics, herbs, potions, and fitness campaigns promising the fountain of youth. Dannon Yogurt hit the big time with a campaign taking off on research that connects eating yogurt with longevity. One commercial featured an ancient Georgian, eating Dannon, with the words "Temur Banacha thought Dannon was really fine yogurt. He ought to know. He's been eating yogurt for 105 years." Of course, virtually all New Age books, tapes, workshops, and products, and many "miraculous" modern technologies—the World Wide Web being only one of them—trade on the image of magic.

The spirit of the Magician is easily evoked when the product has exotic or ancient origins or if it involves some special ritual, such as popping corks, decanting wine, or swirling brandy and sniffing its aroma. (In fact, even the "brown paper bag variety" of brandy drinkers on street corners relish this ritual as part of the experience!) The Magician is also a great brand identity for corporate change strategies, miracle drugs, herbal remedies, spas, exotic travel, and, of course, any product or service that directly affects consciousness—advertising being but one.

Magicians are at the basis of radically new technologies: personal computers, the Internet, organ transplants, and genetic engineering. Think about Ben Franklin with his kite, tapping into the power of electricity, which eventually would help to fuel the industrial revolution. This image is also not so different from the image, in the movie *Frankenstein*, of the doctor bringing the monster to life with electric current as a storm rages outside. From both images, we can see the hope and the fear that are invested in the twin images of scientists as modern miracle workers and "mad geniuses" who try to play god and bring destruction on us all. In some ways, nuclear energy, too, holds both of these potentials: an inexpensive type of energy to heat our homes and the forebearer of a mushroom cloud that threatens to destroy the planet.

While the ancient shaman, medicine man or woman, or alchemist integrated science, spirituality, and psychology, in the modern world we tend to separate them. Advances in the physical sciences, however—especially those that threaten the survival of the planet or of our species—have spurred a strong sense that psychology needs to keep up. Therefore, although different fields and individuals led advances in the natural and physical sciences than in the psychological and spiritual arenas, it is not surprising that the culture as a whole exhibits an interest in all these areas. Moreover, as the Magician archetype emerges in the culture, these fields are beginning to align once again. A wider public is interested in mind–body medicine, the convergence of ideas between psychology, on the one hand, and the physical and biological sciences on the other, psychic phenomena and the occult, and the link between evolved consciousness and success.

Entrepreneurs are often Magicians, as are athletes. Spiritual ideas linking inner consciousness with outer performance are yielding miraculous results in the business and sports worlds. Magical people often have dreams that other people see as impossible, yet it is the essence of magic to have a vision and then walk right into it. When things go wrong, Magicians look inward to change themselves. Then the outer world changes as well. An ad for New Balance shows a man running out into nature. The ad says, "Turn off your computer. Turn off your fax machine. Turn off your cell phone. Connect with yourself." If you do not do this, you cannot do magic, for magic is always accomplished from the inside out.

The most consistent images associated with Magicians are signs in the heavens—rainbows, shooting stars, a beautiful galaxy, flying saucers—which tend to reassure us that we are not alone in the universe. As a symbol, the star over Bethlehem announcing Christ's birth holds this reassurance most palpably. Other images, of course, include caves, crystal balls, magic wands, capes, and, of course, the Magician's tall, pointed hat.

In its positive aspect, the Magician is a wandering angel, like Mary Poppins, the good witch in *The Wizard of Oz*, and Samantha in the television classic "Bewitched"; or the director of the action, like Shakespeare's Prospero (in *The Tempest*), intervening in troubled situations to set things right. Cleaning products such as Ajax and the "white knight" promote their ability to make our homes sparkle, while cultural gurus like Deepak Chopra teach us how to think right in order to become healthy and successful. Sometimes the magic is just in the energy to persist. Witness the remarkable success of the Energizer Bunny, which seems magical because it "keeps going and going."

> The Magician can be known as the visionary, catalyst, innovator, charismatic leader, mediator, shaman, healer, or medicine man or woman.

A number of ads today trade on such imagery, some seriously and others humorously. The American Indian College Fund runs an image of a student senate president, in full medicine woman regalia, dancing on the plains to make it clear that traditional Indian spiritual values govern her school. On a lighter note, McAfree.com, an on-line PC manager, shows a picture of an old woman reading from an ancient text, surrounded by burning candles. The woman appears to be engaged in some kind of incantation, with the caption reassuring the viewer, "Computers enlightened. No hocus-pocus required." There is something so miraculous about modern technologies that they virtually call out for a magical brand identity, even though the companies that sell them may not want to be identified with the more bizarre images associated with the archetype.

Sometimes the magical power of a brand can be communicated negatively—that is, by showing what life would be like without it. For example, JBL, a manufacturer of speaker systems, ran an ad of an empty field (except, of course, for grass), with the caption "How would Woodstock sound without JBL? Moo." The magical result of modern sound technology is powerfully brought home, simply by imagining its absence.

When the Magician archetype is active in individuals, they are catalysts for change. Trusting synchronicity (or meaningful coincidences), they expect that if they do their part, the universe will meet them. To the Magician, consciousness precedes existence. Therefore, if you want to change your world, you begin with changing your own attitudes and behavior. People who have an active inner Magician value experience, seek spiritual help, and, at their best, strive to be true to spiritual guidance.

Such people also typically understand at a deep level how consciousness works, so they are able to influence others in highly effective ways. The Magician archetype is therefore very strong in charismatic politicians, business leaders, and, in fact, the whole field of marketing, trading as it does on the influence of human consciousness on behavior.

You can see the negative potential in the Magician in stories of evil sorcerers, using their power to work their will on unsuspecting victims. Such unflattering images appear in marketing and advertising today, in people who engage in subliminal advertising, or who try to con others into doing things against their better judgment. The negative image of the Magician also shows up in charismatic political leaders who use their power to charm, not to bring out the best in people, but to promote fascist and racist ends. This negative trap within the Magician archetype can, of course, be seen in anyone who uses his or her emotional intelligence to manipulate, rather than communicate with, others.

MasterCard: A Marketing Masterpiece

MasterCard has a wonderful ad campaign featuring magical moments. Most such ads juxtapose the priceless with what MasterCard really does pay for. For example, one reads "Dinner for 37, Chex Marcella: $2,416; one happy 50th birthday card: $1.95; one leopard-print, peekaboo nightie: $45; still being able to make her blush: priceless."

Over time, this campaign has so successfully connected MasterCard with such priceless moments that many ads no longer even contain anything you can really use the card to buy. One such

---

Levels of the Magician

Call: hunches, extrasensory or synchronistic experiences
Level One: magical moments and experiences of transformation
Level Two: the experience of flow
Level Three: miracles, moving from vision to manifestation
Shadow: manipulation, sorcery

---

ad reads, "Speaking your mind: $0; Making friends for life: $0; Trying something new: $0; Believing in yourself: $0; Being young: Priceless." The recurring tag line says, "There are some things money can't buy. For everything else, there's MasterCard."

This ad campaign is brilliant because it is multilayered. At the first layer is the magical quality that resides in the experience of using a credit card. You have this little piece of plastic, and with it, you can get anything you want. Never mind that eventually you will have to pay for it. In the experience of the moment, it certainly does feel like you can have anything you want—and virtually anywhere in the world. Secondly, MasterCard recognizes consumers' ambivalence toward a materialistic culture and identifies truer, magical experiences they can have with their card. Therefore, you can use it to buy things and experience your connection with the card and the company as associated with truer values and deeper experiences than materialism can give you. At the same time, MasterCard is complimenting its customers, letting them know that they know there is more to them than consumption. They are saying, we know you are real, grounded, authentic, and you know what matters in life. So do we.

Magical Moments, Transformative Experiences

Champagne in all brands, recent campaigns for Chanel No. 5, and Polaroid and other instant cameras (capturing those moments) promise magical experiences. The Magician is also the archetype of choice of New Age seminars, spas, chic restaurants and hotels, and many bath products that promise transformative experiences. An ad for Oil of Olay body wash, for example, shows a peaceful-looking nude woman and says, "with only hours until her wedding and her caterer missing in action, Kate felt amazingly calm." The tag line reads, "proven to transform your body and your spirit." This association of luxury bath products with spiritual transformation is quite common. An ad for Acqua de Parmy Blu Mediterraneo says you should "Bring the spa home." Why? Because doing so satisfies "the modern desire for comfort, an excursion to your deepest pleasures . . . those which are born of that perfect balance of body and soul."

In Shakespeare's comedies, characters are transformed because suddenly they find themselves outside the city or the court that defines their roles and identities. In the woods, all the rules and definitions break down. Men and women often disguise themselves as the other sex. People converse with spirits and nymphs. Somehow, by the final act, miracles have occurred, problems are solved, and couples marry. Anichini, an importer of fine linens, has a wonderful ad that plays on this tradition. Renaissance-style linens on a lovely bed are pictured out in nature surrounded by lovely aspen trees. The unexpected setting for a bed gets the customer's attention and promises that magic is afoot.

Similarly, the National Park Foundation shows a picture of a young couple with their little boy setting out to meet the unknown in a beautiful natural landscape promising "10 million acres that couldn't care less what a big shot you are at the office." In the wild, without our normal roles and responsibilities, miracles of transformation happen. They do.

Some ads explicitly promise to deliver the consciousness of the Magician. Stories of indigenous medicine men and women, for example, often portray them as experiencing the laws of nature firsthand. They go on vision quests and discover its mysteries in solitude. The shaman actually may take on the form of a bird or animal and speak its language, because it is privy to nature's secrets. The popularity of Carlos Castañeda's Don Juan narratives, as well as many other studies of shamanistic traditions in New Age research, reflects the willingness of ordinary people to take such traditions seriously as guides for contemporary living.

Bausch and Lomb binoculars connects with the deep meaning of this archetype with an ad that portrays a beautiful landscape, a man with outstretched arms, and the text "I have been awakened by the touch of the sun's first rays. I have been to the solitary places and found company. I have floated on air in lazy circles with eagles. I have seen wild things in the shadows, which to others were mystery. I have shattered the limits imposed by my moral eyes and seen every thread of Mother Nature's gown."

One of Perrier's all-time great ads shows a parched woman face to face with a lion at the top of a mountain in Africa. As the lion bares its fangs and roars, the woman roars back, with the strains of "I put a spell on you" playing in the background. The lion skulks off, and the woman lifts a bottle of Perrier and drinks triumphantly.

Various drinks can be marketed as magic potions, either for healing purposes or as revealing the unseen reality behind the surface of illusion. An ad for Smirnoff features objects seen through the vodka bottle. A flower becomes a Venus flytrap. A lady's fox stole comes fearsomely to life and snarls. A smoker spews fire and a necklace turns into a hissing snake. Two portly gentlemen wearing tuxedos are transformed into penguins, while a demure young woman is revealed to be a veritable Medusa. A couple playing shuffleboard become a dominatrix in black leather and her slave—we hear the crack of the whip. And a harmless black cat sneaking past the bottle changes into a panther—its meow into a growl. The spot ends on a shot of the Smirnoff bottle as script on the screen notes, "If Smirnoff can do this still in the bottle, just imagine what happens when you drink it."

The Magic of the Easier Way

Sometimes the ad is more subtle, merely intimating an outcome so marvelous as to seem miraculous. Zurich Financial Services runs a series of successful ads in which the promised transformation is suggested almost entirely by the visuals. One ad runs the words "Turbulent times" in large block letters, but then shows a picture of a sailboat, completely still on untroubled waters, with the sun setting in the background. No picture could seem more peaceful and reassuring. The copy describes the risks, exposures, volatility, and turmoil of modern economic life, but then promises "a safe haven for uncertain times. Inhale. Exhale." In short, Zurich promises customers a real miracle of calm in the midst of all that pressure. Another, similar ad that also uses language stressing the difficulty of doing business in turbulent times sports a picture of a traditional European café, half full of relaxed customers, with the help looking bored because they have so little to do!

PlaceWare Web Conferencing offers a complex image of two airplanes being drawn (as on a computer screen) toward the trash, together with an ancient-looking image of the earth that might have come from some alchemical drawing. The text promises a respite from pressure as a result of the miracle of modern technology: "This meeting is just about the meeting. There's an entirely new way to hold meetings. It doesn't involve a plane, train, or automobile. All you need is a Web browser and a phone. With PlaceWare, you can hold live, interactive meetings and presentations with up to 2,500 people over the Internet. . . . Think about it next time you're stuck in a holding pattern."

Using less magical imagery, Agilent Technologies also exploits the association with miraculous solutions, writing, "More superhighway, less road rage. Date jams, Internet interruptions. Droops. Crashes. Seems like it's always rush hour out there. But with Agilent systems and technologies, the world's major communications networks move faster, handle more, avoid trouble and merge effortlessly. Happy motoring."

The genius of these ads is that the customer is initially drawn into them because of the discrepancy between the visual images and the large block print. In the ancient tradition of alchemy, magic occurred when elements in opposition were brought together and unified. Similarly, in modern chemistry—remember high school chemistry lab?—changes occur when two substances unify because of the presence of the third, catalytic agent. In the ads, that agent is the mind of the consumer. This sense of the third thing as inherently magical is picked up by a powerful Magician ad run by Saturn (even though its usual brand identity is Regular Guy/Gal) to promote the three-door coupé: "Somewhere between sliced bread and instant oatmeal, there's the third door."

A great lighthearted commercial shows a monk working by candlelight, painstakingly hand copying a manuscript with illuminated margins as a Gregorian chant plays in the background. When he shows it to his superior, he is complimented on his good work and challenged to produce 500 more copies. After a quick trip to the

Xerox machine, the monk produces the copies, and his superior looks heavenward, announcing "It's a miracle."

Vision and Manifestation

Magic is the technology for making dreams come true. American Express Gift Cheques offer an image of an elaborately wrapped present with an American Express check, saying, "I want to make your birthday wish come true. (Even if I don't know exactly what it is.)" The checks have thus positioned themselves as a magical technology of manifestation.

Magicians create from the inside out. Since the publication of Carol Pearson's *The Hero Within*, a host of books, from *The Warrior Within* to *The Child Within*, have helped people learn to transform their inner lives by calling up latent archetypal abilities. Now such ideas are moving, in light and humorous ways, into advertising. An ad for Honda Accord reads

> *You may wonder if you really have Accord potential. But we believe, within every person is a handsome, strong Honda Accord. What can I do, you ask, to unleash this inner "Accord-ness"? Here is a surefire technique. Practiced by many professional athletes and top executives, it's called visualization. You simply close your eyes and picture yourself as the Honda Accord. You are a leader. You are in control. You are dependable. You will become more like the Accord every day. Try it. It works!*

The ad, of course, plays on the way that the Magician archetype's trust in visualization as a precursor to actualization has become commonplace. Although the copy is clearly tongue in cheek, it also provides a way to brag about the Accord in a way that is not off-putting. By suggesting that the consumers identify with the Accord, the ad is congratulating them for being leaders—in control and dependable. Then these qualities are associated with the car.

The ability to realize your dreams is also associated with a certain simpatico association with the environment. Psychiatrist C. G. Jung coined the term "synchronicity" to refer to meaningful coincidences whereby the inner and outer worlds connect. An example would be when you think of someone you have not seen in a long time, and suddenly the phone rings and there she is, calling you. Or, as with one of Jung's patients, who dreamed of a scarab beetle, as she was talking about it, one appeared on the window of the consulting room. When this kind of coincidence happens, it always feels miraculous.

A magical commercial for Volkswagen Jetta shows everything in the external world—including the bouncing of a ball—happening in the same rhythm as the car's windshield wipers. Such an experience of the outer and the inner being in sync is also a symptom of what Mihaly Csikszentmihalyi, in *Flow: The Psychology of Optimal Experience*, calls "flow," a condition he identifies with the achievement of happiness for most people.

Of course, the term "flow" can also describe the fluid movements of an athlete who does not just dream of success, but realizes it. Reebok has captured the whole gestalt of this term in its "flow campaign," which includes ads with this definition:

> Flow (flo) v. flowed, flowing, flows. 1. To move or run smoothly, as in the manner characteristic of a fluid. 2. To proceed steadily and easily. 3. To exhibit a natural or graceful style or continuity: the cadence of the poem flowed gracefully. N. 4. An apparent ease or effortlessness of performance. 5. A mental focus on goals or achievements. 6. Characterized by a natural confidence: 'Give me an athlete with experience, give me another with training, but put my name on the one with flow.'

DuPont's slogan "The miracles of science" celebrates the wonders of technology today. An ad beginning with the text "dreams made real" pictures a father with his daughter on his lap and his "to-do list for the planet." The list includes the following item: "6. Develop medicines that fight HIV. (did that) (Pressing ahead on next generation medicines. Would love to see the day no one has this disease.)"

In ancient times, the Magician—as shaman, medicine man or woman, or witch or midwife—was the healer. Now we have miracle drugs. Bristol-Myers Squibb ("Hope, Triumph, and the Miracle of Medicine") ran this ad:

The little miracle pictured at left is four-month-old Luke Davie Armstrong. The other miracle at left is his dad, Lance. Winner of the 2,287-mile 1999 Tour de France. And of an even more grueling battle—against testicular cancer. By the time Lance Armstrong was diagnosed, his cancer had already spread to his lungs and his brain. But with a regimen of three Bristol-Myers Squibb cancer drugs, doctors worked with Lance first to control his cancer. Then, to beat it. For over three decades, Bristol-Myers Squibb has been at the forefront of developing cancer medicines. Today, advances in treatment are making possible the kind of miracle pictured here.

A basic principle of magic is "as above, so below, the universe is in a grain of sand." Aether shows a picture of a finger almost touching a miniaturized earth, saying, "We're moving the world of business . . . from here [the globe] to here [your finger]." This magical ad then promises, "Today you can hold the power of the office, the Internet, e-mail and e-commerce in the palm of your hand. Indoors or out. Without wires."

Ancient alchemists, moreover, consulted books of wisdom that taught them everything they needed to know to manifest their visions. The first campaign promoting the Yellow Pages, "Let Your Fingers Do the Walking," featured a man in a secondhand bookshop seeking a little-known old book on fly-fishing by J. R. Hartley. After being defeated in his efforts at yet another store, he goes home, where his daughter brings him the Yellow Pages. As he lets his fingers do the walking, he finally succeeds. This ad campaign, lasting over a decade, positioned the Yellow Pages as a source of information, so easy that it seemed magical in its ability to connect consumers with whom or what they needed to make their dreams come true.

The respiritualization of society and commerce during the last two decades of the 20th century and the marketing of New Age products and services demonstrate the palpable vitality of the Magician archetype in today's world. Examples include metaphysical movies and bookstores, the size of New Age and metaphysical sections of mainstream bookstores, Sounds True audiotapes, New Dimension Radio and the Wisdom Channel, New Age catalogues, and the success of numerous spiritual teachers, gurus, workshop leaders, and organizational consultants.

Magician Organization: Lucent Technologies

The Magician organization utilizes cutting-edge technologies in consciousness, communications, and organizational structures. Magician organizations are vision driven, seeking consensus about core values and desired outcomes and then maximizing their flexibility in achieving these goals. Some de-emphasize hierarchy, even featuring self-organizing teams. People need such local authority in order to take advantage of serendipity when it inevitably occurs. Typically, employees brag about how they "pull rabbits out of hats" daily. They may also complain that when miracles come to be expected, they do not even have time to take a bow. The result over time can be burnout, or if they do take the opportunity to celebrate and be grateful, their energy may simply keep building.

When Lucent Technologies (formerly Bell Labs) split off from AT&T, the company was known as an innovator, but it was more connected with basic research than with practical applications. Management determined that the new business had to start fresh, with no baggage from the AT&T culture. The fresh venture, led by an experimental group at Mount Olive, New Jersey, illustrates Magician organization strategies. The firm's new charge was to "Create a new business with paramount speed, cost, and quality—any way you choose to do it." All structures were considered only temporary. What would hold them together was a simple core set of principles: "We live with speed, innovation, quality; a strong sense of social responsibility; a deep respect for the contribution of each person . . . integrity and candor," and "an obsession with serving our customers." New employees actually signed the document with a sense of ritual formality, even using a special pen.

At first, there were few structures. Employees organized themselves around tasks and determined what to make and how to make it. The engineers would meet around a huge table, writing furiously on the white boards surrounding them on virtually every wall. Later, when the number of employees made such informal organization impossible, they established an assembly line, switching people from job to job to be certain they never got bored and their minds stayed fresh, and allowing line workers to organize their own shifts. Other than the core statement of principles, the only rule was that they would have no rules. Employees could log onto their computers, consult statements of policy, and change them if they were not working.

Employees created an "urgents board" to alert anyone who had some extra time to where he or she should be lending a hand. The results of the Mount Olive experiment were spectacular. Thomas Petzinger, highlighting them in his book *The New Pioneers*, sums them up this way:

> In its first several years Mount Olive had never missed a single order deadline, not once. The elapsed time between the conception of each new product version and the first shipments was an astonishing nine months ... with six months soon to come—compared to an industry average of eighteen months. The labor cost of the product averaged 3 percent and was headed lower.... Every worker in the plant knew the name of every customer, the status of every order, and the identity of every competitor. Orders were roaring in—from Puerto Rico, South Korea, Thailand, Canada, and biggest of all, a $1.8 billion deal from Sprint.[1]

The results from the Mount Olive experiment revolutionized Lucent Technologies, helping the firm become a magical organization.

Magical Marketing, Magician Management

In a full-employment economy, when people have infinite access to information through the Internet and other means, and when people expect not just jobs but fulfilling careers, both marketing and management have to be redefined. Jobs are not scarce. Information is not scarce. Money is not scarce. High-quality, inexpensive products and services are not even scarce.

So, in this context, what do people need? People do not have enough time or meaning. Therefore, for people to share their time with you—as customers or employees—you need to provide them with palpable meaning. You can appeal to potential customers by

---

1. Thomas Petzinger, Jr., *The New Pioneers: The Men and Women Who Are Transforming the Workplace and Marketplace* (New York: Simon and Schuster, 1999), pp. 175–177.

associating your products or services with values that are dear to their hearts. To do this, you need to genuinely stand for something. Like Hero marketing, Magician marketing begins with knowing what you stand for.

Wristwatches, Rolf Jensen (*The Dream Society*) notes, are very accurate and reliable. If you want a watch that will keep the exact time, the price is $10—unless you are after a story. If the watch is to appeal to the heart—to bespeak a certain lifestyle, status, or adventure—the price can go up to as much as $15,000. For this reason, Rolex gives awards to customers who tell the Rolex story through their own achievements.[2]

The essence of magic can be defined as the ability to affect consciousness and, in so doing, to affect people's behaviors. In the world of the past, information was scarce. People were hungry for information, so it was not that hard to get them to focus on your commercial. Now, when people are suffering from information overload and over 3,000 commercial messages a day, the problem is how to get them to even notice your message, much less remember it.

We also know that the human mind keeps us from being overwhelmed by stimuli by filtering out much of what comes our way—including ads. This censoring process is not random. Rather, we select for attention the information that is relevant to our concerns and that fits in with the structures of our minds. An easy way to confirm that this is so is to observe that when you learn a new word, you often seem to hear it all over the place. It is not that the word is suddenly being used when it was not before. It is just that you notice it now, whereas you did not notice it before.

Archetypes are the strange attractors of consciousness.[3] You attract customers when your message is congruent with an archetype that is either dominant or emerging in their consciousness. Magical managers understand that the archetypes that give a company its brand identity also preside over the structure of its organizational culture. They also know that you cannot create a company that will

---

2. Rolf Jensen, *The Dream Society* (New York: McGraw-Hill, 1999), p. 35.
3. See John R. Van Eenwyk, *Archetypes and Strange Attractors: The Chaotic World of Symbols* (Toronto, Canada: Inner City Books, 1997), and Michael Conforti, *Field, Form, and Fate: Patterns in Mind, Nature, and Psyche* (Woodstock, CT: Spring Publications, 1999).

attract and retain the most able employees unless you offer them meaning from which they can extract fulfillment from their work. In this way, Magician leaders and Magician organizations can call upon any or all of the archetypes as invisible but powerful strategic partners in managing the meaning level of all aspects of contemporary work.

Jensen therefore cautions executives not to think of contemporary organizations in terms of legal entities, profits, buildings, or anything else really tangible. Nor are they hierarchies. Just as citizens see themselves as peers, rather than subjects, modern employees expect to share decision making. To attract and retain employees, you need to manage an emotional drama that is compelling and makes people want to stay. "If the drama is gripping, many will want to join the show," says Jensen. "The cold company figures, after all, do nothing to reflect the battles for contracts and clients being constantly lost and won. They do not reflect innovations and ideas being hatched at creative meetings. Above all, the emotionless balance sheet does not reflect the social interaction—the conflicts, the friendships, the collaboration, and the jealousy. The balance sheet reveals as much about corporate life as would a word count of William Shakespeare's sonnets."[4]

In the Magician organization, the secret of success is not the management of money, but the management of consciousness within a context that is now radically peer focused. Now that information is not scarce, company and societal decisions are often made not by the leadership alone, but out of a cultural conversation resulting in a quickly forming consensus. Modern medicine tells us that the body works like this. The mind does not tell the stomach what to do. The stomach has intelligence that recognizes food and decides how to digest it. Different parts of the body are in constant communication to retain balance, to defend against foreign bodies, and to signal needs (like hunger, thirst, and fatigue).

At the same time, biologists tell us that whole species moderate their behavior to accommodate to changing circumstances, as, according to the Gaia thesis, daisies change their color to absorb or reflect light—thereby increasing their own survival rate and at the

4. Jensen, p. 135.

same time actually altering the temperature of the earth. Intelligence is no longer understood in a top-down way—in medicine, biology, or the cutting-edge organization. Thus, organizational development scholars such as Peter Senge at MIT (*The Fifth Discipline*)[5] stress the importance of organizations becoming learning systems. It is not just that management needs to be continually learning; rather, everyone at every level needs to be learning and continually communicating what they are learning to every other part of the system.

This is, of course, how it is that the Berlin Wall could come down and the CIA learn of it through the media. Something new is radically afoot. What this means is that the success of your brand depends upon a cultural consensus about its worth. It is no longer possible to control the information the public has about you. Even if you are successful in keeping discrepant information out of the papers, you cannot keep it off the Internet. The trick here is to influence consciousness without the ability to censor or control it.

Marketing to Magicians

According to a marketing study by Paul Ray, there is today an emerging consumer force that he describes as "cultural creatives" who share a magical belief that they are the creators of their own lives through a process by which consciousness fashions concrete reality.[6] As customers and as employees, these magical people believe that who you are is as important as the quality of your product or services. You are therefore always selling yourself, your values, and your own consciousness when you market to them. Of course, because many of these new consumers are chatting with your employees and other customers on the Web, they are likely to find any discrepancy between what your organization espouses and what it really does.

To market effectively to Magicians, it is essential to first engage in enough self-reflection to identify who you are, what you value, and what you want to achieve in the world. If you can then recognize

---

5. Peter Senge, *The Fifth Discipline: The Art and Practice of the Learning Organization* (New York: Doubleday/Currency, 1990).

6. Paul Ray, *The Cultural Creatives: How 50 Million People Are Changing the World* (New York: Harmony Books, 2000), passim.

the archetype that best captures your inner allegiances and develop marketing strategies congruent with those allegiances, you draw people to you who are aligned with your consciousness and with your product or service. The result is marketing a kind of magic.

Everything you do then should reinforce that archetype, which begins to serve as a magnet to organize all the "data" customers, suppliers, and employees have about you. Their own internal filters will likely discard the rest—unless (as in the case of organizational scandals) the information is so blatantly antithetical to your avowed identity as to call attention to the discrepancy. Your archetypal identity can then be expressed not only in ads, but in product design and placement, as a part of your organizational identity, on your Web site, in executive speeches, in company policies, and in orientation programs for new employees. The resulting congruence will attract Magicians to you.

Remember, too, that Magicians are motivated by the desire for personal transformation and for the chance to change people, organizations, and their times. Magicians will appreciate it if you offer them transformative experiences. However, the biggest payoff comes if you can help a customer improve him- or herself. In a very ordinary way, you can see this principle at work in the success of Weight Watchers. Jean Nidetch, an overweight housewife who discovered that getting her friends together to support each other's dieting helped pounds fall off, eventually founded Weight Watchers International in partnership with entrepreneur Albert Lippert. Selling the franchises at low rates in exchange for 10 percent of the gross, they quickly made a fortune. In Weight Watchers, people are empowered to transform themselves from fat to thin, as they also feel good about similarly improving the lives of others.

Magician brands and Magician marketers know that if you give (or sell) a person a fish, they will eat for a night. Teach them to fish, and not only will they eat forever, but they will be loyal to you—forever.

We must add a caveat here. In a more advanced way, you can witness the liberating effect of the women's and New Age movements all around us. Sex roles have changed radically. Most people advocate equal rights. New Age attitudes and perspectives are now mainstreamed. At the same time, people dissociate themselves from feminism and from the New Age because the public has come to identify those movements with their extreme and even bizarre components. The point here is that extreme positions and unusual, shocking, or edgy events, attitudes, and ads compel attention, but they do not ultimately cement identification with your cause or product.

Both the women's movement and the New Age movement were transformative, but neither controlled its archetypal brand identity. As a result, the media defined it for them. In the same way, then, it is important to remember that you can get attention with an extreme or edgy ad, but that flash in the pan will work against you in the long run, unless it is congruent with a solid, archetypal brand identity.

As a result of the women's movement, the lives of millions of women—from all classes, races, ethnic groups, and backgrounds— were changed in positive ways. Women now are more likely to have successful careers; to attain political office; to be taken seriously by their families, friends, and coworkers; and even to have fulfilling sexual lives than they were before the movement. The intrinsic archetype of the movement was the Magician. However, the archetype the media associated with the movement became the angry bra burner—an Outlaw image that was unappealing to most women.

When marketing to Magicians or would-be Magicians, avoid the temptation to generate attention with the edgy and the shocking. Take the time to develop an identity that is aligned with the truth

---

The Magician may be a good identity for your brand if

- the product or service is transformative.
- its implicit promise is to transform the customer.
- it appeals to New Age consumers or cultural creatives.
- it helps to expand or extend consciousness.
- it is a user-friendly technology.
- it has a spiritual or psychological component.
- it is a new and very contemporary product.
- it is medium to high priced.

of your transformative purpose. Unflattering images coming from the media, competitors, or other groups do not have to destroy your message. The antidote is to have a strong enough archetypal brand personality that you can weather dramatic negative publicity. When the Pillsbury Doughboy appeared as an evil spirit in *Ghostbusters*, the brand's Innocent identity was left unscathed. Such is the power of archetypal branding.

No Man (or Woman) Is an Island

Regular Guy/Gal, Lover, Jester

FROM THE EARLY GATHERINGS of cave dwellers and tribesmen to today's popular chat rooms, people's desire to connect, interact, and belong has been a primal urge. Three archetypes help us to fulfill this need by providing a model or structure for doing so. The Regular Guy/Gal helps trigger the behaviors and outlook that allow us both to fit in enough to be part of the group and to place a value on all people, not just those who excel. The Lover aids us in becoming attractive to others and also helps us develop skills of emotional and sexual intimacy. The Jester teaches us to lighten up, live in the moment, and enjoy interacting with others without worrying about what they may think. Symbols and brands

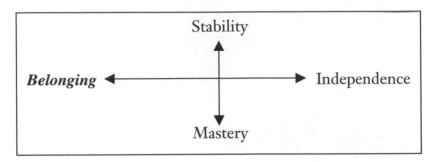

Figure 4.1

that are the embodiments of these archetypes are powerful because they express and affirm a critical sense of likability, popularity, and connectedness.

The three archetypes mediate very different sorts of vulnerabilities than do those related to our need for mastery, control, and power. Instead of worrying about having an impact on the world, the customer ponders the questions, Am I likeable? Attractive? Fun? Will people accept me? Can I be part of the group and still be myself? How do I find true love? And how do I put my life together so that I enjoy it?

The tremendous popularity of television and radio talk shows helps illuminate the appeal of these archetypes, in spite of—or perhaps *because* of—our increasingly individualistic society. People listen simply to hear other ordinary people, not experts, talk, express opinions, and air complaints and issues. They religiously watch talk shows to learn about real-life stories of love and betrayal (the Lover) or to share their time with a late-night Jester such as Jay Leno. The "lesser Jester," David Letterman, boosted his sagging ratings as a result of his cardiac surgery. The combination of the Jester with Everyman/Regular Joe vulnerability sparked enthusiastic support and rekindled loyalty on the part of lapsed viewers.

Customers in whom these archetypes are strong may be especially attracted to brands that help them connect with others. But the nature and form of that connection may take on unexpected dimensions. During the 1960s, middle-class college kids took to wearing farmers' overalls as a way of saying that they wanted to identify with

The special emotion aroused by the Tomb of the Unknown Soldier speaks to the poignant power of the unsung, un- identified "Everyman" or Regular Guy/Gal.

the "uncorrupted" working class. A surprising proportion of owners of Steinway pianos choose to drive unassuming Subarus. Urban yuppies are the most likely readers of gossipy *People* magazine.

It is important here to remember that the Regular Guy/Gal, Lover, and Jester may be a more dominant motivational focus in some customers, but all customers—whatever shows in their surface behavior—have a desire to affiliate with other human beings. In our driven culture, people often do not have much time to hang out together (and doing so may even be seen as wasting time), so people are more and more lonely. As a result, these archetypes have additional power to motivate because they promise to fulfill repressed and unsatisfied needs. The more these three archetypes are under-valued in the culture, the greater is their motivating power.

Consider, for example, the awesome power of sexuality in Victorian England: Whatever went underground gained power in the psyche and in human behavior.

10

The Regular Guy/Gal

Motto: "All men and women are created equal."

T HE REGULAR GUY/GAL demonstrates the virtues of simply being an ordinary person, just like others. You can think of the Everyman figure in medieval morality plays, the idea of the "common man" in political theory and rhetoric, and the emotional impact of the Tomb of the Unknown Soldier. Identification with this archetype has fueled the success of a long line of populist politicians, movie stars, and executives "with the common touch."

The Regular Guy/Gal is evident in Country-Western music, folk music, neighborhood festivals and carnivals, labor unions, diners, and situation comedies about the foibles of everyday people. (Recall "All in the Family," "Roseanne," or "Malcolm in the Middle.")

When the Regular Guy/Gal archetype is active in an individual, the person may dress in working-class or otherwise ordinary clothes (even if he or she is quite wealthy), speak in colloquial ways, and be put off by elitism in any form. The underlying value is that everyone matters, just as they are. The credo is that the good things of life

The Regular Guy/Gal

Core desire: connection with others
Goal: to belong, fit in
Fears: standing out, seeming to put on airs, and being exiled or rejected as a result
Strategy: develop ordinary solid virtues, the common touch, blend in
Trap: give up self to blend in, in exchange for only a superficial connection
Gift: realism, empathy, lack of pretense

The Regular Guy/Gal may also be known as the good old boy, the regular Jane, Everyman, the common man, the guy or gal next door, the realist, the working stiff, the solid citizen, the good neighbor.

belong to everyone as a birthright, not just to an aristocracy or even a meritocracy.

The Regular Guy/Gal is the fundamental archetype of democracy, with the central precept of "One man (or woman), one vote." It is even more pronounced in all progressive movements. You might think of Woody Guthrie assuring people that "This land is your land." It is also crucial to the civil rights movement, the women's movement, gay rights, and every other movement designed to extend the full benefits of social and economic participation to a group or class of people.

Liberation movements, of course, remind us that in real life most societies exclude some people, however lovely their rhetoric of inclusion might be. In ancient indigenous cultures, being exiled or excluded from the group could mean that you would be alone in the wild, prey to all sorts of predators. In practice, exile was equivalent to a death sentence. Even today, people who have poor communication skills and are unable to connect well with others are at greater risk of being unemployed or homeless than are people in whom those skills are more developed. We all still need to create social networks for support. Indeed, it is networks that inevitably position even the disadvantaged for good jobs and support their subsequent success.

Everyone knows the desperation of adolescents to fit in—if not in the "in crowd," at least in some crowd. This sense of loneliness or exclusion—be it on the part of an individual or an entire group—

represents the trigger for the great appeal of the Regular Guy/Gal; the desire is not to be special or different in any way, but simply to melt into the pack. And once that yearning is satisfied, the tendency is simply to revel in the calm reassurance of ordinariness.

Years ago, for example, Margaret Mark was conducting interviews in which she posed the question, "If you had one weekend to explain what you think are the best things about America to a group of people from a foreign land, what would you do?" The group of people she was interviewing in De Soto, Missouri, a small town, didn't mention anything about explaining the Constitution or the Bill or Rights, our system of checks and balances, or the free press. Instead, they reflexively said, "Why, I'd have a barbeque and invite my friends and neighbors!" Clearly, the simple fact of being part of a group of "regular folk" epitomized what is best in America for them.

Affiliation with a group is often further expressed by certain products: caps, T-shirt slogans, bumper stickers, and, more subtly, styles of homes, cars, dress, and foods. Interestingly, at games of the New York Rangers—a professional hockey team that has managed to connect with fans on the "Everyman" level—fans almost uniformly sport Ranger jerseys as a sign of their support, whereas in the very same arena, Madison Square Garden, on a night when the more "glamorous" New York Knicks are playing, most fans come in their street clothes or, in the case of corporate executives, their suits. Rangers fans get to know one another, to watch each other's kids grow up, to celebrate each other's anniversaries. Knicks fans, on the other hand, are united simply by their good fortune in having season subscriptions or tickets to a game. The Rangers are a Regular Guy/Gal brand, whereas the Knicks are more "heroic"; the Knicks' fans are "admirers" more than supporters or "family." Understanding this difference has tremendous implications for how the Garden communicates about each of its franchises.

Americans at large were startled when President George Bush marveled at the scanner at a supermarket checkout counter ("Where has this guy been?!"); later, a cartoon parodying the president showed him driving through a ghetto, inappropriately inquiring if anyone had any Grey Poupon. His failed attempt to be a Regular Guy came off worse than if he had simply retained and expressed his aristocratic

Ruler identity. Like the Knicks, Bush should have understood and leveraged the nature of his appeal, instead of trying to reinvent himself.

Don't Put on Airs

The Regular Guy/Gal wants to be part of the tribe—whether it is a clique, a social class, a workplace culture, a church or temple, a club, or a union. The group may be the one that he or she was "born into," or it might be one quite different. Nonetheless, the desire is to quietly fit in; and, as in the Bush example, the effort must be wholly successful, or it is an absolute failure.

There is a complete absence of artifice in this archetype, as there is a kind of leveling tendency. For example, simply asking for a beer at a party (versus, say, an Absolut on the rocks), choosing to invite a client for a run in the park instead of a power lunch, or wearing your Tevas to work even though you are a Silicon Valley millionaire immediately signals that you value the Everyman principle and lets your Regular Guy/Gal colors fly.

Regular Guys/Gals do not simply cheer for the home team; they root for the underdog. They are likely to prefer hockey to tennis, the perseverance of Cal Ripken, Jr. to the brilliance of Michael Jordan, minor league baseball to the majors. They often use humor to take others down a peg. An ad for Glenlivet whisky says, "In some places, athletes are revered as gods. This is not one of those places. One place. One whisky."

Today, successful people sometimes stave off envy by revealing their neuroses, fears, and difficulties in public. Doing so helps others remember that, underneath the glitz, they are just people after all, the same as you and me. On the TV show, Ally McBeal is beautiful, a Harvard graduate, and a successful attorney, but her appeal depends in large measure on being just as messed up and neurotic as any of us. Seinfeld became a celebration of ordinariness. And even very well-adjusted celebrities can feature their everyday qualities. A classic Gap ad featured Montgomery Clift on a ladder, painting and wearing khakis. The point, of course, is that even larger-than-life celebrities have their down-to-earth side. A driving editorial principle of *People* magazine is to show what's extraordinary about everyday folk (e.g., unassuming couples raising handicapped foster children), mingled with what's "ordinary" about superstars—divorce, anorexia, or struggles with self-confidence.

Regular Guys/Gals love self-deprecating humor, reassuring others and themselves that they are not taking themselves too seriously. Jim Beam whiskey ran an ad with four young men happily talking at a bar. The ad said, "Your lives would make a great sitcom." However, it then acknowledged that the proposed show would not be all that interesting: "Of course, it would have to run on cable." Nevertheless, it also highlighted the real strength of the archetype: "Real friends. Real bourbon." That word, "real," is a defining one for the Regular Guy/Gal. All artifice is suspect, as is the desire for glamour or luxury.

Just the Facts, Ma'am

The Regular Guy/Gal hates artifice, hype, and people who put on airs. Regular Guy/Gal brands, therefore, almost always have a down-home, no-nonsense quality to them that makes them seem genuine. Examples include Perdue or Wendy's (whose folksy owners appear directly in their ads), Snapple (whose first spokesperson was Wendy, the actual Queens-born receptionist), and Saturn automobiles (originally marketed with stories about why the workers in the plants believed in the car and the company).

Paul Newman has had much more staying power than other

Levels of the Regular Guy/Gal Archetype

Call: loneliness, alienation
Level One: the orphan, feeling abandoned and alone, seeking affiliation
Level Two: the joiner, learning to connect, fit in, accept help and friendship
Level Three: the humanitarian, believing in the natural dignity of every person regardless of his or her abilities or circumstances
Shadow: the victim who is willing to be abused rather than be alone, or the lynch-mob member, willing to go along with abuse in order to be one of the gang

handsome actors, largely because his Regular Guy persona, both on and off screen, made millions feel that he would be down to earth and affable if they ran into him in the hardware store on a Saturday morning. Wrangler Jeans protected a Regular Guy/Gal brand identity by wisely avoiding the designer jeans craze and remaining the jeans of choice for those who really love Western wear. The company is associated with cowboys, country, and authentic, well-made products, devoid of hype. Films such as *The Full Monty, Local Hero*, and *Raising Ned Devine* all celebrate the Regular Guy/Gal ethos in terms of characters, story pattern, and the very straightforward way in which they were produced.

The Myers-Briggs Type Indicator differentiated itself from a number of slicker and higher priced psychological instruments to become a best-seller all over the world by presenting itself as the people's psychological tool, even making the most of the fact that the establishment did not initially accept its importance. In differentiating itself from the more elitist image of American Express, VISA took a similar approach, emphasizing more ordinary customers and the ubiquitous use of its charge card. Like the ordinary person, VISA is everywhere.

In the cosmetics industry, Regular Gal ads forgo evocative imagery for practical, down-to-earth functionalism. For example, Nivea face cream sports the face of yet another girl next door, with the words, "Restore your skin's own wrinkle control with a lotion." If you contact most four-year colleges and universities for information about their programs, you get multicolored, professionally packaged marketing pieces. Miami-Dade Community College, one of the most widely successful community colleges in the country, sends only a list of courses in a catalogue printed on newsprint. The message is that this is the people's school. It's inexpensive, down to earth, and without pretense.

The Dignity of the Common Man or Woman

The Regular Guy/Gal is the solid citizen who makes life work. On the frontier, you can think of people who banded together for barn raisings and quilting bees. They did not have to like everyone in order to help them. If they were neighbors, they were implicitly part of the clan. Even today, the Regular Guy/Gal can be readily seen in people who are neighborly, who put in a good day's work for a day's pay, and who evidence a certain solid reliability and grounded common sense.

Many of these qualities are associated with the ordinary American and a shared societal belief in equity. Mutual of America links itself to such values using language explicitly about the importance of equality: "Individuals and groups, companies and partnerships—big and small—receive the same quality service and care." MetLife goes folksier, but with a similar message. A typical ad pictures a girl-next-door type who, we learn, runs a catering business and comes "from a long line of people who don't know how to invest." Her endorsement reads, "I'm not the most seasoned investor, so when I finally got over my fears of jumping into the market, I went to the pros at Met Life for advice. They helped me choose among thousands of mutual funds based on a level of risk I could live with. I'm no Wall Street maven yet, but now I know that investing doesn't have to be as tough as serving soufflé to 400."

Most Regular Guy/Gal brands sport extremely wholesome images. Gap ads, for example, show young people dancing with great abandon, clearly enjoying being together in a positive, upbeat way. Such ads are implicitly in contrast to more typical Explorer ads, which are aimed at youthful alienation, or Guess and Calvin Klein ads that sport images of the young as rather depressed but sexy objects. Our personal favorite Regular Guy/Gal ad is one for an erstwhile eatery, Submarine Sandwiches. The ad started with emaciated, alienated youths talking fashionably about their alienation and yearning for "more." Suddenly a healthy-looking fatherly figure says "Eat something," and the ad continues in full color with images of great sandwiches.

Regular Guy/Gal brands also reassure people that they are OK just as they are. For example, Just My Size, offering large-size clothes, pictures a pretty, but rather heavy, woman, saying "I am a sister. A daughter. A lover. I am not 100 pounds. I am not one-size-fits-all. I am a size 18. 20. 24. I am beautiful. I am over half the women in this country. I am not outside the norm. I am the norm. I am not invisible." August Max Woman sends a similar low-key message, saying simply, "real fashion for women just like you."

Ads frequently assume that the customer's need is pretty basic. Sleep Motels runs an ad with four stars, saying, "The room was affordable. The people were helpful. The breakfast was free. That's all you want from a hotel." Similarly, Quality Inn shows a picture of the McCaughey family—with their octuplets—saying, "We know a thing or two about miracles. Not the least of which is finding a great mattress in a hotel room." That's all they seem to need, even with 10 in a room, except a chance to win a Quality Inn lottery. The popular *Zagat's Guide* to restaurants embodies a Regular Guy/Gal quality, reflecting the opinions of ordinary diners, as opposed to professional restaurant reviewers.

The Regular Guy/Gal is unfailingly frugal, whether or not he or she has money. GEICO Direct says, "You haven't called GEICO Auto Insurance yet? Funny, you don't look rich." An ad for Dryel, run late in 1999, assures people that "In the next millennium, people will care for their 'dry-clean-only' clothes right at home. Hey, isn't that coming up?"

The Third Place

The natural meeting place for Regular Guys and Gals is neither the home nor the workplace. Historically, people met in public spaces that were conducive to conversation about things of general interest—sports, politics, light gossip, or the weather. Sometimes they went places simply to mill about, or to sit quietly side by side. In the past, it may have been the village green, the neighborhood pub, the library, the union hall, the front steps of their homes, or just the bench outside the country store—public spaces where people who do not know each other well congregate and enjoy each other's company. Today, people do not congregate in front of their houses, and neighbors have enough choice in bars or restaurants that they do not predictably congregate in the same places; most of life is either privatized or about business.

The desire for such third places explains the success of the long-running television show "Cheers" ("where everybody knows your name"). When Barnes & Noble and Borders both saw this need and created spaces for customers to congregate, their sales increased 18 and 14 percent, respectively (against an overall U.S. bookstore gain of 4 percent). Hardy's understands that its purpose is not just to provide fast food, but also to offer a community center where people of different ages and classes can all hang out and feel comfortable. The Regular Guy/Gal also explains the survival of many mom-and-pop stores and diners—where the decor is plain and the food and other goods are average, but they greet you by name—even in the world of big chains and successful franchises.

Today, Internet chat rooms create popular third places that transcend the limits of time and space, making people from all over the world into neighbors, at least at the level of the mind. The fact that the fastest growing group of Internet users is more mature consumers defies stereotypes and reinforces the attraction of being connected, even for people who may be somewhat less mobile than they once were. The potential here for brands that can restore a connection between people is immense, even if that connection is simply virtual.

A Regular Guy/Gal Masterpiece: The Launching of Saturn

The launching of Saturn felt like a revival of the best of the tradition of the solid values of the American worker. Detroit was in disrepute, having failed to innovate adequately to rival the Japanese. In fact, customer disaffiliation from the American automobile industry was great enough that General Motors decided to launch Saturn in a way that de-emphasized the car's connection not only with the parent company, but also with Detroit. The decision to move the Saturn plant to Spring Hill, Tennessee, signaled a rejection of the values associated with urban blight and decline in favor of more traditional American rural values.

Moreover, few people believed it was possible to successfully launch a new car, so the brand's success took on a David and Goliath quality. One ad provides a retrospective on the company's success, saying, "About 10 years ago, an American car company named Saturn did what no one expected they could. They succeeded. And, like anyone who's experienced a bit of success, they got a taste for some of the finer things. Maybe that's why they designed their new car line to be faster, roomier, more luxurious and, yes, more expensive. But not too expensive. Because, like we said, that company's name is Saturn."

Saturn is another archetypal name. It is the name of a Roman god of agriculture, thus giving the car rural associations. The planet Saturn has an astrological meaning associated with practical, down-to-earth, slow, and painstaking action. Both associations seem absolutely right for a Regular Guy/Gal brand. Moreover, not too long before the company's founding, a widely printed newspaper article had revealed scientists' dismay that there was no scientific explanation for the planet Saturn's rings. The name then provided a subtle reinforcement of the sense that this company's success was a kind of miracle.

The initial marketing decision to sell the company, not the car, met with great success. Commercials featured workers in the plant sharing their pride at the quality standards of the company and the risks they had taken to believe in a different kind of car company. Ads featured employees reminiscing about cars in their childhood, their sacrifices in moving to a new place in what seemed like a God-forsaken area, their pride in being associated with a new kind of company and watching the first cars come off the line. What GM was doing was selling the car by association with believable, trust-worthy, good-guy workers.

The underlying American values of honesty and hard work were clear in the testimony of the workers who shared their belief in the company. Understanding the vulnerability that ordinary people feel, the company later ran ads showing working-class families of various ethnic groups expressing gratitude for Saturn's one-price-fits-all policy and describing their previous experiences laden with fear that they were being ripped off by manipulative and dishonest car dealers.

Saturn's brand identity was initially consistent and solid, offering a money-back guarantee and demonstrating trustworthiness. When a defective coolant could cause irreparable damage, the firm recalled 1,836 cars and never resold them. Understanding that what is being sold is belonging as much as cars, the company hosted a reunion of Saturn car owners (with country music, rhythm-and-blues, a barbecue, and removable tattoos), while many local dealers held picnics for those who could not caravan to Spring Hill.[1]

In fact, many local dealers have sponsored monthly down-home events for Saturn owners, such as ice cream socials and barbecues.

1. Jonathan Bond and Richard Kirshenbaum, *Under the Radar: Talking to Today's Cynical Consumer* (New York: Adweek Books, 1998), pp. 188–189.

They also get involved in local charity activities, especially those funding playgrounds for kids and local zoos. Saturn's commitment to tracking and meeting the needs of the consumer was dramatized in a commercial portraying one young man showing up at Saturn showrooms throughout the country to eat their donuts. Saturn dealers were seen dutifully informing other dealers that he liked the jelly ones. When a group of dealers suggested a car giveaway as an incentive, Saturn chose instead a contest in which the winners got to go to Spring Hill and help build their own car. This Regular Guy/Gal-brand masterpiece seemed down home even though it was choreographed to the last detail. And it is impossible to pull such a feat off if the organizational culture does not fit the brand identity. In time, the performance of Saturn began to wobble, with its long-term profitability coming into question.

The Regular Guy/Gal Organizational Culture

In organizations, the Regular Guy/Gal archetype reflects these same values and preferences in an aggregate way. Frequently, their sense of group identity is forged in contrast to that of a more elitist group—think of labor unions (and management), worker-owned companies like Avis that establish team spirit by identifying with the underdog ("We try harder"), or companies like VISA that distinguish themselves from brands like American Express that have a more elite image.

Often, Regular Guy/Gal companies are worker owned, and dress is more casual than might be usual in their industry. Managers may wear jeans and a work shirt and chat amicably with employees. If you went to a meeting with management, you might not be able to pick out the leaders immediately, because so few differences of status are apparent. Unions, cause related nonprofits, and progressive political movements are typical Regular Guy/Gal organizations, as is your local health food coop. Generally, these organizations share a strong belief in the importance of each individual and a distaste for differentiating unduly among people. Decisions are made as democratically as possible, depending upon the scale of the organization. In some small organizations or management teams, decisions are likely to be made by consensus. Social occasions are folksy and frequent.

When the organization is healthy, there is a strong sense of camaraderie, a shared sense of purpose and egalitarian values, pride in the work, and commitment to the task. When the organization is unhealthy or when the Regular Guy/Gal archetype is taken to the extreme, egalitarianism becomes bureaucracy. The meritocracy disappears, and people are rewarded similarly regardless of their commitment or productivity.

Marketing to the Regular Guy/Gal Impulse

Today, when virtually all products sport logos, it is important to understand their appeal. To the Ruler, the logo speaks of status. To the Explorer, the logo may be a statement about identity. To the Regular Guy/Gal, the logo is a means of affiliating, a way of demonstrating your connection with others who use that product and identify with its brand meaning.

Author Kurt Vonnegut, in *Cat's Cradle*, coined the word "granfalloon" for our identification with our state (in the Vonnegut novel, a couple identified fervently with Hoosiers), the high school we went to, our ethnic group, a ball club, or a car. This form of belonging—associated with the Regular Guy/Gal—can be quite superficial and still be satisfactory to many people. For example, owners of Saturn cars really do show up at Saturn reunions! Deeper identification—as with patriotism—is triggered if the connection is not just with a car, but with the archetypal meaning of the car. In this sense, some people attending the Saturn reunions were undoubtedly connecting the association with solid, good-citizen values, such as hard work, and quality products in an age of planned obsolescence.[2]

Remember that the urge to belong causes people to make friends with brands. Many people actually form imaginary relationships with companies and their products, just as they do with movie stars and other celebrities. Once they have cemented a friendship, they may experience the changing or phasing in of a product as if they had just lost a friend. This kind of behavior was, of course, most noticeable in the widespread uproar over New Coke, but it is experienced by consumers every time their favorite restaurant or bookstore closes. When Ben & Jerry's was sold, for example, many people ex-

2. Bond and Kirshenbaum, pp. 188–189.

> The Regular Guy/Gal archetype provides a good identity for brands
>
> - whose use helps people belong or feel that they belong
> - whose function is something used commonly in everyday life
> - with pricing that is moderate to low (or that is an upscale version of a product that would ordinarily be inexpensive)
> - produced or sold by a company with a down-home organizational culture, and
> - that want to differentiate themselves in a positive way from a higher priced or more elitist brand

pressed real personal sadness, believing that what was best about the company might be lost—and what they were concerned about had absolutely nothing to do with the taste or quality of the ice cream. Rather, it had to do with a number of things, including Ben & Jerry's efforts to help ordinary folks who might not ordinarily be able to buy a franchise to do so, the company's environmental efforts, and its reputation as a fun-loving place.

In today's fast-paced world, loneliness is a problem for many. People simply do not allot as much time to hanging out with friends, spending long, leisurely hours with lovers, or enjoying quality time with children. The more emotionally deprived people are, the more they seek connection in commercial transactions. Although that is in some way sad, it is also real. You can offer a service and increase profitability to the degree you are able to meet this need.

If you can offer a point of connection for people—as Saturn does with reunions and other gatherings—it will greatly increase their loyalty to you. Although everyone likes best those brands and commercials that present an affable appearance, the appeal is especially strong for the Regular Guy/Gal. This archetype's image is middle class to working class, but it should not be confused with a lifestyle category. What kids now call "credit-card hippies," as well as intellectuals who sport working-class clothing, students at Ivy League colleges who take their fashion cues from inner-city kids, and every one of us who believes in democracy—these tell us that the Regular Guy/Gal is alive and well throughout the society.

The Lover

Motto: "I only have eyes for you."

Lover brands are common in the cosmetics, jewelry, fashion, and travel industries. Think of Revlon. Its ads are sensuous, elegant, even erotic, and the company produces beauty products that help people attract love. Any brand that implicitly promises beauty and sexual appeal is a Lover brand. Victoria's Secret is an obvious example. You also see the Lover in food categories, such as wine and gourmet foods, in which sensuality and indulgence are essential parts of the consumption experience—Godiva chocolate, Barilla pasta, Gevalia coffee, and Häagen Dazs ice cream, for instance. At least two states have based their public identity on this archetype. Virginia states it directly: "Virginia is for lovers." California puts it more figuratively, with the headline, "I'm a test pilot for pleasure."

The Lover archetype governs all sorts of human love, from parental love, to friendship, to spiritual love, but it is most important to romantic love. You might think of the Roman love god and goddess—Cupid and Venus—and of classic cinematic heartthrobs like Clark Gable, Cary Grant, Sophia Loren, or Elizabeth Taylor. This is the realm of hearts and flowers, long strolls on sunset beaches, dancing in the moonlight—of the romantic love story in both its comic (live happily every after) and its tragic forms (torn apart by death—*Titanic*—or circumstances—*Casablanca*).

The Lover archetype also supports the development of gender identity. Revlon promotes products, saying "Feel like a woman." Other products encourage men to feel like men. Whether you are gay or straight, part of growing up is about learning to identify with your gender.

The Lover archetype also inspires the whole genre of romance novels. We all know that most romances follow a very defined plot. The young and beautiful heroine meets Mr. Right, but some circumstance or misunderstanding keeps them apart until somehow the truth is revealed and, after much heaving of chests and protestations of love, they marry and live happily ever after. Some of these novels are quite erotic, while others are more proper, but however much or little explicit sex they contain, the plot is remarkably consistent. And, in spite of this, thousands are sold every year. Some women read one every week and never tire of the same plot. Why? Because these plots call up a deep archetypal yearning for the experience of true love.

> ## The Lover
>
> **Core desire:** attain intimacy and experience sensual pleasure
> **Goal:** being in a relationship with the people, the work, the experiences, the surroundings they love
> **Fear:** being alone, a wallflower, unwanted, unloved
> **Strategy:** become more and more attractive-physically, emotionally, and in every other way
> **Trap:** doing anything and everything to attract and please others, losing identity
> **Gifts:** passion, gratitude, appreciation, commitment

Although women more than men love Lover archetype movies ("chick flicks") and novels, men, of course, are attracted by the archetype, too. For literature aimed at men, the adventure story is often the lead, with the love story occupying second place. Nevertheless, the hero is not quite a hero if he fails to get the girl by the end of the story. For example, in projective techniques used in qualitative research, young women will talk about wanting to "hang out" in a bar with the Camel smoker (the Jester who, like Joe Camel, is a lot of fun), but she will want to leave with the Marlboro man.

The archetype is also reflected in everyday assumptions about the successful life. Parents expect their children to find a fulfilling

---

Levels of the Lover

The Call: infatuation, seduction, falling in love (with a person, an idea, a cause, work, a product)
Level One: seeking great sex or a great romance
Level Two: following your bliss and committing to whom and what you love
Level Three: spiritual love, self-acceptance, and the experience of ecstasy
Shadow: promiscuity, obsession, jealousy, envy, Puritanism

---

career and to marry and settle down. They often do not really see their work of raising the child as complete until the child marries. Although the anticipation is that they will live happily ever after, the reality is that we live in a society where one out of every two marriages ends in divorce. Nevertheless, the search for true love continues to be lived out in most lives. If we cannot live happily ever after with one person, everyone expects us to get going and find someone else. What this means is that, for many, the Lover archetype is active not just in the twenties, but throughout life, involved either in keeping the love of one's spouse (who could leave) or in finding someone new. And, of course, we are all touched and encouraged not only by marriage ceremonies, but also by anniversaries of couples who have grown old together and still clearly love one another.

The Lover as an archetype is also active in intense and personal friendships. In the 19th century, it was more normal than it is today (when people are more concerned about their sexual orientation) to have passionate friendships with people of the same sex. Although modern mores call for cooler friendships (partly because of the keen awareness of the potential for same-sex relationships to become sexual), there is a growing reliance on the part of many young people on friendship as a foundation for intimacy. Lovers may come and go, but friendships last for a lifetime. Jordache runs a lovely ad featuring friends (including boys and girls) with arms around one another in an intimate, friendly way. The connection is not sexual, but it is clearly close. The implied story is that "we really love each other—all of us. We are not lovers, but we really care."

How does Lover friendship differ from the Regular Guy/Gal archetype? For the Regular Guy/Gal, it is important to fit in and belong, but not to stand out. Lovers, by contrast, want to know that you are one of their best friends, that you really know them, and that they are really special to you. In this sense, the Lover can be the archetype of a group of friends who feel like they really know one another. They are connected not just by superficial allegiances, but by something much deeper. Vonnegut named this more intimate connection (than the "granfalloon") the "karass." In his mind, people who enjoy such a relationship are incarnated together for a reason, and they feel a special closeness. For many, this level of intimacy would not necessarily be explained in terms of incarnation. Rather, it might be earned, based on the time invested in building and sustaining it.

Whether the love is romantic or of the friendship variety, the Lover's self-esteem may derive from the sense of specialness that comes from being loved. At its worst, this can lead to a pathetically desperate need to be loved that can drive someone to promiscuity or to stay in an unfulfilling or even abusive situation. When a person has a stronger sense of self, the Lover can be expressed without so much compulsion. At its best, it offers deep, abiding, intimate connection between people—the kind that fuels marriages (or friendships) in which love really does last forever.

Lovers think of themselves as being wonderfully appreciative of others. However, they typically dislike competitors who threaten to supplant them in the affections of others. Associated with the Lover archetype, therefore, may be an underside of competitiveness that is generally unconscious and

> Lovers may be known as partners, friends, intimates, matchmakers, enthusiasts, connoisseurs, sensualists, spouses, team builders, harmonizers.

unacknowledged, with the result that jealousy can lead to very mean-spirited behavior.

When the Lover archetype is active in an individual's life, he or she will want to look not only good, but, indeed, beautiful or handsome. The underlying desire is to attract, give love, and express affection in intimate and pleasurable ways. In friendship and in families, this propensity can include cuddling, sharing the secrets of one's

In this drawing, inspired by a 100 B.C. statue in the Athens Archaeological Museum, the attitude of Aphrodite can be interpreted as a playful rejection of the purely lustful advances of Pan in favor of deeper, more intimate love as Cupid, the mythic matchmaker, looks on.

heart, and bonding through shared likes and dislikes. With a romantic partner, of course, it also includes sexuality.

Sex Still Gets Attention

In today's more open society, sexuality is increasingly bared in advertising. Condoms are, of course, natural props for the Lover's journey. Durex ran an ad with a couple tastefully presented, but clearly making love, with the caption, "The human body has over 45 miles of nerves. Enjoy the ride."

Because wine and spirits decrease inhibition, they are also often associated with sex. Cutty Sark ads sport pinup figures. But many products unrelated to actual sexuality, from power tools to radios, are sold with sexual images. A tough but gorgeous woman wearing only a seat belt is pictured in a Jensen car radio ad with the phrase "Feel the raw naked power of the road." Dior runs edgy fashion ads with women engaging in what appears to be lesbian sexual foreplay so hot that sweat is dripping heavily off their arms and legs.

Bluefly.com, selling discounted fashions for men and women, runs a picture of a woman in her underwear tapping away at her laptop as a naked man holding a towel over his privates steps out of the bathroom. The caption reads "satisfaction guaranteed." The question the reader might raise is, "Was she satisfied by the man or was she not?" She certainly does look satisfied with her laptop. Glenfiddich promises its customers that "tantric sex is a no brainer for a whisky man," explaining that "patience and control are crucial in the single malt business."

Guess Jeans consistently portrays women in come-hither poses. Although they are clothed, the seductive message is clear. Sometimes they look almost orgasmic, but they always have a look of seduction. Playboy has been so successful selling sex directly that it advertises itself as "the most powerful men's brand in the world."

Chanel: The Making of a Lover Brand

Chanel originated in France in the early 1900s. Coco Chanel was the illegitimate daughter of a poor peddler and a shop girl. After her mother died (and her father ran off), she lived in a convent, and as she grew older, she supported herself as a seamstress. She dreamed of more romantic things, eventually running off to become, first, a cabaret singer and, later, the backup mistress of a wealthy playboy who encouraged her to open a dress shop to keep herself busy. Who would have anticipated the magnitude of the success growing out of that modest shop!

Chanel was shockingly daring, often wearing men's clothing and using menswear as an inspiration for a bold line of women's clothes—

clothes that were comfortable and stylish and that forged a new image of a sexy, but also independent, woman. Throughout its history, Chanel has integrated the idea of the independent woman with the sexy woman, undercutting the idea that women who are not dependent on men are masculine and unattractive, as well as the idea that women can have either love or a successful career, but not both.

Chanel herself was known both as a dress designer and as a mistress to famous and wealthy men. When she was the mistress of the Russian Grand Duke Dmitri, he introduced her to a perfumer who was in the process of developing the perfume she later released as Chanel No. 5, having convinced him to give it to her. The initial advertising positioned this fragrance as "A very improper perfume for nicely brought-up ladies."

Legend has it that her nickname, Coco, was short for *coquette*—French for "kept woman." In fact, her reputation as a visible mistress to wealthy and influential men may have enhanced the Lover image of her products. When asked why she refused to marry the Duke of Westminster, who was one of the richest men in Europe, she replied, "There have been several Duchesses of Westminster. There is only one Chanel."[1]

The Cult of Beauty and Romance

The Lover archetype also awakens people's aesthetic appreciation. Suddenly beauty matters—whether it is a natural scene, the ambience of an elegant restaurant, or just the right pair of shoes. Similarly, the senses are heightened, and people take time to savor gourmet food, smell the lilacs, listen to a beautiful melody, and watch the sun go down.

Venus, the Roman goddess of love, was believed to have arisen out of the ocean depths, born of the semen and sea foam. The Lover archetype is there in advertisements for airlines, hotels, and restaurants, ads that often pan out to show a gorgeous beach. You might remember the famous scene in *From Here to Eternity* that ends with a couple lying in the surf kissing as the waves roll in on them. There

1. Thaddeus Wawro, *Radicals and Visionaries* (Irvine, CA: Entrepreneur Press, 2000), pp. 94–95.

is something so erotic about this image that it works much better than more explicit scenes. Learning subtlety is a key to developing ads that evoke the erotic without offending customers. Hot Spring Portable Spas does a good job, simply showing a romantic couple in a hot tub and saying, "Out there, it's bumper to bumper, minute to minute, nose to nose. In here, it's heart to heart."

There is something about the connection between the sea and love, which we see in films such as *Titanic* as well, wherein the romantic love plot is augmented by scenes of visual beauty and by the sheer elegance and indulgence of life on a cruise. Princess Cruises plays it low key, merely showing a young couple in the romantic restaurant, smiling as they choose the wine, implicitly promising the intimacy of a small ship on a large liner. Norwegian Cruise Line is braver, running much more explicit (but still appropriate and relevant) copy: "Sex in the afternoon. It's different out here."

Of course, many love stories have tragic endings. The lovers break up or (as with Romeo and Juliet) are separated by death or circumstances, thus pulling at our heartstrings. The tragic love story works to sell movies, soaps, and romantic novels, but in advertising, the sell is connected to the promise of the happy ending. Or the pull is not necessarily in the ending at all, but in holding the tension of erotic desire as long as possible. Television shows like "Moonlighting" and "Lois and Clark" remain popular as long as they hold the tension between the star-crossed lovers. As soon as the love is consummated, interest in the show wanes. The best ads therefore need to hold Eros without resolving it. An example in a successful ad calls up the classic pickup scene in a bar: B Kool just shows a man's hand holding a cigarette package and a lit cigarette, with the man clearly about to approach a gorgeous woman who is looking back at him in the mirror. The moment is heavy with erotic possibility, but the ad does not tell us where it will go

Cinderella: The Beauty Project

The Lover's fear is of being a wallflower or being cast off by one's lover. Even more fundamentally, the Lover fears not being lovable. That's why he or she is always engaging in self-improvement projects to be ever more worthy of attention. In the original version of Cinderella, her sisters were willing to cut off their toes to fit into the glass slipper offered by the prince. While this may sound extreme, it is not unrelated to the contemporary draw of plastic surgery. People will go under the knife to be more beautiful or handsome. The desire to attract love is deep and strong. Both women and men will go to great lengths to be attractive enough to win love. Beyond the fear is a powerful yearning.

The joy of special occasions—the first kiss, the proposal, the wedding, the anniversary—also appeal to the sentimentalist in all of us. Estée Lauder's "Beautiful" fragrance is marketed with an association with marriage. A lovely bride is embraced by a flower girl. Such a campaign is designed to win the hearts of women aspiring to that special day and of those that recall it.

The Lover archetype is natural for fashion and cars. Cinderella's fairy godmother improves upon her innate beauty and character by providing her with just the right dress, shoes, and carriage to go to the ball and win the heart of the prince. A modern-day Cinderella could get such a makeover with just a trip to the shopping mall. In *Pretty Woman*, Julia Roberts is revealed to be a princess inside when she buys beautiful and expensive clothes. There is hardly any point in chronicling examples of fashion and cosmetics promising such a Cinderella-like transformation. They are all around us, and you know them. However, *Pretty Woman* captured viewers' hearts because Julia Roberts managed to convey a reality of depth and worth to a woman who was making her living as a prostitute. The change of clothes was not just a shallow change; it revealed a truth about the character obscured by her former, trashy attire.

The archetypal plot that grabs attention is deeper than the most frequent commercial message. The archetype does not say that the new hairstyle, outfit, car, or plastic surgery will get you the love of your life. What that archetypal plot says is that it will do so if the change reveals the real beauty of your nature.

Most ads devoted to teenage girls evoke either the Explorer or the Lover—unfortunately, in both cases, the archetypes' lower levels. (The Explorer ads appeal to their feeling of being different and the Lover of wanting to be attractive.) Many of these ads fail to connect with the power of the archetype because they encourage a regressive superficiality. (Just get the new dress!) This perversion of the mythic message has even affected politics: George Bush failed to win re-election in part because he was increasingly associated with a Madison Avenue image rather than some reality about his character.

Ironically, Bill Clinton had an advantage in the public mind simply because people knew about his vulnerabilities. A film shown at the 1992 Democratic convention talked openly about his standing up to an abusive stepfather and his brother's struggle with drugs. In addition, he and Hillary had gone public about "difficulties" in their marriage—which was, of course, code for "We haven't always been true to one another." In the 1990s, it became commonplace for Donahue, Oprah, and other talk shows to host confessional shows in which ordinary people and celebrities would bare their souls, revealing secrets that would never have been disclosed in the past. Our public discourse is increasingly influenced by the Lover's desire to know people's secrets. At the same time, the public has become as accepting of people's vulnerabilities as intimates have historically been. It is therefore a great paradox that they will trust a politician who is open about his defects more than one who claims to have "character."

Baring one's soul now seems almost to be required to win public trust. That's where contemporary advertising falls somewhat short. The superficial message to today's Prince Charming in advertising is that it does not so much matter how his real self connects with appearances, as long as he has the right automobile (carriage). Yet both men and women who are beyond 16 do not feel this way. In extreme terms, the association of cars with romance in ads directed at men even leaves the girl out entirely. It is the car itself that is the love object. One ad by Hyundai shows a bright red satin garter belt just above the automobile, with the caption "Get something just as hot for the garage."

State Farm Insurance also ran an ad with the car as the love object, but with a nod toward some complexity. Front and center is a picture of a red convertible with the caption, "We were there when you found your first love. She was hot. And so-o-o-o choice. Your first real love. Sure she burned more oil than gas. But hey, man . . . love is blind." The truth is, cars are often a man's first love, and loving a car that burns oil is great preparation for loving a woman even though she is not perfect either.

There are innumerable brands helping men and women to look and act like the hero and heroine of a romantic movie. Such ads are particularly effective with the young, who still retain the desire to be perfect and the hope of finding the perfect mate. The fact that so many brands appeal to these desires, however, means that doing so does not provide any meaningful differentiation. At the same time, they have the dubious effect of reinforcing rather negative aspects of traditional sex roles (e.g., women are always gorgeous and men are always in control), messages that the women's and men's movements have attempted to prime people to notice and resent. But most of all, these ads may have less than a maximum effect, because they do not seem authentic enough for ordinary people to identify with them.

While people do love to look at the gorgeous woman and the perfect man, it is also true that almost all of us feel vulnerable when we compare ourselves with them. Not all women look like fashion models. Not all men are totally in-control performance machines. A film such as *The Full Monty* defied Hollywood conventions, using no-name actors and depressing location shots, but won audiences' hearts with its gritty celebration of ordinary guys, stripping down to reveal ordinary bodies. While this movie has a Regular Guy/Gal theme, it also demonstrates how the essence of the Lover is a strip. You gradually let go of your defenses to let someone know you. You take off your clothes to go to bed, thereby revealing what is usually an imperfect body. Over time, in a relationship, the real you surfaces. The real energy in the Lover archetype today is around the truth of this vulnerability, one that is shared by men and women alike. Rather than promising the perfect body and the perfect persona, ads could grab people where they live, as *The Full Monty* did, by connecting with the truth of what they fear (rejection), what they desire (unconditional love), and what they want to give.

Sensuality, Food, and Indulgence

Beyond the anxiety about whether anyone will love us, there is great fun in the Lover archetype simply because Eros, in its pleasure-seeking aspect, enriches life. There is a wonderful scene in the movie *Tom Jones* in which two potential lovers eat lasciviously while staring into one another's eyes. A quasi-sexual feel is often present with particularly indulgent foods. Gevalia Kaffe pictures a woman who looks like she is about to bliss out smelling the coffee. Godiva chocolates branded the connection between sex and chocolate by utilizing the image of Lady Godiva riding naked, clothed only by her long, flowing hair.

Washington Post staff writer Paul Richard shared with us in a phone interview his sense that the white tablecloths, flowers, and candles in virtually all good restaurants are unconscious invocations of a feminine goddess energy, as are filmy curtains and even Superman's cape; if aliens were to land on Earth and study our civilization, they would undoubtedly conclude that humans were unable to eat well without honoring Her. He says that the goddess is all around us, from the woman in filmy clothes stroking the hood of a car in an ad to the luxurious quality of light and shape in a classic still life.

For the lover, Eros is always present—manifest or potentially. Hennessy Cognac runs an ad of two lovers moving in toward the big kiss—that wonderfully erotic moment of anticipation. The caption says, "If you've ever been kissed, you already know the feeling of Cognac Hennessy," thus associating the joy of kissing with drinking the company's product.

Uncle Ben's Rice Bowl ("Uncle Ben's. A Passion for Good Food.") ran a picture of lovers. The woman is feeding the man as she leans suggestively against him, and the caption reads, "Meals so full of excitement, they almost heat themselves." (But does the sensual gratification of the product live up to the promise? And is Uncle Ben's a brand that can promise passion in the first place?)

The Lover archetype is also a natural for spas of all kinds, promising a kind of indulgent, sensory, and healthy time out. C. D. Peacock positions the Concord gold diamond watch by picturing it on the wrist of a beautiful woman, lying naked on her stomach on a white sheet as if awaiting a massage. This image invokes pampering more than sex.

An ad for Caress Moisturizing Bath Products pictures a woman in a towel, looking absolutely ecstatic, with a caption that reads, "You've never been caressed like this before." Such ads evoke the erotic potential within nurturing experiences.

Invoking the strip tease, Absolut Vodka encased its mandarin-flavored vodka in an orange skin that is in the process of being peeled off to reveal the trademark bottle. The ad, saying "Absolut Re-vealed," implicitly suggests the ways that lovers gradually strip to reveal their naked bodies and naked emotions. Absolut ads are re-freshing for their subtlety with an archetype whose meaning is more typically expressed in very blatant and obvious ways. Their most famous and well-known ads—of the vodka bottle blending into the city skyline—reflect the Lover's urge to merge and his or her love of beauty, and have a sensuality to them that is neither forced nor jarring.

The Lover archetype is about passion—not only in our love lives, but also in our work. Chrysler picks up on this with an ad that states, "Without a soul, there's just a shell. Without passion, these would just be cars." The ad goes on to say, "Passion is such a strong emo-tion. It causes us to live, breathe and sweat our hearts out for the things in life we care about. For Chrysler, it's about creating extraor-dinary cars. Cars born from breakthrough design and brought to life through innovative engineering."

What is nice about this ad is the realization that the Lover en-gages our souls, so that passion should infuse our lives. Joseph Camp-bell appealed to the Lover in all of us, inviting his readers to "follow your bliss." Today, any number of self-help and career development books guide people in finding their own personal purpose by rec-ognizing what they love to do.

Hallmark Cards: A Lover Masterpiece

Initially, Hallmark thought of greeting cards as expressing thoughts that were awkward or difficult to articulate. Our insights from heavy card buyers helped the company fine-tune this goal. We discovered that people searched for cards when they wanted to express very specific feelings about the relationship—to communicate something so personal and particular to the self-knowledge of two people that the card was like a gift, the most personal kind of gift. For example, people liked to hunt for cards that demonstrated their knowledge of the recipient—a card with a kitten because their friend likes cats or a card with a message that reveals something real about their mother, father, brother, sister, husband, wife, child, or friend. Finding the card that is just right says, "You are special to me. I notice what you are like and what you like. The card I picked shows I really know you." The line that resulted from these insights, developed by Young & Rubicam, was "Give a little of yourself. Give a Hallmark."

Hallmark realized that its cards needed to be love stories, so it began running love story ads. Some of these ads were about romantic love, but many were about other forms of intimacy—friendship, love between parents and children, and even work relationships. Each ad called up an archetypal story. A young woman is nervous about losing her guy because she wants to go away to ballet school. He encourages her to go, and at a moment when she is feeling very vulnerable in her new and challenging position, she receives a card from him, reminding her of his love.

A young girl, going to her lesson with an elderly piano teacher, slips him a birthday card, and he fights to control how touched he feels, but both tears and a sweet smile begin to show as the young girl begins to play.

In a beautiful Christmas ad, a harried father keeps ignoring his sweet young daughter as he struggles to put up the tree, the trimming, and everything else "perfectly" for the holiday. Then he hears his daughter talking to Santa wishing that instead of ordinary Christmas gifts, she had more time with her dad. He has been a great Caregiver, doing it all right for her. But what she wants is real intimacy—love. He brings her out into the living room, before the fire, and begins to tell her a story that his own father had told him. Priorities are restored; the oral tradition is preserved. In this ad, there is no "sale" at all—only the Hallmark message: "This season, give the greatest gift of all. The gift of yourself."

It is not just that these commercials compel attention. They work because the stories consistently reinforce the Lover identity of Hallmark in a way that relates to the consumer's real feelings. The stories are archetypal, but not stereotypical. They connect the archetype with situations we all know, but which are not simply predictable.

This Lover meaning is also reinforced by the layout of the company's retail stores. In 1998, Hallmark opened over 80 new stores, allowing the Lover theme to drive the shopping experience as well as the cards and the commercial. The new stores offer quiet areas for looking at cards, tables and chairs for writing, boxes of crayons for the kids, and coffee for the adults. Such an enrichment of the shopping experience resulted in dramatic increases in Hallmark's volume of sales.[2]

The Lover Organization

The Lover archetype in organizations results in camaraderie, beautiful surroundings, and attention to the feeling dimension of work life. People are expected to dress well (not for status reasons, but to adorn themselves) and to share their feelings and thoughts freely. A sense of cohesion comes out of a sense of being special—of being beautiful people, appreciating the finer things in life, proficient in communication skills and social graces, and, in many cases, exemplars of good taste or pioneers for new and emerging values. Typically, employees really like one another and have a passion for the organization's values, vision, and products.

Lover organizations like to operate in a power-sharing, consensual manner. Time is freely spent on the process of making decisions, especially being certain that all have had their say, but is often recouped in the implementation phase. When consensus is achieved, everyone uniformly acts to implement the new plan.

At Hewlett-Packard, all decisions of the executive team have to be made by consensus. In many divisions and offices of a variety of companies, decision making involves everyone, and all share their feelings as well as their views. When things are working well, the atmosphere tingles with positive energy, enthusiasm, and enjoyment. When it does not work so well, unstated power struggles and cliques can keep the organization from getting much done. Over time, the unstated business of the organization is just talking through all the emotional issues that surface periodically.

Barilla is a wonderful example of a Lover company. While most pastas are marketed as comfort foods, invoking the nurturance of the Caregiver, upscale Barilla pasta is more consistently Lover in its in-

2. Bernd H. Schmitt, *Experiential Marketing: How to Get Customers to Sense, Feel, Think, Act, and Relate to Your Company* (New York: The Free Press, 1999), pp. 221–222.

vocation of gourmet indulgence and real intimate connection. Barilla consumers are portrayed as real gourmands, enjoying pasta as a sensory experience. Years ago, for example, Barilla ran a commercial, developed by Young & Rubicam, that depicted an elegant and successful-looking man coming home from a long trip to find a party going on at his home. He spots his beautiful wife across the room, smiles, makes eye contact with her, and then signals with his hands that what he really wants is spaghetti. It's clearly implied that the pasta and time alone with her are his main desires, instead of attending the glamorous gathering that's going on. At Barilla, as in many family-owned businesses, work has an intimate quality to it, at least at the top. Beautiful art is on the walls, famous artists and designers have been involved in the design of the firm's packages, and company headquarters is in the Italian countryside. It is no accident that this Lover archetype company is based in Italy—which may be (next to France) the Lover capital of the world.

The Barilla family lives what its ads portray. The family embodies a zest for life and a capacity to live beautifully. The brand that can capture this almost transcendent quality in everyday sensory life can be irresistible to consumers who may ordinarily feel as if their bodies were taxis carrying their minds around. Taste, touch, and smell are related to the Lover's capacity to savor life in a sensory way.

The Lover informs many successful therapy and consulting practices whose success depends on the ability to help people feel safe enough to be vulnerable, on superb communication skills, and on a close and trusting relationship with the client. Even in companies whose primary values emerge from another archetypal perspective, the Lover archetype may be required in times of rapid change or when people are fearful. At such times, team building is not so much about helping people to play their roles better (as on a winning athletic team), but rather, it involves getting people to know one another well enough to develop real trust. Such organizational interventions help diverse populations move beyond superficial differences to relate to the more intimate reality of another complex human being, with dreams and aspirations not unlike one's own. In terms of archetypes, the interventions are related to classic movies such as *Dirty Dancing* or *Guess Who's Coming to Dinner*, wherein love triumphs over divisions of class or race. Ultimately, the Lover archetype expands to spiritual love, as embodied by Christ or other spiritual exemplars of love for all humankind.

Marketing to Lovers

The Lover wants a deeper kind of connection—one that is intimate, genuine, and personal (and sometimes also sensual). Such forms of connection—whether with lovers, friends, or family members—require much greater knowledge, honesty, vulnerability, and passion than the cooler connectivity of the Regular Guy/Gal. Of course, they are deeper, more special, and rare.

Lovers often identify products with certain relationships. One woman declared that she could never drink Harvey's Bristol Cream again after she broke up with her boyfriend. It was "their drink." Another always drinks Diet Coke because everyone did at her all-time favorite job. Lovers also develop relationships with products and companies—especially those that help them feel special and loved. At the Fairmont Hotel chain, a real Lover establishment, room service picks up the phone and calls you by name, evidencing knowledge of your prior requests, likes, and dislikes. A customer may know full well that room service does this because it all comes up on a computer. The customer also knows that the staff says these things because they have been trained to. Nevertheless, it does work. Most people—and especially those for whom belonging is an issue—feel special, cared about, and nurtured in a world that often feels cold and impersonal. People in whom the Lover archetype is dominant are the group for whom relationship marketing and management is the most compelling. Consumers with a highly developed Lover archetype like being singled out for attention. They like the mailing "to our special customers" announcing a sale that has not yet been announced to other customers. They like a salesperson who knows their name and asks about their kids. They like hearing the gossip about the company and what's happening in it. Even knowing about problems can cement the relationship, just as shared vulnerabilities often deepen personal relationships. For Lovers, you don't have to be perfect, but you do need to be real and open.

While Regular Guys/Gals want products that help them fit in

> **The Lover is a promising identity for a brand**
>
> - whose use helps people find love or friendship
> - whose function fosters beauty, communication, or closeness be-
>   tween people or is associated with sexuality or romance
> - with pricing that is moderate to high
> - if it is produced or sold by a company with an intimate, elegant
>   organizational culture, as opposed to a massive Ruler hierarchy
> - that needs to differentiate itself in a positive way from lower
>   priced brands

because those products are identical to what others are buying or wearing, Lovers prefer products that are one of a kind, unusual, or tailored especially for them. Marketing expert Keith McNamara claims that "segmentation as historically conducted by marketers is dead. The future of segmentation lies in the data already collected in organizations' computer systems. The historic data of who buys individual products is the key to creating models that predict future behavior." It is now possible to tailor marketing to the individual purchasing history of customers."[3]

The Lover also expects quality, not as the Ruler does, for status, but for enhanced pleasure in life. A Lover brand like Jaguar can be sleek, beautiful, curvaceous, and sumptuous—but not so much for impressing others as to envelop the driver in a purely sensuous driving experience.

Ideally, then, not only are Lover brands lovable themselves, but they also help the consumer feel special, adored, and doted on. If the attention to the consumer's needs flags, however, he or she may sing, "You don't bring me flowers any more" and seek out a more attentive competitor.

---

3. ICL internal white paper, 1998, quoted in David Lewis and Darren Bridger, *The Soul of the New Consumer* (London, Nicholas Brealey Publishing, 2000), p. 73.

12

The Jester

Motto: "If I can't dance, I don't want to be part of your revolution."

THE JESTER ARCHETYPE includes the clown, the trickster, and anyone at all who loves to play or cut up. Some examples are young children, with their playfulness and spontaneity, Shakespeare's fools, the Yankee tinker in American history and literature, the Coyote figure in American Indian legends, comedians (think Charlie Chaplin, Mae West, the Marx Brothers, Lily Tomlin, Steve Martin, or Jay Leno), and many television and film comedians.

While it is possible to have fun alone, the Jester calls us to come out and play with one another. Jester figures enjoy life and interaction for their own sake. Preferring to be the life of the party, the Jester has as his or her native habitat the playground, the neighborhood bar, the recreation room, and anywhere where fun can be had. While both the Regular Guy/Gal and the Lover censor themselves in order to fit in or attract others, the Jester lets it rip, demonstrating a refreshing faith that it is possible to be truly oneself and be accepted and even adored by others.

Perhaps because we live in such an earnest culture, the Jester tends to be a good brand identification because virtually everyone is hungry for more fun. You can think of the success of ad campaigns for milk, with famous people sporting milk mustaches. If they were being stereotypical, milk would be promoted as being good for you. Instead, this great campaign recognizes how milk can connect any of us with our fun-loving, mischievous inner child.

While all the "Got Milk" ads are great, some of the best show cookies, not milk, allowing the viewer to see cookies and inevitably want milk to go with them. You cannot see an ad like that without it activating the kid part of you that does not associate even the best coffee with cookies. The kid wants milk.

Jester ads often cause us to laugh at situations that would ordinarily be sad,

> **The Jester**
>
> **Core desire:** to live in the moment with full enjoyment
> **Goal:** to have a great time and lighten up the world
> **Fear:** boredom or being boring
> **Strategy:** play, make jokes, be funny
> **Trap:** frittering away one's life
> **Gift:** joy

not humorous (like the comic slipping on a banana peel). One particularly vivid "Got Milk" ad showed a man in a whole body cast. His friends had tried to cheer him up by feeding him cookies. His plight—being unable to ask for milk—leaves the viewer identifying with the frustration of his situation and essentially asking for him. Such a brilliant ad involves the customer in solving the problem by empathizing with what it is like to wish for the product being sold and not get it.

Rules Are Made to Be Broken

Jesters are the archetype most helpful in dealing with the absurdities of the modern world and with faceless, amorphous present-day bureaucracies, partly because they take everything lightly and partly because they are happiest breaking the rules. The Jester's politics are essentially anarchistic, as illustrated by Emma Goldman, the famous anarchist, who said, "If I can't dance, I don't want to be part of your revolution." The Jester's willingness to break rules leads to innovative, out-of-the-box thinking. It also makes for a good brand identity for things like fun foods that are not

> The Jester also may be known as the Fool, trickster, joker, punster, entertainer, clown, prankster, practical joker, or comedian.

necessarily good for you. The Jester identification basically says, "Lighten up on nutrition and health, and have some fun." Candy (M&Ms, Snickers), snack foods (Pringles), cigarettes (Merit, "Lighten up with Merit"), and liquor (Parrot Bay; Kahlua, "Anything Goes") all promise a mini-vacation along with the relaxation of ordinary health rules.

NeoPoint cell phones sport a Jester image, advising the use of the company's "smartphone to boost your IQ" and "make up for the brain cells you lost in college." So Jester brands help you avoid the logical consequences of irresponsible, unhealthy, or even illegal behavior. You might remember the all-time great Alka-Seltzer ad, "Mamma Mia, that's a spicy meatball!" The self-deprecating humor reassures customers that they can eat spicy food with impunity.

The Jester also promises that activities which might ordinarily be seen as tedious or boring can be fun. Kubota tractor, for example, says, "The end justifies the tractor. The smell of fresh-cut grass. The quiet hum of precision. The ability to do more than you imagined. The belief that it's not really work if you enjoy it." Perhaps this is a "tractor thing," because John Deere likens the experience of riding its tractor to "your first pony ride," promising that "You'll never want your first ride to end."

The turn of phrase that changes a negative assumption into a positive one is a great Jester strategy. Trident sugarless gum for kids turns the expectation that gum is bad for kids' teeth on its head. One ad, featuring a cute little boy half hidden by the bubble he has just blown, says, "He huffed and he puffed, and he strengthened his teeth." Similarly, ABC has run an ad campaign for many years that uses the line "TV is good," irreverently defends couch potatoes, and jokes about the allegation that watching TV leads to the disintegration of brain cells. The "yellow campaign," as it is known in the industry, has been noticed and talked about, but the question remains whether anything in the network's lineup or the company's culture reflects a Jester identity, and whether a clever advertising idea that would have been a natural expression of a Jester network simply ended up in the wrong home.

Companies are wise, when expanding services or acquiring new companies, to stay within the same archetypal brand identity. Camel has done this well by expanding from cigarettes to what is described in an ad as "exotic travel" and "pleasure goods." However, while the Jester wants us all to lighten up, have fun, and stop worrying about consequences, this does not mean that the public will always buy in. For example, using a cartoon-image Joe Camel that people feared made smoking appealing to children was serious enough that even a Jester identity could not stave off popular outrage.

Jesters dislike party poopers, people who are overly earnest, and those who are lacking in humor. A downside of the Jester, therefore, can be a tendency to play through life without grappling with issues or thinking things through. When the Jester archetype is your brand's identity, parental guidance is suggested.

Pepsi: A Jester Brand

The Jester as rule-breaker has a long, honorable history. Medieval kings often had fools who not only lightened up the court, but also told the king truths others would be executed for telling. The Jester, therefore, acted as a kind of safety valve for the kingdom. In contemporary times, comedians from Will Rogers to Johnny Carson and Jay Leno poke continual fun at our political leaders in the same spirit that Shakespeare's fools parodied the king. The whole genre of political satire expresses the Jester impulse. This archetype is also a good choice for a brand that is up against a more established one. The Jester (as court fool) has classically been charged with poking holes in the king's pomposity. Therefore, any brand that is challenging another brand that reigns supreme in the marketplace can gain a competitive advantage by making fun of the established brand's smugness—as Pepsi has done successfully with Coke.

Although Pepsi has sometimes strayed into other archetypal territory, its best ads are always Jester ads.

Be Here Now

The Jester archetype helps us really live life in the present and allows us to be impulsive and spontaneous. For example, Hampton Inn advertises its free breakfast bar with questions designed to attract the free spirit within each of us: "Do you still look for the prize in the cereal box? Have you ever taken a sick day due to spring fever? Does your first meeting seem longer on an empty stomach?"

When the Jester archetype is active in an individual, he or she just wants to have fun. The core desire here is to be spontaneous, recapturing the playfulness we all had as little children. Laughter, joking, and even pranks seem appropriate. In this frame of mind, people who are too serious or responsible seem overly uptight. Indeed, the Jester's worst fears are of being bored or boring to others. In addition, the Jester promises that life can be easy. Timex's overall brand identity seems more Regular Guy/Gal, but one ad shows a contortionist with legs intertwined behind his head, whistling while he winds his watch. The caption is "ridiculously easy to use."

The Jester inhabits the egalitarian space of buddies being guys, or gals, together. As with the Regular Guy or Gal, the style is low key and earthy. The Jester has no interest in looking just so. However, instead of blending in, the Jester prefers to look a mite ridiculous. The Jester's motley coat of Shakespeare's time has been succeeded by suspenders, bow ties, and, more recently, baseball caps worn backwards. The overall message is, "You'll want to hang out with me. You'll have a good time." Think of Miller Lite commercials. (Dick Butkus and Bubba Smith are pictured saying, "We're in here drinking Lite because it's less filling and tastes great. Besides, we can't ski.") Teva sporting goods shows a man in a kayak at the front door saying, "Come out and play." The text of one ad goes on to say "Yesterday it was a water fight in the front yard. Today it's your first attempt at 'Brink of Disaster.' Whatever games you play, play them in Teva sandals. Make your feet feel like a kid again."

The Zanier, the Better

The Jester archetype is often a good attention grabber because Jesters like to be zany. eTour.com, for instance, ran an ad with a businessman sitting at his desk with an Olympic swimmer, in dive position, standing, facing him, on his laptop on the desk. The caption read, "Now the things you like find you." The Jester seems to be a great archetypal identity for high-tech firms, because young people, especially, think of high-tech products as fun. eTour.com also promises, "There's no searching. Just surfing." And surfing can be playful. Pocket PC ads picture energetic, outrageous young men and women jovially challenging the reader, "Can your palm do that?" Yahoo!'s bright colors and exclamation point practically shout: It can be fun to surf the Web if you use our service.

Just as children love animals, Jester ads frequently use friendly animal images. Hyundai (whose slogan is "driving is believing") positions the Hyundai Elantra as man's best friend, saying it "does everything but lick your face." Glad zipper storage bags with the double-lock seal shows a cartoon goldfish, happy that the seal is tight enough to keep the water from seeping out.

The WeddingChannel.com pokes gentle fun at the newlyweds in bridal gown and tux in a totally empty house, drinking wine from paper cups and looking shyly at one another. The caption is "Gift Idea: Wine Glasses," but it is clear that they could use anything you might give them!

Finally, many brands succeed in being regarded as more contemporary and fun by associating themselves with a comedian or cartoon figure. IBM overcame an overly stuffy image by using a Charlie Chaplin character in Junior PC ads. MetLife used the Peanuts characters to soften its image and to suggest a playful side to what can be an unsettling category. And Butterfinger successfully updated its image with commercials featuring Bart Simpson.[1]

The Jester Organization

The Jester organization makes enjoyment the bottom line. Ben and Jerry's, for example, prides itself on being a playful place to work. The walls are painted in murals based on ice cream flavors, some floors have a bounce to them, and people get bonuses in ice cream. The company even ran an essay contest at one point to choose its new CEO. At another point, it had an official "minister of joy." Ben and Jerry's also protects itself against the association of the Jester with irresponsibility by its social responsibility program, giving a percentage of revenues to causes much of the public supports.

1. David A. Aaker, *Building Strong Brands* (New York: The Free Press, 1996), pp. 150–151.

Levels of the Jester

Call: ennui, boredom
Level One: life as a game, fun
Level Two: cleverness used to trick others, get out of trouble, and find ways around obstacles, transformation
Level Three: Life experienced in the moment, one day at a time
Shadow: self-indulgence, irresponsibility, mean-spirited pranks

---

At Patagonia, in California, when the surf is up, the plant closes down and people hit the beach. The unwritten expectation in these companies is that employees are motivated by a desire for play. A pompous or dull person, with no sense of humor, is unlikely to thrive there. And, of course, the products the firm produces help people enjoy themselves.

The headquarters of Burger King in Miami has recreational space integrated with work space, including a pool table, roller hockey, an in-line skating rink, and a basketball court (in progress). Employees are known to toss Frisbees past others hard at work, and bunks and showers support those who like to stay 'round the clock alternating work and play.[2]

The Jester helps foster innovation in organizations, whatever their core archetype, by breaking up traditional categories of thinking. For example, Carol Pearson divided the staff of a major cancer hospital into brainstorming groups by archetype in order to generate ideas about how patients' experiences in the hospital can be improved. All of the groups generated good ideas, but the best came from the Jester group; it concluded that cancer patients should enjoy their lives! Instead of wiling away afternoons in waiting rooms when doctors were running behind, patients should be given beepers, so that they can stroll to the shopping mall or, the group added, watch a movie in the special patient theater they also envisioned! To the Jester, no outcome—even saving your life—should mean sacrificing joy in the here and now.

---

2. Rolf Jensen, *The Dream Society: How the Coming Shift from Information to Imagination Will Transform Your Business* (New York: McGraw-Hill, 1999), p. 138.

Marketing to the Jester

The Jester in every one of us loves humor. We like funny commercials because they entertain us, and the attendant good feeling creates a halo effect around the product. Jester ads and packaging highlight bright colors and lots of action—the more outrageous, the better. The Jester also loves to live. For this reason, virtual experiences are great ways to market to Jesters. The Web site for Club Med, for example, links to virtual villages that simulate the experiences you can expect there. You get to begin selecting how you want to spend your time, almost as if you were there. Do you want to play tennis? Go snorkeling? Dance? Making the selection starts your imagination going, and pretty soon you are having a virtual vacation—in fantasy. The Discovery Channel's Planet Explorer also provides virtual travel to exotic places.[3]

Most of all, the Jester helps us get out of trapped, small-time thinking. Jesters excel at brainstorming. The most important aspect of Jester marketing is cleverness. The Jester in every one of us loves outrageous, clever, new ways of seeing the world. The best way to develop such marketing strategies is to lighten up your marketing team. Let the team play, bring in toys, come up with as many wild ideas as you can—no matter how outlandish they might be—to grease the wheels of creativity. The freer your team, the better your new ideas. Jesters love to stand on their heads, seeing the world in unexpected and unpredictable ways.

Jesters are also not as proprietary as other archetypes. If you think about it, you rarely ever hear who invented a joke. Jokes fly around the world via the oral tradition and on the Internet in days, sometimes minutes, and make the whole world laugh. Jester marketing knows that giving things away often enhances a company's reputation. Kinetix, a San Francisco multimedia company, developed the Dancing Baby™ as part of its demo package, before the company was actually established. Somehow it got sent on an e-mail, which was passed from person to person until the image became an underground cult icon. Eventually, it showed up on "Ally McBeal," and

---

3. Bernd H. Schmitt, *Experimental Marketing* (New York: The Free Press, 1999), p. 92.

The Jester is a promising archetype to provide identity for brands

- whose use helps people belong or feel that they belong
- whose function helps people have a good time
- with pricing that is moderate to low
- produced and/or sold by a company with a fun-loving, freewheeling organizational culture
- that need to be differentiated from a self-important, overconfident established brand

the company was launched.[4] If the firm had been able to control the use of this trademarked image, it would have undermined its own success.

Most of all, the Jester simply loves the fun of marketing. This archetype is not frightened by knowing we are in a new time. Rather, it helps us actually enjoy facing a new situation every day. In the process, the Jester helps keep advertising fresh enough to focus the attention of customers, so that their eyes do not glaze over—at least not when they see *your* ad.

4. Agnieszka M. Winkler, *Warp Speed Branding: The Impact of Technology on Marketing* (New York: John Wiley and Sons, 1999), p. 61.

Providing Structure to the World

Caregiver, Creator, Ruler

IN MEDIEVAL TIMES, walls were built around villages and moats around castles in an attempt to maintain order and to protect against marauding Vikings, Visigoths, and Vandals. Later, early American settlers cleared the land immediately around their cabins so that invading animals or Indians could be more easily seen. Today, the threats to one's well-being may be less immediate or dramatic, but people still create lawns and build walls as expressions of the same desire for security and order.

Anthropologist Angeles Arrien sees people with a strong stability orientation drawn to physical shapes that are square, arguing that even physical shapes have an archetypal quality to them. So perhaps it is not surprising that so many people in their family-formation years wish for or purchase "center hall colonials"—square buildings

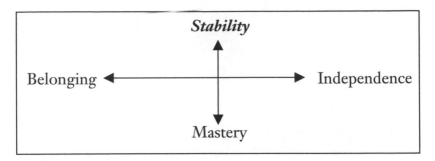

Figure 5.1

with square, symmetrically arranged layouts. And, of course, their car of choice is the squarish, safe Volvo.

Individuals generally relate to these desires from the archetypal stances of the Caregiver, the Creator, and the Ruler. The Caregiver has a heightened awareness of human vulnerability, but is less focused on concern for him- or herself and more preoccupied with alleviating other people's problems. (This is why a 12-year-old may feel more confident baby-sitting than staying home alone.)

The Creator exerts control by creating a poem, a musical composition, a painting, or a product. Consider the film *Shakespeare in Love*. Shakespeare is feeling powerless. His career is not going well. He is in love with a woman who has to marry another. So he has a wonderful love affair with her and then takes his feelings and channels them into the writing of *Romeo and Juliet*. The act of structuring experience into artistic form gives a sense of control and also offers the world great beauty.

The Ruler takes control of situations, especially when they seem to be getting out of hand. It is the Ruler's job to take responsibility for making life as predictable and stable as possible. (The Ruler's very affect communicates, "I have everything under control.") Sizing up the human situation as inherently unstable, Rulers put procedures, policies, customs, and habits in place that reinforce order and predictability. The film *Elizabeth* (a fictionalized version of the life of Queen Elizabeth the First) shows the process by which a young, idealistic woman becomes queen, essentially failing in her role until she learns to embody the Ruler archetype.

The Caregiver, Creator, and Ruler find satisfaction in environ-

The ancient forest was seen as a place of chaos, uncer-tainty, and sexuality. The modern-day lawn or garden, on the other hand, reflects a powerful fear of these forces and a corresponding desire for control, stability, and safety.

ments that seem stable: Old Town anywhere; large, substantial buildings; sturdy cars and appliances; cultivated gardens and parks (rather than "untamed" nature); comfortable and well-made furnishings; anything they themselves have designed, and technology that enhances the control they have over their environment. Together, they help make a profitable business. The Caregiver anticipates people's needs, seeing what will make them feel secure, safe, and nurtured; the Creator takes charge of innovating—new products, new manufacturing processes, new organizational and marketing structures and approaches; the Ruler then manages these new structures, seeing to it that quality is consistently delivered.

Today, the desire for stability and control meets with special challenges as the pace of contemporary living forces each of us to deal with new situations daily if not hourly. CEOs recognize that even though they do all the right things one year, market, economic, and legal conditions will change the next year, and the business needs to be restructured and rethought. Mergers and acquisitions now routinely pull the rug out from under workers' feet, forcing them to reconsider their livelihood and sometimes to seek training in entirely new fields. Funding for culture and the arts is abundant one year and missing the next.

Because of the uncertainty of life in general, and contemporary life in particular, the Creator, the Caregiver, and the Ruler are especially useful archetypes for today's brands. When they are not clouded in wistful nostalgia, but are interpreted in a contemporary and relevant context, they instruct us on how to preserve order and stability and how to reconcile our desires for consistency with change.

13

The Caregiver

Motto: "Love your neighbor as yourself."

T HE CAREGIVER IS AN ALTRUIST, moved by compassion, generosity, and a desire to help others. You can think of Marcus Welby, Florence Nightingale, Princess Diana, Mother Teresa, Albert Schweitzer, Bob Hope entertaining the troops, or any caring mother or father. The Caregiver fears instability and difficulty not so much for him- or herself, but for their impact on people who are less fortunate or resilient. Meaning in life, therefore, comes from giving to others. In fact, the worst fear is that something will happen to a loved one—and on the Caregiver's watch. In *Life Is Beautiful*, the father is so motivated by love for his son that it seems almost immaterial that he himself is killed, as long as the child is saved. The archetype is also related to images of God as the loving father who cares for His children.

Predictable caregiving images are associated with the nurse, the old-fashioned country doctor, the neighborhood cop, teachers, and the like. But the true nature of the Caregiver, and of our relationship to the archetype, is deep and complex, as complicated as our own relationships with the original Caregivers in our lives.

Throughout time, symbols of caregiving, expressed mostly as a powerful maternal figure, have been alternatively sentimentalized and demonized. In an article in *Newsweek*, Anna Quindlen points out

> ## The Caregiver
>
> **Desire:** protect people from harm
> **Goal:** to help others
> **Fear:** selfishness, ingratitude
> **Strategy:** do things for others
> **Trap:** martyrdom of self, entrapment of others
> **Gift:** compassion, generosity

that Mrs. Copperfield and Marmee in *Little Women* are elevated as paragons of virtue, while Mother in *Sons and Lovers*, Mrs. Bennet of *Pride and Prejudice*, and the comical Mrs. Portnoy are all treated harshly by their creators. Bruno Bettelheim describes how in children's legends and fairy tales, the maternal figure is often split into two opposites: the entirely wicked witch or stepmother and the perfectly pure good witch or fairy godmother. It is difficult, it would seem, for us to integrate the complexity of the Caregiver into a coherent whole.

In prehistoric times, people carved little figurines of mother goddesses who, then as now, must have been revered for the power to give birth as well as the capacity to support life through providing food, comfort, and nurturance. Throughout history, the Caregiver as an archetype has been associated with both maternal and paternal feelings of protectiveness toward children and the attendant willingness to do what is necessary to take care of them, even if doing so requires considerable sacrifice—but also, with the darker fears of exerting excessive power and of being controlled.

> The Caregiver also may be known as the caretaker, altruist, saint, parent, helper, or supporter.

One classic Greek myth evoking both the loving and the destructive power of the Caregiver—a myth that formed the basis for a religious cult that lasted thousands of years—recounts the great love of the grain goddess Demeter for her daughter Kore. When Hades, the lord of the underworld, abducts Kore, Demeter is so distraught that she wanders the world over, searching for her daughter and unable to sleep or eat. When she discovers what has happened to Kore, she refuses to allow any of the crops to grow, threatening humankind with massive starvation, which is alleviated only when her daughter is returned. In this story, Kore goes underground every year. We have winter because of her mother's grief when Kore is gone.

Commenting about the desire to sometimes demonize the role of the Caregiver (in this case, the maternal role) as a technique for trying to break free of its power, Anna Quindlen, writing for *Newsweek*, says, "Fat chance, Freudians. Whether querulous or imperious, attentive or overbearing, warm or waspish, surcease or succubus, she is as central as the sun."

Understanding the complexity of the Caregiver and our relationship to it is essential to tapping into the full depth and dimension of the archetype in brand communication. It is also critical to making the archetype useful to contemporary consumers who more than understand that caregiving is a complex affair—fraught with conflict, sacrifice, and the difficult desire to support, rather than suffocate. As Quindlen puts it:

> *Motherhood [and, we would add, most forms of caregiving] consists largely of transcendent scut work, which seems contradictory, which is exactly right. How can you love so much someone who drives you so crazy and makes such constant demands? How can you devote yourself to a vocation in which you are certain to be made peripheral, if not redundant? How can we joyfully embrace the notion that we have ceased to be the center of our own universe?**

In our work on "Sesame Street," it has been helpful for us to constantly keep in mind the natural human tension between mothering and smothering. The metaphor that has proven useful is considering the parent who cries in alarm, "Don't climb that tree! You could get hurt!" compared with the one who says, "Now if you're going to climb that tree, think about it. While you're going up, make a plan for how you're going to get down." The distinction has helped everyone from sales and merchandising people to the show's creators to remember that "Sesame Street" is a decidedly mothering brand. While other shows for preschoolers sugarcoat reality, "Sesame

---

*Anna Quindlen, "A New Roof on an Old House," *Newsweek*, Vol. 135, Issue 23, June 5, 2000, p. 84.

Street" deals honestly with issues such as loss, racial and cultural differences, anger, and so on, but in a totally constructive, age-appropriate way.

A recent campaign for Blue Cross/Blue Shield successfully navigates the same terrain and at the same time provides a contemporary guidepost for parents. A strong and confident mom holds her nine-or-so-year-old daughter, with the accompanying text:

> I check "worry" at the border.
> For I hold the pass that opens doors.
> Wherever we go,
> With our Blue Cross and Blue Shield Plan,
> we're covered.
> My only concern?
> Keeping this vacation forever in memory.
> This is my plan,
> To take care of . . .
> Their mind. Their body. Their spirit. Their health.

Another very contemporary Caregiver campaign which acknowledges that caregiving is a complex task shows a girl of about the same age leaning on her mother's arm, on which the following words are written: "stay involved in my life." The copy goes on to talk about how it would be a lot easier if kids came with directions, but since they don't, we can only hope to laugh with them, sing with them, teach them a joke, listen, and talk. The ad ends with the line, "Parents: the antidrug."

AT&T, a great Caregiver brand, was once famous for wonderful commercials about caring and connecting. Among the most celebrated was a spot titled "Joey Called," in which a sad and somewhat lonely day is made perfect for an aging mother and father because their son, Joey, calls them from abroad. While touching and highly effective, the "Reach Out and Touch" advertising almost welcomed a competitor to parody it. One such MCI ad showed a woman crying and being comforted by her husband—not because she was touched by her son's call, but because she was distressed by how much it cost. Over time, though, MCI realized that an identity based purely on price would impede it from being a true leader in its category. The company cleverly picked up a Caregiver identity by positioning its next big price offer within the context of a program called "MCI Friends and Family." All the people you care about and who care for you could sign onto the plan, and you would all get a discount. The advertising making this offer was warm and emotional, and AT&T was totally blindsided. Not only had its arch competitor usurped the caregiving essence of long-distance calling, but it did it in a more contemporary way—not purely sentimental and wistful, but practical, immediate, and celebratory.

In another contemporary vein, Caregiver brands and campaigns that celebrate the nurturing capacity of men, in spite of the many pressures they face to the contrary, are more than touching; they are powerful social validations of most men's own best intentions. For example, in a Land's End catalogue photo, a man dressed in business casual is in the classic Caregiver posture, slightly bent over his child. (The implied message is, "You are safe with me.") He is going upstairs with his little girl. His hand is on her back reassuringly. The explanatory message says, "Business casual. For when your second most important meeting is with your CEO."

These brands that reconcile the caregiving instinct with a world that often devalues it are not just effective in the marketplace; they play a constructive role in the evolution of our culture.

A World of Caregiving

While more complex or contemporary expressions of the Caregiver instinct help today's consumers reconcile their desire to be generous and caring with regard to their own external conflicts or the pressures of modern life, sometimes a brand can succeed by speaking to the however-impractical wish for a more perfect, caring world.

Campbell's soup is truly iconic, consistently invoking the nurturance of home, family, and mother's love, often in a way that triggers nostalgia. In fact, the company's positioning never waivers. As a result, families stock Campbell's soup in their cupboards (whether or not they actually eat it very often). Visually, the ads look like Norman Rockwell paintings. Sentimental music plays in the background, and parents consistently show children love and affection. In one famous ad, a little boy, proudly bringing his mother a potted flower, drops the pot. She sits him down with a cup of soup and repots the flower in a mug next to him. The music in the background emphasizes happy memories of childhood created by the little loving things mothers do.

In 1998, the campaign was updated with a "Good for the Body, Good for the Soul" theme. In a pivotal ad, a little child arrives at her foster home for the first time and is overwhelmed and shy. When the foster mother brings her a bowl of soup, she is comforted and says, "My mommy used to fix me this soup." The mother bonds with her, replying, "My mother used to make it for me, too."[1]

Stouffer's positions itself similarly with the tag line "Nothing comes closer to home." A typical ad shows a family sitting at a table, chatting warmly. The littlest boy is on his dad's lap, and the mother is looking lovingly at the teenage daughter. The text reassures mom that Stouffer's tastes "just like homemade." Midwest Express Airlines, which pampers its customers with extra-roomy seats and lots of attention, also actually delivers an experience that triggers the nostalgic connection with home and mother, one that may be particularly important for people who are phobic about flying. Someone must have looked for an inexpensive way to make people feel cared about. The answer he or she lit upon was chocolate chip cookies. Partway through the flight, you begin to smell them cooking. Then the flight attendants come around with baskets of them, helping passengers to feel like happy kids, just home from school, with mothers who greet them with cookies.

Many people today identify caregiving relationships as providing experiences so real that, in contrast to more shallow pursuits, they are what make life worth living. A lovely cosmetics ad from Eckerd.com shows a happy little girl running through the grass, with lipstick in the form of a kiss on her cheek. The ad continues, "I vow to spend less time looking for ruby red lipstick and more time leaving it behind." The copy continues with this promise: "You'll find just what you need quick and easy—so you can get back to something more important . . . like living."

Often, Caregivers take much better care of others than they do

---

1. Bernice Kanner, *The 100 Best TV Commercials . . . and Why They Worked* (New York: Times Business, 1999), p. 196.

of themselves. Sunsweet sells pitted prunes with the picture of a healthy-looking adult woman and the message "To your health . . . and happiness." It goes on: "Get in shape with a personal trainer, learn to cook healthier, rejuvenate at a spa resort, take off on a photo adventure, or attend a professional driving school." Lincoln Financial Group shows a picture of a man happily fishing in the ocean, overlaid with these words: "I've been devoted to my business. I've been devoted to my clients. And I've been devoted to my shareholders. Now all I want is to devote a little more time searching for bonefish." Clearly, this man is saying that he has given a lot, and now it is his turn.

Perhaps the most elegant and understated message today regarding self-care is being proclaimed by Concord Watch. The simple words "be late" overlay an uncluttered image of an adult's arm rubbing up against a child's or a photo of a woman serenely sleeping in her bed. Brands that care for the Caregiver do well, as they also provide a wonderful service to the world.

Levels of the Caregiver

Call: seeing someone in need
Level One: caring for and nurturing one's dependents
Level Two: balancing self-care with care for others
Level Three: altruism, concern for the larger world
Shadow: martyrdom, enabling, guilt-tripping

Natural Caregiver Categories

The concern of Caregivers for their children and other dependents makes this brand identity a natural consideration for medical care, health products, insurance, banks, and financial planning—so much so that it can lead to undifferentiated identities. Within the field of banking alone, for example, the following all have Caregiver identities: Sallie Mae, BankOne, Fleet, First Union, and Bank of America. Many ad campaigns speak to the responsibility people feel for their families and their fears of not being able to care for them properly. HealthExtras insurance ran an ad with a picture of Christopher Reeves and the copy, "You could lose everything you've worked your entire career for. EVERYTHING." The ad then goes on to say, "I've seen too many families destroyed, not from the disability, but the financial drain. Please, protect yourself. Protect your family . . . with HealthExtras."

A very touching ad run by Bayer for a home blood test (which uses just a tiny drop of blood) for people with diabetes shows a vulnerable-looking little blonde girl. The copy dares the reader to "Ask this diabetes patient to give even more blood for yet another test. Go ahead, ask her." Of course, who could respond to this ad without wanting to make life a little more comfortable for the girl?

The Caregiver's fear includes a concern about neglecting those you love. Zomig painkillers shows a woman in bed, with her little boy standing by her side, looking sad and bored, holding a baseball and mitt, and saying, "Mama has another migraine." Clearly, the mother is motivated to buy the product not to free herself from her own pain, but to make certain that she is a good mom and does not neglect her child. A less distressing ad for Health Source Soy Protein Shake shows a toddler with big brown eyes and says, "Just one little reason to take care of your heart."

An ad for Merrill Lynch shows a picture of a cute little girl, daughter of mezzo-soprano Vicky Hart and conductor Valery Ryvkin. Vicky is quoted as saying,

> The arts is [sic] not the most stable career; then, when you have a child, the uncertainty really hits home. But little by little, Leila [their financial consultant] taught us how to balance this sometimes-precarious life in the arts with the need for long-term financial well-being. She took the time to find out who we are . . . what's important to us. . . . we couldn't be doing this if we thought we were compromising Amanda's future.

Right in the middle of the page, in large letters, the key words tell us, "Amanda's needs are not negotiable."

Nuveen Investments also appeals to parents' love for their children. One ad shows a sweet and bright-looking boy with height marks on the wall, marking his growth. The copy reads,

These are the height marks of the little boy
that keep track of his lifetime growth
which should be matched by lifelong investments
which are the hallmark of our Rittenhouse customized managed
  accounts
which means your adviser can help you
manage the wealth of a lifetime
which will fund the education of the little boy
who could reach heights no one can mark.

Often, Caregivers do not just worry about their children. They worry about their parents, about anyone sick, about people in poverty, and about their pets. An ad for Revolution dog medicine shows a young woman hugging her big dog and promising, "I will throw a ball for you every day, take you on long walks, protect you from heartworm and fleas." The ad continues, "Of all the promises you make to your pet, none is more important than protecting him from harm."

Children also worry about their parents—about disappointing them, about seeming to reject them by being different, or even by surpassing them in some way. An ad for Rogaine baldness treatment shows a young man with his father in the background. The copy says, "Your dad wants you to have things he never had. Like hair." The father reassures the son that parents are fulfilled by their children standing on their shoulders and having more than they have had—education, money, opportunities—even hair!

At their worst, these brands skim the surface of the Caregiver stereotype. At their best, they convey the essential qualities of the caregiving relationship:

- Empathy—seeing and feeling things from another's perspective, not just our own
- Communication—listening—to what they say, what they don't say, and especially, what they mean
- Consistency—wholesale, reliable, unquestioning commitment
- Trust—the bedrock of true attachment.

Great mini-stories within ads can feature any of these elements of attachment and still trigger archetypal recognition.

Instrumental and Societal Care

Much of care, however, is not at all about direct, empathic nurturance, but rather, is instrumental. In *Defending the Caveman*, comic Dave Becker has a great skit about a couple visiting another couple who are going to have a baby. The two women talk very intimately about the baby and their feelings. The two men work quietly together, making a playhouse in the backyard. The women's typical response is to think that the men are out of touch with their feelings. After all, the women seem to be really connecting, while the men are just playing with power tools. Becker reminds the audience in a poignant moment that that young father-to-be must have a great deal of love in him to be building a playhouse for a child who is not even born yet.

The concept of the Caregiver as protector is evident in a commercial that helped launch Volvo's reputation for safety and made it possible for the brand to have an identity so strong that it could translate from the company's economy car to its compact, to its full-size sedan and finally, to a real luxury car. The ad began with a worried father and mother on a stormy night, pacing around the living room. Their daughter is supposed to be going out on a date in horrible weather, and she really wants to go. The date shows up, the parents let him in, and Dad says, "Jeff, do me a favor, will you? Take my Volvo." What a dad! What a car![2]

Of course, much of parents' caregiving is instrumental—cooking, cleaning, driving kids to lessons, doing all the things which create an environment that is nurturing and safe for children. Whether couples have traditional or nontraditional sex roles, ideally, both men and women bond with children, and both also do a lot of just plain work that is the result of a caring intentions. Products that help them with this work are naturals for a Caregiver identity.

The Caregiver archetype is present in all the jobs related to taking care of people and the physical world—gardening; cleaning

2. Kanner, p. 204.

clothes, homes, offices, and streets; mending clothes, bridges, or anything at all that is broken; caring for the sick and the elderly; chauffeuring; etc. At New York's Yankee Stadium during the seventh-inning stretch, the maintenance crew comes out to sweep the field, Surprisingly, the guys perform a synchronized "dance" to the song "YMCA," and the crowd goes wild—one of the few times such humble Caregiver work is publicly celebrated. Typically, Caregiver employment is not well paid, as it is expected that caring for others is its own reward.

Businesses, however, can become enormously successful doing maintenance functions for people—like picking up the trash. H. Wayne Huizenga made a veritable fortune setting up a waste collection service. At 25, he began hauling garbage himself in the morning, after which he showered and put on a suit to go out and sell his services. From Southern Sanitation Service, his first company, he eventually built Waste Management, the largest garbage removal company in the United States. From there, he leveraged his money into other industries, becoming one of the wealthiest men in America and thereby demonstrating how a willingness to fill a humble need can lead to great things.[3]

General Electric (GE) has consistently tied the value of its products to their utility in improving life in the home. GE was a spin-off from Thomas Edison's research lab. Edison's vision was to invent products that improved the quality of life on farms, in households, and in factories at the rate of one every 12 days. The GE name and logo were intended to look like the "initials of a friend," and the tag line "living better electronically" underscored the helping-people theme. In 1955, GE ran a commercial showing Ronald and Nancy Reagan happily using modern appliances. By the 1960s, the company had diversified to the point that it was building jet planes and medical equipment, as well as offering financial services way beyond the financing of appliances. At that time, a new tag line was needed, because not everything the firm did was related to electricity. So the new catch phrase became "Better living through technology." Finally, in 1979, a marketing study revealed that the public associated GE

3. Thaddeus Wawro, *Radicals and Visionaries* (Irvine, CA: Entrepreneur Press, 2000), pp. 215–217.

with men in hard hats. To soften the company's image, the tag line was altered once more, to "GE—we bring good things to life."

While GE has thrived, in part, by its commitment to research, innovation, and expansion, its Caregiver brand identity has consistently tied the brand less to innovation than to helping people. This focus on the benefits of the company's products provides an image that it cares about its customers. GE's history has further tied the whole concept of progress to helping people, thus connecting the concept of technological progress with positive qualities—such as home, family, care, love, and wholesome enjoyment.

We often think of care as important only for children, the elderly, the sick, and the poor. But the truth of the matter is that our entire well-being is also dependent on a kind of continuous, behind-the-scenes caregiving that has become all but invisible in contemporary life. Mothers and fathers take care of their children and loved ones. People take in friends and relatives in trouble. Social services help the poor. Teachers, principals, and bus drivers care for kids. All the sanitation people, repair people, taxi drivers, waiters, and cleaners—all of these people take care of the details that enable everyday life to function. Similarly, the people who staff the 911 numbers 24 hours a day, the ambulance drivers, the hospital orderlies, and the doctors on call, all have caregiving functions.

Not so long ago in American life, little kids viewed neighborhood cops as friendly protectors (not pigs), Bob Hope was bringing holiday cheer and "Silent Night" to faraway American soldiers who "sacrificed their Christmas to keep us at home safe," and TV doctors were represented as dedicated father figures (e.g., Marcus Welby), as opposed to misguided thirtysomethings confused and conflicted about how much they should care. Mothers were portrayed somewhat stereotypically, but with honor for their homemaking role. On a community level, people viewed their institutions as providers of care. Generally speaking, they believed that the school cared for their children, the church or temple cared for their souls, and the bank cared for their money. Ironically, today, with homeless people lining our streets and children and elders suffering neglect, the image of the Caregiver has become less celebrated, more thankless. And it is possible that the low status accompanying the Caregiver is in part responsible for how alone people in need often are.

Yet a whole new industry of virtual Caregivers has arisen. An example featured by the *New York Times* is a nonprofit Internet 800 number that answers parents' day-to-day questions, including: "How do I start potty training?" and "How do you control a two-year-old's biting and hitting?" Child-care experts respond on the spot and, in the case of serious problems, refer the parents to others who can help them. Not surprisingly, contemporary parents, often bereft of the grandmothers, older sisters, and aunts who used to counsel them, are using the service in droves. In addition, caregiving activities— like child care, elder care, doing laundry, and food preparation—that used to be handled in the home as unpaid activities have now entered the paid economy, providing a whole array of services and products that are naturals for a Caregiver brand identity.

While caregiving has lost status generally, if you think of the high regard placed on figures such as Ronald Reagan, Walter Cronkite, Princess Di, and Mother Teresa, you can readily see that the Caregiver still holds a relatively high place in people's hearts and minds. At the higher level, the Caregiver is not just concerned with his or her own family. That concern grows in concentric circles to encompass, in turn, the community, the nation, humanity, and the planet. One beautiful fact about mammals is that the old and infirm will sacrifice their lives for the young and fit. Humankind takes this one step further: The young and fit often will sacrifice themselves for the old and infirm. Furthermore, humans, as a species, are capable of concern for other species as well, even those very different from us.

The highest level of the Caregiver is the altruist, which is why the Caregiver can be a powerful brand identification for non-profit organizations. Habitat for Humanity, the Salvation Army, and the United Way are but a few examples. It is also encouraging that philanthropy is increasingly an expected part of corporate life, as is a high level of generosity and care directed at employees and customers.

Nordstrom and Marriott Corporation: Caregiver Organizations

When department stores are dropping like flies, why is Nordstrom expanding? It is successful partly because it has a superb reputation for customer service, including a no-questions-asked return policy. The company has even been known to accept returns that did not come from its store in the first place. Then, of course, it also has a reputation for selling shoes in odd sizes to fit real feet and for training employees to treat customers well. Nordstrom actually engenders an atmosphere in which acts of exemplary service become legends, passed around in the store and to customers. The firm even has a marketing budget for helping to create a buzz. The point is that Nordstrom's real marketing strategy is not its ads: It is acting in ways that cause customers to tell others about how well they were treated.

The habits of mind that characterize the Caregiver not only help with customer service, but also help companies anticipate customer needs and preferences. Caregivers like to do nice things for others. Their desire to anticipate customer needs and to accommodate them is not simply about good business; it defines their basic motivation in working. J. Willard Marriott was a Mormon, trained, as Mormons tend to be, to care for others in the community. In addition, he was born to a poor sheepherder and helped tend the sheep from the age of 8. What a wonderful training that must have been for industries in which tending the customer is the first order of business! At 19, he traveled to Washington, DC to preach the gospel (his required Mormon missionary year). In Washington, he suffered with the heat and imagined how much money someone would make who could provide a cool drink to sell there. During his senior year at the University of Utah, an A&W Root Beer stand opened nearby, and Marriott loved it. After college, he bought the Washington-area A&W franchise. When business flagged in the winter, he opened his first Hot Shoppe, innovating to provide drive-in service.

Like any good Caregiver, Marriott was always attuned to anticipating people's needs. He noticed that people would pick up food from his Hot Shoppe on the way to the airport. So Marriott negotiated to pre-box meals and sell them to the airlines, initiating the in-flight catering industry. After 30 years in the food business, he opened his first hotel, which he described as "the logical extension of Hot Shoppes' traditional concern for the American family on wheels." Over time, he acquired Big Boy restaurants, developed Roy Rogers fast-food outlets and Sun Line Cruise Ships, and offered food services for many colleges and universities, as well as three Great America theme parks. By 1999, Marriott International was the second-largest hotel chain in the world. Throughout all of this business activity, Marriott's success was always attributed to recognizing people's needs, providing good customer service, paying exemplary attention to detail, and treating employees well. Marriott advised other business leaders to "take care of your people and they will take care of your customers."[4]

Many Caregiver organizations are non-profit cause- or charity-related enterprises. The bottom line is helping the client group. Typically, management assumes that employees will do whatever it takes to meet client needs, often leading to burnout and, over time, demoralization and disengagement. In healthy Caregiver organizations, employees as well as clients are taken care of, so they are able to keep their enthusiasm for the work. As with hospitals, often the organization is highly bureaucratic, in part because people want to be certain that no harm is done. Therefore, policies and procedures need to be clear, new policies must be well studied over time, and staff must be well educated or well trained. Because the client group either is, or is envisioned as being, vulnerable, every effort is made to provide an atmosphere that seems solid, stable, and without undue surprises. Care is demonstrated not only by a warm smile or a touch of the hand, but also by a commitment to high standards of quality in every interaction. For the Caregiver, it is much more important to show you care by tangible actions than it is to mouth empty words. Put another way, it is not so much about saying you love the customer as about bringing him or her a warm blanket or a cup of tea.

Aetna U.S. Healthcare says, "Lots of companies have a mission statement. How many have a mission? Our mission? Create better ways to reach out and help make sure people get the health care they need." After identifying many of its initiatives, Aetna concludes, "Simply said, we're putting our money firmly where our mission is."

Marketing to Caregivers

As you might imagine, one of the least effective ways to market to Caregivers is to tell them straight out that you care. Doing so in the modern cynical world just raises the response "Tell me another one."

---

4. Thaddeus Wawro, *Radicals and Visionaries: Entrepreneurs Who Revolutionized the 20th Century* (Irvine, CA: Entrepreneur Press, 2000), pp. 292–293.

But if you *show* people you care, that is another thing entirely. If you do so, they will spread the word. Jonathan Bond and Richard Kirshenbaum, in *Under the Radar*, share a story about a nameless Palm Beach jewelry store. A client calls to ask about a brooch. A salesperson hops on a plane and delivers it to her personally, just in time for her to wear it to a charity ball that night. For one plane ticket, the jewelry store developed a wonderful reputation with every person at the function—and they were all very rich. Perhaps in a less dramatic way, but a consistent one nonetheless, places such as L.L. Bean and Nordstrom have built their reputations by offering customer service that is so unusually friendly that people spread the word about it.

A long-term issue for people today is how to balance concern for oneself with concern for others. In our society, parents often invest heavily in their children's education at the same time that they are paying for their parents' care and at the same time that they should be putting money away for their own retirement. They have a similar concern about time and health—that is, how to find time to care for others and still have a life and good health habits themselves. Addressing these concerns can provide a great brand identity for enterprising companies.

As you can see from many of the ads quoted thus far in this chapter, effective marketing to the Caregiver stresses not the brand's caring, but the customer's concern for others. The customer is portrayed as being someone who cares about other people. The product or service helps the customer be more effective in caring and also offers greater ease in doing so.

Responsible people who exert a lot of their energy caring for others often really appreciate companies that care for them. Such people often have a nurturance gap: They are giving more than they are getting, and they need support. Any company that helps people care for themselves or that helps them meet their obligations with greater ease has the potential to be extremely successful in a society where both women and men are carrying caregiving responsibilities over and above their work obligations.

Rolf Jensen, in *The Dream Society*, quotes *Time* magazine, which in 1997 declared that although for decades it was cool to be cool, suddenly it wasn't anymore. These days, there is a passion to show that you care. If you go to commencement ceremonies today, even prestigious graduate schools, you will see both male and female students carrying their infants and small children across the stage when they go up to receive their diplomas. Men and women are making time for their families a major factor in choosing jobs and in negotiating salaries and other conditions of work. We have just come through a time when the literature about codependence and enabling behaviors suggested that the Caregiver may be primarily dysfunctional. At the same time, the need for care was spiraling. Dual-career couples and single mothers were expected to perform as long and as hard at work as if they had no other responsibilities. Homeless individuals were beginning to line our streets. And people were complaining of feeling like strangers in a strange land, wishing for home. But, of course, the archetype of the Caregiver is fundamental to the human species. People do care about one another, and a strong sense of meaning comes from that care. You could then imagine that the Caregiver archetype would make a quick comeback. It is, once again, cool to care.

The style of that caring, however, has changed. The success of a movie such as *Mrs. Doubtfire*, and of men who transcend traditional masculine and feminine roles (like Michael Jackson, Robin Williams, and Colin Powell), tells us that, although caring was once seen as a primarily feminine pursuit, it is now generally acknowledged as important to men as well. (Of course, it always was, as anyone who had a loving father or grandfather knows.) The similar success of films like *The First Wives Club* tells us that Caregivers today do not want to be pushovers. They are willing to be tough if they have to be. They expect to be respected, and they get angry if they are slighted. The old martyr is gone, and in its place is a more balanced aspiration: giving with receiving, and caring with being cared for.

Remember *It's a Wonderful Life*? The Jimmy Stewart character sacrifices for others all his life and then despairs when it seemed that he would lose everything. This is a classic Caregiver story. As a culture, we have just turned the corner from becoming cynical about caring. What people want is reinforcement that if they care, others will care for them. In the film, the contributions come in, and George Bailey's building and loan association is saved. The emotion expressed at the death of Princess Di and, to a somewhat lesser extent, Mother Teresa tells us that this archetype is powerfully present in the human psyche today. However, since Watergate and Vietnam,

The Caregiver is a good identity for brands

- for which customer service provides the competitive advantage.
- that provide support to families (from fast food to minivans) or that are associated with nurturance (such as cookies).
- for services in the health care, education, and other caregiving fields (including politics).
- that help people stay connected with and care about one another.
- that help people care for themselves.
- for non-profit causes and charitable activities.

we have been living in a very cynical time. What Caregivers want to hear is that they are not losers if they care about others. Our guess is that brands which avoid portraying the Caregiver in stereotypical ways, but that reinforce Caregiver values, are well positioned to thrive. Any archetype that has been repressed always has energy. That energy can propel winning brands today, but only if the level of the archetypal expression is both androgynous and self-actualized.

Moreover, just as there has been a proliferation of services designed to help members of contemporary organizations work well together, the next frontier will be similar services to help families not only stay together, but develop the emotional ability to thrive in a community. Furthermore, community development activities are on the rise. We have moved out of a time when our group affinities are defined by our ethnic or racial identity. We now live in somewhat more integrated settings. Although there is also a counter–trend, people want to make a pluralistic society work, for the most part. Wise brands will understand that the Caregiver archetype is now being expressed not only in the family, but also in the world. In some ways, it seems to us that brands can count on people to be better than we have thought they were—and more capable of expanding the circle of care than had been thought. The Caregiver is always related to the Innocent, because it is usually the Caregiver who makes the Innocent's desire for a safe and beautiful world come true. It is a short step between the Innocent Coca-Cola brand singing, "I'd like to buy the world a Coke and keep it company" and the Caregiver reaching out to give some substance to that wish.

14

The Creator

Motto: "If it can be imagined, it can be created."

THE CREATOR ARCHETYPE is seen in the artist, the writer, the innovator, and the entrepreneur, as well as in any endeavor that taps into the human imagination. The Creator's passion is self-expression in material form. The artist paints a picture that reflects his soul. The entrepreneur does business her own way, often flying by the seat of her pants. The innovator in any field turns away from business as usual, tapping into his unique ability to imagine a different way. In the arts, you may think of Georgia O'Keeffe or Pablo Picasso; in film, you may remember *Amadeus* exploring the eccentricities, as well as the genius, of Mozart.

Creator brands are inherently nonconformist. The Creator is not about fitting in, but about self-expression. Authentic creation requires an unfettered mind and heart. Creator spaces include workshops, kitchens, gardens, social clubs, and workplaces—any place creative projects take place. Creator brands include Crayola, Martha Stewart, Williams-Sonoma, Sherwin-Williams, Singer, and Kinko's ("Express yourself"). They also include foods, such as taco kits, which have, as part of their attraction, an invitation to kids to create their own "personal" version of the taco, as well as quirky, iconoclastic brands like Fresh Samantha, which almost shout, "I'm imaginative and different."

The Creator
Desire: create something of enduring value
Goal: give form to a vision
Fear: having a mediocre vision or execution
Strategy: develop artistic control and skill
Task: create culture, express own vision
Trap: perfectionism, miscreation
Gift: creativity and imagination

When the Creator archetype is active in individuals, they often are compelled to create or innovate—anything else and they feel stifled. Authenticity will seem extremely essential to them, as great art and society-changing inventions typically emerge out of the depth of soul or unfettered curiosity of someone who, in many ways, is a cultural pioneer. Indeed, artists typically see themselves as such, creating the world of the future. They may be pessimistic about the culture at large, but they trust the creative process and believe in the power of imagination.

Generally, they express their creativity in artsy clothing, homes, and offices. Creators fear that their creations will be judged harshly by others. They often have a punishing inner critic and censor that says nothing is ever good enough. As a result, they also fear giving in to this voice and failing to express their gifts at all.

People who are high in the Creator archetype, moreover, think of themselves as desirous of freedom, which they are. In this way, they are like the Innocent, Explorer, and Sage. However, a deeper motivation is the need to exert aesthetic or artistic control—to be, in a way, like God, to create something that has never been there before. Ultimately, what the Creator desires is to form a work of art so special that it will endure. And, in this way, the Creator achieves a kind of immortality.

Employees frequently make jokes about how every new boss decides to reorganize, yet every Creator knows that structures determine outcomes. If you do not have the right structure, your vision will not be realized. Creative types love the process of dismantling old structures and creating new ones. That's what most consultants, especially those in the field of organizational development, most prefer to do. In marketing, the fun is coming up with something new—some innovative approach that will catch the public eye while it also expresses your own or your company's vision. In research and development, the Creator provides the impetus to develop new products and services.

At its best, the Creator archetype fosters real innovation and beauty. At its worst, it provides an excuse for irresponsibility and self-involvement. The Creator tends to be intolerant of shoddy, mass-produced merchandise

> The Creator may also be known as the artist, innovator, inventor, musician, writer, or dreamer.

and the attendant lack of both imagination and attention to quality. Accordingly, purchases are a way that Creators demonstrate their taste and their values.

The part of each of us that is drawn to the Creator archetype finds out who we are by what we create around us. Whether or not we have any artistic talent, our homes, our offices, and our lifestyles mirror back to us some core of who we are. The Creator therefore consumes, not to impress—but to *ex*press. The Creator within us is also drawn to other people's artistry, so we enjoy not only art museums, but also consumer goods with excellent design.

Re-Creating Yourself

The fields of fitness, beauty, and education often present themselves as helping people to re-create themselves. EAS ("The Performance Nutrition Advantage") fitness bars and shakes ran a two-page ad. The first page shows Michelangelo's David, the second a handsome, contemporary man. The copy reads, "It took Michelangelo three years to sculpt a masterpiece. It took me only three short months (and I have better abs)." Nordstrom runs an ad for fitness clothes for women with a picture of a gorgeous woman, apparently nude and with attractive muscle definition. The copy says, "She always had a sense of inner strength. And now it showed." Nordstrom also ran a very simple, plainspoken ad for red high-heeled boots with the simple injunction, "Reinvent yourself."

Cosmetics can be marketed as the tools to help you become a work of art. M·A·C Make-Up Art Cosmetics shows an arty picture of a lipstick case going off like a rocket. The copy says,

Make up Your mind. What inspires? Over the past 12 months flaunt and M·A·C have created a portfolio of images depicting the works of some of the world's top photographers, stylists and makeup artists. Inspired by the colors, textures and the hip, self-expressive, non-conformity of M·A·C Cosmetics' own creative attitude, this portfolio allowed top talents unlimited scope to use the tools, textures and impressionistic possibilities of cosmetics in nontraditional and far-out ways. Look. Think about it. Are cosmetics more than just beauty aids? M·A·C says: Makeup your mind.

Levels of the Creator

Call: daydreams, fantasies, flashes of inspiration
Level One: being creative or innovative in imitative ways
Level Two: giving form to your own vision
Level Three: creating structures that influence culture and society
Shadow: overly dramatizing your life, living a soap opera

In a more down-home way, Color Me Beautiful offers consultations that help women and men determine what colors best suit them. The company promotes its line of cosmetics on its Web site, promising that "Beauty is always revealed . . . Never applied."

Gateway.com promises: "Bring out all your hidden talents. Whatever they may be." By using Gateway's computer equipment, you can "Nurture your inner _____." The firm offers the following as choices to fill in the blank: "Rock Star, Master Photographer; Blockbuster Director; Gaming Warrior." ISIM University of Denver, Colorado, says "eCreate yourself" by "earning your graduate degree online."

Mondera.com jewelry runs ads showing unconventional, creative women as so winning, that men want to buy them beautiful jewelry. One such ad pictures a woman laughing with a little girl, together with the words, "because she appreciates preschool finger painting more than postmodern sculpture," give her "fine jewelry as unique as she is."

Props for Beautifying Your Life

Artifacts from the most ancient times show that people are inherently artistic creatures: There are cave drawings, sculptures, baskets, elaborately painted bowls, totem poles, jewelry items, tattoos—the list is endless. Even the most basic tools were typically decorative as well. In indigenous societies, everyone is involved in art all the time. If we consider the history of craft, even in today's world most people have some creative outlet, whether they think of themselves as creative or not. People paint, sew, do woodworking, garden, decorate their homes, wear makeup, and generally beautify their surroundings.

Creator products help them with such tasks. The industrial revolution provided all sorts of technologies to help people create more easily. Elias Howe invented the first sewing machine in 1845. I. M. Singer then modified it so that it could be used in the home. He launched sales of the machine in 1851. They were still expensive for the average household, so he also invented the time payment plan. In the early 1920s, in India, Mahatma Gandhi exempted sewing machines from his sweeping ban on Western machinery, because they seemed so essential to self-reliance.

Sherwin-Williams was the first paint company to offer pre-mixed paint for do-it-yourselfers. Before that, professionals painted homes and mixed their own paint. Sherwin-Williams wisely supplemented paint sales with all sorts of how-to materials. Home Depot and all design, fabric, and craft stores cater to people showing creativity in their homes, dress, and gardens, as do magazines such as *Good Housekeeping* and *House Beautiful*.

Upscale furniture and carpets are particularly likely to be marketed with appeal to the Creator archetype. Lees, for example, shows a carpet that seems to emanate from a Greek temple with the face of an artistic-looking woman (who might be a Greek goddess). The copy reads, "Refined by architecture. Created by you." X Quest Wall Surfaces from Omnova (motto, "where 'what if' becomes what is") ran an ad showing a man in a top hat, up to his chest in what seems to be a lagoon. He is walking toward an intricately patterned square object, emerging from the water, that looks like it is either some ancient treasure or a relic from extraterrestrials. The ad then asks,

"Adrift in a sea of the mundane? Look to a new horizon. A wall covering range as vast as your imagination is within your grasp."

Many such ads connect home decoration with high art. Furniture manufacturer Dauphin shows two arty-looking chairs next to paintings of the chairs (like Andy Warhol's Campbell Soup painting), saying "Life Imitates Art." Donghia, maker of furniture, textiles, and wall coverings, shows a beautiful pile of different gorgeous fabrics topped with one ballet shoe. B&B Italia furniture ("Timeless and Treasured") shows two very classic, modern tables, saying, "The choice for quality, harmony and modern living." Bombay Sapphire Gin portrays a martini glass that is a work of art. In the martini are beautiful flowers. The caption says, "Pour something priceless."

The Creator at Work and at School

At work, the capacity for innovation is particularly valued, simply because we live in such competitive and fast-changing times. All fields are innovating all the time. At the same time, technological advances offer incredible resources for doing so. Homestead.com shows a picture of a potter's wet hands forming the lip of a vase. The potter reflects, "Of all your great creations, your Web site will be the easiest." Texas Instruments promotes digital signal processors with the words, "where voice meets video meets words meets your imagination" and a picture of an ecstatic woman at a keyboard.

The story of how Post-its were developed by mistake has become a modern legend about creativity. The secretaries figured out what to do with a glue that would not really stick, and the rest is history. An ad for Post-it Self-Sticking Easel Pads says, "Think of it as a Post-it Note on steroids." In smaller print, the copy goes on to say "You're in a meeting, capturing ideas on your easel pad. But then everything grinds to a halt as you search for tacks or tape. Unless you're using a Post-it Easel Pad." Its pages stick to the wall by themselves, with a strong adhesive. An ad for Canon Image Runner 600 challenges the consumer to "Imagine creating 200-page, three-hole-punch documents right from your desktop." And, of course, you now can. Kinko's sees itself as in the business of supporting customer creativity, with the motto "Express yourself." The implication is that it is Kinko's job to help you do so.

Palm Pilot got almost instant brand recognition marketing the device with pictures of artistic and successful people holding it. In these ads, the company was not just selling the Palm Pilot and what it could do; rather, they were selling the glamour of the artist's life. One such ad featured Catherine Hennes, textile designer. It read, [Icon for address book] "My favorite weavers and embroiderers; all my friends from art school." [Icon for date book] "Haute couture showings, Monday, 9:00am; lunch w/Max, Friday, 1:00pm." [Icon for memo pad] "Preliminary ideas for spring–summer patterns; novels I plan to read." [Icon for to-do list] "Meet with architects, re: new studio plans; plant bulbs before it rains." [Icon for HotSync] "Synchronize and back up my Palm Vx handheld with my PC. With just one touch." This approach provided an interesting, and highly differentiated, antidote to the more common Ruler imagery surrounding technology in general and business tools in particular.

How creative can we be? Want to make a Disney movie—by yourself? An ad that looks like a news note features Matt and Dan O'Donnell, twins who created a software program called Mexico, a package that helps create animation with great shading and facial details. Quoting Matt, the ad says, "The characters respond to stage direction. . . . You create a model, and you say, 'Snookie: walk to Captain,' and it will compute the subanimations."

Of course, we all want our children to be creative. Apple promotes iMac with an ad featuring its compatibility with a digital camcorder: "Now students and teachers can tell stories in ways they never could before—by making experiences outside of the class come to life vividly in class. Best of all, it's so easy; anyone can be a director." Crayola is a Creator-brand icon. One ad shows a box of crayons with a caption next to the sharpener that says, "Built-in Mind Sharpener." The explanatory copy continues: "Studies show that kids who grow up participating in the arts score higher on the SAT by an average of 51 points on verbal and 38 points on math. That's the power of creativity. . . . It starts here" (with a box of crayons). To encourage parents to provide coloring opportunities so that the brand delivers on its promise of creativity, ads frequently suggest different coloring activities—such as creating a Father's Day card cut out like an arm and a hand. The ad promises "A wild and wacky day for dad: an egg dish not made from eggs! Coffee made with yogurt?

A hug hidden in a card. We've got some surprising and crazy ways for you to say 'Happy Father's Day.' "

Kellogg's recognizes that making Rice Krispie Treats (by adding melted marshmallow and margarine) is one of the first things many children learn to cook. To reinforce the connection with creativity, Kellogg's offers recipe sculpturing contests for schools. The 1998 winning sculpture was "a six-foot wide by three-foot high replica of a coral reef and its related ecosystems . . . edging out sculptures from 65 other schools in more than 30 states."

"Sesame Street": A Creator Brand

Few television shows make it past their premier season. Not so for the much-acclaimed "Sesame Street," which is now entering its thirty-second year on the air and which has grown into one of the most widely recognized and respected brands in the world. In a much more competitive era than the one in which it was launched, it is still watched by millions of children around the world, and the show has garnered 76 Emmys (more than any other show in history!) and eight Grammys. How did this idea manage to sustain itself and thrive?

Much of its success lies in the fact that the show's powerful approach to learning and its carefully developed curriculum have taken life in a uniquely charming and innovative expression of the Creator.

Every episode of "Sesame Street" is based on a complex, holistic curriculum, designed to support young children's cognitive, social, emotional, and physical development, and expert educators and researchers work hand in hand each day with the writers and producers. Clearly, were it not for all of this educational research, it would be just another kiddy show. Yet at the same time, all of this high-minded educational expertise could have been translated into an uninspired lesson that preschoolers would wander away from to play with their dolls and toys. Instead, the concept of "Sesame Street" is presented in a wonderfully creative way: on a street where a key character lives in a garbage can, another inhales cookies like a vacuum cleaner, one of the stars is an eight-foot-tall bird, and there is an ongoing segment called "Monsterpiece Theater," among others. During a special series about space, the venerable Tony Bennett belted out "Slimey to the moon . . . ," and it is not surprising to see Itzak Perlman or another famous person cavorting with one of the Muppets. As Gail David, "Sesame Street's" Director of Corporate Communications, comments, "It's amazing that anything can be so grounded and yet so effervescent."

The creation of "Sesame Street" in and of itself is a wonderful example of the creative process and the birth of a Creator brand. Joan Ganz Cooney, one of "Sesame Street"'s founders, relates in a soon-to-be published essay that it was during a dinner party conversation in March of 1966 that the idea for "Sesame Street" was first raised. Cooney, then a documentary producer at WNET, a local educational television channel in New York City, was talking with Lloyd Morrisett, then a vice president at the Carnegie Corporation of New York. The two were so excited by the proposition of doing something about the great untapped potential of television as an educator that they met again some days later. Morrisett had long been interested in children's cognitive development. And as a father of two small children, he had been astonished once to find them watching the test patterns on television, waiting for the cartoons to come on— such was the dearth of engaging, quality programming for kids in those days. Ganz Cooney had been deeply concerned about poverty, civil rights, and the educational deficit that poverty created. The dinner-party conversation had had an electrifying effect on both participants. As Ganz Cooney now reminisces, "I just suddenly saw that I could do little documentaries on Channel 13 for the rest of my life and have no impact on those in need, or I could use television to help children, particularly disadvantaged children, learn. I saw it so clearly, it really was a kind of St. Paul on the highway." The two joined forces, armed with the conviction that television could be a positive force in children's lives, assuming that an educational curriculum could be delivered in a fresh and relevant way.[1]

It was the Sixties, the "Laugh-In" era, and a time of great creative license in terms of what was on the air, including advertising. Ganz Cooney had noticed that children, in particular, seemed to be mesmerized by the quick-cut, whacky formats of television commercials

1. Joan Ganz Cooney, in "The Top Fifty Women in American Radio and Television," in press.

and that they were learning the commercials' jingles faster than their ABCs. Not afraid to take advantage of the prevailing sensibility of the times, she wanted to direct it in a way that would benefit pre-schoolers. Describing the show's premise in *The New York Times*, she said, "Traditional educators might not be nuts about this, but we're going to clip along at a much faster pace than anyone's used to in children's programs. [Kids] like commercials and banana-peel humor and avant-garde video and audio techniques . . . . We have to infuse our content into forms children find accessible."

A kind of creative dream team was formed that ultimately included Jim Henson and his inimitable Muppets; Joe Raposo, a talented musician and composer; Jeff Moss, a brilliant young writer; Jon Stone, who would be the show's producer and director for more than 26 years; and a group of formidable researchers, including Gerry Lessor and Ed Palmer. But even beyond the sheer assemblage of talent, the concept was driven from the beginning by a quest for authenticity and innovation.

In "Sesame Street, Unpaved," a retrospective on the show, Jon Stone says that the creators "didn't want another clubhouse or treasure house or tree house . . . my proposal was that this should be a real inner city street, and we should populate it with real people."

A big part of the emergence of the Creator in this work was that the show was thought of as a grand experiment, as it continues to be. Children were among its original casting directors, so to speak. For example, the Muppets were first intended to be in entirely different segments than the ones using human characters, so that kids would not be confused; but when research showed that children were most involved when the Muppets were on the air, the Muppets were integrated into scenes with humans. Humor was not only encouraged, it was required. According to Arlene Sherman, supervising producer of "Sesame Street," pure comedy was always an essential ingredient of its creativity: "When people ask for a thumbnail sketch of what 'Sesame Street' is, I always say that it's a comedy show that teaches. We have the best comedy writers on TV working for us. That's why it works." Developers were encouraged, even expected, to take chances and to innovate.

The creators' willingness to be zany shows up in segments like the following: WASA (Worm Air and Space Agency) searches to find five physically fit, internationally-renowned worms to send to the moon (but only the worms with the "right squiggle"!), and a chicken who believes she is a worm sneaks on board the space vehicle; a farmer knows when a bad storm is coming, because his sheep dance the cha-cha beforehand; Big Bird hires the leading animal architectural firm, Pig, Pig & Pig, led by the world-renowned I. M. Pig, to advise him on reconstructing his nest. According to legend, Henson's and Stone's ideas were sometimes so far out that there were frequent struggles with the researchers, whose responsibility it was to keep the curriculum on track.

But a healthy tension between unbridled creativity and the educational work of "Sesame Street" is at the heart of the success of this Creator brand. Rosemarie Truglio, vice president for Sesame Street Research, describes a kind of friendly tug-of-war at each session to review scripts, with writers delighting in some hilarious new segment and researchers painstakingly pointing out adjustments that need to be made to ensure child safety, preclude negative modeling, build a foundation for learning, and so on. Yet, the collaboration is a happy and successful one, because, as Truglio says, "We have a mutual respect for each other's craft. I'm not a comedy writer, so sometimes the writers feel they need to teach me 'comedy 101.' But I'm not insulted; I respect their talent. On the other hand, I do know about children, so there are times I teach *them* child development 101. I hold the voice of the child."

The results work. Academic research has shown that as long as three years after their pre-school years, children who regularly watched "Sesame Street" and other children's educational programming performed better on a host of standard measures. A separate study showed that even in high school, children who had regularly watched educational programming had higher grade-point averages in English, science, and math, as compared with children who watched educational programming infrequently or not at all. These studies controlled for parents' education levels, income, and so forth.

Qualitative research illuminates some of the other positive byproducts of watching "Sesame Street." It seems that the show operates on many complex levels, even for preschoolers. A unique ideology comes through that viewers remember all of their lives. First-generation "Sesame Street" watchers—people who grew up on the original show—often recall that the first time they were exposed to people different from themselves was on "Sesame Street." For example, Sesame Street may have provided their first exposure to an African-American person (who might have been sporting a huge Afro to boot!). Or, it may have been through "Sesame Street" that they learned to count in Spanish, before they even understood the concept of "another language." Mothers and other caregivers who watch "Sesame Street" with their children often encounter a momentary reference to some contemporary event, offered in a way that delights preschooler and Mom (or other caregiver) alike. "Sesame Street" announces that "this show is brought to you by the number 3 and the letter Q," and suddenly, all seems right with the world.

Today, in its thrity-second season, the show is being developed to include an even greater emphasis on art and music—not so much as skills that are ends in and of themselves, but as vehicles that help children learn and cope. For example, in an upcoming series of episodes that will feature a hurricane coming to Sesame Street, Big Bird is distraught to learn that he has lost his nest in the storm. Other members of the community counsel him, which helps, but the real support comes when one of them suggests that if he misses his nest so much, he should draw a picture of it. Not only is his picture a comfort to him, but it also suggests a plan. If it can be drawn, it can be recreated, which teaches children not just how to cope, but also to begin to deal with adversity.

In today's complex world, in which the problems of adult life have begun to infiltrate the province of childhood, it is good that this wonderful Creator brand continues to provide such a rich and engaging way for preschoolers to learn and grow.

Creator Organizations

The prototype of the Creator organizational culture is an artist's collective. People want great latitude to express their creativity, with a minimum of controls. The function of the collective structure is to provide a place to promote, develop, and market an artistic product. Dignity comes from the collective agreement about the importance of the creative process, so that people avoid "selling out" to the marketplace. Generally, quality is regarded as more important over the long run than maximizing immediate sales. Underpricing is avoided because the employees would view it as denigrating the importance of their work.

Creator organizations are found in the arts, in design, in marketing, and in other fields requiring a high degree of imaginative and "out-of-the-box" thinking. A reasonable amount of worker autonomy is viewed as essential to the creative process, so employees often control their own time and the way they undertake a task. Styles of dress and modes of behavior can be flamboyant or simply unconventional, as employees express themselves rather freely in how they behave. Freedom reigns as long as the result is a high-quality product.

Many companies position themselves by stressing their creativity or by comparing their product to the quality you find in fine art, whether or not they exhibit traits of real Creator organizations. Saab, for example, ran an ad for its convertible that stated, in large letters, "Saab vs. Vivaldi," asking the customer,

> Can a car compete with a musical composition? The Four Seasons by Antonio Vivaldi is as good a test as you'll get. Concerto No. 1. Spring. The top comes down, a sense of freedom floods in. Summer arrives and calls the road to come play. The turbo engine proves more than its equal. Fast forward to Autumn. An aerodynamic body keeps the wind at bay. Winter comes on with a vengeance. Front-wheel drive responds. The triple-layer insulated top, heated front seats, and heated glass rear window all do their jobs. Vivaldi meets his match. Let the music play.

The Biltmore Estate, with its house, gardens, and winery, runs a picture of the mansion with the words, "From Canvas to Masterpiece. . . . Its Wonders Never Cease," explaining,

> He began with bare earth. With an artist's eye, he sculpted forests, parks, and farms. Then George Vanderbilt created a home for the ages: Biltmore House. From Renoir to Barye, Whistler to Duer, he filled this architectural wonder with the works of masters: paintings, sculpture,

*books, and furnishings shaping centuries of artistic endeavor. Celebrate.
. . . at Biltmore this summer as we unveil four newly restored guest
rooms, called the Artists' Suite.*

More modestly, Serta ("We make the world's best mattress") runs
an ad that shows a bare mattress in a lovely, ornate room by an open
window, featuring a sliver of a new moon. You see all this in a framed
mirror, so it appears that you are viewing a painting. At the bottom
of the page you read, "Somehow 'good night' seems like an under-
statement."

Movado positions its watches as art objects in part by promoting
the company's contributions to the arts. An ad features a ballerina
performing in the street, juxtaposed against a lovely watch and the
words "pushing the art form." The ad goes on to say, "For 60 years,
American Ballet Theatre has awed international audiences with the
most innovative choreographers, designers and dancers known in the
world of ballet. Movado Watch is proud of its decade-long role as a
principal Benefactor of ABT." The ad then links the firm's own artistry with the ballet: "Throughout its history, Movado has been recognized for its innovation: 99 patents; over 200 international awards;
watches in museums on five continents." The point that this is a
Creator archetype brand is driven home by larger letters at the end,
saying, "Movado watches are exhibited in the permanent collections
of museums worldwide."

The larger message of such ads is that Creator organizations want
not just to *appear* as a work of art, but to *embody* one. In the past, a
metaphor that inspired such companies was often the orchestra, with
each member of the organization following the conductor (CEO) to
harmonize most effectively with the other players. More recently,
the field of jazz improvisation has spoken to managers and organizational development professionals, offering a model for staying so
attuned to the music that leadership can be rotated as needed, with
people so connected to one another that they know when to take the
lead and when to follow. In a Creator organization, the bottom line
is not money as much as it is beauty. Overall, the experience of
working for the company and the quality of the product need to
satisfy the aesthetic sensibilities of the key players. Then all is well.

Marketing to the Creator

Who would have thought that an empire could be built on women's traditional creativity in the home just at the time when women were going back to work in droves? It appeared that women were turning their backs on making wonderfully creative centerpieces for dinner parties, decorating the house all over for Christmas, or making meals that take all day to cook. Yet, somehow Martha Stewart intuited that domestic creativity was alive and well. In fact, a great way to succeed is to catch the wave of an archetype that is being repressed, but whose flames are still alive. All you have to do is fan those flames, and you are in business. Martha Stewart caught that wave and became an industry. Not only does she teach women how to excel in the domestic arts, but she now has a whole line of products. The association with the Creator gives them an upscale feel, even though she has designed a whole line for K-Mart, thus improving that company's image.

The truth is that both men and women love brands that help them release the Creator within. This affinity has to do with how out of control the world seems. At the most obvious level, people know they need to be constantly inventing and innovating to keep up. At a deeper level, the process of creation requires the ability to focus and gives a sense of control. When you are creating something, you are generally completely engaged in doing so, and the process also allows you to form colors, or music, or data, or anything at all into a structure that gives you a sense of control and pleasure. The more out of control life becomes, the more people crave the outlet of creativity. A man loses his love and feels better after he crafts a sonnet about it. A woman is yelled at by her boss and comes home and sews a lovely dress. Doing so heals them. A teenager is not chosen for the team and goes home and creates an animated cartoon and feels so satisfied that he no longer cares about the team. Any kind of artistic endeavor satisfies the human desire for form and stability.

Art also fosters self-esteem. What people create is a mirror of who they are. As they look at the product they make, they feel good about themselves because they have made something worthwhile. Marketing that engages the customer in creating the product is smart

> A Creator identity may be right for your brand
>
> - if your product's function encourages self-expression, provides the customer with choices and options, helps foster innovation, or is artistic in design
> - in a creative field, like marketing, public relations, the arts, technological innovation (such as software development)
> - when you are seeking to differentiate it from a brand that "does it all" for the customer, leaving little room for choice
> - when a do-it-yourself element saves the customer money
> - if your customers have enough discretionary time for creativity to flourish
> - if your organization has a Creator culture.

business. Your customers are innovative experts, and you can often reach them with an e-mail. Read their responses and give them feedback when their ideas influence the mix.

The very speed with which brands need to establish an identity today is phenomenal. All components—design, manufacture, marketing—need to tap into their full creative potential. Agnieszka M. Winkler, in *Warp Speed Branding*, describes how, for most products today, marketing strategies are being thought through at the same time the product is being designed. The design, marketing, and production teams need to be in constant communication with one another. The creativity that is necessary in this new world makes hierarchy and elaborately planned meetings obsolete. The new, more collaborative business strategies require emotional intelligence, great communication skills, flex-time, real-time decision making by the players involved, and comfort with permanent ambiguity.[2]

Moreover, people in the field of marketing need to recognize that they are in the arts. We all know people in advertising, for example, who are always bemoaning the fact that they are not making great films. We think of playwrights and songwriters, authors and directors of films, and visual artists and others in the fine arts as, in a very real way, creating culture. Outside of religion, the arts exert the primary

2. Agnieszka M. Winkler, *Warp Speed Branding: The Impact of Technology on Marketing* (New York: John Wiley and Sons, 1999), pp. 93–95.

force that makes collective meaning in a society. However, today we need to recognize that commercial communication in its various guises has become an art form that profoundly influences our culture. People may never go to an art museum, a concert, or a play, or they may never read a great poem or novel, but everyone is exposed to marketing communication. The amount of care and quality that goes into ads today is staggering. They are crafted with great care and funded lavishly.

If you are willing to see advertising and other marketing communication as an art form, you will understand that nowadays marketing is a major influence on the society in which we live. Marketing with the Creator in mind requires us to rise to this occasion and to be as aware as we can of the impact of the images, symbols, and stories on the collective psyche. As with the fine arts, this awareness in no way requires Pollyanna images. The whole of life—positive and negative—can be reflected in art. What it does require is that we take responsibility for clarifying our own values, for understanding those related to products being promoted, and for expressing them in a compelling and artistic way that sells the product while it also ennobles society. Art has always done so. Ads can do so now. Recognizing this possibility dignifies the profession and the people in it, defining them as the reigning artists of our time.

CHAPTER

15

The Ruler

Motto: "Power isn't everything. It's the only thing."

WHEN YOU IMAGINE the Ruler archetype, think of the king, the queen, the corporate CEO, the president of a country, the super-efficient soccer mom—or anyone with a commanding, authoritative manner. To think of someone with power, imagine Winston Churchill, Margaret Thatcher, or any Supreme Court justice. Somewhere in between is the boss, the father, or the mother who acts like someone born to rule.

The Ruler knows that the best thing to do to avoid chaos is to take control. While Innocents assume that others will protect them, the Ruler has no such faith. Gaining and maintaining power is therefore a primary motivation. To the Ruler, it is the best way to keep oneself and one's family and friends safe. If you think of the royal court, impressive possessions and surroundings are desirable because they provide the trappings of power. Ruler environments are therefore substantial and impressive—think buildings with big columns and plenty of scale. Materials are meant to last and suggest timelessness—like granite or concrete, fine paneling, and heavy draperies.

Ruler brands include the IRS, the White House, E. F. Hutton, Brooks Brothers, Microsoft, IBM, American Express, The Sharper Image, CitiBank, Cadillac, and Day-Timers, as well as most HMOs, old-style banks, insurance companies, and high-status law and investment firms. President George Bush could be seen as a presidential Ruler brand in part as a result of a prep school education and in part because his campaign stressed his insider status and his long experience in government. Ruler products also include home alarm systems, intercoms, zoned heating systems, and automatic lawn-watering systems.

The Ruler
Desire: control
Goal: create a prosperous, successful family, company, or community
Strategy: exert leadership
Fear: chaos, being overthrown
Trap: being bossy, authoritarian
Gift: responsibility, leadership

When the Ruler archetype is active in individuals, they will enjoy taking on leadership roles and being in control as much as possible. Thinking about the best way to organize activities and setting in place policies and procedures provide a sense of self-mastery and power over the world that is very fulfilling. Rulers also have a heightened fear that chaos will ensue if they fail to take control. You might think of the Greek god Atlas carrying the world on his shoulders for an image of how responsible Rulers tend to be. For this reason, they tend to dislike people who are loose cannons and threaten to disrupt the order the Ruler has so carefully developed.

The Ruler also is known as the boss, leader, aristocrat, parent, politician, responsible citizen, role model, manager, or administrator.

Levels of the Ruler

Call: lack of resources, order, or harmony
Level One: taking responsibility for the state of your own life
Level Two: exerting leadership in your family, group, organization, or workplace
Level Three: becoming a leader in your community, field, or society
Shadow: Tyrannical or manipulative behaviors

The columned homes of modern-day Rulers echo those of their Classical counterparts.

People with high Ruler archetype tendencies are concerned with issues of image, status, and prestige—not because they are superficial, but because they understand how the way things look can enhance power. They act with a natural sense of authority that makes it easy for others to follow them. At their best, Rulers are motivated by a desire to help the world. At their worst, they are just domineering or controlling.

If you think about kings, queens, and presidents, you will quickly see that they are charged with helping society remain peaceful (or, if they fail, sending out the military to head off threats), for establishing and maintaining the rule of law, and for putting into place policies and procedures that foster prosperity for as many people as possible. The Ruler as an archetype, then, helps individuals become wealthy, powerful, and established in their fields and their communities.

The Ruler archetype likes hierarchical organizations because, in them, you know where you stand. Your role is clearly defined by a job description that tells you what you are supposed to do. You know who reports to you and who your boss is. The people you supervise are not supposed to go over your head to talk to your boss, and you do not go around yours either. Roles and relationships are stable and defined—until and unless anyone actually changes their job.

The New Royalty

Many Ruler brands and ads appeal to the desire we all have to be successful and important. In ancient times, kings and queens were often the thought of either as gods or as having a special relationship with the gods. Modern advertising sometimes makes this connection between success and a godlike stature. An ad for Lotus shows a woman walking purposefully down the street, reading papers (likely a spreadsheet). The copy reads, "Mere mortals manage people and money. You manage the knowledge of thousands." Furniture maker Thomasville runs an ad with a lovely sofa on a veranda with white columns and a Grecian statue overlooking the sea. The caption reads, "In order to seduce, the gods were known to take on shapes irresistible to mere mortals (approach with caution)." We then learn that "Thomasville takes comfort, luxury and style to a realm that even the almighty Zeus would envy."

Phoenix Wealth Management has been running ads with women wearing crowns as if they were queens. Some of the ads include pictures of a woman in full regal dress who looks like she may have reigned in the Renaissance. The copy reads, "Some people still inherit wealth; the rest of us have no choice but to earn it. The good news is, a lot of us know how. But then what? Phoenix has been showing people innovative new directions for nearly 150 years. We understand that making money—and knowing what to do with it—are two different skills. It's one reason high net worth people turn to Phoenix for help." Acutron shows two watches circling the globe. They reassure you that "Acutron has traveled to the moon, been presented to royalty and flown on Air Force One. Perhaps it's worthy of your wrist." Park Avenue Buick ran an ad that was unflinchingly frank regarding its car being about status: "It says everything before the meeting even starts."

Jones of New York typically portrays women modeling the company's clothes who are confident, in control, and in charge. You can tell by their carriage that they are important. DKNY runs a series of pages in succession with no text at all—just very successful-looking young men doing business. The series simply ends with "DKNY." The pictures say it all. Harter promotes its executive office ergonomic chair with the lone word "Never."

Van Kampen Funds pictures a little boy, just out of a portable swimming pool, reaching for an inflatable ball. The ad says, "The palace grounds. The prince. The royal ball." Although Van Kampen's service is managing money, the company makes the point that true royalty is about an approach to life, not how much money you have: "With the right investments, anyone can appreciate life's TRUE WEALTH. . . . Because enjoying life is what life is finally all about."

Many charitable and good-cause organizations appeal to the noblesse oblige of the Ruler. Heralds of Nature, a society of the National Wildlife Federation, enjoins readers to "Rise above the crowd. As a member of National Wildlife Federation's influential Heralds of Nature, you will take a lead role in helping NWF secure a lasting place for wildlife in today's modern world." In addition to helping wildlife, you also get "benefits and privileges," including "insider reports," "exclusive invitations," "advance notice" of events, and "your name listed in NWF's annual report."

Volvo promotes its cross-country all-wheel-drive models by flattering the customer, suggesting that he or she is like the car: "The trick to having power is being able to use it effectively. So along with their muscular, turbo-charged engines, these Volvos have intelligent all-wheel-drive. The Volvos don't just power through obstacles. They give you the option to avoid them. So if you like a little finesse with your power, stop by for a test drive." Bell Helicopter Textron takes a similar approach, picturing a tall, confident man who looks like he must be a CEO of some big company. The text reads, "Your mission is our mission. You know what it takes to be successful. So do we. That's why we develop and produce only the safest, most reliable products and services. Just like you. We also know the importance of being in the right place at the right time. After all, our goal is to stay on top, too."

But what happens if people do not know how important you are? American Express ran a successful campaign in which famous people use an American Express card so that they will be treated like royalty, whether or not they are recognized. One great ad featured writer Stephen King in a ghoulish old mansion. He confesses that however famous he is as a novelist, "When I'm not recognized it just kills me. So, instead of saying I wrote *Carrie*, I carry the card." Without it, he says, "Life is a little scary." Of course, one of American Express's most memorable ads featured Bob Dole being warmly greeted in his hometown, until he tried to cash a check. The message is clear: If you want to be treated well, show your AmEx card. OneWorld plays on a similar concern. Representing several major airlines, the firm offers access to many airport lounges. An ad showing a distinguished-looking businessman says, "Some people never worry about a lounge being available for them. Are you one of them? Wouldn't it be nice if your status preceded you, no matter where you fly?" Obviously, it doesn't, so they suggest it is wise to join OneWorld.

Although we think Jaguar is, overall, a Lover brand, one ad is quite direct about status being a primary motivator for a person to buy the car. The ad positions a Jaguar as being "for those seeking power, performance, and visible signs of envy." In another ad, the Lincoln Navigator is shown surrounded by a vivid sunset and the words "Tread luxuriously." Crystal Cruises pictures a waiter in a black suit, with the words "minister of every little detail." The company promises to be "at your service. . . . We will tend to your every desire. Throughout 2000, our uniquely friendly style of service will place the great cities of Europe, and the rest of the world, at your feet."

George Washington University positions itself as a Ruler school, saying

William Jefferson Clinton moves in around the corner [at the White House], and the world press makes GW its headquarters; former President Ronald Reagan returns to GW to accept an honorary degree on the anniversary of his life-saving care at the GW Medical Center;...

> *The presence of prominent international figures on campus is a near daily event at GW because our neighbors are some of the most powerful national and international corporations, organizations, and agencies in the world, and because the University has a special global reputation.*

The implied promise is that if you go here, you will be important and successful, too.

Be in Control

The Ruler is in charge and in control. Typically, he or she is portrayed as extremely responsible and juggling many important responsibilities. Ruler products help them be managed in an expedient way and also reaffirm the customer's power and status. NEC projectors feature, in huge letters, the injunction "Rule the Room," explaining, "with a variety of optional lenses, you're ready for just about any production scenario imaginable." Saab (which wobbles in its advertising, but is generally a Ruler brand) ran an ad for the Saab sedan that says, "In order to release your emotions, must control be relinquished as well?" "Not if you drive the Saab 9–5 Aero," the company reassures its high-status customers. Hewlett-Packard and Intel run an ad calling on customers to be as "in charge" with their computers as they are with their employees: "If your computer is not your most reliable employee, fire it. Get angrier when your computer crashes. Stop accepting 'the server is down' as a legitimate excuse. It's time to change the level of reliability you accept from computers. Demand a better computer."

Delphi Automotive Systems promises you that you can be in control even when you are stuck in traffic: "What do you call a company that can bring you MP3 playback, e-mail, and Internet access—all while you're sitting in traffic? Wired." By comparison, www.autobytel.co.uk tells you that you can "buy your next car from the comfort of your P. C." PayMyBills.com, advertised as "the most powerful bill-paying tool ever created," promises, "There's only one thing better than a stack of bills neatly arranged on your desk: a stack of bills neatly arranged on your desktop."

How do you amass power? Partly by networking. Bizzed.com

offers resources for small businesses to help them compete. One ad shows a confident and smiling woman. The text says, "GOOD. Join a professional organization. BETTER. Attend industry events. BIZ-ZED. Post your business card online, interact with potential clients and colleagues, sign on for major trade shows and get industry news as it breaks."

Power is also the ability to take decisive action. MySAP.com shows a successful-looking woman with a laptop at an airport and presents a mini-story. It begins with the words "Five empty seats. Twenty-five anxious passengers. One woman with a laptop. Make that four empty seats." The ad goes on,

> Sara Berg had a problem: a cancelled flight, a strange city, and a strong desire to sleep in her own bed. So she logged on to mySAP.com. With a few clicks, she went right to a travel booking system and grabbed a seat on the next flight out. And with those same few clicks, her expense report and travel plans were also updated. Instantly. Easily. Automatically. . . . Want to find out how every person in your organization can be more powerful? Visit www.sap.com/mhsap, and we'll show you how.

If power is that important, then you can bet that one person's success annoys others who have less of it. Some brands show you how to curry favor with the successful and, in that way, advance yourself. *Fortune Small Business* magazine shows a woman driving a car, with the caption, "She's the type you love to hate. Rich. Successful. Her own boss. But turn her into a customer and it takes the edge right off it." ThirdVoice runs an ad with a picture of an arrogant but beautiful woman, clearly in charge of her life, with the words, "Wonder how I get what I want from the Web? (Hint: I don't search.)" Of course, she doesn't search. She looks so regal that everything must come to her. Her secret? "I just use ThirdVoice 2000 to bring the entire Web to me."

Then there is the Advil ad, showing an African-American female executive talking authoritatively into the phone. Under her picture runs the caption, "I don't have time for that time of the month." Rulers don't have time to wait in lines either. So Hertz #1Club Gold promises, "No waiting in lines. No worries."

Often, Ruler ads focus less on status than on control and the ability to meet one's responsibilities— to work, family, and one's health. Solgar Optein Wellness Beverage shows a woman jogging in the rain with a fierce determination. The copy recounts her day: "Walked the dog. Took kids to school. Signed deal with new client. Organized fundraiser. Dropped son at soccer practice. Went to acupuncturist. Prepared the dinner. Went for usual evening run (in the pouring rain)." Now this woman is in charge of her life, perhaps to the point of being a stereotype more than a real human.

A less upbeat ad (for beef) shows a mother doll being pulled in all directions. It says, "The bendable-stretchable-pulled-in-all-directions modern mom. Go to the game. Go to the client. These days, you have to do it all. Fortunately, beef can help you find the strength to stay on top of it all." Post Shredded Wheat cereals and *Prevention* magazine put out a booklet for women on how to "balance your life," providing tips on making it all work. Such manuals, of course, have their public-service component. They also position the brand as helping high-achieving Ruler moms continue to keep it all together.

As with the Caregiver, a grid of individuals and organizations that willingly take responsibility for the good of the whole keeps the society working and running. The first job of the president is to keep us all safe and to call out the military if necessary. Alan Greenspan keeps an eye on the economy and takes action when it is needed. Bankers, business leaders, union bosses, police, lawyers, and community leaders are continually making and enforcing policies that stabilize our society. If they do their jobs well, the society succeeds. If they fail, it fails.

Heads of businesses hold a sacred trust to keep their employees, stockholders, and customers safe. Whole industries help them do so. Epoch Internet appeals to this concern, running a picture of a pyramid and arguing that "the Pharaohs knew how to keep their treasures safe and secure. Shouldn't your company do the same?" The ad continues: "Like the pharaohs, we understand the importance of securing valuable assets. Especially when it comes to hosting your company's Website. . . . Of course, when your site resides in one of our highly secure data centers, your business has a better chance of becoming the next great wonder of the world." Similarly, Iomega computer insurance shows a wild-looking young man grabbing a computer. The text reads, "You've got insurance if Johnny crashes your car. But what if he crashes your computer?" Of course, if there is anything the Ruler hates, it is any kind of change he or she cannot control. An ad for the world's first handheld global satellite phone and paging network (www.iridium.com) says, "The food changes. The water changes. The language changes. At least your phone number won't have to change."

Driveway reassures you that even if you are the ruler of an evil empire, it will help you succeed. Running a picture of what looks like an alien emperor dressed in a black cape, the copy offers, "Access your files from anywhere. Including your secret base in the volcano." In case you are vacationing, Hilton Hotels promises you that "Everything you need for business is right at hand, including high-speed Internet access from CAIS Internet."

The Ruler has a natural connection to patriotism. We like our countries because we are proud of their laws and their traditions. In an emotional way, to the degree that we abide by the rules—written and unwritten—of our societies and cultures, we share responsibility for their leadership. We become role models for proper behavior and enforcers of the status quo. You can think of mother reminding you to be a good example to others.

Black Currant Tango soda has been marketed as a notably British drink (in spite of the fact that the tango is a dance that originated in Argentina). A famous commercial begins with the Black Currant Tango spokesman waving a letter from a French exchange student who tried the drink and did not love it. The commercial goes on to suggest that the student's failing to appreciate the soda was a sign of his lack of understanding of the force of British culture. The spokesman gets so upset, he begins to shred his clothes, ranting, "Yes! Black Current Tango is a change for the taste buds. Yes, it's feisty! Yes! It's got guts! But so have we, Sebastian. Look at us!" The ad ends with a flag-waving crowd cheering as the spokesman enters a boxing ring and offers to take on France, Europe, and the world.

The Ruler archetype is not just about wealth and power. Rulers are about being models for ideal behavior in the society. Thus, propriety and taste are of the utmost importance.

Ralph Lauren: A Keeper of the Ruler Style

Ralph Lauren and his brother Jerry grew up in the Bronx. When other kids their age were into popular movies, Ralph and Jerry were watching the films of Cary Grant, Ginger Rogers, and Fred Astaire. When the others were listening to Elvis, Ralph and Jerry couldn't get enough of Ella Fitzgerald. And when the others were wearing tight black chinos, Ralph and Jerry were captivated by crewneck sweaters, khakis, and the just-right, button-down shirt. They dreamed of Princeton and Yale, and what it would be like to toss a football on the beach in Hyannisport, looking fabulous and looking like you didn't give a damn how you looked.

Ralph started as a tie salesman at Brooks Brothers and then moved on to create his own ties and, eventually, a brand icon of a company. But what might not be so obvious is that Ralph Lauren, in his studious examination of how the "better people" live, made at least a part of that life accessible to virtually everyone. Like Ralph and Jerry observing every detail of what made Cary Grant so effortlessly graceful, consumers today from virtually every walk of life could "learn" a certain kind of dress and, more importantly, behavior from every Ralph Lauren sub-brand. From the highest-end clothing, with the purple or black Ralph Lauren label, to Lauren, the brand for comfortable suburbanites, to Ralph, the brand for the young and the hip, to Polo Ralph Lauren, the classic sportswear line, and, ultimately, to the more affordable Polo Sport Company, Ralph Lauren presents a coherent view of "life as it should be"—civilized, orderly, and always gracious.

People and places live up to their highest mythic potential. Cape Cod lives up to our imaginings of clambakes on the beach at sunset, everyone tanned and healthy, with their collars pulled up, and children running bare-legged into the surf. It is the good life as we always dreamed it—and it is not just about money. It is about heritage and feeling that you have a safe place in the world; it is the certainty that the life you are living is the very best one that you could hope to realize in this one chance at existence that you have.

At its best, Ralph Lauren is also about the responsibility of the Ruler. Ralph Lauren himself has contributed substantial funds to restoring the original American flag involved in Francis Scott Key's poem—which, of course, became the inspiration for our national anthem. Today, at the Smithsonian Museum, you can see the craftsmen and -women painstakingly sewing the fabric by hand, an arduous task made possible by Ralph Lauren's commitment to order, stability, and heritage.

At Polo Ralph Lauren, people joke about "drinking the Kool-Aid"—becoming such believers in the spirit and values of the founder that they kiddingly wonder if they're losing perspective. But Ralph himself inspires them on an almost daily basis. At every ad shoot, or whenever he is first reviewing a concept for a new line, his signature question is "What's the story?" What's the mood and feeling and narrative of what we are presenting to the public? Employees feel that they are part of that story, and they are.

Also, Ralph is committed to knowing about where his story should go next. He has, in a sense, solved one dilemma: How can people who were not born into "old money" learn the some of the accompanying social graces? But perhaps now the question has changed: How can we all take time to enjoy the pleasures that the good life offers and also not lose sight of the values that make life worth living in the first place? The overnight success stories of Silicon Valley and Seattle are spawning a new kind of Ruler, expressing a more laid back West Coast style and sensibility. Might it be that the code of the Ivies is morphing into something entirely new?

Whatever the questions, and whatever the answers, Ralph Lauren is a self-made Ruler who will take the time and the effort to make sure that the "kingdom" of his followers does not stand still. He's out there to bring everyone along on his remarkable journey of discovery.

Ruler Organizations: The U.S. Government and Microsoft

A different kind of Ruler organization is often found in insurance companies, banks, regulatory and government agencies, producers of office products designed for executives, and numerous very large global firms. Many Ruler organizations are involved in setting standards that govern how things are done. For example, the insurance companies now govern managed care in the medical field, and the resulting friction comes from a collision of archetypal values. Medical service providers tend to be Sages, Magicians, or Caregivers and, therefore, have different values than the companies that often tell them what they can or cannot do.

Generally, Ruler organizations are quite hierarchical, with clearly defined power relationships as well as some checks and balances between and among divisions or other units. With great power comes a heightened sense of the cost of making a mistake. For this reason, decisions often have to be approved by a chain of command up the hierarchy. Generally, there are policies governing everything, but Catch-22 situations are common because there are so many regulations that they are not well integrated together.

A strength of these organizations is that they are stable, productive, and orderly, and they function smoothly with timely procedures and policies. However, they are appropriate only in situations where neither a fast response nor high-level innovation is required, as they are very slow to act. The currency of such organizations is power—both internal and external. People know and care who has the corner office. Nuances of power may even be reflected in how people dress. In some cases, dress is formal and conservative. Even when it is casual, clothes are likely to be favored that promote an aura of power and that, generally speaking, are traditional in cut, conservative in color, and substantial in feel.

Politics, of course, exists in every organization, but following the politics in Ruler organizations is the major spectator sport. If the organization is not a veritable dictatorship, then it works on balancing constituency interests, just as in government. This means that real consensus is often reached. Sometimes checks and balances are so extreme that 10 or more people have to sign off on the same decision or report. This process slows things down, but it also provides a way that managers in different areas can come to terms with one another and make things work.

The classic Ruler organization is the U.S. government or, perhaps we should say, the government of any stable country. The civil service protects workers' jobs, so the workers feel secure. Checks and balances between parts of the government focus on slowing down decision making to ensure that quick and harmful changes do not get made. In today's organizational climate, even government is not exempt from changing organizational structures. Organizations in every sector are becoming less hierarchical, more flexible, and more able to make quicker real-time decisions. Efforts to "reinvent" the U.S. government, accordingly, decreased the levels of hierarchy by eliminating much of middle management, simplifying decision making, and eradicating levels of red tape, thereby cutting costs and making efforts more efficient.

A more modern version of a Ruler organization can be seen in the growth of Microsoft. Bill Gates and Paul Allen began as hackers, but their first big break happened when IBM needed an operating system for its new line of personal computers. Gates and Allen purchased an existing system from another company, developed it, and entered into a partnership with IBM that was highly advantageous to Microsoft. IBM could use MS-DOS, but Microsoft kept ownership of the software and was also allowed to license its use to other firms. As a result, every time IBM sold a PC, it promoted Microsoft. Meanwhile, Microsoft kept developing the operating system and selling it to all the IBM-compatible computer companies. In doing so, in true Ruler fashion, they also created industry standards. The upshot was that all the other computer companies became dependent on Microsoft, so much so that Microsoft eventually eclipsed IBM in importance. Later, when Microsoft developed Windows, it used the same tactics. Windows Office provided integrated systems that worked wonderfully for business applications and quickly gained market dominance. Microsoft then convinced leading computer producers to preload Windows, eventually achieving such preeminence in the market that the company was slapped with an antitrust lawsuit.

Microsoft demonstrates both the positive and the negative potential of Ruler organizations. On the plus side, it understood how to partner with other parts of the market and to leverage the partnerships to its own advantage. In short, Microsoft knew how to play industry politics. Moreover, while its competitors were focusing on selling software, Microsoft placed its emphasis on setting (and then meeting) industry standards. If you can think of the imperialistic quality of many kings and queens, it will come as no surprise to you that the Ruler organization likes to take over other companies and other product lines. Ruler companies therefore often grow by acquisition. The downside, of course, is becoming an industry bully by suppressing competitive technologies. Over time, such actions can cause an expensive antitrust case and a publicity nightmare.[1]

Ruler Marketing

In the old economy, Ruler institutions frequently treated customers and clients as their "subjects." No more. Customers want to be Rulers themselves. A very effective ad for LiveCapital.com ("Business financing made easy.") reflects this transition. The ad starts with a picture of a man sitting across a desk, staring at a skeptical-looking banker. The text reads, "Option A: You sit in front of this guy, justifying why the past two years of your life's work are worthy of a business loan. Option B: You fill out one short, online application and get financing offers from multiple lenders." Of course, appealing to the Ruler, you always want to let the customer have power. And you never want to humiliate the customer.

Rulers like control, and they do not like to be told what to do. Microsoft ran a great ad that leaves customers with the decision whether to work on their vacation. You see a small boat out to sea, on a beautiful day. You see just the bottom half of the owner—his laptop, legs, and bare, crossed feet. He looks totally relaxed. Across the page are the words, "Now you have the technology to work during your vacation. Does that mean you'll be doing more work, or taking more vacation? . . . . The decision is yours." Either way, the picture shows him relaxed, in control, enjoying his life.

In the old days, companies operated for the most part as if they existed in isolation. Sure, they needed suppliers and they were aware of their competition, but on a day-to-day basis, they assumed autonomy. Agnieszka M. Winkler, in *Warp Speed Branding*, makes a compelling case that those days are really over. In a global economic system, nations have to recognize their interdependence upon one another. Similarly, companies are dependent on all the companies with which they do business. In addition, "it's the increasingly complex set of interrelationships of all the stakeholders and brands in-

---

1. Thaddeus Wawro, *Radicals and Visionaries* (Irvine, CA: Entrepreneur Press, 2000), pp. 137–139.

volved in putting together a product or service" that Winkler says defines the crucial ecosystem that determines how they operate, at least ideally. "Take a typical software product," she says.

> *The application probably has to be Microsoft Windows-compatible. It has to be able to run on all computer brands, and the box will usually specify which Pentium processors have enough power to run the application. Now, add Pentium and Intel to the brand effect. We already have five brands involved, and we haven't yet begun to think about distribution or promotion. Every brand with which our brand allies has an impact on the brand.*

Bill Gates had not only a genius for understanding this current reality, but the political smarts to turn it consistently to his advantage.

If you run an HMO, you'll see that the situation is similar. Your "ecosystem" includes employers of companies that belong to the HMO, your own employees, insurance companies, all the independent contractors (clinics, doctors, labs) that do work for you, the state insurance commission, state and company retirement systems, and pharmaceutical companies—and you haven't even begun to take account of the patients! Making business decisions in such a climate requires a holistic understanding of the ecosystem and your niche in it—and also requires the Ruler to have the political skill to gain the support of diverse constituent groups. Clearly, your brand identity needs to work not only with your primary customers, but with the whole ecosystem.

Ideally, brands should contribute to the health of the entire system to ensure needed cooperation. Modern biology tells us that species which survive are not necessarily the fittest, in the usual way of thinking about that term. In fact, those that thrive do so because they have maximized their position within a niche and have participated, in general, in an ecological give and take that strengthens everyone. Winkler suggests that

> *your brand strategy, brand promise, brand essence, character and personality should be well thought out and articulated in writing, so that it can be passed on to all of the stakeholders. That's the only way to keep your brand from becoming diluted by the impact of all its other*

brand relationships. Your brand will grow and change as it adapts to its environment, but your job is to make sure that it continues to be strong and healthy.[2]

And we would add that you should also make sure that it continues to be true to one compelling and identifiable archetype.

The expression of the Ruler archetype has evolved over time from the monarch to the politician and from absolute local rule to global interdependence with other Rulers. The Ruler's contribution to our lives has also been revolutionized by changes in the scientific paradigm, especially, as we have seen, in the evolutionary and biological sciences. In the nineteenth century, it may have made sense to industry giants to aspire to achieve market dominance at any cost; but the Microsoft antitrust case tells us that if this were ever so, it certainly is not now. There is no limit to how much money a brand can make or how big its company can be. However, brands are now expected to be good global citizens. If you play to win—at others' expense—you may, ironically, lose. It's just like politics: Win–win outcomes are the safest strategy for lasting success. Great brands know how to be good citizens of the world.

Ruler symbols that become too extreme in their expression of the "separateness" of the Ruler can become vulnerable to a kind of ridicule. Once the super-expensive leather attaché case became a symbol of maniacal corporate zeal, self-conscious top executives began to sport economical canvas cases from Land's End, or even casual backpacks. The Philfax, similarly, is being replaced by the hipper Palm Pilot—which is cleverly being positioned as a Creator's tool, not a Ruler's. After the "Beamer" became such a symbol of the excesses of the go-go Eighties, many owners actually became embarrassed to drive them, even though they loved their handling and construction. This is not to say that symbols of the Ruler are irrelevant, but it may be that they are subject to a special kind of sensitivity. The country that brought the world the Boston Tea Party will, perhaps, allow only a certain degree of obvious symbols of class distinction. Also,

---

2. Agnieszka M. Winkler, *Warp Speed Branding: The Impact of Technology on Marketing* (New York: John Wiley and Sons, 1999), pp. 148–149, 159.

the new Seattle and Silicon Valley breed of Ruler is more likely to wear his khakis to the office than a suit from Saville Row, setting a new standard for what expresses true confidence at the top.

Both the traditional Ruler and its new, more populist form agree on the importance of good management systems. It is this archetype which insists that it is chaotic and unsafe to try to manage meaning without a system for doing so. The Ruler demands that decisions be made by the book. But the trouble is, most branding decisions have no "book" helpful enough to truly monitor the evolution of the meaning of the brand. As you implement the recommendations in this book for settling on one compelling archetypal identity for your brand, it is also important that you put an infrastructure in place to communicate that meaning to all stakeholders and to any or all marketing consultants, advertising firms, or other people involved in marketing decisions. If you add to that a sense of your "ecosystem," then you will also see your customers less as just consumers to be convinced to buy your product and more as constituents. In this sense, your endeavor prospers in a symbiotic relationship with theirs. At the most basic level, if your customers are faltering economically, they may not be able to buy your product. At a more everyday level, if your product does not enhance their lives, they will not continue to purchase it. If you are always seeking to know your constituents and to understand their needs, you will naturally produce products that enhance their lives. They will then reward you with their loyalty. The Ruler would tell you that this is not just a matter of semantics; it is a paradigm shift of massive dimensions.

It is not just about market surveys, asking customers what they want. Often, they do not know. It is knowing them so well that you know what might help them before they know. Akio Morita explained that did not customers request the Walkman before it was introduced. In getting to know Americans, he socialized a lot and generally paid attention to what they said and did. In this process, he noticed that Americans loved music, also loved walking around, and were generally too polite to offend others by playing music publicly. Morita noted that people did not ask for such a portable tape player because they did not even know it was possible.

The great Ruler brand knows its constituents so well that it an-

The Ruler identity might be right for your brand if you have

- a high-status product used by powerful people to enhance their power
- a product that helps people be more organized
- a product or service that can offer a lifetime guarantee
- services that offer technical assistance or information that helps maintain or enhance power
- an organization with a regulatory or protective function
- a product at the moderate to high price range
- a brand seeking to differentiate from a more populist (Regular Guy/ Gal) one or that is the clear leader in the field
- a field that is relatively stable or a product that promises safety and predictability in a chaotic world

ticipates their deepest needs. Understanding archetypes is a powerful tool for helping you go beneath the surface and meet invisible and emerging needs.

Parts 2 through 5 were designed to help you recognize the archetypes that, like constellations in the sky, make order out of seemingly erratic data having to do with meaning. Our hope is that by this time you will recognize them all around you—in movies, music, political debates, ads—and, most of all, great brands. Parts 6 and 7 will help you apply this wisdom to positioning your own brand.

Finding True North

Positioning an Archetypal Brand

Ancient navigators used the stars to guide them, and even in these days of radar and sonar, pilots still rely on the horizon to maintain their perspective while flying. And, truth be told, it was the Moon that guided the almost-doomed astronauts of the *Apollo 13* space mission back to earth. Without fixed and steady reference points, we are almost sure to become hopelessly lost.

Too often, even the most sophisticated marketers feel totally at sea as they try to manage the meaning of their brands because they lack any meaningful reference points or framework to provide a system or structure. Frequently, the absence of a guiding framework leads them to overcompensate by using complicated forms or formats to try to capture and express brand meaning—"brand pyramids" loaded with descriptive adjectives, "brand wheels" highlighting concentric levels and layers of meaning, multipage brand essence or equity statements—as though a painfully detailed schematic will somehow compensate for the fact that the brand meaning itself was arrived at in a careless or haphazard way.

But there is an alternative to the kind of "adjective soup" that constitutes the primary "meaning management" process currently practiced. This alternative navigational system makes it possible to find the meaning that is right for your brand and to preserve, nurture, and enrich that meaning over time. The meanings you will be considering and exploring are fundamental, timeless, universal "reference points," like the stars or the horizon, which are each *clear and coherent* concepts that require no wheels or pyramids to grasp or to apply. They force you to make a choice, embrace an idea, and immerse yourself in the depth and breadth of that concept, as opposed to being caught in an endless and often meaningless debate about a litany of attributes or adjectives.

This section will (1) help you identify the most ideal archetypal identity for your brand; (2) explore ways to use mythic story patterns and other means to effectively tell your brand's story; and (3) provide a case study of how one organization—the March of Dimes—reclaimed its archetypal identity, identified the relevant story patterns, and built a compelling campaign around them.

16

The Artichoke

Uncovering the Archetypal Meaning of Your Brand

As with eating an artichoke, the goal here is to pull away the inessential leaves and get to the heart of the matter—the core of indisputable brand meaning. You can start by familiarizing yourself with the archetypes described in Chapters 4 through 15. Then, take the steps to view your business, your brand, your category, and your company through this new lens. It will no doubt clarify and illuminate the way for you to chart the brand's course into the future. The five steps that are most critical to the discovery of a brand's archetypal identity are summarized in Figure 6.1.

Step One: Searching for Brand Soul

Begin by conducting the equivalent of an archaeological dig to discover your brand's deepest, most meaningful equity—its essence or

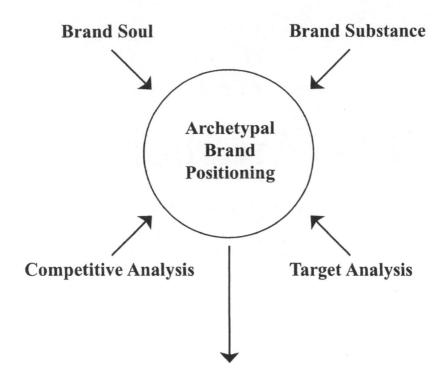

Telling the Brand's Stories

Figure 6.1

soul. Approach the exercise as though you were the brand's "biographer," addressing questions such as: *Who created it, and why? What was going on in the broader culture at the time? How was it first positioned? What was the best or most memorable communication ever created for it? How have customers related to the brand over the years? How do they relate to it now? What within its essence or equity makes it stand out from the competition?*

Just like a biographer, you will be exploring both the rational and the emotional, the "documented" history as well as the folklore about the brand.

For example, a "brand biographer" would learn that the original formula for Oil of Olay, a leading mass-market skin care line, was developed by Graham Gordon Wulff in South Africa in the 1940s. Company lore, handed down orally and written about secondhand, says that the original formula was developed as a salve to treat the dehydrated skin of British pilots who suffered burns during World War II. It was a kind of "secret weapon," countering the terrible effects of battle, and was alleged to be so successful that it was almost magical. When the product was acquired and then marketed by Richardson-Vicks in 1970, its early stewards were wise enough to know that they must not sell this "secret" in conventional ways, or it would lose its specialness. In the beginning, subtle, informative print ads were used in place of prime-time television advertising, based on the feeling that the product should be "discovered" by women, not "sold" to them. The content of each ad was specifically designed to fit in with the editorial style of each magazine in which it was placed. Later, when advertising moved to TV, the commercials showed beautiful women from all over the world who used Oil of Olay. But the print retained a feeling of woman-to-woman intimacy, with headlines such as, "Do you see your mother when you look in the mirror?" The deliberate strategy was to make the user feel that while the brand's "public" identity might be glamorous when she is watching with her husband or family, she and Oil of Olay share their "secrets" when she is looking at the print ad in a magazine.

The visual and verbal language surrounding the brand also had an air of mystery. The initial product was never even called a "moisturizer"; rather, it was referred to in the copy as a "beauty secret." A Madonna figure graced the logo. In ad copy, the product was never "applied"; it was "lavished on." People new to the business, at both the company and their advertising agency, were required to read and live by the Oil of Olay "white paper," which explained the special history and culture of the brand.

Those early marketers of a powerful Magician brand understood and leveraged the unique origin and spirit of their brand and its archetype (even if they did not understand the underlying theory of archetypes or consciously recognize Olay as a Magician brand). They sensed that they were dealing with magic and that magical traditions such as alchemy are often secret, passed on to initiates only.

More recently, the task of designing and then launching the new Volkswagen Beetle must have been a daunting one. How could you recapture the iconic spirit and essence of the 1960s Beetle's success and still reinterpret it in a fresh way at the turn of the millennium?

Archetypes could have helped provide the way. Jay Mays, the creator of the new Beetle and now head of design at Ford Motor Company, likes to say that the car's design concept is as simple as three concentric circles, invoking, but reinterpreting, the spirit of its earlier incarnation. But looking at the design through the archetypal lens, we see that the "face" of the new Beetle is virtually identical to the face of an infant—with big eyes and a high, smooth forehead. Research has shown that throughout both the animal and the human kingdom, those same baby-faced characteristics, the characteristics of the Innocent, signal that there is no threat and that the creature is in need of care. They are the facial characteristics of the koala bear, the teddy bear, Mickey Mouse, and, most recently, the little television creatures from the United Kingdom called the Teletubbies. They are faces that win hearts the world over.

Now that face, the face of the Innocent, has found expression in a unique and charming automotive design. But is it the right expression for the brand?

To answer that question as brand biographer, you would need to examine the deep meaning of the original Volkswagen Beetle in its time. As we have discussed earlier, to many of the middle-class college students in the throes of antiwar, antiestablishment, proenvironment sentiment, automobiles were anathema—especially the gas-guzzling, living-room-on-wheels varieties their fathers favored. But being young Explorers, they had to get around. Quite a dilemma. Then along came the answer in the form of a small, quirky-looking, fuel-efficient vehicle: the "un-car," the Innocent.

Today, we look at the reincarnated Beetle and want to smile. We may not know exactly why, but we feel that it would be really great to drive one, to own one. For some inexplicable reason, we would want to own one in a primary color. What we intuit as consumers, but cannot express, is our delight that the Innocent has been resurrected in such a clever new way.

When you are branding a company or an organization, taking an extra step is wise. Take some time to access your organizational culture and its values. Look at the brand or the company's "creation stories." How did it start? What were the core values of the founder? If there were a documentary film made about your brand, what would it be called? What would its plot be?

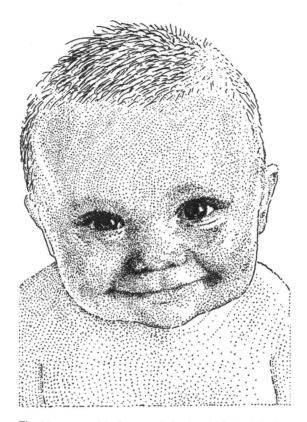

The big eyes and high, smooth forehead of a baby's face are echoed in the faces of the teddy bear, Mickey Mouse, and the Teletubbies, and, most surprisingly, the "face" of the reincarnated Volkswagen Beetle.

The origin of Ford, for example, links to the creation of the assembly plant and the possibility of car ownership for everyday Americans. In retrospect, Henry Ford represents a kind of American folk hero, a spirit that could continue to differentiate the motor company that bears his name from its competition. The history of General Motors, on the other hand, is associated with American power and clout, suggesting that a very different kind of essence might be carried forward. History is not irrelevant to iconic brands; they were shaped by the time and place in which they were born, and in turn, they have shaped the culture as well.

Often, discovering the deep essence or soul of a brand—especially when that essence is congruent with the organization's values—leads to an archetypal identity that feels so true, so right, that it seems unnecessary to go any further. But even if it is the right answer, pursuing the recommended five steps in their entirety is necessary, because the interpretation of that essence must be both relevant and differentiating in a contemporary context.

Step Two: Searching for Brand Substance

The second step of the analysis ensures that the archetypal identity suggested by "the dig" is also grounded in some truth about the product or service—ideally, a physical, contemporary truth. For example, many banks and savings and loan associations originated as Caregiver institutions. Recall again *It's a Wonderful Life*, in which the townspeople are taken care of by George's bank and, in turn, they empty their wallets and their piggybanks to help bail out the bank when it's in trouble. Not just in the movies, but in real life, many neighborhood and small-town banking brands once had warm and supportive relationships with their customers, grounded in a sense of real trust and stability. William Bradley, father of former Senator Bill Bradley, once claimed that his proudest achievement in his role as president of his hometown bank in Crystal City, Missouri, was that he never foreclosed on a customer's farm or home during the Great Depression—the bank and the customer found a way to work it out.

But if such a bank wanted to assume a Caregiver identity today, we would need to explore the contemporary authenticity of that concept. What's the basis of the bank's relationship with its customers? Is there a real relationship or just a series of transactions? What is the character of the bank's internal employee policies? Its customer complaint policies? What happens if a customer who is generally responsible is suddenly late with her mortgage payment because she has lost her job?

It could well be that a Caregiver identity is out of the question, even though it probably would offer a relevant and differentiating communication position. On the other hand, honestly exploring what the bank truly delivers consistently and well may lead to other symbolic avenues that are equally compelling.

Sometimes these physical or functional points of leverage are obvious and clearly link up with an archetypal meaning. For example, technologies that are entirely new to a culture often have an obvious "Magician" quality to them until they become commonplace. Think about the telephone when it was new, or TV, or the microwave oven. Early advertising for long-distance calling—which seemed downright miraculous to people—clearly evoked the spirit of the Magician. Instant photography did this as well. For example, a commercial that ran in the early days of the Kodak Instant Camera showed little children in their classroom on the first day of school, looking apprehensive and timid. Then the teacher comes in with an Instant Camera, and they all begin to take pictures of each other and watch them develop. The musical score evokes the transformational power of the Magician ("Suddenly you're closer than you've ever been before") as we see the children begin to warm up to each other and to their new teacher.

The physical product itself can provide meaningful clues as well. Caregiver products are often soothing and calm, like hot chocolate. Innocent products are often simply constructed or white in color, like talcum powder. Outlaw products might have some "bite"—like Tabasco sauce. Magician products may be shimmering, translucent, and changeable.

When the characteristics of the product do not so clearly indicate an archetypal identity, sensitive, in-depth consumer research is necessary to uncover the truth about what has been called "the inherent drama of the product" as it is as experienced in real-life, day-to-day use. This kind of research goes beyond providing data or even information—it assumes the skills, perspective, and analytic ability that lead to real insight.

Ethnographic studies are one means of getting closer to that kind of human truth. Adapted from cultural anthropology, this approach involves the researcher spending time with the target customer in his or her environment, observing, interacting, and discussing the product and its benefits in the larger context of the consumer's life. It may take a few hours, or even a few days, but the opportunities for learning are endless. How does the prospect decorate his or her home? What's in the cupboards? When is the household most tense? When is it most relaxed? What are the interactions between its members like? What, in the home, is most expressive of the prospect's values? What would he or she run back to save in a fire? Often, this kind of up-close-and-personal perspective yields surprising results.

For example, "Sesame Street," the popular and respected educational show for preschoolers, was developed to appeal to mothers and other caretakers, as well as kids, because the Children's Television Workshop's (now Sesame Workshop's) research had shown that children learn better from television when they are interacting with their parents. Acting on this principle, the producers developed much of the show on two levels: well-researched educational entertainment for the little ones and a layer of clever, well-written double entendres or cultural references to amuse and entertain mom.

Mothers and other caregivers in focus groups talked about enjoying the show when they watched it with their children, supporting the long-held principle. But when we went into people's homes early in the morning to observe what was happening, the dynamic was somewhat different. Once "Sesame Street" came on, busy mothers (many of whom were racing to get older siblings out to school or to get out the door themselves) felt free to dash about, taking care of all that they needed to do, relieved in the knowledge that their preschooler was in good hands with quality programming. They would occasionally pop in to check on things, perhaps chuckle at a fleeting segment of the show, and then pop out. Were they watching? Sort of. Did the behavior conform to the belief that they were relaxing with their preschooler in front of the set, enjoying the show from end to end? Hardly.

Observations from these ethnographic studies led the production team and writers to rethink how much of the content should be relevant to adults, versus purely kid driven. Much of the show's hallmark cleverness and adult sophistication remains, but the research helped explain the tremendous popularity of a new segment called "Elmo's World," which has been developed solely with the three-year-old in mind.

Another ethnographic perspective on mornings in American households led to a different kind of realization regarding product truth. Operating on the very reasonable assumption that women were frantically busy in the morning, a major food manufacturer had been focusing on portable, healthy "breakfasts on the run" for a certain segment of the female population. To help refine this product idea, we conducted general focus groups, probing what morning was like in these households. Rather than simply exploring the context, however, we asked each woman to describe in detail what she ate each morning and where and how she ate it. To our surprise, no matter how frantic the woman's morning might be, her so-called breakfast on the run was, instead, a precious moment of calm. It might only be for three or four minutes, and it might be at the kitchen counter instead of at the table, but every woman we interviewed talked about how her time with that bagel or cereal and a cup of coffee was a moment to collect herself, take stock, and brace herself for the day. Almost to a woman, she got up even earlier than she had to, before anyone else in the household arose, just to have that calming moment over her breakfast. Our asking the right questions and listening well saved the client from making a big mistake and led the company to rethink the proposition entirely.

Some questions that might lead to a deeper exploration of the relationship between consumer and brand include the following:

Is the brand's role functional or value expressive for its users?

Is the brand part of a high-involvement or low-involvement product category?

Is use of the brand episodic or routine?

Do consumers tend to use the brand exclusively or as their dominant brand, or is the brand part of a portfolio of brands that consumers find equally acceptable?

What is consumers' level of attachment to the brand?

Are you trying to hold onto your current franchise or attract users who favor other brands to move to your franchise, or are you trying to expand use of the product category overall by way of attraction to your brand?

Do you simply want to increase frequency of use of your brand among those who already use it?

Step Three: Finding the Competitive Leverage

After several iterative explorations and some well-done and sensitive consumer research, steps one and two have generally led clients to develop a hypothesis about the archetype or archetypes that are right and true for the brand they are interested in. Step three ensures that the "answer" is not just a comfortable fit, but that it will offer significant and sustainable differentiation in the marketplace.

Young & Rubicam's BrandAsset Valuator model and database show that relevant differentiation is the "brand engine"—the quality that keeps a brand vital and strong. In today's cluttered marketplace, brands that feel undifferentiated fall to commodity status, and by default, price becomes the consumer's primary criterion for choosing.

To begin to assess whether the archetype provides a basis for your brand's uniqueness, examine the competitive set in terms of archetypal meaning:

- Have any brands stumbled into archetypal territory? If so, which archetypes? Are any clearly related to the archetype most suited to your brand?
- How well are the competitors supporting and living up to their archetypes?
- At what level are the competitors expressing the archetype? Is there an opportunity to move to a deeper, more relevant, or differentiating level?
- Is everyone in the category expressing the same one or two archetypes? Is there an opportunity for a truly new archetype in the category?

For example, when coffee brands were all variations of the Caregiver, General Foods' line of flavored European-style instant coffees offered an Explorer identity that presented consumers with an exciting new way to experience the beverage. More recently and more successfully, Starbucks did the same thing.

Often, as will be discussed in a later chapter, the leading brand in a category comes to own the dominant "category archetype" (e.g., Ivory has "branded" the deep, archetypal meaning of cleansing). If the leader is doing that, and is doing it well, differentiation can be created from some other secondary or perhaps altogether new category archetype. For example, in contrast to Ivory's Innocent identity, Dove is more of a Caregiver brand, which is linked to the fact that Dove has emollients that Ivory does not have and therefore "nurtures" the skin.

The category leader also sometimes presents the opportunity for a "challenger" archetype, or foil. Joe Camel was the Jester to Marlboro's serious Hero and, at its best, Pepsi has been another kind of Jester brand, good-naturedly poking fun at sometimes sanctimonious Innocent Coke.

Another opportunity for differentiation can be found in identifying a new *level* of the archetype that has been overlooked in the category. For example, if you skim through magazines targeted at teens and young adults, you will find advertising absolutely flooded with Explorer imagery for everything from apparel to entertainment. This is probably because the Explorer–youth link is such an obvious one, even to those who know little of archetypes. But on closer inspection, you will likely discover that virtually every brand is not only on the same archetype, but they are all operating at the same *level* of the archetype—the most shallow and obvious one. Ad after ad features the rebellious outsider, when that is just the tip of the Explorer iceberg. Beneath the surface are deeper aspects of the archetype that are highly relevant to young people, but that the advertisers are ignoring: the Explorer as seeker of truth, true to him- or herself, who doesn't sell out or compromise and who cares about principle. In Europe, Levi's has been positioned as the brand for young people who have the courage to embark on the journey of discovering what they believe in and why—but in the United States (the land of immigrants, the great frontier, and rugged individualism, where the Bill of Rights protects "life, liberty, and the pursuit of happiness"!"), this kind of deeper interpretation of the archetype is ironically hardly ever conveyed to our youth.

This competitive assessment should illuminate your thinking and narrow the field of archetypes to the one that is clearly best. It may be tempting to "borrow" a little from one or another archetype, but then the essential power of the clear, coherent concept of one archetype is compromised. Instead, once an archetype seems to be the right one for your brand, plumb the depths of that concept. Examine the levels of your archetype as highlighted in the previous chapters.

Sometimes it is useful to make a simple chart of how your competitors are positioning their product at a particular time. The chart in Figure 6.2 roughly identifies the archetype in ads for running shoes that were current as we were writing this book. Of course, only a few of these brands have a consistent identity. If you were surveying

Charting the Territory		
Archetype	**Brand**	**Picture and/or text of ad**
Creator	Diadora	"Someone Get Darwin on the phone. He's gonna want to see this. Mythos 300. The most significant genetic leap in running since the foot."
Caregiver	Fila	Picture of two bare feet at the end of the bed, sticking out from under the covers. Copy: "Your feet will be as comfortable as the rest of your body."
Sage	Avia	Picture of runner with bag over his head. "What we saved on endorsements, we spent on technology."
Lover (as companion)	Oasis	"Have you ever worn a pair of shoes that felt like you weren't just wearing them, but felt like they were actually running with you?"
Jester	Brooks	Pictures of toes with happy faces on them and smiling faces of happy young people. "Run happy."
Hero	Nike	"Just do it."
Outlaw	Tattoo	Runner with tattoo, running in a barren terrain. The picture of the shoe shows flames and a monster on the sole.
Magician	Reebok	Emphasis on achieving flow.
Magician (or Explorer)	New Balance	"Turn off your computer. Turn off your fax machine. Turn off your cell phone. Connect with yourself."
Innocent	Saucony	"Quietly making great fitting shoes since 1898."

Figure 6.2

your competition, you would, of course, want to differentiate between established brand identities and ephemeral campaigns and, to
the greatest degree possible, identify their archetypal levels.

When the development of new products is the key, analyzing the
category from an archetypal perspective can lead to some decidedly
out-of-the-box thinking. The framework forces you to think about
some surprising possibilities: What would an Outlaw bank provide?
A Lover beer? An Explorer magazine for parents of preschoolers?

Whether your product is a new venture or an established brand,
determine the level of its archetype that is best for you to leverage.
Then, explore how you might express that archetype in every aspect
of the brand. For example, the McDonald's Innocent archetype
comes to life in much more than its restaurants and its advertising;
the archetype is expressed in the McDonald's All School Marching
Band, a wholesome symbol in a cynical time; the Ronald McDonald
Houses, supporting "innocents" who are in pain; the golden arches;
and the promotions McDonald's features. And Budweiser, the Regular Guy and Gal beer, brings back the Clydesdales from time to
time as a symbolic reminder of the importance of tradition and hard
work. Brainstorm where your archetype can lead you, in every possible communication discipline. Then, go on to further enrich your
direction by infusing this new or clarified brand identity with a deep
understanding of your customer.

Step Four: Know Your Customer

The final stage of the analysis ensures that the archetype is likely to
be powerfully relevant and meaningful to your target prospect. While
some part of us responds to each and every archetype, particular
contexts, situations, or transition points in life make an archetype
especially potent.

First-time parents learning how to be Caregivers need Sages and
Caregivers themselves. Young people just breaking free from their
parents need Explorer brands that can help them express their newfound autonomy. And sometimes parents in the "full nest" stage of
their lives need Explorer brands, too, just so they can feel a little
young, independent, and free.

"Lifestyle" marketing has led to an assumption that people want

to see mirror images of themselves in advertising, or else they will not identify with the advertisements. Archetypal marketing assumes quite the opposite—that unfulfilled yearnings might lead people to respond on a deeper level to what's missing, as opposed to what's already there.

Eric Erickson's stages, summarized in Figure 6.3, highlight the fundamental conflict or issue at each stage of life. Each "struggle" calls forth issues that are powerful but conflicting: the goal or mastery that represents forward motion, versus the one that perpetuates the status quo. For example, children in their elementary years struggle with industry versus inferiority, whereas people in the later stages

Visually based projective techniques often prove useful, such as this one used in a study for the National Parenting Association intended to explore the priorities and preoccupations of parents versus non-parents when they vote. Such approaches often reveal deeper and more authentic insights than does direct questioning.

of life face either integrity or despair. While both urges will be powerful, we could argue that archetypes that tap into and instruct the more healthy, positive desire will meet with even greater success than archetypes that appeal to the negative desire. In a sense, the use of the positive archetype models the healthy instinct for the prospect.

Erickson's Eight Stages of Man and Related Personal Conflicts

	1	2	3	4	5	6	7	8
VIII.				"The Bridge Years"				INTEGRITY VERSUS DESPAIR
VII.							GENERATIVITY VERSUS STAGNATION	
VI.						INTIMACY VERSUS ISOLATION		
V.	Temporal Perspective versus Time Confusion	Self-Certainty versus Self-Conscious	Role Experimentation versus Role Fixation	Apprenticeship versus Work Paralysis	IDENTITY VERSUS IDENTITY CONFUSION	Sexual Polarization versus Bisexual Confusion	Leader- and Followership versus Authority Confusion	Ideological Commitment versus Confusion of Values
IV.				INDUSTRY VERSUS INFERIORITY	Task Identification versus Sense of Futility			
III.			INITIATIVE VERSUS GUILT		Anticipation of Roles versus Role Inhibition			
II.		AUTONOMY VERSUS SHAME, DOUBT			Will to be Oneself versus Self-Doubt			
I.	TRUST VERSUS MISTRUST				Mutual Recognition versus Autistic Isolation			
	1 Infancy	2 Early Childhood	3 Play Stage	4 School Stage	5 Adolescence	6 Young Adulthood	7 Adulthood	8 Old Age

Figure 6.3

Consideration of your customers' life stage is a good starting point for examination of their relationship to the archetype you're thinking about using.

Beyond your prospects' own individual stage in life, it is also wise to consider your prospects' stage in the family life cycle. Are they younger or older singles, or are they elderly solitary survivors? If they are in the "nesting" stages, are they in the early "full nest" (youngest child under 6 years of age) or the later (youngest child 6 to 18 years of age)? Given the fact that people nowadays tend to delay marriage and child rearing until later in life, it is entirely possible that individuals in one of Erickson's later stages of personal development might still be in an early stage of family formation.

Similarly, sometimes the dominant or most visible aspect of the target market population does not necessarily present the best opportunity for connecting with them. For example, our research among fortyish women in the "full nest" stage of their lives reveals their dominant tendency to reflect the Ruler archetype—chauffeuring kids here and there, arranging play dates and parties, maintaining harmony in the household, and, at the same time, holding down jobs of their own. Their commitment to order, stability, and control makes it all possible.

Countless advertisers have discovered these same tendencies (although they probably don't understand the deeper roots of the Ruler archetype, especially in the context of harried moms!). In response, they have jumped on a bandwagon of "lifestyle" brand positioning and advertising that shows women dashing here and there but heroically holding it all together.

However, our research reveals that Ruler moms don't necessarily need that part of themselves reflected or validated—they are well aware of what their lives are like and all that they have to do! More importantly, deeper archetypal analysis indicates that new "burgeoning" identities and tendencies—dormant urges that speak to the person she *wants to become* when all the pressure subsides—the little voice that says, "What about *me?!*"—do need critical support and validation.

Deep within many of these women are strong Creator urges, perhaps visible now only through occasional artistic projects or a "self-indulgent" visit to a crafts show. Within others are strong strains of Sage tendencies, as they unconsciously begin to integrate and make sense of the experience of their years. And within others are powerful Magician urges and capabilities, as they silently prepare for a time when they can transform aspects of their home, their marriage, and their community or, perhaps, themselves.

So it is no wonder that Martha Stewart, by dignifying and reinforcing the Creator urge; Oprah Winfrey, by validating and supporting the Sage, and numerous spas and self-help books have become powerhouse industries. At the same time, it is no wonder that so many brands that have jumped on the obvious "soccer mom" lifestyle bandwagon have become undifferentiated also-rans.

Often, the equivalent of these dormant urges exists in the entire culture, creating an enormous need—and an opportunity. It could be argued that during the go-go eighties in America, the Creator archetype was less esteemed in our entire culture—which instead favored the Ruler ethos: control, responsibility, and success. So Martha's determination to swim upstream with the concept of domestic creativity may have encouraged the adoption of that concept within both the primary target audience and the culture at large.

Sinister forces can fill these vacuums as well. For a culture desperate to feel any vestige of national pride, Adolph Hitler was an easy sell—a Ruler tapping into the desire of a people to feel powerful, important, and in control. In the increasingly secular society of postwar America, the dark side of the Magician—the need and the vulnerability—was so deep and so broad that delusionary and greedy "priests"—in the form of Jim Jones and those like him— were easily able to command the loyalty and commitment of thousands.

When archetypal forces are less visible in a culture, they are all the more powerful—like black holes actively searching out the life forces that will fill them. Hucksters and charlatans intuitively understand this, but marketers tend to favor a more rational and literal route, struggling to chase down the latest "trend."

The system of archetypes can offer a more substantive route to our understanding of individual customers and the culture that surrounds them by enabling us to focus on "trends" in a far deeper and more meaningful way than is now practiced. We are not talking here of swerving from one archetype to another, based on what is in style and what is out of style. At the time a brand is launching its identity, it may do well to ride the wave of a suppressed but emerging archetype. Once that identity is established, then determine how to stabilize that expression of a basic human need in a way that can endure over time.

In either case, it is useful to reflect on questions such as: "Which fundamental human needs are being well served at this point in our individual or collective history, and which are being underserved?" These questions will lead to real insight and inspiration.

And so, the final step delves much more deeply than conventional approaches into the wishes, fears, conflicts, and aspirations of the target audience in order to thoroughly understand how the archetype will resonate with them.

Step Five: Staying on Course: Managing the "Brand Bank"

By the end of this unique analytic process, companies have an unprecedented degree of confidence regarding their potential iconic or

Brand Building

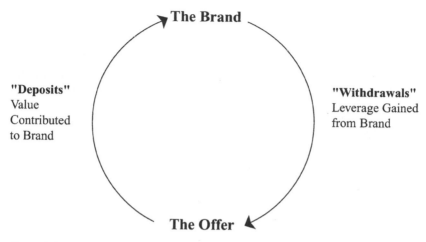

Figure 6.4

archetypal place in the world—which results in both marketplace success and an exciting and invigorating focus for the whole organization.

Once the brand's archetypal place in the world has been clarified, the process of nourishing that identity—and *benefiting* from it—must be managed carefully. One metaphor that has been helpful to both brand managers, who make day-to-day decisions for their businesses, and corporate leaders, who are responsible for long range planning, is Margaret Mark's concept of the brand bank illustrated in Figure 6.1.

A brand is a repository of rich meaning and goodwill on the part of consumers. Any action taken in the name of that brand or "offer"—be it a short-term price promotion to attract new users, a customer relationship program, or an extension of the product line—enhances or nourishes the essential archetypal meaning of the brand, or it trades on it. Trading on the meaning, in this case, is not necessarily a bad thing: When Disney or Ralph Lauren elects to extend their names to yet another new line or concept, they are justifiably "cashing in" on years of carefully nurtured and nourished archetypal identities. And more and more companies are electing to try to similarly leverage strong existing equities to the max, as the cost of launching a new brand escalates along with the risk of failure in highly competitive marketplaces.

It's not that simple, however: Companies must have invested heavily in creating strong, consistent archetypal associations over time before assuming that they can cash in on them through brand extensions. For example, for some time, the Levi's brand has seemed a bit lost, having wandered away from its original Explorer archetype and into the Outlaw, the Hero, the Regular Guy and, more recently, the Lover. So if it were to launch Levi's Theme Vacations, what would the consumer expect? Sexy getaways? Down-to-earth budget trips? Or rugged adventures in the wild? Once, we all would have jumped at the third answer, but lately it's not so clear, creating a negative situation for trading on the parent brand identity. Consider, alternatively, the launch of Polo Ralph Lauren vacations. Or L.L. Bean trips? Don't you instantly get a sense of what each might be like? This comparison provides a fairly decent litmus test.

Beyond being sure that we have consistently nurtured a strong identity, we have to be sure that actions which "withdraw" from the Brand Bank are accompanied by commensurate actions which "deposit" the desired meaning into it. For example, Ronald McDonald Houses, the McDonald All Schools Band, and uniformly immaculate restaurants together go a long way toward compensating for the fact that McDonald's runs less heartwarming brand advertising and more competitive, opportunistic price promotions than it once did. But if all they had done were to switch the emphasis in their national advertising—with no compensatory "deposits"—the balance sheet would tip, and Americans would begin to feel very differently about the brand. Similarly, one brilliant *Lion King* production on the part of Disney and a theater that triggered the cleanup of Times Square, and the Disney/ABC versus Time Warner battle for dominance goes all but unnoticed by the consumer.

This kind of brand bank or balance sheet can be managed almost intuitively in the case of smaller one-product brands. But as more and more brands become multiproduct "superbrands," the need for more conscious "banking" is necessary.

Brands like Jell-O and Ivory each have more than one product, but the physical similarity of the products bearing their names helps to simplify matters. For instance, all Ivory offerings are associated with cleaning, so sustaining and supporting the Innocent brand archetype can be fairly automatic. But consider the brands mentioned earlier—Disney, Ralph Lauren, and others like them, such as Virgin. Each has numerous products, dissimilar to each other in both form and function. Now the burden falls entirely on maintaining some kind of *conceptual unity* across offerings and ensuring that that meaning is not depleted by continuous "withdrawals," but is constantly reinforced and replenished.

Perhaps it's not surprising that maintaining that conceptual unity seems to be best accomplished when the owner is a living icon him- or herself, as is the case with both Virgin and Ralph Lauren, or a legendary figure such as Walt Disney. The sensibility of the leader infects everything that he or she touches.

But systems need to work in the absence of cult of personality, and the Brand Bank is the best we have come across yet. As opposed to developing only linear marketing plans, brand management is also asked to organize plans for the brand in terms of likely "deposits" versus "withdrawals," to assess the "evenness" of the balance sheets, and to adjust accordingly. The process of managing the brand is given equal weight with the process of managing the business, an imperative if the archetypal identity is not to be squandered.

17

Telling Your Brand Story

MUCH CAN BE SAID about the qualities and characteristics of good marketing communication. But truly great communication—communication that creates, builds, and sustains the power of great brands—embodies an elementary paradox. Like all extraordinary literature and art, it lies at the intersection of time*less*ness and time*li*ness. It captures or taps into a fundamental, enduring truth about the human condition. And, at the same time, it expresses that truth in a fresh and contemporary way.

Like brands that stumble into archetypal identities, brand symbols, events, public relations efforts, and advertising campaigns sometimes wander onto this powerful turf, echoing patterns that have captivated people throughout the ages. The Clydesdales for Bud, Ronald McDonald, the Good Housekeeping seal, the Jolly Green Giant, and the Nike swoosh—symbols like these endure, while most others get zapped into oblivion after a few weeks or months of exposure. People don't tire of archetypal ideas after years—even decades—of seeing them, time after time. Multiple generations of consumers, lifestyle and life-stage segments, and global markets—as different as night and day—are still universally drawn to them. And, most relevant to the mini-stories we call advertising, the archetypes are often powerfully communicated in story form.

When the film *E.T.* became a rip-roaring success, many of us marveled at the fact that a homely little extraterrestrial could win so many hearts. But our archetypal analysis identified a pattern of story elements that had been recurring in stories throughout the ages: the "Tale of the Foundling," a Caregiver story for children.

In this tale, a small person, usually a child, starts out feeling dislocated and lonely, but then discovers a creature even more vulnerable than he. The child immediately becomes the protector. The child begins to feel stronger, minute by minute, as he and his charge are able to communicate with each other magically, defying differences in species or kind. Their relationship is kept secret from the more powerful creatures (usually adults), but expands to include a circle of other vulnerable ones. Together, they are able to fend off the threats to the little creature's well-being. One adult—usually a mother and always a woman—is allowed into their protective circle, becoming their ally. Eventually outwitting their predators, the little folk themselves willingly part from their beloved charge, returning it to its natural home so that it can develop freely and properly.

Almost every generation of children has its Foundling stories. Such stories help the children realize that while they must eventually separate from what they love and need the most—their mothers— they can not only survive that separation but even thrive. They can do so because learning that they can care for another helps them know they can eventually care for themselves.

Experiencing the story vicariously helps children develop. And *remembering the story*—even unconsciously—helps us cope, even as adults. We are probably not even remotely aware of the source of our strong feelings at the end of *E.T.*, but it is there. Deep within us, the memory of that separation, as well as the triumph of surviving it, is stirred.

Given the tremendous value of the foundling myth, it may come as no surprise that when Margaret Mark and Paul Wolansky, a film professor at the University of Southern California, reconstructed the story patterns of over 500 successful films over the past 50 years, a popular Foundling story repeatedly emerged at regular intervals. Almost every generation needed, and got, its own Foundling. (And we might wonder about the lost opportunity during the period which no blockbuster Foundling emerged.) The details of these archetypal stories are varied, but the basic structures are remarkably consistent.

It was *The Yearling* in 1946, *Old Yeller* in 1958, *E.T.* in 1982, *Free Willy* in 1993 . . . an astounding reflection of the power and importance of mythic stories. The foundling may take the form of a horse or a dog or a "politically correct" 1990s whale, but the fundamental architecture of these stories and the purpose they serve remain inviolate. The details are simply updated to fit the times. But in each era, people love to learn the stories, again and again, because they serve some important psychological purpose for their audiences, whether they realize it or not.

Let Me Tell You a Story

There are only two or three great human stories,
and they go on repeating themselves
as fiercely as if they had never happened before.
Willa Cather

As the storytellers for archetypal brands, we should be capable of understanding and expressing the great human stories, providing a "voice"—to be communicated through advertising, points of sale, Web sites, public relations, and so on—that is worthy of a mythic identity. In many cases, these stories may be the narratives that reveal the essential dilemmas and issues surrounding your archetype. However, great story patterns can often be used by more than one archetype. For example, the Cinderella story is a Lover story, so it is a good story to tell for a Lover brand. However, if your brand has a function similar to that of the fairy godmother, then the story could be used by a Magician brand, casting the brand in the role of the magical helper. If your brand has a Hero or Explorer identity, you would focus on the role of the prince, searching everywhere for his lost love and, in the process, rescuing her.

But what are the great stories? And what is the meaning and purpose of stories in our lives in the first place? It pays to consider the early role that stories played in our own lives and in the evolution of the culture.

If you have had children, or if you can remember being a child yourself, you know that one of the first sentences you uttered and that you repeated again and again and again was "Can you tell me a story?" And if it was a good story, you wanted to hear it over and over and over.

The conventional wisdom is that children crave simple familiarity. But does that alone explain why certain children's stories have been cherished generation after generation? Or, for that matter, why modern, busy adults will watch *It's a Wonderful Life* every year of their own lives, even though they know every turn of the plot? Or why the original *Star Wars* trilogy or the "Star Trek" TV series developed huge cult followings who watched these movies and shows dozens of times? Or, even more revealing, why the great religions the world over reflect the same stories, characters, and themes?

Working with Margaret on the analysis of story patterns, Wolansky explained: "Before the invention of writing, stories were passed down from generation to generation as campfire, ghost, and bedtime stories. Over time, as stories were told, memorized, and retold, certain stories, ideas, themes, characters, and situations would resonate deeply with listeners and would be saved. Other story details would be found lacking and tossed aside. In film terms, these stories had good 'word of mouth' over the generations, and ultimately became the enduring, distilled, universally 'truthful' fairy tales, legends, and mythological stories that have come down to us today."

Bruno Bettelheim, in *The Uses of Enchantment*, described the same kind of "sorting process" occurring when children distinguish between very good stories and merely ordinary ones. The child wants to hear a *good* story over and over again because she intuitively recognizes some deep truth in it; she has a vague feeling that the story has something important to tell her.*

The best stories, then, the stories that transcend time and place, are more than simply entertaining—they are in some way *useful* to us, children and adults alike. They help us work through unconscious pressures and deal with fear, anger, and anxiety, and they lend expression to deep yearnings we are often unable to articulate or even identify. They may be cloaked in quite contemporary dress—and the "delivery system" may be a film, a well-told joke, or a 30-second

* Bruno Bettelheim, *The Uses of Enchantment* (New York: Alfred A. Knopf, Inc., 1976).

commercial—but if it provides this kind of profound value or utility, it will move us powerfully. Like children, we want to understand the lesson, the "gift" of the story, to "get it," and to integrate it into our lives.

Great Stories, Great Ads

The idea of the story in advertising is as old as the "slice of life" construct first pioneered, to great advantage, by Procter & Gamble. It was assumed, and often proven, that the vehicle of the story did more to engage viewers and involve them in the inherent drama of the product than did a simple exposition of features and benefits.

But the principle of the advertising story providing more than an effective sale—in fact, providing a "gift"—was first studied in a systematic way years after the Procter & Gamble invention, in the work of Mary Jane Schlinger at the University of Illinois at Chicago Circle. Analyzing viewers' responses to hundreds of television commercials, Dr. Schlinger discovered that the most effective ads demonstrated a principle of "reciprocity": When the viewer was "given" something (beyond the information necessary to consummate the sale) in return for his or her time and attention, the running of the ad constituted a "fair exchange," a kind of *quid pro quo* in return for the viewer's time and attention. Viewers were then more likely to consider rewarding the advertiser with their business. On the other hand, if there was nothing in the ad for the viewer beyond a self-serving sale of merchandise, the exchange was shallow, unfulfilling, and ultimately ineffectual.

Working with Dr. Joseph Plummer at Leo Burnett, Schlinger identified numerous dimensions of "viewer reward" and developed a unique instrument, or testing system, for quantifying subjective responses to television advertisements.* Using that technique to repeatedly explore different consumer groups' responses to a huge range of commercials for wildly divergent categories of products, the two researchers demonstrated that advertising was not exempt from the principle of "story utility" that Bettelheim or Joseph Campbell applied to legends and tales or—the principle that Carl Jung used to

---

* Mary Jane Schlinger, "A Profile of Responses to Commercials," *Journal of Advertising Research*, Volume II, September 1984.

decode the recurring dream patterns of patients from different parts of the world.

The best commercials, like all truly effective communications, strike a deep nerve or reveal a deep truth, and the responses to that universal and timeless power can be codified and understood. For example, consider the characteristics of empathy, one of the seven dimensions of viewer reward examined in the Viewer Reward Profile (VRP) technique. Empathy reveals the extent to which the viewer participates in the events and feelings in the ad, assumes some imaginary role in the situation, and feels an emotional involvement with what is happening. Empathy can be an emotionally rewarding experience, allowing the viewer to enhance his self-image or express his values. Rituals and rites of passage, the depiction of close, warm relationships, and larger-than-life characters often engender high empathy scores, but the situations, relationships, or characters do not have to be slavishly realistic to engender empathy.* (Mythic figures and places such as the Pillsbury Doughboy and the "valley" of the Green Giant generate above-average ratings on empathy.)

The Leo Burnett Company, one of the original participants in this research, used the testing and the theories to support and extend its legacy of creating deep, enduring advertising campaigns and symbols, such as the Marlboro man, the Jolly Green Giant, and the Keebler elves, to name a few. Later, Joe Plummer brought the technique with him to Young & Rubicam, using it to support and enrich that company's understanding of creative work guided by insight—great, story-driven campaigns that won industry acclaim and marketplace success for brands such as Hallmark, AT&T, Merrill Lynch, and Johnson & Johnson.

Other agencies got there in their own way as well. Under the leadership of Phil Dusenberry and Ted Sann, two of the great storytellers of the commercial world, BBD&O was turning out one delightful and enduring story after another for the Pepsi brand.

When they were intuited by brilliant art directors and copywriters, these little "brand stories" were phenomenally successful, and the VRP gave agencies a tool to quantitatively assess and defend advertising that moved minds and hearts while it sold products. But these creators and writers, even the best of them, often came up dry,

---

* *Ibid.*

having little inspiration to draw on. What Madison Avenue still lacked, Hollywood was catching on to.

Star Wars and the Hero with a Thousand Faces

In the 1960s, when George Lucas was a student at the USC Cinema School, he made a discovery that would influence his fate and would irrevocably change the art and craft of filmmaking: He stumbled across the writings of Joseph Campbell. Lucas's *Star Wars*, created over a decade later, drew heavily on that discovery and on the Arthurian myth cycle. In the myths, the farm boy Parsifal must become a knight and find the Holy Grail, lest the land die; in *Star Wars*, the farm boy Luke Skywalker must master the Force and uncover the secret to destroying the Death Star in order to save the galaxy. The wizard Merlin is mentor to the young Arthur; the Jedi Knight Obi-Wan Kenobi becomes Luke's mentor. Arthur pulls the sword Excalibur from the stone in which it is lodged; Luke learns to use his father's light saber, which he will use to set things right.

As codified by writer, producer, and story analyst Chris Vogler, the deep structure of *Star Wars* reveals an almost perfect parallel to Campbell's model of the Hero's Journey, summarized in Figure 6.5.[1] Yet, unlike the parallel of *E.T.* and the foundling myth, *Star Wars* seems to have been modeled in a more deliberate and conscious way.

Star Wars, of course, became the box office winner of all time. And what Lucas did paved new ground. There had been countless "script templates" before. Aristotle had codified the first principles of drama in his *Poetics* in 321 B.C., and over a millennium later, Lajos Egri's *The Art of Dramatic Writing* (1946) also emphasized the importance of the lesson or the premise. In 1979, Syd Field offered a simple, easy-to-grasp three-part paradigm in *The Screenplay*, and great filmmakers such as Akira Kurosawa and Jean Renoir had long recognized the similarity between film structure and symphonic structure—three or four movements, including exposition, development, and resolution.

But what Lucas did with Campbell's work went far beyond improving the "craft" or narrative flow of the story: As Wolansky points

---

1. Christopher Vogler, *The Writer's Journey: Mythic Structure for Writers* (Michael Wiese Productions, 1998).

The Hero's Journey	Star Wars
THE HERO EXISTS IN AN ORDINARY WORLD	Luke Skywalker as a bored farmboy, dreaming of going to the space academy
HE GETS THE CALL TO ADVENTURE	Luke receives distress hologram from Princess Leia
HE ALMOST REFUSES THE CALL	Luke delivers the message to Obi-Wan but decides to go back home
THE WISE ELDER ADVISES HIM TO HEED THE CALL	Obi-Wan advises Luke to come with him
HE ENTERS THE SPECIAL WORLD . . .	Luke follows Obi-Wan into the Cantina
WHERE HE ENCOUNTERS TESTS, DISCOVERS ALLIES AND ENEMIES	Luke meets Hans Solo, they escape from Imperial Storm Troopers, fight a laser battle, jump to hyperspace, emerge in a meteor storm
HE ENTERS THE INMOST CAVE	Luke and company are pulled into the Death Star
WHERE HE ENCOUNTERS THE SUPREME ORDEAL	Luke and company in the "trash masher"; Obi-Wan "killed" by Darth Vader
HE SEIZES THE SWORD	Luke gets the plans to the Death Star
TAKES THE ROAD BACK	Luke and company pursued by Darth Vader
ALMOST DIES, BUT IS RESURRECTED	Despite being wounded, Luke hits the weak spot and destroys the Death Star
AND RETURNS WITH THE ELIXIR	Luke learns the message of the film; not to rely on machines, but to "trust the force"—his intuition, which is already within him. He is transformed from a boy to a hero, a fully realized human being.

Figure 6.5

out, Lucas benefited from the realization that it is the *inner struggle* of the character that provides the deep structure. And his act also paved the way for a whole new source of inspiration and validation for creative people of all stripes who intuitively thought and felt in archetypal terms, but had no tools to guide and structure their work.

Bringing the Myths to Madison Avenue

Margaret Mark had long believed that archetypal story patterns could be studied, codified, and applied to the development of advertising and other commercial communication. She also felt that the marketing community suffered from a kind of insularity, in that it didn't fully benefit from what could be learned from how the public responds to art and literature—not just the stuff of universities and intellectuals, but in their most common and everyday forms. If we are the "image makers," why aren't we continually examining and trying to understand the appeal of prints that are chosen to hang on living room walls across America and beyond? Or, for that matter, why aren't we studying the pictures and sayings in the most popular greeting cards, or the postcards tourists are most likely to buy when they visit Washington, DC, or New York? (Which symbol of America is spontaneously favored by ordinary Americans and visitors to the United States? Isn't this something sophisticated marketing communicators should know?) Or shouldn't we be continually analyzing the content of the lyrics of the most popular songs? And most importantly, why wouldn't we feel some urgency to understand the stories that people have loved and cherished over the ages and around the world?

Working both independently and with Young & Rubicam, Margaret teamed up with Wolansky to systematically examine the patterns of the most "popular" of our story "delivery systems," movies. Film by film, Wolansky deconstructed stories, not by superficial categories of "genre" (romantic comedy, horror/suspense, etc.), but in terms of their deep architecture or "bones" of the story. Their work deliberately focused on films that met with marketplace success, as opposed to movies that were critically acclaimed but rejected by the public.

In the end, their analysis showed that virtually all of the leading box office hits of the past 50 years reflected mythic patterns in whole or in part. In most cases, these patterns had antecedents in literature, sacred stories, myth, and legend. But in some cases, interestingly enough, film seemed to be required to make some adaptations in order to satisfy the public. This was most notable among what they called the "cautionary tales." Religions and literature abound with a category they titled "Paradise Lost": The Innocent, unsatisfied by the beauty of the world around him, reaches for forbidden fruit and, as a result, loses all that was good about his life. In the Bible or in medieval morality plays, no one got the chance to gripe about "ticket prices" just because there was a stern warning and an unhappy ending. But in films, the "warning" must be delivered in a more oblique way if it is to be accepted. So, for example, the ending of the movie *Fatal Attraction*, a clear Paradise Lost tale (like the story of Adam and Eve or that of Dr. Faust), was changed from one of absolute doom to a last-minute second chance for the protagonist, resulting in a kind of "Paradise *Almost* Lost" adaptation. For the most part, though, the story structures of successful films are remarkably consistent with fables, myth, and legend. Consider, for instance, our "Ugly Duckling" construct:

The Ugly Duckling
- The special beauty, virtue, or power of the protagonist is hidden by ordinary clothing or a disguise.
- The character is trapped in stasis.
- No one realizes the character's true inner capabilities or virtues, except for one individual, who *suspects* them.
- The key moment is the change of costume or "externals" that reveals the true inner self.
- The character can begin to realize his or her special identity.
- Forces (or internal obstacles) conspire to bring the character back to his or her original role.
- The character overcomes those forces and gains deserved recognition.

The psychological "gift" or appeal of the Ugly Duckling story is that it reflects a deep yearning we all feel from time to time: If only they knew how good or how smart I am deep inside, if only they understood the *real me*, I'd be accepted, promoted, loved, etc.

We see the Ugly Duckling tale realized in stories as disparate as *Zorro*, *Moonstruck*, *My Fair Lady*, *Superman*, *Sabrina*, *Working Girl*, *Pretty Woman*, and, of course, one of the favorite stories of all time, *Cinderella*.

If a screenwriter or advertiser didn't understand the importance of the "change of clothes" in this story—the moment in which the "inside" and the "outside" become aligned—we would never have had Clark Kent in the phone booth, Julia Roberts on Rodeo Drive, or the magic of Cinderella's rags transformed into a ballroom gown. More significantly, if the writer misinterpreted the pattern as "realizing your fantasies," she would distort the value or message of the story, as might have happened with a star-studded flop called *The Mirror Has Two Faces*. In that film, Barbra Streisand becomes something she's *not* in order to win love—not a terribly useful template for living one's life. In the great Ugly Duckling stories, on the other hand, we are shown how to understand and express who we *are*, and then everything falls into place.

The total inventory of these rich story patterns can be understood as either guides or warnings, imparting corresponding messages or "gifts," as shown in Figure 6.6.

The lifelong process of maturation and development is reflected in the "arc" of the story patterns on the grid. Like the archetypes, each fits primarily in one quadrant, but in stories there is a built-in assumption of character development, of change.

For example, the stories in the lower left-hand quadrant reflect an appreciation of the status quo and a fear of change—feelings reflective of an individual's or a whole culture's desire to remain "safe." Transformation stories, at the intersection of the map, deal with a quantum leap, the moment of transition when we become ready to pursue our destiny. Moving to the upper right-hand quadrant, we see that the Hero's Journey reflects the quest for self-actualization and wholeness; Paradise Found is the realization of that wholeness.

The Wandering Angel structure, shown on the arc, involves the catalyst for helping the protagonist make the transition from one stage to the next in the process of maturation and self-development.

In a classic film such as *It's a Wonderful Life*, or in contemporary ones like *Heaven Can Wait*, *Mary Poppins*, and *Jerry McGuire*, it is a mystical or transient character who "shows the way" for the protag-

The Guides

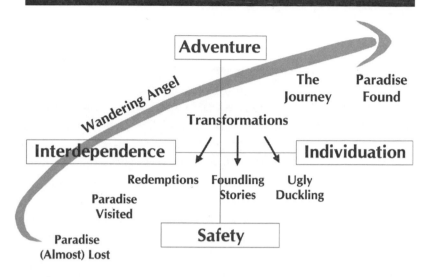

The Warnings

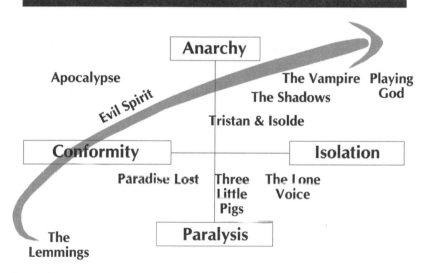

Figure 6.6

onist to get unstuck, get on with it—treasure the circumstances of his or her own life. The shifts that are undertaken may be related to one's life stage and development, or they may be related to an evolution of needs, independent of the stage in life. Throughout our lives, all of these structures are useful, but, depending on the cultural zeitgeist or more personal issues that we are dealing with, one or more of the structures will seem more relevant.

For example, the Paradise structures may be very compelling to the overwrought Ruler who is wishing that he or she could simply exit that life, cast off the trappings of success, and enjoy everyday pleasures—in short, the wish of the Ruler to become the Innocent. The Paradise Visited story pattern speaks to this pining: The protagonist inadvertently stumbles into an earthly paradise, savors its simplicity for a moment, but then reluctantly realizes that he or she must return to business as usual. Films such as *Witness* and *Local Hero* speak to this yearning and realization—"You can have a taste of a simpler, better life, but then you must return to where you belong."

Vacation sites targeted to the Ruler can tap into the Paradise Visited story. The story pattern reminds us of the enormous appeal pure simplicity holds for people with overly complicated lives. Like Harrison Ford living among the Amish in *Witness*, the ability to savor pure Innocent pleasure, however momentary, is irresistible.

The Paradise Found structure takes that yearning to another plane. In this pattern, the protagonist is in stasis. He may have a problem he needs to deal with or a vague sense that things could be better, but he has no plan. Then he stumbles into a perfect place, where life is simple, priorities are in order, and he can take time to smell the roses. At first he struggles with the strangeness of it all, but over time, its beauty begins to reveal itself to him. He is called back to his ordinary world and reluctantly leaves the Innocent paradise. He attempts to return to the life he was living, but he can't cope as he did before; now that he knows too much, he has been irreversibly transformed by the process. He finds the Utopia again and chooses to stay there.

The stories that reflect this pattern go far beyond the idea of just breaking the surface and putting a toe in the water: The protagonist takes the plunge and changes his or her life. Consider the film *Baby Boom*, with Diane Keaton.

Keaton's character has a high-powered glamour job and lifestyle, but is caught up in a passionless relationship and a brutally competitive career. When an orphan baby (a distant cousin's child) is dropped into her life, she loses her job and is forced, in desperation, to move to a farmhouse in Vermont. Keaton finds the house, the country, the baby, and the only single man in town, a veterinarian played by Sam Shepard, too alien for words. But little by little, she falls in love with the baby, the vet, and Vermont. She starts a business, but an Innocent business—creating natural, premium baby foods—called "Country Baby." She feels avenged when her former company, impressed by her entrepreneurial prowess, offers to buy "Country Baby" and reinstate her to her former position. She is momentarily tempted to fall back into the rat race, but, in a moment of epiphany, chooses to return to Vermont, her baby, and her new love. Of course, the implicit message of this story is that a simpler, better, more fulfilling life is possible if you have the guts to throw away all of your prestige, power, and status for the real thing.

Investment houses could tap into this pattern. For every high-achieving Boomer saving for a future of private jets and luxury condos, there's one who yearns for the luxury of being able to fish every day if he wants, to stay at home to be a full-time dad, or to become an inner-city elementary school teacher.

The Interplay of Guides and Warnings

Understanding the interplay of the guides and the warnings plays an important role in helping us to understand which story to use when. For example, the March of Dimes, in trying to communicate about the important work the organization is doing in genetic research, is considering both the positive and the "darker" stories that relate to reaching beyond customary boundaries. On the "dark" side, related stories fall into the category of Playing God, expressed in films like *Frankenstein* and *The Fly*—science so seductive that it leads human beings to overstep their circumscribed bounds and venture into the realm that rightly belongs only to the deities. But, on the positive side, the corollary to these urges, taken as a guide, shows how the healthy and appropriate reaching for success is the story of the Hero (who rescues the vulnerable ones), the Magician (who transforms people and things for the better), and the Sage (who provides wisdom and knowledge). Informed by both types of story patterns, the organization thus is in a position to communicate in inspiring, rather than frightening, ways.

This newly developed inventory of story patterns is now helping communicators of all stripes to benefit from the inspiration offered by timeless, beloved tales. And it is finally working its way into the little stories we call advertising.

One Archetype, Many Stories

Our approach recommends identifying the most appropriate and effective single archetype for your brand. But having done that, you will likely find that a myriad of story patterns, or different aspects of one story pattern, can inspire your brand's communication over time. Start by revisiting the motivational needs that underlie your brand's archetype, and then find the corresponding concepts that relate to the story patterns.

For example, Nike, once a strong Hero brand, did a great job of expressing *some* parts of the Hero's journey: the call to adventure ("Just do it"); entering the special world (magnificent vistas, the private space of the runner); and the supreme ordeal (the implication that, by testing yourself, you are taking on your own inner demons). But much opportunity for plumbing the depths of the story further was left unrealized: Who is the runner's Merlin, or wise elder? Who are his or her allies and enemies? What is the "elixir" in this case, and how do you find it?

By way of comparison, Pepsi, over time, has richly milked its Jester archetype with a myriad of fresh and interesting stories: Michael J. Fox, our modern-day Puck, sneaking out of his apartment window and running down the fire escape to get the can of Diet Pepsi for his pretty neighbor waiting at his apartment door; Pepsi being accidentally delivered to the old folks' home, prompting a wild party, while everyone snores at the frat house that got the delivery of Coke; and an "archaeology" spot, in which a professor and students of the future uncover artifacts from the 1990s, identifying their historic significance one by one until they come to a bottle of Coke, an article so long extinct that nobody knows what it is. (Of course, they are all drinking Pepsi as they marvel at this unknown object.)

The Guides		
Psychological needs	**Message/Gift**	**Story patterns**
Interdependence and Safety	Appreciate your world and your place in it	*Paradise (Almost) Lost* *Paradise Visited*
Wish for Adventure and Individuation	Maturation and growth are difficult, but achievable; you have it within yourself to change	*Redemption Stories* *Foundling Stories* *The Ugly Duckling*
Realizing Adventure and Individuation	If you have the courage to grow, you can achieve true happiness in this life	*The Journey* *Paradise Found*

The Warnings		
Fear	**Message/Warning**	**Story patterns**
Conformity and Paralysis	You will lose yourself in an excessive desire for security and conformity	*Lemmings*
Isolation and Paralysis	Only the disciplined and courageous individual can restore order	*The Lone Voice* *The Three Little Pigs*
Anarchy and Isolation	Without discipline and interdependence, destruction is inevitable	*Tristan & Isolde* *The Shadows* *The Vampire*

Pepsi's—and BBD&O's—intuitive understanding of the spirit of the Jester archetype has successfully translated into a fairly steady image of the good-natured, puckish mischief maker poking fun at sanctimonious Coke. The stories never get old—from the original "Pepsi Challenge" to today's campaign featuring the little girl with the Godfather voice, challenging people when they think they can trick her into drinking Coke.

Other brands have successfully stayed true to their identity by telling stories that express the relationship their archetype has with other archetypes. For example, the deep equity of AT&T makes it a strong Caregiver brand. While the industry has profoundly changed since divestiture (and continues to change daily), AT&T's deep roots and its best leverage lie in the company's being the telecom brand that most cares about, and cares *for*, its customers. Its original nickname was "*Ma* Bell." During divestiture, recognizing that the customer was confused and anxious, AT&T set up an 800 number and ran an advertising campaign inviting people to call, with the tag line, "Let's Talk." AT&T's telephone operators answered the phone by saying, "How can I help you?" and for a time, AT&T's national advertising used that line as well. The operators were famous for going far beyond the call of duty to help their customers out, and stories were legion of operators saving children who called during emergencies.

Even in the confusion of more recent times, when AT&T's true Caregiver colors fly, it stands out from the pack. Such was the case during a phase of the national advertising campaign in which Caregiver AT&T intervened on the part of other archetypal characters. For example, in a spot featuring a superharried, superachieving Ruler mom, the Caregiver makes it possible for her to soften, relax, and temporarily revel in an Innocent world (Paradise Visited): She blows off a day at the office to take her little girls to the beach. Her AT&T cell phone helps make that possible, since she can call in later in the day.

In another spot in the AT&T series, the Caregiver leads the orphan to shelter in a Redemption/Wandering Angel story structure very much like the one expressed in *It's a Wonderful Life*. A young runaway in deep despair on a dark street corner finds his way home, both spiritually and literally, because of a mystical experience of hearing a beautiful woman singing "Amazing Grace" into the cold night air. The music triggers memories of his home, with his dad loading the Christmas tree onto the car. He goes to a pay phone and tells the operator that he wants to call home, but has no money. "Stay on the line. I can help you," she says, as she puts him through to his stunned and tearful mother. The commercial, run during the Christmas season, ends with the words, "If you're lost or stranded, we can help. Call this toll-free number. Greetings of the season. AT&T."

The number of calls to the line was so overwhelming that even AT&T's powerful switchboards were overloaded. In yet another spot in the series, Caregiver AT&T enables the lonely and isolated Explorer to feel connected. To the strains of Elton John's "Rocket Man," a man in a plane sends a fax to his wife, inviting her to go out on their front porch at a certain time that night. When she does, she sees the very plane he is in flying overhead amidst the stars.

The "stories" campaign beautifully demonstrates how one archetype, the Caregiver, helps a range of others. The stories themselves are powerful narratives, rooted in deep structures that are at once both familiar and new: We immediately recognize the profound human truth they contain, and yet we are surprised that they are being retold in such a fresh and unexpected way. In fact, it is the surprising familiarity of archetypal stories that makes us instantly recognize them, even in the flash of a 30-second spot.

Carl Hixon, one of the creative greats from the glory days of Leo Burnett, summed it up this way:

> It took me many years and many lumps to value the familiar, because, as a young copywriter, my instincts were to shun the familiar and to embrace the contemporary. But I learned. One of my teachers was Jimmy Durante, "the schnoz," with whom I worked for several years in the 1960s. Durante applied the theory of familiarity to his humor. There are two kinds of humor, he believed. There's humor of surprise that confronts you with something unexpected, and there's humor of the familiar—the kind that people love to hear over and over again, like kids listening to a familiar bedtime story. The one wears out the instant the surprise is over. The other improves with age. Durante's performance was built on the latter—on the beloved familiar—old routines the audience knew by heart, and would have been disappointed not to hear.

"Archetypal brands and stories are familiar because they belong to our inner life," Hixon put it, "just as surely as the memory of the toys we had when we were kids, or the music that was woven into our first love affair, or the way our old dog smelled when he was wet and warm." We recognize and embrace them because the concepts they represent are larger than the product or service; the product or service is simply one aspect of their meaning.

The story, of course, can be told in print as well as on TV. Some of the best print ever has evoked a story, even if it could not fully tell one. Consider, for example, the long-running campaign featuring the "Hathaway Man," who wears a patch over one eye. Why does he have the patch? Who *is* he really? The not knowing—the having to "fill in the blanks"—demands that the reader build a story around the ad. More recently, Foster Grant's "Who is it behind those . . . ?" campaign does a similar thing: We are required to participate in the advertising by imagining the story that accompanies it.

Today's Story Becomes Tomorrow's Icon

Archetypal brands are classless, ageless, and regionless, and their deep meaning must be inviolate. That's why it matters that the brand's story (not just its advertising, but the whole myth or legend surrounding the brand) must be congruent with the brand's core archetype. Brands are trusted to the degree that everything they do is consistent. Products seem right when everything about them is aligned with their informing archetype. This obviously includes the product's logo, tag line, product design, packaging, and placement in stores, as well as the design of the story, the environment surrounding the sale of the product, and the look and story line of all promotional materials, including your Web site. They all should tell your story.

Brands make history, and they become history. They may be part of our shared story or our personal and individual narratives. Generally, if you ask an American three-year-old to draw a cookie, she will draw an Oreo, and if you ask her to draw a dog biscuit, she will draw a Milk Bone. Sketching the "ideal home," many baby boomers will create the two-story Colonial the Cleavers lived in. Etched deeply in our collective and individual memories are stories of our ancestors and our first loves, our dreams realized and unfulfilled. The commercial world is comingled with these deepest memories and longings. We need only study and understand these road maps of the unconscious to find the surest paths for our brands.

18

The Case of the March of Dimes

Lessons in a Lobby

T HE LOBBY of the national headquarters of the March of Dimes Birth Defects Foundation, in White Plains, New York, is a quiet, pleasant, and nondescript place, unless you happen to wander around a corner behind the staircase and notice a display along the wall. There behind the glass case are relics from another time: newspapers and packages that tell a story that is as chilling as it is inspiring. The front pages of the *New York Times* and the *Journal American*, now yellowed with age, scream out with double-sized headlines proclaiming that a vaccine has been found to be effective against a deadly epidemic called polio. Packages of the Salk vaccine, wrapped in brown paper with "RUSH" imprinted everywhere, lie next to the papers. And if you turn around, there is an iron lung, once used in a desperate effort to keep victims alive until that vaccine could be found, and then, until it could reach them.

It is hard today to imagine the terror that seized the United States during the polio epidemic. Victor Cohn, in *Four Million Dimes*, describes the summer of 1916: "Panic froze the East, particularly New

York City, where 2000 died and another 7000 were attacked (three fourths of them children under 5). Thousands tried to leave—police at highways and railroad stations halted them. Few hospitals would take polio cases. Police had to break into apartments to take dead children from their mothers." The disease was unpredictable, inexplicable, and indifferent to social station—even Franklin Delano Roosevelt, a well-off young man who would someday become president of the United States, was its victim.

Over the next several decades, the American public would become aroused to take on the fight against polio with a fervor tantamount to a war effort. Medical researchers, feverishly trying to find the cure, often died themselves in the process of experimenting with the new drugs. Under the leadership of President Roosevelt and Basil O'Connor, millions of dollars were raised for medical research, and millions of dimes were sent from all corners of America to contribute, piece by piece, to America's other war. And at the heart of all this unprecedented public intervention was a new organization called the National Foundation for the Prevention of Infantile Paralysis, later known as the March of Dimes.

That terrifying time, the quietly pleasant White Plains headquarters of today's March of Dimes, and the *new* dangers that the organization confronts can all be understood and unified through the archetypal lens. What's more, an understanding of its archetypal identity is helping the March of Dimes become an even more effective force against the powers of disease and ignorance.

A New Enemy

Today, the March of Dimes confronts a different, but equally devastating, threat than the infantile paralysis that plagued America during the first half of the twentieth century—birth defects. The March of Dimes underwrites major new studies of premature birth and groundbreaking research on gene therapy. It sponsors a major public service campaign encouraging all women of childbearing years to take the B vitamin folic acid, which has been shown to help prevent birth defects of the brain and spinal cord. It lobbies for health insurance for the 11 million children who currently have none. It manages the March of Dimes Resource Center, through which the organization's health information specialists provide expert answers to questions about pregnancy and birth defects.

The problems the March of Dimes is trying to prevent and, when it can't, the problems it has to deal with are very real, and they are widespread. Each day in America, 151 babies are born so small that they have to fight for their lives. Ninety-three are born with hearts that do not work properly. Seventy-seven die. But unlike polio, these threats, and the tragedies that often result, are more private and personal. The death of an infant or a lifetime of caring for a severely disabled child is a devastating experience for the family that must endure it. But it is fairly "invisible" to the rest of society. This is terrible, but it is not a contagious disease. Accordingly, until it happens to one of us, we like to think that we are somehow "immune." As a result, it is much harder to arouse the kind of immediate passionate public support for "the prevention of birth defects" than it once was to rouse the public to defeat polio. And so, ironically, understanding the public and understanding how to connect people to this cause with some sense of urgency and passion are almost as important to today's March of Dimes as is the breakthrough medical research that it sponsors.

Again ironically, this non-profit organization (like many others) faces an even tougher challenge than most *for*-profit ventures—a challenge that demands a higher level of marketing sophistication: The March of Dimes is "selling a product"—prevention of birth defects—that people don't even want to think about, let alone actively support. The organization is fighting faceless enemies: denial and apathy. Yet, it manages to stir up a tremendous amount of public support. Walk America, the March of Dimes' major annual fundraising event, involves about 1 million participants stepping out to support children on a single day each year in the spring—average Americans in 1,400 communities across the country. Last year, WalkAmerica raised over $85.5 million. And since the event started in 1970, the organization, in total, has raised more than $1 billion. In spite of all the obstacles, how do they do it?

A New Positioning

In 1995, the March of Dimes Board of Trustees initiated a market research project intended to help understand and deepen the organization's connection to its target audiences—the women, children, and families who benefit from its mission, along with its current and potential donors and volunteers. The Board wanted to explore perceptions of the March of Dimes and to learn how it might present its mission more powerfully.

The major result of the initial work was a change in positioning—from "preventing birth defects," which led people to imagine an already handicapped child in a wheelchair, to "saving babies, together," which led people to think about innocent infants and the possibility of squandering human potential. While both concepts were emotionally potent, the latter was far truer to the present work of today's March of Dimes. While the March of Dimes advocates for services for disabled children and their families, the bulk of the organization's fund-raising and research is devoted to *preventing* these problems in the first place.

But all marketers know that prevention is a difficult sale, especially when what is being prevented is as unsettling a prospect as birth defects. The fear of bearing an "imperfect" child is a primal one—since time immemorial, mothers of newborns count fingers and toes, and myth and legend are filled with terrifying images of aberrant children.

But could this primal or archetypal fear be turned to a *positive* emotion—one strong enough to trigger a *preventative* call to action? Susan Royer, then Planning Director at the Lord Group, the advertising agency for the March of Dimes, thought it might be possible. She had seen the work Margaret had done with archetypes and archetypal stories, and she thought it might be powerfully applicable to the cause of the March of Dimes.

The day it was first presented to the senior managers of the organization was a pivotal one. Margaret took them through the presentation of the concept of applying archetypes to brand identity, followed by brief descriptions of the archetypes and of archetypal story patterns. Royer followed with a short piece recommending her initial thoughts as to where the archetypes might guide them. What happened from there was an incredible example of how this type of thinking can prompt organizations to recognize, and act upon, their deepest cultural values.

Not a minute after the presentation, Dr. Jennifer L. Howse, president of the March of Dimes, proclaimed to the group that the thinking had led her to an inevitable conclusion about the "soul" of the organization and that she was curious as to whether others had had the same immediate reaction. She said that she had written down the archetype she felt was at their core on a piece of paper before her. Others responded that they had done the same. And when they lifted their papers to show their instinctual thinking, the word "Hero" appeared simultaneously on each one.

This unanimous selection was really quite astounding. Nonprofits that are in the business of helping children almost inevitably are drawn to the gravitational force of the Caregiver, and to all of the imagery that surrounds that archetype. Research about the competition had reinforced how prevailing the Caregiver identity was in organizations helping children. Even the March of Dimes, in its earlier positioning work, had adopted a corporate logo that shows a line drawing of an infant in the soft embrace of a mother figure.

But what led Howse and the other executives of the organization to write "Hero" on their charts was quite different from the emotion surrounding the Caregiver. Every day, as they went through that serene lobby, whether they noticed it or not, they had filed past that iron lung and those headlines proclaiming victory over polio. And every day they went to work to try to wrest a victory from today's silent and unseen enemies: youth and ignorance leading to unhealthy pregnancies, premature births, emotionally and physically debilitating birth defects, and the unnecessary deaths of little babies. Whether they had acknowledged it or not, these people were working for a *heroic* cause, and there was something wonderfully validating and inspiring in acknowledging that this was the case. The Hero archetype also spoke to them as people—in some real way it expressed values that they held in common, that motivated their collective actions. But could it be effective in today's cynical age?

Howse could not have been clearer on that subject and on the potential power of the archetypal approach. Following the presentation and the discussion that ensued, she cautioned the group, "This is powerful stuff, not to be reckoned with lightly. If we are to pursue this approach, if we are to adopt the 'Hero' archetype, we are to do it as carefully and responsibly as possible. We have to be sure it is right for us, right for the cause we serve, right for the public." So we set out to live up to her challenge.

Becoming Heroic

The first major test of this premise turned out to be the March of Dimes' most important annual event: Walk America 2000. The organization's agency, the Lord Group, had developed several approaches to encouraging people to come out and participate in this year's version of the original walking event. Some focused on the pure fun and sociability of the event—for example, a TV approach that used the old Fred Astaire song "Stepping Out with My Baby" and showed walkers high-fiving each other, enjoying good times for a good cause in the fresh spring air. Another approach challenged viewers with the idea that "You've talked the talk, now walk the walk"—with a silhouette of a baby taking its first step.

Finally, one approach was developed to directly express the idea of the March of Dimes as a "Hero"—and to invite members of the public to become Heroes themselves.

The research we conducted on these ideas was most illuminating. While many people talked about a "good time, with good people on a Spring day," the ideas that simply captured this feel-good experience underrepresented the true emotional reward of the event. Instead, the walkers revealed a deep and abiding desire to protect babies. For some, the feeling was prompted by the experience of having lost a baby or come close to it; for others, by having struggled to conceive a baby themselves; and for still others, by simple gratitude for the health of their own children. But beyond that, people who had never had children or even thought about it were profoundly moved to participate in the event by the archetypal concept of the Innocent—unborn babies, pure and entirely undeserving of serious threats to their well-being, vessels for our collective dreams and ideals, able to remind us of what's good in life and what's still good in *ourselves*—vulnerable and entirely dependent on our unselfishness and our goodwill. In Margaret's interviews, most people said things like

> "We've had our chance. Now we have to be sure that they have their chance."
>
> "There are babies in need. They could be anybody's baby."
>
> "These babies can't help themselves, so they need us to help."

"This isn't like other causes that my company has gotten involved with. With this one, you can't blame the victim for what has happened. . . ."

Not surprisingly, in terms of the archetypal story patterns that have inspired people since ancient times, the plight of the vulnerable Innocent aroused the dormant heroic spirit in people. While they were first uncomfortable thinking of themselves as heroes, they were instinctually drawn to heroic heights by the need to protect Innocent babies. Moreover, the overall concept of the March of Dimes was interpreted as a heroic one. On reflection, they saw the March of Dimes as the embodiment of the essence of the Hero and the heroic cause:

"Willing to tackle huge challenges."

"If they cured polio, they can do this!"

"Able to envision possibilities others simply cannot see."

"The March of Dimes can envision a day when no baby is born with a birth defect. . . . Wow!!!"

"Unselfish and self-sacrificing."

"The doctors, the parents, the survivors who go beyond the call of duty."

"People doing this to help babies who aren't their own."

"People walking for strangers."

"Inspiring others to leave their narrow lives and join the movement, the force."

"The more people that walk, the more money we raise, the more babies we save."

"I do only a little something, but there are a lot of us."

"We're part of something big, something important."

"Gives me a feeling of fullness, purpose."

We learned, though, to avoid Hero messages that were too explicit. People who are heroic, we found, often do not identify as Heroes. They see themselves as just doing what needed to be done. It became immediately clear that a somewhat more subtle approach was necessary that recognized the Hero's reluctance to identify with such a grand archetype.

The advertising agency translated these insights into a wonderful campaign that built on the idea that even if contributors and walkers are too humble to think of themselves as Heroes, the thousands of children whose lives they have saved are more than eager to think of their benefactors as heroic figures, and the cause they have served is heroic, indeed.

Child after child is featured in posters, print ads, and brochures that show actual situations in which a baby whose life was endangered was saved by surfactant therapy, folic acid supplements, or special neonatal equipment made available by the March of Dimes. And in each case, the headline proclaims that even if you don't think you're a hero, "Jennifer does."

Perhaps most dramatic was a television commercial inspired by the insights the March of Dimes gained. It began with the pounding feet of dozens, then hundreds, and then thousands of walkers—the heroic "army," fighting for children. As the walkers turn a corner around a building, the camera slowly pans up its side, focusing on a window in which we view a tiny infant hooked up to lifesaving neonatal equipment, and we hear another pounding sound: the pounding of the baby's heart. The point is clear, and it is powerful: Unknowingly, the walkers just below that window are saving that baby's life.

The Hero's Journey

Critical elements of the March of Dimes campaign naturally reflect the classical story of the Hero's journey, which Joseph Campbell so eloquently identified as the pattern reoccurring in the great epochs and religious stories throughout the ages and, in fact, the trajectory that will describe our lives, should we pursue the heroic course. Campbell, later interpreted by Chris Vogler, identified key elements of the Heroes' journey, mirrored in the Walk America communication:

THE HERO STARTS OUT IN AN ORDINARY WORLD

Throughout the year, potential walkers go about their day-to-day business, hardly feeling heroic.

THE HERO IS CALLED TO ADVENTURE, BUT ALMOST REFUSES THE CALL

The campaign clearly acknowledges the fact that the potential participant is not especially anxious to do something heroic and is even reluctant to be called a Hero.

BUT WISE COUNSEL ENCOURAGES THE HERO TO HEED THE CALL

The child or baby in need—the wisdom of the Innocent—is inarguable.
 "Don't think you're a hero? He does."

THE HERO ENTERS A SPECIAL WORLD WHERE HE OR SHE IS TESTED AND FINDS NEW ALLIES AND ENEMIES

The walk itself, as depicted in the commercial, is physically challenging. People from all walks of life who would not ordinarily come together find common ground and common cause while they unknowingly protect the infant above them from a lethal threat.

THE HERO CONFRONTS THE ENEMY, SEIZES THE SWORD, AND RETURNS WITH THE ELIXIR

Seeing and feeling this communication, past walkers are reminded of the feeling of "uplift" and transformation that they experience when they participate; first-timers are provided with a glimpse of what the transformational experience will be like.

Evoking the Hero's Journey at All Points of Contact

Not only the advertising was changed. The March of Dimes, which relies on thousands of "field-workers" to carry forth its message to local communities across America, created a "One Voice" kit, encouraging these ambassadors for the cause to adopt a heroic stance themselves, demonstrating how the organization could use a heroic visual and verbal vocabulary at the all-critical grassroots level.

And if you call the national headquarters and have to wait on hold for a few seconds, you will hear a recording that conveys a dramatic, urgent message about babies' lives "hanging in the balance"—awaiting the simple heroism of ordinary people to intervene on their behalf.

The total communication package is as different in form as it is in substance. The words and images surrounding the Caregiver are soft, nurturing, soothing, and reassuring. The visual and verbal vocabulary of the Hero is energetic, dramatic, inspirational, and purposeful.

As a result of this more urgent "voice," the adoption of the Hero archetype has not been without its challenges, both within and outside of the organization. For instance, the folic acid awareness campaign used a commercial called "Traffic Baby," in which we see a little child crawl right into a chaotic intersection, as trucks and taxis whiz by. The concept, which proved in research to be a highly effective one, conveys that if you don't take folic acid even before you might be pregnant, you future baby will be subjected to this kind of risk. But many members of the organization became skittish about such a dramatic metaphor, and some public-service directors at stations throughout the country thought the ad might be "too disturbing" for their viewers. Such reactions are not at all surprising, because it seems that whenever a company or organization decides to really put a stake in the ground and establish a meaning, someone, somewhere, will take issue.

But the process moves on. Today, the thousands of brochures, videos, ads, and other kinds of public service messages the March of Dimes creates are passed through the "Hero" filter, to be sure that they indeed reflect "one voice." Very soon, as the culture fully embraces its heroic origin and destiny, the Hero's voice will be its automatic and natural one.

On the one hand, these are difficult times to embrace a heroic identity and to call attention to little lives "hanging in the balance." The economy is strong, most Americans feel some participation in the boom, and we are generally at peace. The trend experts tell us that we are a cynical lot and that we have been disappointed so many times that we no longer believe in Heroes. That's what people who merely scratch the surface predict. But the archetypal lens tells us that the need for Heroes and the desire to feel heroic ourselves is as old as the human species and that, no matter what, we will find some outlet for fulfilling that need. By acknowledging and tapping into that deep human truth, the March of Dimes was able to resurrect its heroic identity, re-energize its organization, and fulfill its valuable service more effectively.

VII

Deeper Waters

T HE FIRST SIX PARTS of *The Hero and the Outlaw* have focused on how to harness archetypes in order to maximize your brand's power in the marketplace and successfully manage its meaning over time. Part 7 deepens the well of meaning from which you can draw.

Chapter 19, "May the Force Be with You: Capturing Category Essence," describes how product categories themselves can have a unique archetypal identity or essence and that this core meaning is both discoverable and the secret of the success of many brand icons. Within the chapter, we describe how consumers' first encounter with a product or service can be a kind of "imprinting experience," forever influencing how they relate to it, and how the role that a product or service plays within a culture can take on a significant meaning. We also describe innovative ways of understanding category essence and of capitalizing on it as a kind of "tailwind" that can give your brand added momentum. Chapter 20, "The Real McCoy: Branding and Organizational Congruence," takes us further into exploring the ways that archetypes help us define the soul of an organization, providing a focal point to organize all its activities. Chapter 21, "Leaving a Legacy: The Ethics of Archetypal Marketing," delves deeply into the ethical domain, providing technical assistance to professionals grappling with the thorny issues raised by the marketing of meaning.

Ultimately, Part 7 explores issues concerning what it means to be in the business of meaning management, particularly in a world so fundamentally hungry for substance.

Among other things, it leads the reader to consider how the deep archetypal meaning of both their brand and the business they are in can inform decisions as far-reaching as the philanthropic or cause marketing that might be most appropriate for them.

19

May the Force Be with You

Capturing Category Essence

Every CONTEMPORARY CATEGORY that has stood the test of time has an antecedent from the preindustrial age that reveals its true, deep meaning or purpose. Before cars, we had horses and donkeys; before washing machines, stream beds and ritual baths.

Understanding the *original purpose* of a product—in the life of an individual or of a civilization—gets us closer to its primal meaning. "Branding" the primal meaning and claiming it as your own gets you closer to market dominance. This is because category meaning is like a strong tailwind or current; it's not the "engine" of the brand, as is relevant differentiation, but it can be the force that accelerates the brand's power and increases its momentum.

This idea goes far beyond the old concept of owning the "category benefit," which ordinarily was perceived in objective, functional terms. Archetypal brands instead come to represent the meaning beneath the benefit. Ivory is not just about getting clean; rather, it is associated with the deep meaning of cleanliness: renewal, purity, and innocence. (It is for this reason that such publicity and outrage surrounded the discovery that an actress who had once been in pornographic films was the model for the drawing of a mother's face on the box of Ivory Snow. Procter & Gamble immediately replaced the model and the packaging.) Eastern Airlines did not just get you from here to there; it was "The Wings of Man." Nike did not say it was a better athletic shoe; it said, "Just Do It," summoning the discipline and determination required to finally "go for it"—to get in shape and to win. And even its name—the name of a winged goddess, as we have discussed previously—taps into a deep archetypal meaning associated with being fleet of foot. Just wearing Nike shoes might encourage a runner to push to run faster or longer, simply because the shoes carry the association of heroic effort. Because owning the category meaning can propel a brand to a leadership position, we have been conducting archetype studies across a range of categories. Both qualitative and unusual quantitative approaches have been employed. In the process, we are discovering new ways to get at the *essential meaning and experience of a category*. Much of the research in this section of the book was conducted by Margaret Mark in her position at Young & Rubicam and as a private consultant.

How to Identify Category Essence from Consumer Memories

In a major study we conducted for the automotive industry, we were determined to avoid the usual rationalizations and clichés common to asking drivers about what they want from an automobile brand. Instead, we began with a framework of fundamental psychological needs: achievement, aggression, belonging, independence, sexuality, status, etc. For each need, we generated adjectives, phrases, images, and descriptions of situations, summarized in Figure 7.1, which were then incorporated into a questionnaire.

In the actual interviews, respondents were first asked to free associate, recalling their earliest memories of first getting behind the wheel of the car, putting the key into the first car that they ever owned, and the like. Following this exercise, they responded to the

Examples of Derived Words and Phrases	
Psychological Need	**Derived Words and Images**
Achievement: to do better than others, be successful, do a difficult job well	Successful Competent Driving successfully under very challenging circumstances Driving better than most people Winning, overcoming challenges, rising to the occasion, feeling competent and on top of my game
Independence: to do things without regard for what others think, make independent decisions, avoid obligations, be unconventional, nonconforming	Independent Free My own person Driving wherever I want to The open road stretching out before me The wind blowing through my hair Feeling like a real free spirit Wandering, going on an adventure, or searching for and maybe finding something new The sense that anything can happen An open road, with no limits
Security: to be socially or psychologically safe, to be correct in behavior, not to make errors or be otherwise looked down upon	Secure Driving the kind of car all your friends and neighbors drive The safe, snug feeling of being in a car with people you care about, at night or in bad weather Feelings of security, peace and togetherness Feeling like I'm surrounding people I care about with a strong vehicle, and knowing that I can protect them and ensure their safety

Figure 7.1

battery of questions derived from the psychological needs framework, indicating the degree to which each word, phrase, or image described how they related to the experience of driving. Finally, they were asked to indicate which car company or nameplate they associated with these situations, images, and feelings.

The results were quite astounding. Drivers who, in more conventional approaches, might have talked about gas mileage and sticker prices, offered memories of early driving experiences that were far richer and more authentic than surveys of customer preferences generally yield. One man simply recalled "hot summer nights, blondes, cops, [and] the color red."

In responding to the words and phrases, some people related to cars and driving from a Caregiver perspective. Men tended to view the selection and proper maintenance of their cars as an opportunity to protect and care for their families. Women tended to take a slightly different Caregiver perspective; many revealed that in their frenetic family lives, the car has become the one place that people actually are forced to be in one place at the same time together and catch up on each other's day. They sensed a feeling of intimacy when driving with their families, a finding that we later termed "carcooning."

But the response that was most overwhelming and intense with respect to the deep meaning of cars and driving related to the Hero and the Explorer. In reacting to the words and phrases, many drivers indicated that, for them, the experience of driving was about testing themselves, driving in bad weather, rising to challenges, and overcoming obstacles. No insulated living-room-on-wheels experience for them—even though this type of experience is often featured in automotive advertising and emphasized at the showroom. Their earliest memories of cars and driving conformed to this finding and helped to explain the fundamental importance of cars in our culture.

It was clear that for many Americans—especially, but not exclusively, men—cars and driving are our first "true loves," and the act of earning one's driving license is one of the few true rites of passage in our culture, marking our passing into adulthood.

Long before we leave our parents for our friends or our mates, we leave them for our cars. This is because the essential meaning of the car is utterly compatible with our developmental needs at that stage of our lives. The car accompanies and accelerates the act of separating from one's parents, reinforces and supports individualism and ego development, and equips youths' natural belief in unlimited possibilities. Even if it's a hand-me-down or a jalopy, our first car becomes tangible evidence of our autonomy and our independence—the expression of our Hero and Explorer yearnings.

In many respects, the car is the first "place of our own" as well. Many young people sit in their cars for spells, savoring the feeling of being in their own space. To help shed further light on the deep meaning of cars and driving, Margaret tapped into the expertise of cultural anthropologist Grant McCracken while she was at Young & Rubicam. McCracken wrote,

> Americans mark their rise to maturity by the possession of a driver's license. In fact, in our culture, there is no other rite of passage. Some cultures ask their children to spend a week of hardship in the desert. Others put on a ceremony in which the child is covered with paint and feathers. In our culture, we do not have rituals of this kind. In our culture, we have cars.
>
> The logic of the car-ritual is clear enough. We are tested by the state. If we "pass," we are endowed with the right to have the self dramatically increased. We get our license and, with it, access to a car, and with this we get new freedom from our parents and new, almost adult, powers of control. If we fail, nothing happens. We remain immature, "just a kid."
>
> But, what is worse, the self must remain as it is, unaugmented by the powers of the machine.

McCracken went on,

> This rite of passage is about mastery. The test here is to see if we have mastered the car, the measure of our maturity. The question is "Have we gained enough mastery to be given more mastery?" Our rite of passage is about assessing whether we have grown sufficiently to take on the one instrument in our culture that will expand our mastery dramatically. The question is not just "Can you drive the car?" but "Are you ready for an adult self? Do you have enough mastery to deserve more mastery?"

As we mature and assume responsibilities—particularly raising children—our relationship with cars changes profoundly. The sense of pure freedom and independence driving once aroused is compromised by the constraints and responsibilities of marriage, maturity, and, especially, parenthood. Our research showed that driving becomes associated with deference to others, as opposed to pure self-indulgence: driving to work, hauling the kids around, and coping with traffic.

And yet, we also saw that beneath the surface lies our middle-aged yearning for the essential meaning of the car—and for the youthful, freer Explorer within us. Our research revealed that simple design elements, such as a sunroof, a CD player, the color red, or sporty off-road characteristics, take on a disproportionate degree of importance to the harried soccer mom who still needs to feel like she hasn't lost her *self*, even though she has four kids in the car. And successfully taking a tough turn on wet pavement (or watching professionals do it at breakneck speeds) provides a heroic thrill that is hard to come by these days. These deep insights were used by our client to help spur the phenomenal growth of sport utility vehicles in the industry—vehicles whose off-road characteristics are hardly necessary in our cities and suburbs, but *do* preserve an important part of our inner lives.

Of course, cars have other meanings that can be used to differentiate brands: status, luxury, rebellion, and sophistication, for example. But each of these meanings must be understood within the larger context of the essential meaning of the category and, ideally, should be fused with it. In this category, the spirit of the Hero and the Explorer is the tailwind that can provide an unexpected source of energy and velocity in the marketplace.

The carcooning phenomenon, moreover, suggests that there is a strong alternative essence for cars. The historical antecedent of the category essence of the car is most likely the Explorer's trusty steed—like the Lone Ranger's Silver. But for a sizeable, yet smaller, number of people, the alternative predecessor to the car's essence is more likely the enclosed, safe, communal carriage. While the latter identity carries less punch than the primary category essence, it still offers a strong point of differentiation and an opportunity for improving product design. How can the minivan, for example, better facilitate a feeling of intimacy or coziness for families whose best opportunity to be in one place at one time is when they are driving?

Beers and Banks

Other techniques for discovering category essence have proven useful in industries as far ranging as beers and banks. For example, we have given young beer drinkers some "starting cues" and then asked them to "write their own stories" about a "perfect night" involving beer drinking. Analyzing the structure of these stories and then connecting the patterns with recurring patterns found in literature and myth sheds further light on what the category does for these individuals and means to them.

In one such study, given a range of respondent-generated stories, young men almost universally chose one that best captured their feeling about beer:

> A place where life is easy, with no cares, no worries.
> Everyone is treated equally and gets along.

In archetypal terms, this "third place," connected neither to the home nor to the workplace, is the pressure-free environment in which you are unconditionally accepted for being who you are, where everyone is equal, and where beer is the great leveler—the ideal environment for the fun-loving Jester.

When that concept was embodied by a television show, "Cheers," the show became one of the longest–running in television history ("Where everybody knows your name, where your troubles are all the same"). The fact that it's highly unlikely that a psychiatrist and a postal worker would actually hang out in the same bar every night is irrelevant, in fact, it's part of the magic of the concept. While the outside world may draw clear lines regarding social standing and status, in this perfect place, for this moment suspended in time, everyone is ordinary and everyone is equal.

The same mythic concept of the Jester's "best place" was evoked in a very successful early campaign for Miller Lite: the Miller Lite "All Stars." In the early 1990s, Young & Rubicam wanted to help its client, Philip Morris, understand how that landmark instance of advertising was able to lift the product out of the realm of ersatz "diet beer" and position it as the real thing for fun guys. Our research showed that the advertising tapped into the powerful flow of the category's essence. Grant McCracken cleverly labeled the character of this "best place" as "Riggins's World," describing the essential nature of beer and a certain kind of Jester American maleness.

Grant McCracken's "Riggins's World"

Here's the image to keep in mind. It's a quintessential moment in American culture. And it contains the secret of the Miller Lite "All-Star" campaign. The image is a simple one. It's a man asleep under a table. Mr. Riggins goes to Washington. It's the early 1980s. We're sitting in a Washington stateroom. All the world is there.

Baker's at one table. Kissinger's at another. Hollywood stars dot the room. We are here for one of the grand fetes that make up ceremonial Washington and the imperial presidency. We are here to honor the new Reagan era.

The place is crowded with local worthies, all of them splendid in their fine evening dress. Tables groan with crystal and china. Candelabra sparkle above us. This is Washington at its most sumptuous. The president himself is about to speak. The crowd, noisy until now, begins to quiet. The president makes his way to the podium. The crowd falls silent.

Well, almost silent. From a far corner of the room comes a sawing sound. It sounds a little bit like snoring. God in heaven, it *is* snoring. Someone has fallen asleep at the most important social event of the season. Someone has pegged out in front of the president of the United States. The great ceremonial order of Washington has been breached. The new imperial presidency has been wounded.

People are annoyed, really annoyed. Who dares affront the president? Eyes search the room for the author of the outrage. They are looking for some poor schmo who had one too many gin and tonics and fell asleep in his salad. And they are looking for revenge. Just wait till they get their hands on this guy. They're going to rescind his career, hound him from Washington, and make him live in abject humiliation for the rest of his life.

What they find are two legs sticking through the rich linen folds of a tablecloth. A great snoring comes from within. Someone has managed to fall asleep under the table. Naturally, there is consternation. Who the hell is this guy? Someone parts the linen folds and has a look. He comes up smiling. And as the word spreads, everyone is smiling. The snorer, it turns out, is John Riggins, running back for the Washington Redskins and Super Bowl MVP.

What's important here is what happened next. Everything that should have happened didn't. Security did not come and haul away this vulgar, stupid man. No one sniffed his disapproval. The world did not recoil in horror. No one in this status-conscious town trotted out their contempt. No one leapt to restore the honor of the president.

In fact, everyone just smiled. Everyone simply nodded, smiled, and said, "Well, that's John Riggins for you," and that was the end of that. Not only was Riggins not ridiculed or vilified for this gesture, he was celebrated for it. As it turned out, everyone loved it. They were charmed as hell. Riggins fell asleep listening to the president. Wonderful!

Riggins, it turned out, had done nothing to embarrass himself. Snoring through a presidential address was apparently something glorious, entirely in character for Riggins, and perfectly endearing. And why? Partly, it made everyone think of the old joke about "where does an elephant sleep?"

In Mr. Riggins' case it was, of course, "pretty much anywhere he wants to." There was also the sense that the guy who brought home the Super Bowl had the keys to the city. If he wanted to sleep while the president was talking, well, that was okay. After all, next to the Super Bowl, Washington hadn't really accomplished anything for years.

But what really protected Riggins from ridicule? What really made the gesture so profoundly endearing was that it tapped deep into the very cultural foundations of American maleness. This little nap beneath linen was immediately seen to play out the most fundamental meanings of maleness. It was quintessentially what a certain kind of male does. It was quintessentially what a certain kind of American male is expected and entitled to do. Riggins's nap may not have been good etiquette. But it was the defining image of the American male. This is what the American male, the most elemental version thereof, is supposed to do in the face of ceremony, formality, civilized niceties, and politesse. He is "supposed to" crawl under a table and go to sleep.

After all, football players are works of nature. They are men who have been relatively untouched by civilization. They are men who do not know and do not care for the niceties of polite society. These are guys who are tapped into fundamental forces. They are guys who are an elemental presence in the modern world. Football is, after all, the practice of barely mediated violence. It is an exertion of the most primitive physical and emotional kind. Take football players off the gridiron, take them out of the violent male company, introduce them to polite society, and they are bored witless. Remove the elemental man from his elements, and all he wants to do is to find a soft spot beneath the nearest table and wait out the tedium.

From a technical marketing point of view, the probable development of this campaign looks pretty clear. A decision was made to beef up the masculinity of the brand in order to counteract all of the associations of "liteness." Large, mean football players were chosen to reposition that meaning of the brand and to make it more acceptable to the traditional beer drinker.

But what makes these ads so effective is that they zero in on a very particular kind of American maleness. These ads are not just about tough-guy maleness. They are about Riggins maleness. And they are even more particular than that: The ads are about the way in which a Riggins male doesn't care about polite society and the civilized world. They are about a type of American maleness that sets itself apart from the civilized world.

The Miller Lite ads captured a particularly virulent, powerful, elemental version of American maleness. And it just so happens that this is the type of maleness that men most care about when they are out with one another. This is the type of maleness that men build and act out when they spend time together. And this is the type of maleness that men cultivate when they are drinking beer.

In other words, the Miller Lite campaign zeroed in on just the type of masculinity that guys care about when they are drinking beer. The campaign said that this brand contains exactly the meanings you go looking for when you go drinking beer. The campaign said, "We know you are looking for Riggins maleness. Miller Lite is the place to find it."

Mr. Riggins Comes Home: How the Miller Lite Campaign Links the Consumer and Riggins

I want now to broaden my theme. The Miller Lite campaign summoned Riggins's maleness. But what makes it really effective as a piece of advertising is how well it manages to connect this world with the world of the consumer. In fact, this is, I think, the real genius of the ad. Not only does it play out Riggins's masculinity, but it actually manages to put that masculinity within the grasp of the consumer. The campaign succeeds in getting Riggins's maleness off the football field and into the bar.

Let's face it, what's the single greatest problem with sports marketing and the endorsement of athletes? It is that the athletes who get chosen as the endorsers are often larger than life. Their heroism makes them inaccessible. It is as if they have mythical standing. It is as if they occupy another universe. This is precisely the problem with the Bo Jackson ads. Sometimes you say, "Wow, that guy is my hero." And sometimes you say, "You know, I don't recognize anything about that man." Worship is one thing. Identification is something else again. If the object is to establish an identification, the sports hero has to be given a human scale.

And look at how the Miller Lite campaign gives its heroes human scale. First, the campaign used ex-athletes. This tack may have been driven by legislation about current athletes and alcohol association. But look what it does for the message of the ad. Suddenly, they look a little more recognizable.

And second, look at where all these ads take place. They are right there in the neighborhood bar. None of this Bo streaking across a rain-slicked pavement on a bicycle. They are right there, in a world I know. Surrounded by guys who look like you and me.

Third, look at what they are doing. They are not doing heroic things—slam-dunking, running marathons, or hitting the ball out of the park. The ad does not document just how little they have in common with the average guy. Instead, it shows them doing all the things that average guys do: competing (the Ben Davidson ad), boasting (the "tall tales" ad by Brian Anderson and the Brits Gresham ad), making fun of one another (the Deford and Billy Martin ad). All of this is regular-guy stuff. And the fact that it is being done by athletes lets the campaign actually deposit Riggins's meanings right into the lives of regular guys. All of this builds a connection.

Fourth, look at the role that some of the athletes play. To be sure, Butkus, Smith, Davidson, and Deacon Jones are there to make sure that the ad captures Riggins's masculinity. But John Madden, Rodney Dangerfield, and Bob Uecker are there for another reason. Each of these guys works in the ad because it helps the ad duplicate the world of the average consumer.

Every group of guys has a guy like John Madden (at least, as he appears in Miller Lite ads). Madden always appears at the end of the commercial in a lather, saying "Hey, we can break this tie; we can take these guys." There is a John Madden–type guy in every group, a guy who never knows when to quit. These are guys you admire and indulge because they take the "force of nature" thing to the limit. They just can't stop. These guys endear themselves to other males because they capture this Riggins quality.

And that's part of the role for Rodney Dangerfield and Bob Uecker. Every group of guys has a klutz and a faker on its margin. These guys would like to be closer to the center of the group, but in fact, the Riggins males won't let them in because they cannot make the grade. They stand as lessons in how *not* to be a Riggins male.

In other words, this campaign does more than just play out the world of the superhero; it also plays out the world of the average beer consumer. It plays out the known universe, with its characteristic activities, places, and people. And in all of this, something remarkable is accomplished: The campaign succeeds in persuading the viewer that what is true of the Riggins male can also be true of the world of the Miller Lite drinker. This is how the best "meaning transfer" in advertising always takes place. In order to give the world of the consumer the properties of the world of the sports hero, a campaign must first give the sports hero the properties of the consumer. This is how the "All Star" campaign succeeds in making Miller Lite stand for "Riggins's world."

Banking may seem like a radically different category from beer, and it is, but the concept of category essence is equally relevant and powerful. In research conducted to understand the deep meaning banks hold for middle-class versus more upscale consumers, we deployed a powerful technique called "laddering." Adapted from clinical psychology, laddering uses a series of systematic probes to move respondents from articulations of attributes that are relevant to them to objective benefits, to more subjective benefits, and, ultimately, to the deep meanings or values that connect them to the category. We want to go "up the ladder" from attributes to benefits to values.

Interviews are conducted individually by highly trained professionals, but the idea of going "up the ladder" is as basic as behaving like a three-year-old. All parents are familiar with the following routine:

Parent:	It's time to go to bed.
Three-year-old:	Why?
Parent:	It's 8 o'clock and you need your sleep.
Three-year-old:	Why?
Parent:	So you can grow up to be big and strong.
Three-year-old:	Why?
Parent:	So you can play for the Yankees and get rich!

The three-year-old has just "laddered" his parents from attributes, to benefits, to revealing their Ruler values!

When we conducted our research in the banking business, it became clear that the values working-class folk associate with investing are very different from those of the upper class. The more upscale consumers quickly laddered to Ruler (control) values and, sometimes, to Explorer (freedom) values. The ultimate benefit of saving and investing, for them, is the self-determination and freedom that money can provide—the ability to do what you want, when you want to. The ultimate benefits desired by middle-class folk, on the other hand, all centered on affiliation and security needs—holding things together for the family and preserving its stability and security.

We also explored early "imprinting" experiences, memories of when people were little children accompanying their moms and dads to banks. The more upscale consumers remembered it as an exhilarating "grown-up" experience, especially the memory of getting their own bankbooks. The more middle-class people, on the other hand, remembered banks as cold and forbidding places, places where you couldn't bounce your ball or finish your ice cream.

These findings on category essence forced our client and us to face the very different category meanings held by different segments of the population, decide on some targeting priorities, and, finally, position the bank effectively.

Masculinity, Femininity, and Category Essence

In some languages, masculine or feminine pronouns are used to describe inanimate objects, as a tacit acknowledgment that even non-living things may have a spirit or "energy" that is either inherently malelike or femalelike. Similarly, some, but not all, product categories can have a "gendered" energy influencing their archetypal identity. In identifying the gender of your product, it is important to remember that "masculine" and "feminine," as used in this context, do not imply that a masculine product is only, or even primarily, for men or that a feminine one is for women. Rather, we are using masculine and feminine sensibilities or qualities of consciousness, not sex role prescriptions or descriptions.

Gender is, of course, a complicated concept. Both the masculine and the feminine distinction carry a wide variety of attributes. Although Virginia Slims has defined an identity as a woman's cigarette, the gender of smoking is decidedly masculine, and so a tough, aggressive posture appropriately found its way into their communication. Marlboro first became successful and, eventually, iconic when it changed its positioning from a women's cigarette to the cowboy's cigarette, capturing the tough, stoic quality of smoking. Marlboro's image of masculinity stands in sharp contrast to Riggins's world, carrying more of the Hero archetype than the Riggins Jester.

Carla Gambescia, a talented and creative marketing consultant, often finds food categories in which it is important to recognize a gender identity. For example, in her work with the dessert and snack categories, she has found that salty snacks, like potato chips, have an inherently masculine nature, while ice cream has an inherently feminine nature. How does she get there?

Starting with either a consumer-based or mental laddering exercise, Gambescia examined the physical attributes of salty snacks versus those of ice cream. Salty snacks, she found, are angular or bumpy; crisp, dry, solid, and sharp. They are crunchy and noisy to eat, often have strong, savory flavors, and can even be spicy or zesty. In terms of their benefits (the next step on the ladder), salty snacks set a party tone, stimulate the senses, spice things up, make them "hot," and provide some "kick." They require eating with the hands and active chewing, and they induce a kind of nonstop eating until the bag is empty.

On a meaning level (the highest rung of the ladder), these snacks provide an antidote to boredom by breaking the routine. They are associated with testing limits, feeling kind of irresponsible, shucking your inhibitions, and feeling free. They provide a kind of permission to let go, a release.

How does the ladder for salty snacks differ from the ladder for ice cream? In every way. Starting on the attribute level, consider the contrast. (See Figure 7.2.)

Moving further up the ladder, Gambescia continues to draw the contrast. The benefits are shown in Figure 7.3.

The meaning-level contrast continues, as seen in Figure 7.4.

These differences in masculine versus feminine energy may automatically lead us to consider some archetypes over others for brands in either category. Outlaw, Explorer, and Jester all feel like good reflexive considerations for a salty snack, whereas Lover, Innocent, and Caregiver all make intuitive sense for an ice cream. The choice of archetype within each frame examined would be based, as we described in Part 6, on many considerations having to do with

Contrast	
Salty snack	**Ice cream**
Salty	Sweet
Starch/grain-based	Cream/milk-based
Crisp, dry	Moist
Solid	Soft
Angular or bumpy	Round or lumpy
Crunchy, noisy	Quiet, melting
Coarse	Smooth
Strong, savory flavor	Delicate, luscious flavors
Available anytime	A special treat
Spicy, zesty	Rich, creamy

Figure 7.2

the brand's equity, prospective target(s), source of competitive leverage, and so forth. But regardless of the specific archetypal identity, it would be wise to consider the feminine or masculine "sensibility" of the category itself in developing communication for the brand.

Gambescia helps this process along by contrasting consumer associations with each of the two categories of snacks. (See Figure 7.5.)

While both men and women may like salty snacks and ice cream equally, in some food categories the qualities of femininity and masculinity do attract more of one sex than another to the product, but even then, this does not require the brand to exclude the other sex. For example, years ago, in its advertising, General Foods International Coffees featured primarily women, taking a moment to themselves or engaged in a heart-to-heart talk with another kindred spirit. The surroundings were always beautiful, soothing, and a little bit elegant. The flavored coffees were drunk from delicate cups, never mugs. The feeling was decidedly feminine. Men used the coffees as well, but they were in the minority. Of course, the client, wanting to expand usage, asked the agency to include more men in the commercials. The challenge in doing so, however, was to include male–female situations and still not lose the wonderfully delicate sensibility of the category. (Flavored coffees were then quite special, more expensive, and outside of the ordinary "mindless" consumption of reg-

Benefits	
Salty snack	**Ice cream**
Sets a party tone	Sets a party tone
Stimulates the senses	Pleases the senses
Spices things up, makes them hot	Soothes and cools the palate
Provides some excitement, some "kick"	Provides satisfaction and comfort
Requires the hands	Engages the tongue
Induces nonstop eating until the bag is spent	Involves a luxurious experience to be prolonged
Requires active chewing	Permits "passive" eating as it melts

Figure 7.3

ular coffees.) In fact, when male users were interviewed about why they liked the international coffees, they talked about their "special-ness," or delicacy, in much the same way that women did. If, instead of just including men in the advertising, we had included a masculine energy or sensibility, in it, we would have been violating the essence of the category.

Sometimes category gender works against what an individual brand is trying to accomplish, and this must be taken into account and understood. For example, within New York City's Madison

Meaning	
Salty snack	**Ice cream**
Happiness	Happiness
Antidote to boredom, breaking from routine	Enhancing and transforming the occasion
Testing limits	Retreating into a cocoon
Exhilaration, speeding up	Luxuriating, prolonging
Feeling sort of irresponsible	Feeling childlike security
Letting down your reserve, feeling free	Momentary suspension of time and reality
Permission to let go	Indulging self (or others)
A release	Sweet surrender

Figure 7.4

Salty snack	Ice cream
Staccato	Melodious
Percussions	Strings
Energetic	Languid
Anytime	Special
Change of pace	Reward
Stimulating	Comforting
Invigorating	Relaxing
A shower	A bath
Childlike transgression	Regression to a childlike state
Fast forward	Pause
Asserts	Envelops
Freedom	Serenity
Aggressive	Soothing
Independent	Nurturing

Figure 7.5

Square Garden, one of the most well-known sports arenas in the world, there is a lovely, little-known theater called the Theater at Madison Square Garden. Delicate, sentimental productions like *The Wizard of Oz* and *A Christmas Carol* are performed there, and the people who attend these performances are astounded that such a nice little theater exists right in the Garden building.

People who aren't aware of its existence, however, have the hardest time imagining a theater there, even when they are told about it. They regard the Garden as exciting, boisterous, rowdy, and down to earth. They associate it with the best of class in athletics: the fiercest and most powerful competitors in the world. The Regular Guy or Gal goes there to see the world's revered Heroes and Warriors slug it out.

Both men and women turn up at the Garden, and both male and female athletes compete there, but its spirit and energy are decidedly masculine. How can consumers be helped to reconcile this masculine energy with the very feminine sensibility of a theater?

Understanding this conflict helped us find the beginnings of a solution. Our research showed that families who have been there especially appreciate a unique kind of child and family friendliness at the Theater at Madison Square Garden. People are allowed to bring food and drinks to their seats, strollers in the aisles are tolerated, and the productions are designed to have no intermission, a break in the action that usually forces kids to disengage from the story, get antsy, and want to go home.

Even the productions themselves often have a special kind of child-friendliness: At *A Christmas Carol*, "snow" actually falls in the theater over the audience at the uplifting conclusion of the show. This relaxed, more down-to-earth atmosphere of the theater, besides being conducive to parents' and kids' appreciation of the performance, begins to help mediate the cognitive dissonance between the Garden and the Theater. It's as though a little bit of the Garden's exuberance has seeped in—not enough to undermine the specialness of a live theatrical performance, but enough to begin to help people "make sense" out of the relationship between the two.

This is one area in which "projective" approaches can help you be sensitive to, and understand, the gender undertones of category essence. "If salty snacks were a film star, who would they be? If ice cream was a character from a book, who would it be? Which historical figure might represent the 'spirit' of the theater? Which historical figure might represent the 'spirit' of a sports arena?" These kinds of questions, often posed in qualitative research, can help reveal the inherent nature of the category from a gender perspective.

Category essence, then, in all its forms, gives us a jump start by revealing the archetypal forces that drive the category, not just the brand. If we ignore this powerful force, we do so at our peril. Young & Rubicam once marketed a new laundry detergent from Colgate called Fresh Start. It was one of the first liquids, and it came in a handy, easy-to-use container. The agency and the client decided to link the contemporary nature of the brand and product to contemporary women's outright rejection of defining themselves in terms of housework. A commercial, "Red Dress," was developed, in which a husband calls home to invite his wife out to an unexpected dinner and the wife tosses her red dress into the wash and is ready in a jiff. The idea of the ad was that life is too short to worry about laundry—we have better things to do—and this brand understands and facilitates that. The spot was lively, energetic, and very contemporary.

But the business did badly. In subsequent research, we interviewed our modern, intelligent prospects about their attitudes toward household chores. As we all expected, they saw them as tedious and unfulfilling, and their satisfaction and identity were derived from other things.

But interestingly, the nature of the interview changed when we talked specifically about doing the laundry. Women described how much they loved the feeling of taking freshly laundered towels and clothing out of the dryer; how they always took a deep whiff of the wonderful, clean smell; and how they loved to fold the laundry while it was still warm to the touch. They said that finishing the laundry gave them a feeling similar to getting a clean, new black-and-white notebook in September at the start of school—a new beginning, a fresh start.

Fresh start! We had a product *called* Fresh Start! But instead of adopting the Innocent essence of the category for our brand—the spirit of purity and renewal, the sensory gratification of feeling "cleansed" and renewed—we had squandered an incredible archetypal association by trying to connect with a valid, but essentially irrelevant, "trend."

Researching the Mythic or Original Uses of a Product

Category essence can also be discovered through research into the original use of a product and the mythology associated with it in both ancient and modern times. For example, if you are marketing a cereal line, you might research the origins of agriculture and the nature of grain gods and goddesses. In Greece, the Eleusinian mystery cult taught the secrets of agriculture, as well as provided sexual and spiritual education. The primary deities associated with this cult are the nurturing mother (Demeter) and her virginal daughter (Kore). From this information, you might conclude that the category essence of cereal could be Caregiver or Innocent, which are the archetypes under which most healthy cereals are marketed today.

If you wanted to differentiate your brand from other brands with a Caregiver or Innocent identification, you might want to look further into the story of Demeter and Kore and the teachings coming out of Eleusis. There, pubescent girls were initiated into womanhood, and their mothers were prepared to part with them. (Marriage happened early in ancient Greece.)

Briefly, as recounted in an earlier chapter, Kore is abducted by Hades, the lord of the underworld, and lives underground until her mother's grief and refusal to allow grain to grow cause a famine. When this famine occurs, Zeus, the chief god of Olympus, sends Mercury to take Kore back to her mother. When Kore returns, spring comes, and the crops grow. In this agricultural myth, Kore is like a seed being planted and sprouting in the spring. At Eleusis, this pattern was interpreted as explaining the miracle of both agriculture and birth (the seed is planted in the womb, develops, and eventually is born into the world), as well as the miracle of immortality (bodies are buried, but the soul is resurrected or reincarnated).

If you are acquainted with the ancient mythos at this level, cereal might sustain an identity of Magician—focusing on the miracle of seeds becoming plants that sprout grain, which is then made into cereal that fosters healthy minds and bodies. It could also position itself around faith—that when things look bleakest, new life will always prevail. Similarly, the fact that the Merrill Lynch bull is so memorable may be related to the category essence of banking. Cave paintings from prehistoric times have been found. It is possible that, at first, bulls were chosen as the subject of the paintings because they were prey that the painters hunted. If you think, however, of some of our modern impressions of bulls—powerful, somewhat threatening, and good for breeding, and hence very sexual—you may surmise that these factors inspired people to paint bulls. In ancient times, the bull was a commonly used symbol that represented behaviors associated with fertility. Today, we might interpret the bull's symbolism as the power to make things happen.

Archaeologist Marija Gimbutas says that bull sculptures and paintings "are consistently allied with energy symbols—snake coils, concentric circles, eggs, cup marks, antithetic spirals, and life columns." "According to Lithuanian folklore," she continues, "lakes follow bulls; wherever the bull stops, a lake appears." The regenerative power of the bull is also "manifest in plants and flowers springing up from the bull's body. This belief is recorded as late as the 16th century AD. It occurs in Simon Grunau's Old Prussian Chronicle

Starting as early as 16,000 B.C., primitive hunter–artists such as those who created drawings in the Lascaux cave (which inspired this one) depicted the strength and virility of the bull, as does Merrill Lynch today in its corporate symbol. Feelings of power associated with the bull since ancient times are linked to the power that results from financial success—an effective example of "branding" the essence of a category.

2.4.1., compiled between 1517 and 1521. The author tells of a fabulous ox whose body is made in part of plants and which, when killed, gives birth to plants."[1]

1. Marija Gimbutas, *The Language of the Goddess* (New York: Harper & Row, 1989), pp. 270–273.

A prominent myth from Crete tells of King Minos' wife, who fell in love with a white bull. She felt such passion for this beast that she mated with him, producing the Minotaur. Daedalus, the Magician, created a labyrinth to contain the Minotaur, so that he would be of no danger to the land.[2] If you think about this story symbolically, the Minotaur—half human, half bull—personifies energy, but is safely contained in the bowels of the castle, perhaps even providing the energy for the island's prominence.

What an image for banking—holding the awesome power of money, safely contained, ready for use! The point here is that people do not have to know such background stories for the archetypal power of the image to be effective. Such is the power of an archetype.

The search for category essence is really a search for the ways in which animals, plants, places, and physical things hold intrinsic meaning for people. In his best-selling book *Care of the Soul*, Thomas Moore reflects on the meaning nature has for most of us, talking about the sorrow he would feel if the road near his house were widened, requiring the beautiful chestnut trees that line it to be cut down. Most of us can think of some place in nature that matters to us and that in some way feeds our souls. Moore identifies the human willingness to despoil the natural landscape as resulting from an unfortunate blindness to the soul in the world. The current ecological crisis, he concludes, is felt by all of us even as we go about our daily lives, acting oblivious, but really jointly experiencing an underlying sadness. What if the progress of civilization does come down to "They paved paradise and put up a parking lot," as Joni Mitchell's powerful song suggests?

More to the point of marketing, Moore continues, "Made things also have soul. We can become attached to them and find meaningfulness in them, along with deeply felt values and warm memories."[3] The modern preference for splitting the sacred from the material makes the world seem dead and meaningless. Such attitudes are re-

---

2. Pierre Grimal, ed., *Larousse World Mythology* (New York: Gallery Books, 1965), p. 171.

3. Thomas Moore *Cure of the soul: A Guide to Cultivating Depth and Sacredness in Everyday Life* (New York, N.Y.: HarperCollins Publishers, 1992), p. 270.

sponsible for the twin problems of materialism and the anticonsumption backlash.

Moore reminds us that business and products used to be sacred. "In the medieval world," carpenters, secretaries, and gardeners did not see themselves as doing menial work, because "each had a patron god—Saturn, Mercury, and Venus, respectively—indicating that in each case matters of profound significance to the soul are encountered in daily work." He concludes that the problem of modern manufacturing is not a lack of efficiency; rather, it is a loss of soul.[4]

By seeking out the meaning activities and objects had in the ancient world, we unlock powerful human motivators as we simultaneously re-ensoul the world.

When the Archetypal Expression Is in Flux

There are times when the fundamental essence of a product is in full force, but its *expression* is changing in meaningful and important ways. Take, for example, the work that Margaret Mark, Gambescia, and insightful researcher Bill McCaffrey did in the bread category in 1995.

Denise Larson, then Research Manager at Entenmann's, a leading bakery, was concerned by declines in packaged sliced bread, given that her firm was heavily invested in the category. While others in the organization were almost ready to get out of the business, Larson commissioned our team to delve deeply into the consumer dynamics of the decline, on the principle that unless it was fully understood, course corrections would be made in a kind of strategic vacuum.

What the team found was that the decline of sliced bread distorted a much more important reality: The bread experience had changed profoundly. Whereas bread had once been eaten (as coffee was drunk) functionally and habitually, it was now eaten (again, as coffee was being drunk) experientially and experimentally: People were trying scones, bagels, muffins, biscuits, and the like. Whereas previously choices had been limited (white or rye), there was now an explosion of variety. People had once favored mass-produced brands; now they favored authentic sources. The bread category was not

4. Thomas Moore, p. 182.

declining, we concluded, it was "morphing" into a different expression of its essence (yet again, not unlike coffee).

But what made this case so fascinating, and so unique, was that bread, in many respects, was morphing *back* to its truer, more authentic essence. In this evolving role, bread products provided a "permissible indulgence." Americans' preoccupation with weight, health, and the avoidance of certain ingredients was depriving them of guilt-free food pleasure, either because they avoided heartier, more satisfying food altogether or because they were so guilt ridden when they did indulge. As a result, the texture and density of the "morphed" breads (especially bagels and muffins) were providing one of the few remaining sensory indulgences that they could enjoy with abandon.

Also, hectic lifestyles and meals on the go had given bread a new prominence as the "main event" at many eating occasions (e.g., eating only a bagel for breakfast), compared with its previous role as a simple carrier or complement (e.g., eating toast as a mere accompaniment to bacon and eggs). This change went hand in hand with the previous one and required that bread provide a more satisfying, substantive, and sensory eating experience.

As a result, bread evolved from "filler" to "real food." After decades of being relegated to the role of simple carrier, bread was once again assuming its time-honored role as "the staff of life"—a physical expression of the Caregiver. Consumers weren't rejecting bread; they were rejecting a kind of "deviant" time in the latter half of the 1900s in which the true role of bread had gone "underground." They were demonstrating their receptivity to what bread could be—indeed, what it used to be at an earlier time and what it still is in many parts of Europe. People were showing how bread could be more of a part of daily eating experiences.

However, little in the "mass" marketing or retail environment had yet supported and guided consumers' natural, emerging enthusiasm for the true essence of the category. The supermarket bread aisle was simultaneously boring and overwhelming. Unlike the appetizing new cheese sections or even what was beginning to happen in the coffee aisle, consumers had to deal with a plethora of unappetizing, relatively undifferentiated choices of bread. What little advertising existed treated bread products as commodities, as opposed to indulgences. We concluded that, rather than abandon the bread category, Entenmann's was in a position to act upon a significant unrealized opportunity.

And it did. Entenmann's encouraged us to move on to a second stage of our work, in which we systematically examined combinations of attributes that best delivered "the bread experience" to consumers. The company aggressively began to develop new products and to lend support to those already in its portfolio that were "on target." Entenmann's adjusted its expectations for the sliced-bread business to more realistic levels and focused its energies on growth opportunities. Early signs of marketplace success and its renewed strategic vigor made the company an attractive buyout target. Entenmann's was happily acquired by giant CPC/Best Foods, which could lend more extensive manufacturing and distribution strength to this "renaissance" of the bread category.

Ignoring category essence is like swimming out far into the ocean, oblivious to the natural currents. You may think you know where you're going, and through sheer force of will, you might even get there, but it's a dangerous expenditure of energy nonetheless. On the other hand, acknowledging, understanding, and *using* category essence to your advantage is like the wind beneath your sails.

With some products, ignoring category essence would be fatal. For example, colleges and universities establish distinct identities in order to differentiate themselves from others. Liberal arts colleges often have a Caregiver cast to them. Elite colleges often have a Ruler ambiance, for they know they are recruiting and educating the next generation's leadership. Progressive schools typically highlight the Explorer, appealing to nontraditional students who want to chart their own course. Community colleges more typically emphasize their Regular Guy/Gal openness or their Magician capacity to transform lives.

But the category essence of colleges and universities is indisputably Sage. All these higher educational institutions are selling knowledge and wisdom. To violate the decorum of the Sage would be to discredit the school. This means that whatever marketing strategy a college uses, it has to take into consideration the values and sensibilities of the Sage.

The most competitive position in most cases is to own the category essence of a brand. However, that is not always possible. When someone else gets there first and does it well, there is good reason to choose a quite different archetypal identity (unless you are capable of understanding the archetype at a deeper and more relevant level than your competition). Even here, it is wise to remember what the category essence is so that the style and tone of your marketing communication do not violate its most salient attributes. Yahoo!, for example, presents a Jester identity within a Sage category. Making the customer feel that surfing the Web will be fun is great so long as the fun does not interfere with getting needed information. If that were to occur, the consumer would likely turn elsewhere.

> **Tools for Understanding Category Essence**
>
> - Psychological needs
> - Exploring "imprinting experiences"
> - Consumer stories
> - Laddering
> - Projective techniques
> - Anthropological and mythic perspectives and research

The category essence is the soul of your product line or field. Connecting with this soul can add special meaning to your whole industry. You may have heard the story about three construction workers, each of whom is asked what he is doing. The first says he is breaking up big rocks into little ones. The second says that he is doing what his boss wants. The third says he is building a cathedral!

Which worker is most likely to have job satisfaction? Which is most likely to be absent the least? Which is most likely to be loyal to the company? The discovery of the soul of one's product or craft not only attracts customers; it also adds meaning and value to the lives of executives and employees. When the product or service has soul, the work of everyone involved with it is ennobled.

The Real McCoy

Branding and Organizational Congruence

J AMES C. COLLINS and Jerry I. Porras, reporting on their long-term study of very successful companies in the *Harvard Business Review*, assert that "Companies that enjoy enduring success have core values and a core purpose that remain fixed while their business strategies and practices endlessly adapt to a changing world." Studying effective companies, Collins and Porras discovered that those with strong and positive core values had outperformed the general stock market by a factor of 12 since 1925. Among the examples they cited were Hewlett-Packard, 3M, Johnson & Johnson, Procter & Gamble, Merck, Sony, Motorola, and Nordstrom.

The authors argue that the core ideology of any organization defines its enduring character, providing a "consistent identity that transcends product or market life cycles, technological breakthroughs, management fads, and individual leaders." Core values are, therefore, "the glue that holds an organization together through tough times."[1]

It is not enough to get together, write up your values, and then put them in a drawer or even post them on the wall. You have to mean them. They have to be the driving force in the organization, or they are essentially useless. Beneath any set of values lies an archetype. When that archetype and your stated values inform your real behavior, people recognize that you are the "real McCoy." You do not just spout empty words; you walk your talk.

Such was the case with the Johnson & Johnson Corporation during the Tylenol crisis. For years, the Caregiver credo of Johnson & Johnson was admired in the industry as being one of the most inspirational and outer-directed mission statements in the corporate world. It was an expression of the company's commitment to "give care" to doctors, nurses, mothers, babies, and others all over the world. The company's products, by and large, reflected that commitment, and its advertising for products from baby shampoo to painkillers like Tylenol was a lyrical expression of the company's apparent concern for the well-being of its customers. Johnson & Johnson, like other highly successful companies, had intuitively and effectively embraced an archetypal identity and had managed it in a consistent way.

However, the best test of Johnson & Johnson as a genuine Caregiver resulted from a real-life tragedy. When criminal tampering with Tylenol resulted in deaths throughout the country, Johnson & Johnson CEO Jim Burke spent sleepless nights reviewing hard evidence, but also going over countless stories of people who had trusted the brand beyond the normal measure of product reliability—had trusted it to be a Caregiver and a friend.

It was these stories, along with a high ethical standard, that led Burke to order the most massive recall in history to protect, or care for, Tylenol's loyal customers. Cynics in the industry claimed that the recall amounted to an admission of culpability and that it would destroy Tylenol's credibility. Consumers knew better. They intui-

---

1. James C. Collins and Jerry I. Porras, "Building your Company's Vision," *Harvard Business Review* (Sept./Oct. 1996), p. 65. See also James C. Collins and Jerry I. Porras, *Built to Last: Successful Habits of Visionary Companies* (New York: Harper Business, 1994).

Tell Your Story on the Web

Travelers driving along the interstate in South Dakota have very little to amuse them. The terrain is pretty desolate. The boredom is only moderately relieved by sign after sign advertising Wall Drug. If motorists are curious at all, they stop there and find that it is a restaurant, not a pharmacy. The placemats tell the story of the Walls going west and setting up their pharmacy. Almost nobody came, and they were about to go out of business, until Mrs. Wall realized that in the 100° plus summer weather, travelers must be thirsty, so they advertised free ice water. And the business boomed. Soon they added ice cream and one thing led to another. People read the story and liked it. It is an old-time Innocent story that warms the cockles of your heart.

If a small business in South Dakota can tell its story in a way that makes it thrive, why can't more international corporations tell their own creation story on their Web pages, thereby delighting the thirsty souls of consumers surfing the Web? People generally go to a Web page to find out about a product or a company. Why not use this medium to share your company's soul?

---

tively recognized a story expressing the self-sacrifice of the Caregiver in the service of the higher good. Burke, Johnson & Johnson, and Tylenol all lived up to an authentic Caregiver story, and the way that Johnson & Johnson responded to the crisis was the proof of the pudding. The business soared back after the recall to levels that exceeded those prior to the tampering incident.

Companies and their leadership cannot stand behind their values in trying times if those values are only skin deep. How does a leader instill values that stick? You tell your company story and retell it. Tell it to the public, to your board, to investors, to your employees, and to your leadership team, and make sure someone tells it to all new hires during their orientation. By all means, tell it on your Web site, too!

These stories must, of course, distill organizational values and inspire enthusiasm—even passion. Where do you find such stories? Most organizations have their own sacred mythology: creation stories (two hackers in a garage, for instance), stories of crises weathered, tales of exceptional performance, jokes that capture and defuse the organization's human frailties, and visionary images of longed-for future outcomes. If your company—or your client—does not tell such stories, then it is not too late to take people down memory lane to reclaim the lost company heritage.

For people who were there at the start, help them remember what captured their imagination when they dreamed of the company. If they are no longer around, do research and find out what it was like for the founders. Have people remember when they were hired and what attracted them to the organization. Enlist them in detailing what they like best about the company—not just in the abstract, but in anecdotes that provide the substance and the feel of what is going right.

It is easy to think that all stakeholders in your organization know the deeper and more high-minded values that inform your actions. However, in the hustle and bustle and rush of daily life, it is natural for them to forget why they care about what they are doing. Sacred stories—of a religion, nation, family, or company—bear repeating. The repetition helps the values to sink in and continually inspire belief and loyalty.

Branding and Organizational Coherence

Branding, if done well, can help large and complex organizations to sustain coherence during quickly changing times. The current high-pressure, fast-paced economic climate has required companies to shrink their internal structure. Hierarchies are modified: Often, everyone required for a project gets involved in ways that cross both status and unit lines. In addition, with virtually full employment, workers expect to be treated with respect and to make autonomous decisions within their own areas of expertise. Standard organizational development practice now encourages flexibility, self-organizing teams, and other strategies that bring out the full intelligence of the group and that increase the company's flexibility in solving problems.

It is a most interesting world. However, in many organizations, this greater fluidity often goes to the edge of chaos, especially if no one knows what anyone else is doing. Frequently, marketing plans are drawn up for products that are still at the design stage. Different teams work on research and development, design, manufacturing, sales, and marketing—with very little interaction between and among them.

A clear archetypal identity not only for the product, but for the company, acts as the "strange attractor" that allows an orderly pattern to emerge even in chaotic conditions. Margaret Wheatley, in *Leadership and the New Science*, explains: "As chaos theory shows . . . if we look at such a system long enough and with the perspective of time, it always demonstrates its inherent orderliness. The most chaotic of systems never goes beyond certain boundaries; it stays contained within a shape that we can recognize as the system's strange attractor."[2]

The growing consensus in organizational literature today is that the equivalent of the strange attractor in a company is its values— not necessarily its stated values, but its real values. We would add to this the understanding that foundational to these values is an archetype that defines them. Therefore, it is the archetypal structure of an organization that keeps it from spinning out of control.

You undoubtedly know this from experience. In values-based businesses, people have a compass to guide their actions, even when the boss is not around. They also have a bond with one another. They are not just random strangers working together, but people committed to the same ends. People who share such convictions, moreover, have an advantage over those who do not in being able to trust one another and to work out problems when they arise. Of course, this happy result occurs only if people know what those values are and what it means to live by them.

Clearly, good communication and collaborative systems are also necessary in today's fluid environments. But it is even more important that people live the same archetypal story. Then they will not be loose cannons going off in their own direction to take actions that are incongruous with the overall meaning structure of the brand. Different units and teams may also have active archetypes that relate to their function. For example, people in the financial area often

---

2. Margaret Wheatley, *Leadership and the New Science: Learning about Organization from an Orderly Universe* (San Francisco: Berrett-Koehler Publishers, 1992), p. 21.

unconsciously assume Ruler values, while those in training or organizational development units are more likely to be Lovers or Magicians. Members of these different groups may miscommunicate unless they learn to be archetypally bilingual, speaking across group boundaries in the language and from the perspective of the organization's unifying archetype.

Obviously, in a free society, people cannot be compelled to have the same values and resonate with the same archetype. However, if a brand identity is clear, they do not have to be compelled. A company will attract employees, investors, suppliers, and customers, like metal filings moving toward a magnet.

Wheatley argues that the fast pace of today's world means that our desire to control organizational processes and to put permanent structures in place will inevitably be thwarted. When we take the larger view, we can see the implicit order. Rather than trying to impose order by an act of will, we recognize that we can get "order for free." The point, then, is to work in harmony with the natural order, which we can recognize by its archetypal qualities.

Although everything is changing very fast, archetypes are eternal. They can evolve in the level of their expression in us, but they themselves do not change. If we share an archetypal perspective, we are anchored in permanence, even as the material structures of our lives shift their shapes around us.

What Story Are You Living?

Each of the preceding chapters described organizations stamped with the narrative structure of an archetype. In working with organizations, we have been enthralled with how fundamentally different one is from another. The bottom line often appears to be money, but rarely actually is. Certainly, people want to make a good living, and some want to make a killing. However, most of us also want our lives to matter in some deeper way. Examining Figure 7.6 will familiarize you with inherent values that motivate people in organizational cultures with a defined archetypal cast to them. As you look over the categories described in the figure, you may be able to identify the kind of organization that is the best match to what most effectively motivates you.

Organizational Cultures Valuing Individual Fulfillment, Growth, and Learning			
Archetype	Innocent	Explorer	Sage
Strength	Job security	Employee autonomy	Analysis, planning
Weakness	Employee dependence	Insufficient coordination	Slow to act
Values	Loyalty	Freedom, Independence	Learning
Taboo	Rocking the Boat	Conformity	Naïvete
Leadership Style	Parental	Pioneering	Collegial
Shadow	Controlling behaviors	Antisocial acting out	Enforcing dogma

Organizational Cultures Emphasizing Risk, Mastery, and Achievement			
Archetype	Hero	Outlaw	Magician
Strength	Courage	Divergent thinking	Vision
Weakness	Hubris	Ethics	Connecting with ordinary people
Values	Achieving goals	Nontraditional	Evolved consciousness
Taboo	Weakness	Conformity	Shallowness
Leadership Style	Coach	Revolutionary	Charismatic
Shadow	Ruthlessness	Criminal	Manipulation

Organizational Cultures Emphasizing Belonging, Enjoyment, and Community			
Archetypes	Regular Guy/Gal	Lover	Jester
Strength	Surviving	Community	Playfulness
Weakness	Leveling	Conflict avoidance	Accountability
Value	Equality	Closeness	Fun
Taboo	Being special	Stoic withdrawal	Being boring
Leadership Style	Authoritarian	Facilitative	Troubleshooting
Shadow	Cruelty	Free-floating Eros	Con artistry

Figure 7.6

Organizational Cultures Emphasizing Stability, Control, and Permanence			
Archetypes	Caregiver	Creator	Ruler
Strength	Service	Innovation	Structure
Weakness	Requiring accountability	Routine	Flexibility
Values	Caring	Integrity	Power
Taboo	Selfishness	Mediocrity	Irresponsibility
Leadership Style	Crusading	Visionary	Political
Shadow	Devouring, controlling	Critical perfectionism	Tyranny

Figure 7.6 (Continued)

Sometimes, people within an organization are not even aware of the strength of the values that underlie the story they are living until one is violated. As an example, suppose a certain gas company in the Midwest is privatized. New leadership realizes that the company's having been a monopoly for so many years has undermined customer service. It is not that the employees do not care about the customer; they do. In fact, they think of themselves as kindly people who are heating the homes of their neighbors. They are, in fact, Caregivers. Because they know that the customer has no choice of servers, however, they might schmooze so long with one that they have to put off the next call till the next day. This will not do, of course, in a competitive situation.

The new managers rightly decide that everything needs to be streamlined and made more cost efficient. They are not skilled in meaning management, however. They do not know that the bottom-line value to their employees is caretaking. They even begin to cut off the gas to people who do not pay their bills—including little old ladies. The winters in the area are fierce. People without heat can die. The Caregiving employees are devastated. Morale plummets. The result is less effectiveness.

In a higher education association operated according to collegial Sage values, high competence and professionalism were expected, and people were treated in a manner which indicated that management believed that the workers knew what they were doing. Hierarchy was minimized, and interactions across levels of management were easy and comfortable. People loved their jobs and willingly worked long hours. A new CEO came in and established a more hierarchical structure, alienated some of the best people, and showed indifference to some of the core ideas that had energized employees to work so hard. Within a year, many of the best staff left the organization, and others began taking off each day at 5:00 p.m. Suddenly, instead of a culture of commitment, the organization had a culture of "I just work here."

The archetypal structure of culture is generally invisible and unarticulated. Sometimes new hires fail—even at the top—because they do not read the culture adequately. In a Jester organization, you can be ostracized if you have no sense of humor. In some Lover organizations, the unspoken rule is that everyone knows everything about everyone else. They all share stories about their lives, their kids, and even their fears and their dreams. Anyone who wants to keep to him- or herself may have a very difficult time succeeding. In a Hero culture, you do not want to seem like a wimp. In an Outlaw culture, it is not wise to appear too goody-goody.

In all these cases, many of the employees, and certainly those who fit in the best, find their self-esteem through the same story. Caregivers feel good about themselves to the degree that they are caring; Creators by producing something beautiful, imaginative, and cutting edge; and Rulers by establishing and maintaining systems that make life more orderly and predictable.

So what do you do when there is a real need for a culture change—as with the aforementioned gas company? Ideally, you introduce a new story while also valuing and honoring the old one. This is a little like having one brand identity while recognizing the power of the category essence. An organization's fundamental story is usually derived from its product line, its founder, and early decisions that were made and encoded in an oral history that becomes its story. Over time, the company hires people who have the right chemistry—meaning that they live by the same story. You can introduce new stories, but they are like new software. At this point, it works best to think of the historic brand identity as the operating system, which is inevitably still defined by the old story. All the new software needs is to be compatible. You can update the operating system, but replacing it requires you to start over, losing your brand equity.

However, you *can* move from a lower level to a higher level of an archetype relatively easily, especially if that change is required by circumstances or supported by cultural change. For example, the contemporary workplace is more democratic and egalitarian than it was two decades ago. This influences the level of many archetypes. There is pressure for autocrats to become politicians, for instance. Caregivers are likely to expect others to do more for themselves. The lone Hero is being replaced by the heroic team. Moreover, for the brand identity to remain vital, its expression should keep up with the consciousness of the time. If the archetype's expression is evolving in your customers, the level of the archetype in your commercial messages and in your organizational culture need to keep pace.

Most importantly, even when new qualities and habits of mind need to be introduced into a culture, its brand identity must remain clear—not only to keep faith with customers, but also for internal congruence and effectiveness.

Staying out of Trouble

If you understand the archetypal underpinnings of an organizational culture, you can also recognize the company's shadow. When individuals and groups typically identify the positive qualities of an archetype, they may repress other archetypes that can surface in unpleasant and unconscious ways. For example, in a Caregiver culture, everyone wants to seem kind and compassionate. Aggressive urges, then, go underground and can surface as very petty and manipulative politics. No one admits to wanting power, but power struggles go on all the time. Because the power dynamic is not an open subject for discussion, those contests do not have to follow any kind of rules of fair play.

That's how the shadow operates. In a Ruler bank, everyone seemed very respectable and responsible. The Lover went underground and emerged as unbridled Eros. Everyone was sleeping with everyone else, and sexual harassment was commonplace; yet, on the surface, people could not have seemed more proper. (It was a bit like Victorian England.)

As we have seen in the preceding chapters, each archetytpe also has its own negative temptation. That is, the archetype itself has a shadow, too. As has been apparent with Nike and Microsoft, public relations nightmares often germinate in the shadow of an archetype. It is prudent to remain vigilant, to note when the archetype is moving into its more negative potentialities and take preventive action to redirect it into its positive form before trouble surfaces.

The antidote to shadow possession in an organization is to bring the behaviors out in the open, where they can be looked at and reflected upon. This gives the organization a chance to express the suppressed archetype in a more appropriate and integrated way.

Making the Unconscious Conscious

The branding process provides a wonderful opportunity for analyzing your organizational culture and clarifying its values, mission, future vision, and core archetype. Doing so makes the unconscious conscious in a way that helps you make better staffing decisions, orient new employees more effectively, and retain talent. Your analysis can help different units within the organization to talk the same language with one another and increase the chances that the information customers get informally from employees (socially, in chat rooms on the Web, and in actual business interactions) is congruent with your intended brand identity.

We have a series of instruments that can help (1) organizations assess the archetypal roots of their culture, (2) teams collaborate more effectively, and (3) individuals understand how to be successful within a given organizational culture.[3] However, you can also diagnose a culture by walking around, listening, watching, and asking some questions.

Begin collecting examples of the organization's sacred stories.

3. For information about the use of these instruments, contact Carol Pearson at The Center for Archetypal Studies and Applications (CASA) at 301–277–8042, or e-mail cspearson@herowithin.com.

Notice what archetypal plot they represent. Then ask yourself the following questions:

- What is the name of your company and what does it mean?
- What are your company's logo and motto? What do they symbolize or suggest?
- How do people in your organization dress and interact?
- Sometimes the actual architecture or the office layout is informative. Use your imagination to answer the question, "If this were a setting for a play or movie, what would it be called?"
- Look at the promotional materials that are popular in-house. Ask people what they most value about the organization? Ask them what is difficult about it?
- If this is your organization, think deeply about its function in your life. Does it give you stability and respectability (which might suggest the Ruler or the Innocent)? Does it make you feel cared for or give you a chance to care for others (which might suggest the Caregiver)? Ask similar questions about the other archetypes. If the organization is your client, ask people at different levels these questions.
- Conduct or review consumer research. How do the customers see the organization?

Understanding the archetypal dimension of an organizational culture gives you greater power to recognize the invisible forces at work within it. As a company aligns its brand identity with the truth about its real cultural values, it is easier for it to be, and to be perceived as, a "real McCoy." Doing so provides a winning brand identity powerful enough to withstand great difficulties—as Johnson & Johnson did with the Tylenol crisis. Most importantly, the exercise of branding allows a company to know itself and its loyalties at a new level by decoding its core archetype.

If you are starting (or helping to start) a new enterprise, look inward and clarify your values. Notice the structure of your daydreams, and decide how you want the plot to develop. Monitor your dreams by writing them down. Overall, pay attention to what archetype answers the real yearning of your soul—one that could do the same for customers.

The ancient Greeks and Romans often went to the temple of a certain god or goddess to gain certain virtues. They might seek out the temple of Artemis if they hoped for an easy labor, the Temple of Zeus if they wanted political power, or that of Aphrodite if they desired love. We no longer visit the archetypes in temples, but in a very real way, we need to recognize what "shrine" we are metaphorically inhabiting. Doing so helps us take conscious responsibility for the impact of our messages on our customers, our culture, and ourselves.

CHAPTER

21

Leaving a Legacy
The Ethics of Archetypal Marketing

THE IMPACT OF BRAND MARKETING, especially advertising, is immeasurable. To a great extent, attention determines history. That is, what we focus on and resonate to reinforces patterns of consciousness that, in turn, direct action. Television advertising wins attention because so much talent, energy, and cleverness go into the ads that they may be more entertaining than the shows during which they are played. As *Washington Post* columnist David Ignatius puts it, "It is not simply that ads sell products. Overall, the media has [sic] a magical effect on the cultural consciousness for, by and large, the best thing on television . . . is the advertising. It's hip, it's funny, it's beautifully produced and it doesn't make any pretenses. Who wants to channel click, just to watch another dopey show?" Advertising, he notes, is the art form of our age, and he even asserts that if "Michelangelo were alive today, he'd probably be working on Madison Avenue."[1]

For those who are working on Madison Avenue or its equivalent,

1. David Ignatius, "And Viewing Pleasure," *The Washington Post* (July 7, 1999).

Ignatius's concept may be appealing, but it is also intimidating. Long called "Captains of Consciousness," marketing communication folk have been simultaneously elevated and vilified. But what could they do? Their charge was to sell the product, and often the most that could be hoped for was that they would do so in entertaining or at least innocuous ways.

The study of archetypes, though, invites us to contemplate another avenue: Thinking more deeply about individual consumers, the culture at large, and our own organizations allows us to entertain possibilities that could be winning strategies for management or for clients and, at the same time, provide a theory that helps us resolve or even anticipate and defuse ethical problems that arise in advertising.

When You Wish upon a Star

The field of marketing inhabits the world of dreaming. When we enter the world of what we want to be true, rather than what is true, we are allowing ourselves to feel human yearnings that reveal our vulnerabilities. Think for a minute about children's stories that continue to capture the heart, however much they are repeated. Gepetto wishes for a son, and the Blue Fairy appears from the sky to bring life to the puppet Pinocchio. Cinderella wishes to go to the ball, and the fairy godmother appears to change the pumpkin into a carriage, the mice into horses, and her rags into a ball gown. Kermit the Frog sings about wishing on the morning star ("The Rainbow Connection" in *The Muppet Movie*), and an agent appears in the swamp to call Kermit to Hollywood, adventure, and the promise that he will be able to make millions of people happy.

As marketers, we trade in the realm of human dreams and aspirations. Corporate executives want to create brand icons that launch their companies into extraordinary success. The underlying forces behind these motivations go far beyond the need simply to do their job well or get a return for their stockholders. Such desires are not just about making money. They evoke a passion for success that originates in issues of self-esteem, in deep needs to prove oneself to one's parents and others, in a desire to avoid the experience of powerlessness by winning really big, and so on.

These matters are not trivial. So, too, customers buy products that appeal to their most deeply cherished hopes and dreams. Unconsciously, people expect professionals in the marketing field to be fairy godmothers, turning products that are sow's ears into silk purses or fulfilling customers' dreams that no real product can satisfy.

All of us have dreams and yearnings. If we could be granted three wishes, most of us might begin by wishing for the fulfillment of our personal desires, but if we took some pause before making all of our wishes, at least one of our wishes would likely express some hope for the world. We might wish for world peace, the protection of the environment, or a renewed sense of community in the world. Virtually everyone has some altruistic desire to make a difference in the world. However much we comprehend the enormous impact that commercial messages have on the culture of the time, we understand that we cannot necessarily make even our own dreams come true through the work we do day to day.

The truth is, however, that we exist in the *real world*, where we cannot always control the outcome of our own actions, much less the fate of the culture. We cannot transform an inferior product into a winning one, nor can we provide the kind of meaning in people's lives that they truly crave. If we look at the basic categories of human motivation, we might safely conclude that the real fulfillment for customers will come from spiritual faith, true love, a genuine experience of familial and community engagement, genuine accomplishments, self-awareness and acceptance, a sense of making a difference in the world, and some sense of genuine rootedness in place, time, and space.

For the first time in human history, a shared mythos has broken down, and commercial messages are now taking the place of shared sacred stories. We know in our hearts that a profession designed to sell products cannot fill this gap. If we take the time to think of how many people are finding the only meaning they have in their lives from consumption of various sorts, we do not feel proud; we feel sad, or even outraged.

The field cannot be the fairy godmother of the culture. We do not really have magic wands, and, when it comes down to it, the bottom line is that we are paid to sell products.

What can we do? Outside of our paid work, many of us do volunteer work to help churches, temples, charity organizations, community projects, or political candidates reach out to make a deeper difference in people's lives than most products can.

If we are corporate or organizational leaders, we might also have directed our company to contribute to good causes—no matter whether we do so to reinforce positive associations in the public mind with our brand or out of generosity and a desire to give back to the world. Most likely, we are doing so for both reasons.

Of course, we know that linking such philanthropy to a brand identity reinforces the identity. We might also recognize that contributing to causes that fulfill the meaning promise of a brand in more powerful and direct ways than the actual brand can ever do is a way of filling this gap and demonstrating real integrity. For example, if your brand is an Explorer brand and you trade on the Explorer's delight in nature, you might choose to get involved in environmental causes, donating your time and money to ensure that the natural world will still be there for future generations to explore. If your brand is a Caregiver brand, you may want to take on the project of feeding, clothing, or housing the homeless. If your brand is a Sage brand, you might want to invest in primary research that furthers knowledge for everyone, not simply that develops new product lines for your company. If you are a marketing professional, working for an advertising firm, your pro bono work might appropriately involve bringing marketing skills to organizations that promote good causes.

Many issues of ethics and social policy that are beyond the province of this book, among them unhealthy, harmful, or environmentally unfriendly products; inhumane corporate and labor policies; and the issue of First Amendment rights versus the need to protect children from violent and pornographic materials. Such issues, of course, can be addressed through civic and political engagement, and, at a personal level, each professional makes his or her own decisions about whom he or she will work with and for.

We have also stopped short of conducting any systematic analysis of the impact of the artificial stimulation of commercial activity on the values and priorities of the time, providing any speculations about the real and potential role of consumer advocacy, or undertaking any true study of the impact of current images on any particular social

group. The opportunities and concerns we raise in this chapter con-
fine themselves to ethical issues and situations that are immediately
relevant to the everyday practice of marketing. The upcoming mus-
ings are intended to help professionals manage meaning in ways that

- avoid harm and prevent public-relations nightmares;
- increase options, rather than put people into boxes; and
- foster positive social and psychological outcomes.

Do No Harm

Of all the issues that consumers and marketers face, the one they
generally feel the strongest about is the impact of ads on children.
Children are so impressionable, and the power of the image affects
them so deeply; that's why there was such a backlash against Calvin
Klein and Camel cigarettes. The most egregious offenses are clear
and glaring, but on a day-to-day level, there are many gray areas.
Working with archetypes puts a positive perspective on the task of
assessing the appropriateness of ads; rather than focus on what to
avoid, we can remember that kids need to have all the archetypes
awakened in them. By consciously aiming ads at the positive pole of
each archetype, it is possible to positively influence kids while also
leaving ample room for brand positioning and creative expression.

Many influential books bring up concerns about the fate of boys
and girls today. *Raising Cain* points out that, in spite of our best
efforts, boys are still being "systematically steered away from their
emotional lives toward silence, solitude, and distrust."[2] Who is tending to the heroic impulses of little girls? The argument presented in
Reviving Ophelia asserts that social pressures lead girls to lose their
"true selves" once they enter adolescence.[3] Most of us are caring
mothers, fathers, aunts, and uncles. Could we attempt to address
these issues in the work we do and still feel that we are giving our
businesses or our clients our all? All knowledge requires responsi-

2. Dan Kindlon and Michael Thompson, *Raising Cain: Protecting the Emotional Life of Boys* (New York, N.Y. Ballantine Books, 1999).

3. Mary Pipher, *Reviving Ophelia: Saving the Selves of Adolescent Girls* (New York: N.Y. Ballantine Books, 1995).

bility. Can we understand the plight of our young people and recognize our role as arbiters of consciousness, but still not present the kinds of images that can help our young people channel their energies in a positive direction?

One strategy that can help enact this positive intent to systematically consider, during the development process of a product, the product's impact on the consciousness of children. This procedure can include gaining a full understanding of the archetype the product evokes and its impact on consciousness, just as companies now routinely screen for possible safety hazards of any new product.

For example, many mothers and fathers, as well as psychologists, are concerned about the potential impact of the Barbie doll on young girls. This enormously popular doll has longer legs, a thinner waist and hips, and generally a more elongated shape than any real woman could possibly achieve. Many fear that the doll reinforces the trends in society that influence girls to diet chronically, experience low self-esteem, and even develop dangerous eating disorders. Illustration 7.2 shows the remarkable similarity between Barbie and an Egyptian Sky goddess, who is associated with creation, destruction, and the process of metamorphosis. Her legs are long because she both reaches up to the sky and lovingly enfolds the world. Is this archetypal shape one of the reasons for her appeal?

Archetypes exert a powerful pull that children are unlikely to have the awareness to counter. For this reason, it is especially important that the potential fallout from the meaning, as well as the function, of products be studied before the products are launched. Doing so can avert public relations nightmares and prevent brands from harming people.

The Pearson-Mark collaboration began out of Margaret's concern with the impact of advertising primarily on children, but secondarily on individuals of all ages. We began by looking at Calvin Klein ads, which at the time were showing young teenagers in seductive poses. Of course, we were not alone in our concern. This ad campaign was widely decried as "kiddy porn." Looking at the Gap ads of the same period, Carol recognized that they appealed to the same feeling of alienation in kids that Calvin Klein was targeting, only Gap showed teenagers leaning up against their peers in groups in a really friendly, and age-appropriate, way. We were pleased that

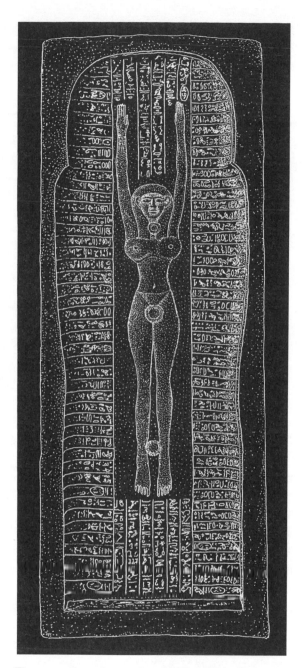

The unusually top-heavy, elongated form of the Barbie doll echoes that of the Sky Goddess Nut, depicted here. The form reflects the image inside the sarcophagus of Princess Ankhnesneferibre, from around 525 B.C. Did Barbie's creators consciously reflect an archetypal form?

the Gap ads addressed the same underlying issues but hinted at a more positive resolution of the issue. When you feel lonely, don't seduce someone (as the Calvin Klein ads implicitly suggest); get together with your friends and commiserate instead.

As we examined a number of other ads, we realized that archetypal ads that appeal to a real need tend to be successful. To get the customer's attention, it is simply not necessary to resort to ads that may have negative consequences for the consciousness of individuals and/or result in a backlash against the brand. Then why take chances? People in the marketing field can use this system to consistently find ways to take the high road while still being successful selling products.

Accentuate the Positive, Eliminate the Negative

There are wonderful ads out there that reinforce the cutting-edge potential of archetypes. However, many run-of-the-mill messages currently reinforce their negative or lower-level aspects of archetypes. For example, so many commercial messages appeal to the Ruler's desire for power and status. However, the Ruler archetype at its higher level is willing to take on huge responsibilities, not just for money and status, but to make the world a better place. People with a high degree of Ruler tendencies also have a knack for putting together the infrastructure of policies, procedures, rules, regulations, and laws that make the world function. You can think of such people as great citizens who help make things work for all of us. Is it really necessary that so many ads to appeal simply to the more crass Ruler desire to incite envy or dominate situations? You can sell products using either approach—in the first case, with the potential for reinforcing shallow tendencies in people or, in the second case, for reinforcing something greater and nobler within them. If you can sell a product either way, why not take the high road?

Particularly when marketing professionals may be pressured to create commercial messages designed primarily to get attention, with no thought given to other factors, it is important to recognize that there is a great risk that these stereotypical ads can reinforce the negative potential within an archetype.

In the field of medicine, doctors and pharmaceutical companies are charged with the task of making people well. However, if, in the process, they induce side effects that are harmful, they are held accountable. Recent government and class-action suits against cigarette companies may be only the first step in the growing social consensus that business is responsible for the impact of its products on consumers.

Marketing can also have unanticipated consequences on the consciousness of individuals and of the time, however well intentioned marketers might be. It is therefore helpful, in developing a marketing campaign or constructing an ad campaign, to monitor the level of the archetype you are reinforcing and to deemphasize its shadow or negative aspects. If you remember from Part 1 how the placebo effect works, it is apparent that a product can become so associated with negative attitudes and behaviors that its use promotes them. Figure 7.7 includes summary information, which can be supplemented by revisiting Parts 2 to 5 of this book, about the shadow aspects of the 12 archetypes. This information is meant to provide a means to routinely consider the ethical domain, which tends to be nebulous and difficult to pin down.

Quality Standards in Marketing

There are other ways, too, in which the ethics of working with archetypes gets dicey. Sometimes, one positive feature conflicts with another. For example, one might argue that showing off-road vehicles tearing through a wild terrain holds important Explorer values that are threatened by modern life. Some part of us is tired of cities and wants to go back to nature, but we don't. Such images vicariously give us an experience we crave. However, one might also argue that this kind of commercial encourages behavior that is damaging to the environment. How to resolve this issue undoubtedly requires serious thinking about the ethics involved.

Archetypes have their positive and negative sides. On the positive side, they enhance our lives. Archetypes by their very nature, are amoral. Like nuclear power, or even hydropower, they can be tapped for good or ill. Part of what it means to be responsible is not to let such energies take you over and just do what they will you to do. For example, if you let the Outlaw take you over (especially in its

Quality Standards in Marketing: Do No Harm		
Archetype	**Virtue**	**Vice**
Innocent	Faith	Denial
Caregiver	Compassion	Martyrdom
Ruler	Responsibility	Dictatorship
Jester	Fun	Cruel humor/tricks
Regular Guy/Gal	Equality	Lynch mob
Lover	Love	Promiscuity
Hero	Courage	Arrogance
Outlaw	Revolution	Destructiveness
Magician	Transformation	Manipulation
Creator	Innovation	Mad Scientist
Explorer	Authenticity	Self-indulgence
Sage	Wisdom	Dogmatism

Figure 7.7

negative form), you might end up in jail! The Caregiver can get you martyred, the Hero can get you killed, and the Innocent can get you swindled. The archetypes need to be harnessed by a powerful moral sense. This bridling, however, is not simple: It requires intelligence and mindfulness.

That responsibility also means that we should not see management of meaning as just "adding an archetype and stirring." In researching the chapters on the various archetypes, we were surprised by how much advertising tends to graft a trendy meaning onto a product whose function cannot hold that meaning. The most effective products anchor the meaning in something that is true and an actual benefit. While it may theoretically be possible to graft a meaning onto an unrelated function—like grafting the Lover onto a lawnmower, or the Ruler onto talcum powder—when such associations are attempted, they are usually unconvincing at best and ludicrous at worst.

When meaning differentiates very similar products, there should be some functional difference between the products for the message to be credible. This difference between products does not have to be huge to work. For example, although Coke and Pepsi are both colas, their slightly different tastes are now inextricably linked with different meanings. Ivory and Dove are both soaps, but Dove's addition of moisturizers helps it honestly sustain the meaning of nurturance rather than purity.

When, in fact, there is no basis at all to the archetypal meaning associated with the products, savvy customers not only remain unconvinced by the message, but their incredulity reinforces the cynicism of the times and, eventually, undermines the status of advertising as a field. Such ads feed the public misconception that people in the field of marketing are trying to manipulate the consumer.

Respect Religion and Spirituality

It is always tempting in advertising to jump on whatever bandwagon is trendy. However, it is best not to do so unconsciously. For example, today's emerging consciousness is more overtly spiritual than in the more secular seventies, eighties, and the early nineties. Within various religions; a refreshing ecumenicalism; any people of all ages have experience of, knowledge about, and respect for numerous spiritual traditions. For example, a Presbyterian might take a Zen meditation class, attend a Native-American ritual or go to a New Age workshop.

As spirituality has become "in," there has been a tendency simply to drop religious symbols into ads. Of course, this practice has engendered a backlash from people who strongly feel that their religious traditions should not be exploited to sell products. American Indians are particularly sensitive about this trend, because many of their traditions have already been commercialized. Most of us will handle our own religious stories and symbols with appropriate sensitivity, but we may not be as immediately aware of other traditions and what might be seen as exploitative or disrespectful to them.

Todd Stein, in an article in the *Shambala Sun* called "Zen Sells," raises serious issues about how casually religious symbols are dropped into ads, citing Lancôme's Hydra Zen (a moisturizer), Apple showing a picture of the Dalai Lama in its "Think different" campaign, and, his personal least favorite, Abba shampoo. Stein notes that Zen is ubiquitous in ads today—even in ads that have nothing at all to do with Buddhist thought. He also notes that "Abba"(meaning "father" in Aramaic) was the word used by Jesus for God the Father and also the name used for the first Christian monks. He cites an ad for Abba in which a woman is dressed like a monk and raising her hands to the heavens. Stein argues that the "healing power" of Abba, in a religious sense, is about something much greater than split ends![4]

The point here is that spiritual imagery *can* be used in ads. Probably very few people were offended when Xerox portrayed a monk becoming ecstatic over the miracle of photocopying a manuscript, so that he would not have to laboriously copy it by hand. It was clear that no disrespect was intended—and the ad was funny. Everyone could identify with this situation and the convenience offered by the product. Similarly, when Apple shows a picture of the Dalai Lama, the "Think different" tag line limits the association of the image to his independence both from the Chinese and from conventional ways of thinking. Most of us do not infer that Apple computers hold the secret to enlightenment.

However, religious symbols do carry power. Our encouragement to use archetypes appropriately would, therefore, caution against using imagery, however archetypal, that might be seen by people within a particular religion as truly sacred.

Moreover, the danger of commercial messages substituting for real spiritual meaning is minimized to the degree that people have some kind of genuine faith. Using religious symbols in commercial messages trivializes the symbols and, in that way, undercuts the very institutions and teachings that might genuinely fulfill the deeper spiritual hunger in the world today.

Conscious Marketing: Be Real, Be Current, Expand Options

Anthropologists and psychologists alike agree that there is a profound sense of fragmentation, isolation, and loss of meaning in contemporary life. As cultural anthropologist Grant McCracken puts it,

> The first conclusion you come to when anthropologists study contemporary society is that we're not looking at anything that looks like society here. In a traditional society, every individual is born into this

4. *Shambala Sun* (Spring 2000).

wonderful cocoon of cultural meanings. The myths and legends that they hear at the knees of their parents as they're being socialized make a kind of geodesic dome (i.e., a structure with identical segments that fit together perfectly and support one another) for themselves and their culture, so that they find themselves constantly living in a coherent world.

That wonderful geodesic done of myth, legend and cultural meaning does not exist in our culture. Our contemporary culture insists that the individual is both free and forced to make up their [sic] own geodesic domes. Our culture says you may and must choose the meanings of your world. Instead of a geodesic dome, what we do is lay out a kind of smorgasbord of possibilities and you choose among those possibilities and you build a world for yourself.[5]

Accompanying such enormous need is enormous opportunity. We can do good without compromising effectiveness; in fact, we are very apt to *increase* effectiveness by tapping into some unfulfilled or latent need.

For example, at the height of the New Age beverage craze, Mark conducted interviews among groups of young urban consumers— New York City street kids, mostly black and Hispanic, dressed in baggy, grungy black leather and understandably suspicious of a focus-group setting and an unidentified white moderator. But after being shown a few ads, those same kids were waxing enthusiastically about Wendy, the ongoing spokesperson in the Snapple commercials. Many chuckled about how she reminded them of their grandmothers and aunts, sitting in their kitchen and telling them what to do. Almost every kid spontaneously recalled a favorite commercial that was especially goofy, but really rang true. The fact that Wendy was a middle-aged white receptionist seemed irrelevant to her connection to these kids—all Snapple fans, incidentally. Archetypes made the kids momentarily "colorblind."

On the other hand, ads for another brand that showed kids who looked just like themselves "chilling" and drinking beverages had no impact at all on them, and a campaign for another brand using neon

---

5. From an interview conducted by Margaret Mark for Young & Rubicam and used with its permission and that of the author.

psychedelic graphics they found downright laughable to the kids. Apparently, Wendy, by authentically evoking the Regular Jane archetype, did more than just put Snapple on the map and avoid the transparent clichés of "target marketing." In a subtle but meaningful way, Snapple also took a step toward bridging a tremendous racial and cultural chasm by truthfully showing how a Queens receptionist and a Harlem kid's grandmother could be exactly alike.

People in marketing are criticized frequently for presenting limited or stereotypical images of women and racial minorities. In a world where social roles are changing rapidly, it can often seem hard to find the balance between showing respect for a group's history and honoring its promise. For example, women want to continue to increase their access to work and political realms that were traditionally masculine, but they do not want their historic and present commitments to home and family to be trivialized.

Working with archetypes does not make this issue go away, but it does provide a way to keep some balance. Generally, any group that is shown reflecting the higher levels of an archetype is unlikely to feel diminished or demeaned. Many products have a masculine or feminine feel that can be deduced by using the "laddering" technique described in Chapter 19. This feel, as well as other preferences and behaviors, is associated explicitly with historical sex roles. The masculine or feminine character can be honored in the style of both the message and the visuals while not creating a gender-exclusive message. In fact, the other gender may be the one that finds the brand most attractive, because breaking out of confining roles tends to be liberating and creates a special kind of bonding with the opposite sex.

Most products are not associated with one race or ethnic group, but some are. For example, Barilla pasta's brand identity emphasizes its Italian heritage—yet we are all invited to share in the Italian experience by eating the pasta. This same strategy can be used even with products or experiences that come from the heritage of groups that may have special sensitivities because of a history of oppression, as is demonstrated by a rock favorite: "Play that funky music, white boy."[6] Of course, with consumers coming in all colors, great ad campaigns now generally include people of different races.

6. *Play That Funky Music*, performed by Wild Cherry, 1976, for CBS/Epic.

Stereotypes limit people by "putting them into boxes." Qualities and virtues that make genders and ethnic groups special both represent those groups in positive ways and help others emulate their gifts—thus expanding options for everyone. This doesn't mean that marketers are expected to become evangelists—about gender or racial diversity or any other social goal. In fact, the situation is quite the opposite: No one wants the field of marketing to become the nursemaid of the culture, preaching about what people should and should not do. That would be offensive—and boring. But just as negative social messages are subtle, so, too, are positive messages. The more real and the more effective commercial messages are, the more they tend to empower people and bring them together.

The media in all its forms, including advertising, has a powerful effect on the ongoing socialization of every one of us. We tend to think of socialization as something that happens to us as children, but actually it is an ongoing and interactive process that occurs throughout life. At every level, most successful people are attuned to the social cues around them. In a world where a high degree of emotional intelligence is expected, people who lack such sensitivity cannot succeed. Yet, sometimes that attention to context goes too far. In our work with organizations, we have noticed a troubling phenomenon. In the hall, before a meeting, we may have a deep, fascinating conversation with one or more people. They are funny. They tell us where the bones are buried and what the real issues are that will not be talked about. They share ideas from all kinds of contexts, from the New Age or religious retreat they just went on to some idea in the new sciences that seems relevant to how their office runs.

Then we go into the formal meeting, and the conversation is so judicious and careful that most of the real life in people's thinking is absent. Most of the time, it seems as though there is a ghost in the room of some old expectations about acceptable conversation that has little or nothing to do with where the individuals really reside in terms of the vitality of their minds and hearts. The result can be that problems are not solved and new opportunities wane because the lively, insightful truths that are so easily shared in a casual one-on-one conversation never make it into the room in which business decisions are made.

At a deeper level, our societal collective discourse works in the same way. People often take their cues from the media about what is "in" and "out," what they are allowed to talk about and what not. This phenomenon is, of course, even truer for people who have not had strong role models who anchored their behavior in a sense of possibility. We have an opportunity today to create more commercial messages that connect with the emerging intelligence and consciousness of the times. Such ads grab attention, so they are good business. As with the Snapple ads, they feel real.

We are in no way implying in this book that edgy ads are necessarily unhealthy. A positive side effect of edgy ads is that they give social permission for cutting-edge side conversations to enter our public discourse. For example, the Benetton Group has gained some notoriety for running politically provocative advertising. One ad showed an AIDS patient on his deathbed. A more recent campaign feature photographs of inmates on death row, accompanied by their names and the dates on which they were sentenced to die. Is the advertising offensive to many people? Absolutely. But at the same time, it provokes a healthy dialogue about life-and-death issues.

The list of possibilities goes on and on, because once we free ourselves from the constraints of typical "businessthink," the possibilities of finding a match between fundamental human needs and marketing objectives become endless.

Cause Marketing: Where Myths and Legends Live on

When the archetypal and mythic dimension is utilized in cause marketing, it has the potential for moving us out of "me first," narcissistic, bigoted thinking into caring about the whole human family. Our work with the March of Dimes has revealed that when the Innocent—a helpless infant—is shown in ads and other promotional materials, the race or gender of the baby becomes immaterial; people are called to their heroic selves and simply want to help.

In fact, archetypes have found a natural home in the realm of public-service advertising. Unencumbered by the need for the "hard sell," creative people seem to intuitively tap into their own deeper instincts and feelings and gravitate to archetypal stories and characters. In the process, they often develop advertising more effective than that which exists in the commercial world, advertising that taps into the richer mines of archetypal energy and that calls people to act out of their higher and better selves.

Some of the most effective advertising—ever—has been created in this more "free-form" environment: Rosie the Riveter, Smokey the Bear, and the tearful Native American. The Jester archetype made seat-belt compliance acceptable by featuring the ever-funny seat belt dummies, instead of horrifying images of crashes.

Research showed that fellow drinkers didn't especially care if another reveler got behind the wheel intoxicated; the person, in a way, "deserved" what he or she got. Then the Ad Council learned that by evoking the Innocent—all of the blameless children and families who were killed by drunk drivers—it was able to trigger a tremendous "heroic" response. People were determined to stop their friends from driving drunk—not only out of concern for their buddies, but for what they might do to the Innocents. The advertising campaign that resulted was as effective as it was heart wrenching: In each commercial, we see actual rough and imperfect home movies of babies, mothers, and fathers just hanging out, followed a scroll that outlines the circumstances of their death—in each case, killed by a drunk driver.

Also tapping into the desire to be heroic was an Ad Council campaign for a coalition hoping to encourage parents and other citizens to get involved in school reform. We learned that many people felt ambivalent about their own school years and were reluctant to get involved in issues involved with changing the schools of today. Our breakthrough resulted from an understanding that we were not really appealing to their desire to save schools, but instead to their natural protectiveness of children. The advertising resurrected the story of Baby Jessica, whose plight mesmerized the nation during her rescue from a well in Midland, Texas. How is it, we asked, that this one little girl was able to get an entire town to pull out all the stops and the whole nation to hold its breath, while countless other children were being neglected and forgotten in schools throughout the country? After news footage of this incident was shown (in which the film was linked to the subject of school reform), interviews reported that even the toughest working-class men and women teared up and resolved to get involved with their local schools and find out how to make them better.

Telling the Stories You Want to Tell

If you are true to your brand's archetypal identity, there are many stories, images, and symbols that can keep your campaign interesting and also help you update your message to fit the time—without either reinforcing the negative possibilities within the archetype or downgrading the archetype into a shallow stereotype. The richest sources of inspiration for your endeavor might not be the latest Harvard Business School treatise so much as remembering your favorite novel and why it so touched you, noticing the pattern of today's most popular TV shows and wondering why they are so widely watched, going to an art museum, or reading a magazine review of a brilliant piece of theater. Your knowledge of archetypes will enable you to see the patterns in these expressions of timeless themes—patterns that you can use in your own work. Rather than treating everyday activities as irrelevant to the work we produce, or treating the arts and the social sciences as unrelated to business, our approach suggests that we "take it all in." No field of study could be more important than the simple observation of human truth. The larger your vision and experience, the better you can be at managing meaning.

Suddenly, in the last decade, it has become normative for business leaders to invest a good chunk of their time in clarifying their company's values as the anchor for everything that they do. When those of us who work in marketing face the huge impact that commercial messages have on the consciousness of the time, it can be truly intimidating. It requires us to consider not only our own personal values, but also the more nebulous issue of how certain value-laden images might affect not only individual customers, but the times in which we live.

The current generation of marketers could be the first to show concern for the *impact* of the *meaning* that their product conveys. It is not so confusing to consider the moral domain if there is a simple tool to use in doing so, since most of us are not going back to school to get advanced degrees in philosophy or theology. *The Hero and The Outlaw* provides a vocabulary and a way of thinking that makes possible an informed consideration of the ways in which commercial messages affect people.

Some say that the reality of our society is that marketers have become contemporary priests and priestesses tending the sacred fires of cultural meaning. We have that assessment is not entirely true, and we still value the religious leaders, artists, and philosophers, as well as Jungian and other transpersonal psychologists, who can more legitimately fulfill this role.

In the meantime, it is important to understand that the creative talents who spin out wonderfully designed, artistic commercial messages are a bit like the ancient medicine men or women who sat with members of the tribe around the campfire and told stories filled with practical significance. Such stories instructed people about the world around them and taught them how to live.

Margaret's research for Sesame Workshop tells us that when ordinary folks are asked to take a picture of the "heart of their home," they send in a snapshot of the television or media center—which, in a technological age, seems to have taken on the ancient role of the tribal fire, as well as the more recent one of the family kitchen. Even though interest in the spiritual domain of life in undergoing a revival, we still have no sacred orthodoxy that holds us all together. In large measure, the stories presented by television, popular music, movies— and, yes, commercial messages—shape our culture. Like it or not, the messages we create or pay for affect the quality of the consciousness of our time.

You can utilize this system for the management of brand meaning, not only to sell products, but also to leave a meaningful legacy. You always have many choices in the images you evoke and the stories you tell in selling any product or service. Making the management of meaning systematic allows you to practice your craft in a way that, at the very least, does no harm and, at best, ennobles the customers you serve. We are not calling here for industry standards or censorship. We are merely asking our readers to grapple with rather profound questions, like, What do you want your legacy to be? And what stories do *you* want to tell?

Index

About the Authors

Margaret Mark leads a unique consulting firm specializing in innovative ways of developing, implementing, and evaluating strategic directions for businesses and brands—directions that provide significant and sustainable competitive advantage. She focuses on approaches that uncover the fundamental, even primal, basis for consumer motivation, which then is translated into powerful positionings.

Prior to launching Margaret Mark Strategic Insight, Margaret was an Executive Vice President of Young & Rubicam, where she played several roles over the course of sixteen years: Worldwide Director of Consumer Insight, Director of Y&R New York's Strategy Review Board, and Managing Director of the agency's AT&T business around the world. Before joining Y&R, she was with Ogilvy & Mather and Dancer-Fitzgerald-Sample.

Today, her ongoing clients include numerous Fortune 500 companies spanning industries ranging from food, to fashion, to computer software. She also is involved with a variety of non-profit organizations, including Sesame Workshop and the March of Dimes.

Carol S. Pearson, Ph.D. is the President of CASA: the Center for Archetypal Studies and Applications and a consulting faculty member in the Organizational Systems Inquiry and Change Program at Saybrook Graduate School. A pioneer in the field of applied Jungian psychology, she is the creator of archetypal systems that are widely used by psychologists, educators, executive coaches, and consultants. In her integrated marketing/organizational development consulting practice, she helps values-based organizations establish a compelling brand identity, inspire customer/employee loyalty, and build optimally-performing teams.

Carol is the author of numerous books, including *The Hero Within: Six Archetypes We Live By; Awakening the Heroes Within: Twelve Archetypes that Help Us Find Ourselves and Transform Our World; Magic At Work: A Guide to Releasing Your Highest Creative Po-*

tential; and *Invisible Forces: Harnessing the Power of Archetypes to Improve Your Career and Your Organization.*

Carol also has designed instrumentation that identifies the archetypes most active in individuals, families, teams, and organizations, most notably the *Pearson-Marr Archetype Indicator (PMAI)* (Center for Applications of Psychological Type, 2000) and the *Organizational Culture Index (OCI)* (CASA, 1998). Carol can be reached at CASA, P. O. Box 73, College Park, MD 20741–0073; phone: 301–277-8042; fax: 301–864-2977; Web Site: www.herowithin.com.

Pearson and Mark Collaboration: In addition to their own consulting practices, Carol and Margaret team up to provide uniquely powerful interventions to companies seeking sustained and consistent archetypal meaning management in today's challenging and turbulent times. Their e-mail address is: PearsonMark@Earthlink.net.